Consumer Economics

By

JAMES N. MORGAN

Associate Professor of Economics, Department of Economics, Assistant Program Director, Survey Research Center, University of Michigan

Prentice-Hall, Inc.
Englewood Cliffs, N. J.

L.C. Cat. Card No.: 55–8370

Second printing . . . . *June, 1956*

16942

Preface

You, as an American consumer, are an extremely important person. With a high and rising income you have a good deal of discretion as to how you will use your money in spite of your fixed commitments.* [1] The efficiency and the nation's stability of economy depend on the wisdom with which you select your purchases and the restraint you show in alternating between buying a lot and feeling saturated with goods.[2]

This book concentrates on important choices you make as a consumer. Direct advice-giving, and the presentation of transient facts, are reduced to a minimum. It concentrates on the understanding necessary for your own decision-making, and on understanding the larger economic problems that arise because of the way all of us behave as consumers.

This book could not have been written much earlier. Our knowledge of consumer behavior, motivations, and aspirations was limited until the development of the personal interview survey with a representative sample of consumers.[3]

The reasons people gave for using installment credit are more interesting than a logical "demonstration" that they are wasting money in so doing. The fact that many people are still dreaming of a better house, or a new car, or something is more revealing than a theoretical discussion of saturation.

* Throughout this book the footnotes are at the end of each chapter, for ease in reading and in finding references afterwards.

iii

I am indebted to many colleagues, and to students whose ability to sense the irrelevant or the incomplete has often been uncanny.   In particular, I am indebted to Professor George Katona for many broader and new insights into the motives of consumers.   The Board of Governors of the Federal Reserve System and the Survey Research Center of the University of Michigan, who co-operatively conduct the Surveys of Consumer Finances, have graciously permitted me to use both their published and unpublished tabulations.   Some of the special tabulations were made by me while under a grant from the Carnegie Corporation; others, under a Faculty Research Grant from the University of Michigan.[4]

Parts of the manuscript have been read by Professors Z. K. Dickinson, George Katona, and George Anderson, and I am indebted to them for many helpful suggestions and criticisms. I also extend my thanks to the following who read the book in manuscript form and made many helpful suggestions: Russell A. Dixon of the University of Pittsburgh, Mary M. Crawford of Indiana University, Warren J. Bilkey of the University of Connecticut, and Mrs. Juanita Kreps.   Finally, my wife provided necessary encouragement to me, diversion for three, and then four, children, a considerable amount of typing, and numerous suggestions for improvements.

J. N. M.

FOOTNOTES TO PREFACE

[1] George Katona and Eva Mueller, *Consumer Attitudes and Demand*, 1950–52, Ann Arbor, Michigan: Survey Research Center, 1953. (Survey Research Center Monograph # 12), pp. 53–55.

[2] *Op. cit.*, pp. 90–91.

[3] L. Festinger and D. Katz, eds., *Research Methods in the Behavioral Sciences*, New York: The Dryden Press Inc., 1953; see also, George Katona, *Psychological Foundations of Economic Behavior*, New York: McGraw-Hill Book Co., 1951.

[4] Detailed results of the research done under the Carnegie grant, as well as other research findings by colleagues at Survey Research Center, can be found in *Contributions of Survey Methods to Economics*, L. R. Klein, ed., New York: Columbia University Press, 1954.

Table of Contents

chapter I

Introduction

As a consumer in a modern capitalist society, you need to know a great many things if you wish to avoid mistakes you will later regret. This is not easy, because the facts change. They cannot be passed down from father to son, nor learned once for all, nor placed conveniently in a book for ready reference.

Nor do the facts speak for themselves. Much interpretation is involved before facts become really useful, and this means that you must understand some general principles. Hence, this book attempts to show, first, what facts are needed and where they are likely to be available; and, second, how these facts can be analyzed by you the consumer to help you make decisions that will make you happy. Facts will not be avoided, particularly those which change slowly or which are extremely important, but the facts presented are transitory. The lasting benefit from this book should be an increased ability to find and to use the facts when you need them in making decisions.

Types of Consumer Decisions

This book is organized around typical consumer decisions, though chapters on governmental aids to consumers and on some larger economic problems of importance to consumers have been included also.

1

Chapter 2 deals with choices between spending on current consumption, saving for the future, or investing in future consumption by buying equipment (cars, durable goods, houses, and so forth).

Chapter 3 analyzes the social significance of these choices.

Chapter 4 deals with budgeting analysis, planning, and record keeping, not only in terms of the choice "what" and "how," but also in terms of its effects on the choices discussed in Chapters 2 and 3.

Chapter 5 discusses consumer information, shopping, and detailed choices.

Chapter 6 analyzes the risks the consumer faces, the choices he makes in dealing with risks and insurance, and some larger economic problems that arise from the cumulation of individual behavior.

Chapter 7 deals with health and medical care.

Chapter 8 discusses choices about housing in terms of buying or renting, selection of community and types of housing, and the larger problems of community development that must be understood in order to make sound choices.

Chapter 9 deals with other major consumer expenditures.

Chapter 10 describes governmental and other aids to the consumer, particularly those involving direct protection of his interests.

Chapter 11 analyzes some important economic problems where the consumer's stake is large, understanding is difficult, and choices have to be made (if only at the polls).

Chapter 12 discusses the problem of maximizing consumer satisfaction from a somewhat broader point of view and discusses choices which are important and frequently neglected in discussions of the consumer and his problems.

Ways of Looking at Consumer Choices

Where possible, each area of decision is looked at from several points of view.

A. One is the individual's attempt to find a satisfactory solution to his personal financial affairs. What understanding does he need in making decisions? What facts are relevant? Is there any standard for the "best" decision?

B. What theories do economists and others have concerning how consumers actually make this type of choice, and why?

C. What do statistics and research findings indicate that most consumers actually do?

D. What problems arise for the consumer and his family because of the way choices are customarily made?

E. What problems arise for other consumers or for society as a whole because of the way a consumer makes his choices?

F. What remedies have been proposed or adopted when consumer choices have led to important social and economic problems?

All these dimensions are not relevant in every chapter, of course, but keeping them in mind helps you in treating your choices systematically.

Basic Principles and Distinctions

Even the direct economic choices you make as a consumer involve rather complex problems. The ability to analyze these problems well and to make good decisions depends on knowing what distinctions to make in order to separate each problem into simpler component parts, and on knowing how and when to apply some rather elementary principles. These principles may seem obvious when stated, but they are frequently neglected, and it seems worth while to list some of the most important of them.

A. The real cost of any decision is the value of what was given up—what the economist calls the "opportunity cost." Making choices in terms of the most important alternatives available has two advantages. First, it avoids the necessity of thinking in terms of dollars. It is difficult to keep in mind what a dollar is worth, and some costs and values are difficult or impossible to put in money terms. Second, it is easy to forget some of the opportunity costs of a decision if one thinks only in money terms.   In deciding whether to buy or rent a house, it must be remembered that one of the costs of ownership is the loss of potential interest that could otherwise be earned on the money tied up in the house.   A $15,000 house with $5,000 still unpaid on the mortgage involves $10,000 so tied up, on which the owner could be earning at least $300 a year.   This $300 is a part of the cost of owning the house.

B. The distinction between the real value and the monetary value is important.   That same house just mentioned may be depreciating in value by 2 per cent each year.   Even with adequate maintenance, this means that the house is costing you another $300 a year, even though you are not paying out this much cash.   In recent years of inflation, of course, depreciation is hidden by the inflation of property values, and houses may increase in value rather than decrease.   A "capital gain" more than offsets the depreciation.   But depreciation exists, and will go on, whether the inflation does or not.   There are many other examples where monetary measurements are insufficient. Money spent on a college education may bring a reward not only in future earning power, but also in capacity to enjoy life or in an ability to be a good citizen, both of which are difficult to assess in money terms.   Again, if you sell your house or car, the money you receive is not income—you cannot use it up without reducing your total wealth.   In many economic problems that appear extremely complex and difficult, things fall into line if you try this simple experiment—Pretend there is no money, and work out the problem in terms of real goods and services, satisfactions, resources, production, and so on.   Once the "money veil" is removed, a good many complexities disappear.

C. Time is money.   This is a special case of the opportunity cost principle.   Since you can always earn an interest return on money you control, a dollar now is not the same as a dollar ten years ago or ten years hence, even apart from changes in the price level.   This means that the spacing in time of receipts and payments is important.   A system, as in insurance policies, where you put in money now and get back more later, has to be interpreted in terms of the rate of interest you are earning on this money, because if you kept it, you could earn the interest directly. For the ordinary consumer, this matter of interest is more complex because the rates you can earn are far below the rates you must pay if you borrow money. In addition, there are costs in lending or borrowing that make it cheaper to do neither. In comparing a series of receipts and payments, it is necessary to choose an interest rate, and then convert them all to values at some point in time, usually the present. Ten dollars, ten years in the future, discounted back to the present at 3 per cent, is worth about $7.50 now. This is obvious since a $75 U.S. savings bond purchased now will be worth $100 in ten years. The mathematics of discounting or accumulation of interest are complex, but since there are available interest and annuity tables, you should have little difficulty looking up the answers.

D. What is true for the individual may or may not be true for society. The effect of too many people trying to do the same thing may be quite unpleasant, as anyone who has been in a week-end traffic jam can testify. There are two ways in which the discrepancy between individual and social interests diverge. First, there may be social costs or benefits from an individual's action which he does not pay for and cannot collect for. If he fires his furnace improperly, it may be his neighbor whose clothes are soiled. If, on the other hand, his efforts to make his house and ground look pleasing increase his neighbors' happiness and property values, he can hardly charge them a fee for it. Secondly, the cumulation of individual behavior may have consequences in the aggregate which are unwanted or unexpected. Economists refer to the confusion here as the "fallacy of composition." If everyone tries to save half his income, the ensuing depression may make it impossible for anyone to save. If everyone tries to spend all his income, competing spenders will bid up the prices, and, aside from some redistributions, the average man will consume no more than before. On a simpler level there are cases where a single water well or septic tank works fine, but in a crowded neighborhood, such facilities may all fail.

E. It is impossible to avoid value judgments, but important to make the attempt, and to think separately in terms of equity and efficiency. On the individual level, it is important to separate what people want out of life from a discussion of how they might get it efficiently, even though one thing people often want is the freedom from being continually efficient. On the social level, things to be considered separately include (a) the effects of consumer behavior or policies of government on the distribution of income and wealth, and (b) their effects on the efficiency with which resources are allocated and used.

A good many problems, particularly those where government policy affecting consumers is involved, are made almost impossible to analyze because the policy in question involves effects on the productive mechanism, the allocation of resources, the efficiency with which these resources are used on the one hand, and redistribution of income on the other. The polemic literature about such issues as subsidized low-rent housing, multipurpose federal power projects, prepaid medical care, and so on, becomes a great deal easier to understand and analyze if this distinction is kept in mind.

I should add that the distinction between efficiency and equity is impossible to make completely. The adequacy and fairness of an income distribution depends on the price structure, while the definition of efficient and optimum allocation and use of resources depends on the valuations of the things that are produced—which in turn depend on the distribution of income. For instance, if the necessities of life such as food are cheap and luxuries are expensive, the poor people are better off than they would be with the same income distribution in a market that demanded high food prices but offered cheap Cadillacs. But the distinction is still useful analytically, and must be kept in mind.

Facts and the relations between facts, stated in the form if

A then B may seem devoid of moral implication, but their selection and the conclusions drawn from them are not. Any statement must be interpreted in the light of the particular interests and motivation of the person who makes it. The author, like most economists, makes an attempt to avoid advocating particular forms of behavior based on value judgments about what people ought to do, but like most people, he has some deeply ingrained value judgments. Some of these are: Consumers should have a consistent set of preferences, should collect the facts, and should be able to analyze them so as to "maximize their satisfactions," or at least make major decisions in ways they will not regret; should plan for the long run; and look out for their own interests as consumers.

A consumer will often find it wise to make a few major decisions or choices in such a way as to keep himself from making day-to-day decisions badly. This may seem like a value judgment, too, though it is partly based on observation of consumer behavior. One frequent and generally accepted way of outwitting yourself in this fashion is by making contractual saving commitments through life insurance, mortgage payments, or even installment credit. This enables you to save money without the necessity for eternal vigilance. Most schemes of this sort cost something—they lead to somewhat less over-all efficiency in use of money, if only through lower interest yields on your savings—but the return in ease from worry and certainty of saving is real enough to many people. It may be rational not to try to be rational all the time.

There is an old story about a worker in a plant who was so reliable and hard working that the foreman thought he would do the worker a favor. He assigned the worker to an easier job where he merely stood watching a conveyor belt of potatoes moving past, and was instructed to remove the bad ones. When the foreman returned after a few hours, the man was standing there shaking his head and letting all the potatoes go past. He asked to be taken off the job. When the foreman asked why, he said, "I just can't stand this job. It means making up my mind all the time, and I just can't do it. Every potato is another decision."

Most of us want to avoid the necessity for making a real decision over every potato, and we develop habits and rules. We may even make a few major decisions in a way calculated to reduce the necessity for a lot of decision-making and help ourselves develop habits that are not too inefficient.

F. Finally, we are all learning all the time. Not only do we find new, different, and sometimes better ways to achieve our goals and satisfy our needs, but such goals and needs may themselves change. We usually find it difficult to overcome resistances and do something different, and these resistances will either be increased if our first experience is unsatisfactory, or decreased if the first experience is successful and pleasant.

Piano teachers have long since ceased to spend the first lessons on scales and keys and exercises. They start out teaching their pupils to play a tune. The pupils enjoy this, practice is fun, and the motivation to go on and learn more is increased.

The lesson is clear. If we want to develop habits we can live with, it is essential to begin with successful, pleasant experiences, and gradually work into the more difficult ones. For instance, our first budget should be one we can easily stay within, and our first record-keeping should be simple and easy.

A second conclusion from knowing that people's goals may change is that you may want to concentrate on developing successful experience in areas where you will be happy to see your own standards and aspirations increasing. We all enjoy owning expensive things, but it is possible to concentrate on this to the virtual exclusion of other sources of satisfaction.

chapter 2

Present or Future Consumption?

What people do with their income, whether they spend it or save it, is probably the most important choice they make both from their own point of view and from the point of view of society. Let us first look at this choice from the point of view of the individual family.

For most people, the pattern of income through life is not the same as the pattern of needs for money to spend. Income is likely to increase for a time as the worker gets better at his job and is promoted. Then it remains fairly steady, and finally, drops to nothing when he retires. Of course, it is difficult to predict income, and the peak is reached at different times in different occupations, but the general pattern of steady income increases and final retirement with no income from work remains.

Needs are of course primarily a matter of standard of living, but if we fix some arbitrary standard, we can usefully ask how such needs are likely to vary over the life cycle of the typical family. We shall see this in the next section. Here it is enough to notice that we as consumers may feel pressures at any time to spend more than our income by borrowing. Or

we may want to spend less than our income and save for the
future. These decisions must be made in the light of the fact
that there is an interest rate by which savings increase and that
a somewhat larger interest rate must be paid on borrowed
money. So borrowing and spending more than income means
paying back more than the amount borrowed. Even if spending more than our income means simply using up our bank
account, there is a cost in foregone interest we could have
earned on the money.

When you are young, there are four major reasons why you
might want to keep some of each year's income for future use.

First, because income and needs are both unpredictable, you
may want some reserve for emergencies—a backlog of cash so
you will not have to borrow at high interest rates, or be a nuisance to your friends or relatives.

Second, earned income will drop to zero when you retire, but
you and perhaps others dependent on you will still need money
for many years. The amount of saving necessary for this need
is great, particularly with the low interest rates at which your
savings increase, and the longer time you can now expect to
live.

Third, there are foreseeable needs for large expenditures:
rearing and education of children, accumulation of household
equipment, purchase of a car, down payment on a house, vacation, and other necessities and luxuries for which you must
save.

Fourth, you may want to accumulate some estate to hand on
to your children.

Reserve Funds

Accumulating reserve funds is a method of taking care of
emergencies: some of which can be insured against, such as
medical bills, or accidents; some of which are partially insured
against for some people, such as unemployment. All of these
can be taken care of by borrowing or relying on charity, but we

like to avoid these methods if possible. Theoretically, the amount of reserve funds should depend on the amount of uncertainty as to income, and the number of unforeseen expenditures that are not covered by insurance. Borrowing is likely to be expensive, and ready cash sometimes allows us to take advantage of bargains.

Saving for a reserve fund is a one-time thing. It may mean the difference between continual interest charges and difficulties without such a fund, and a more pleasant life with it (even at the same level of spending), once the reserve is accumulated. This is a simple idea, but important. One person may borrow $200 to buy something, and as soon as those payments are finished borrow another $200 to buy something else, and so on. He is actually putting $200 or more of his income each payment period into these items, but is always in debt and always paying interest. Another person who accumulates $200 first ends up buying for cash, and accumulating another $200 in cash each period to buy the next item. Instead of paying out 6–20 per cent interest, he is earning a few per cent, is not in debt, and has a liquid reserve he can use for other emergencies. When he wants to buy a house, his ability to make a substantial down payment widens his choice and may enable him to get a house large enough to meet his needs. There is no way of determining an optimum amount of reserve. Some people suggest one month's income; others, two; others, six; others, twelve.

What do most people actually do? Table 1 shows that more than a fourth of them have neither savings bonds nor money in the bank, and that even in the middle income groups another third have less than $500. (See next page for Table 1.)

In addition, nearly two-thirds of those people with no liquid assets also have some personal debts, even after excluding mortgages, and business and farm debts. This does not mean that credit is used only by those who have no reserve fund, for more than six-tenths of the people with personal debts also have liquid assets.[1] These people have presumably chosen to keep a reserve fund even if it meant borrowing or buying on credit. More than a third of those with personal (non-mortgage) debts in early 1953 had liquid assets (U.S. bonds or bank accounts) sufficient to pay off all their debts.

TABLE 1

AMOUNT OF LIQUID ASSETS IN EARLY 1954 HELD BY SPENDING
UNITS IN DIFFERENT INCOME GROUPS

	TOTAL INCOME				
Amount of Liquid Assets	All Spending Units (per cent)	Under $1,000 (per cent)	$1,000– 2,999 (per cent)	$3,000– 4,999 (per cent)	Over $5,000 (per cent)
None	26	59	41	24	5
$1–499	28	18	28	33	27
$500–1,999	24	12	19	26	30
$2,000–4,999	13	6	8	12	20
$5,000 & over	9	5	4	5	18
	100	100	100	100	100

Source: 1954 Survey of Consumer Finances, see Federal Reserve Bulletin for July, 1954. A spending unit is defined as a group of people who are related, live together, and pool their incomes for major items of expense.

Saving for Predictable Needs

There is usually a pattern of needs which changes over the life cycle of the family, and which can be predicted at least in a rough way. Of course, "needs" are partly social and psychological. We all have certain "standards" of life that we regard as minimal, and others to which we aspire, but these are necessary only because we think they are. Even the published budgets for minimum cost of living in the United States are generally based on standards of nutrition, sanitation, and comfort that a large part of the world has no likelihood of attaining in the near future.

Hence, added to uncertainties as to our future income and the number of our dependents, we have reason to suspect that our standards of living are subject to change and generally in an upward direction. Although this makes the prediction of our future needs difficult, it makes planning more important if we don't want to get accustomed to standards which we cannot maintain.

Finally, inflation or deflation add further complications.   If prices continually rise and the consumer can find no adequate method of proportionally increasing the value of his own savings, he is forced to save more to provide adequately for his old age, but he is discouraged from doing so because he saves dollars that are valuable, only to have dollars which are worth much less later.

At any rate, it is useful as an example to take some standard of living which seems feasible and acceptable now, put it together with some other assumptions about family income, number of children, and so on, and see what it would mean in terms of expenditures over the lifetime of a family.   Our concern here is with expenditures, even if some of them are for durable goods.   Later on we shall want to consider carefully how to look at changes in the real economic position of the family.

Let us make the following assumptions, not because they are typical or reasonable, but because certain important principles will show up under almost any reasonable assumptions.

Our hypothetical family consists of a man and his wife of the same age, who will have four children, one when the parents are 22, one at 24, one at 27, and one at 30.   They plan to send all four to college.

Let us assume food will cost $30 per month per person, and half of this will be for children less than six years old.   This assumes that there are few if any economies in feeding larger families.   There are no available statistics as to whether there are economies of scale in feeding families.   Indeed, the problem is difficult to investigate, because a larger family at the same income has a lower income per person and is bound to spend less per person on food.   It might be suggested, however, that the present methods of handling and packaging foods reduce the amount of preparation time and the problem of leftovers, and also reduce the possible economies from buying in volume. It is difficult to see offhand any reason why one could feed more people at the same nutritional level for substantially less per person until one got to large enough numbers to be buying food wholesale. In addition, let us assume that food costs drop to $25 per person after retirement.

We allow $10 per month per person for clothing, but only half of this for those under six, and $7.50 for the parents after they are 65.

For rent or housing cost, we allow $75 per month until the second child arrives, then $100 a month until the fourth child is born, then $125 a month for 21 years when the last child leaves home (and the parents either move to smaller quarters or have the mortgage paid off). After this, the rent drops to $50 per month. Again after the wage earner retires and can do more around the house, rent drops again to $40. These figures are of course only rough guesses and are easier to predict for rental quarters than for an owned house, because they represent expenditures, not estimated real expenses. (See Chart 1.)

CHART 1

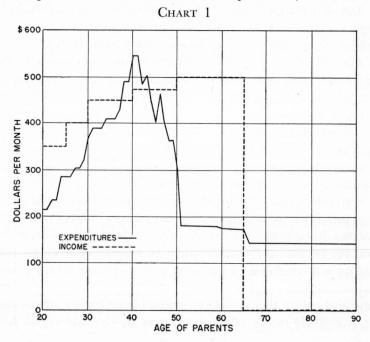

For utilities, household operation, cleaning and so forth, we allow $15 a month until the second child is born, then $20 until the fourth child, then $25 until the children leave home, and $20 after that.

For transportation, gifts, charity, and recreation, we allow $20 a month until retirement, then $15 (probably a gross underestimate).

For durable goods, including purchase of automobiles, we assume expenditures of $25 a month for the first ten years, $20 a month for the next ten, $15 a month for the next ten, $10 a month for the next ten, and $5 a month after that. Except in higher income groups, where there is some tendency to replace many durables when the parents are in the 45–54 age group (and the children have left home, perhaps), this is the prevailing tendency that appears in the data from the Surveys of Consumer Finances. It makes sense in terms of rapid accumulation of "necessary" furniture and household appliances.

Cost of college education (excluding food) is guessed to be $720 per year or $60 per month.

With these particular assumptions, Chart 1 gives the estimated expenditures at various ages of the parents. It can be seen that they become extremely large at the time the children are in college, amounting to some $6,540 a year in expenditures. Now, of course, things are not this simple. It is possible to delay certain expenditures, or borrow money, or for the children to work their way through college, and so on. But even as a rough indication, the particular family would want to save a great deal when the children are small, count on borrowing, or "borrowing from their savings" for a few years just before the children leave home, and hope to save a great deal from then until retirement.

Suppose we also estimate earned income for the same period. We have drawn on Chart 1 an expected income pattern of a rather optimistic nature. It looks as though this family could save a great deal after the children leave home, and would need most of it for the large and indeterminate needs of retire-

TABLE 2
FAMILY FINANCES OVER THE LIFE CYCLE [1]

	UNDER 45	UNDER 45	UNDER 45	UNDER 45	45 OR OLDER	45 OR OLDER	45 OR OLDER
	Single	*Married No Children*	*Married Children Under 18 (Youngest child under age 6)*	*Married Children Under 18 (Youngest child age 6 or over)*	*Married Children Under 18*	*Married No Children*	*Single*
Proportion of population in this group [2] (early 1954)	11	7	22	10	10	21	14
Median income, 1953	$2,600	$4,800	$4,300	$5,000	$4,300	$3,900	$1,700
Median net worth [3] (early 1953)	$700	$3,100	$3,100	$5,200	$7,800	$11,000	$5,400
Median proportion or income after taxes used for fixed payment [4]	13	25	28	25	20	16	29
Proportion with some personal debt (early 1954)	42	46	79	73	66	38	25
Proportion with some debt (personal or mortgage) (early 1954)	43	71	88	83	77	49	31
Proportion who bought one or more large household items (furniture or appliances) in 1953	22	52	58	58	48	39	22
Proportion who bought a used car in 1953	11	22	23	18	14	11	4
Proportion who bought a new car in 1953	5	11	11	20	11	9	2
Proportion owning a television set in early 1954	19	49	62	65	56	51	27
Proportion with some medical debt (early 1954)	14	12	35	19	25	9	9
Proportion with personal debt 10% of income or more (early 1954, excludes farmers and owners of businesses)	23	33	41	42	31	20	13

16

ment. We cannot show on this chart the possible additional desire to leave an estate for the children.

No matter what assumptions we made, provided they were reasonable, we should probably find about the same pattern: a possibility of saving in early years, tremendous pressures to spend during the period of the growing family, greatly diminished pressures after the children leave home. Table 2 provides some indications of the effects of this pattern of needs on the spending, the assets, and the debts of people at various stages in the life cycle.

Some consumer debt is for emergency purposes, and there is usually about a billion dollars or more outstanding in debts to doctors, dentists, and hospitals. Most debt is for the purchase of items for which people either do not have the cash or liquid savings, or do not wish to use what savings they have. Dramatic evidence of this is the way debt varies over the life cycle. (See Table 2.) The typical family accumulates a good many physical assets. They use credit to speed up this accumulation, since after all a washing machine is most useful when there are babies and small children. The family has a rapid increase in its total assets, but an increase in debt too, so that its net worth increases slowly. As the debts are paid off faster than the assets depreciate, net worth increases. Finally, during these periods, but afterwards also, monetary assets such as U.S. savings bonds are accumulated directly. Net worth should then show an increasing pattern over the life cycle of the family, while debt first increases, then decreases. Table 2 tends to show this pattern, although such a cross-section survey must be care-

---

NOTES ON TABLE 2

1 Data from the 1953 and 1954 Surveys of Consumer Finances.

2 Five per cent of the spending units do not fit into the pattern and are omitted.

3 Includes value of house, car, farm, business, other real estate, liquid assets, and stock, minus all debts. Does not include value of household furnishings, life insurance, annuity, or pension rights. Estimated from bracket data.

4 Rent, mortgage or debt payments, insurance, social security, annuities, and property taxes. Estimated from bracket data.

fully interpreted, because at any point in time, those who are at different stages of the life cycle will have had different experiences. Some grew up during a war and prosperity; others during a depression. Their assets and debts reflect this experience as well as their stage in life. Second, it is not possible to estimate all the components of net worth, and net worth in Table 2 includes only bank accounts, U.S. government bonds, common stock, value of house and car, investments in a business, farm or other real estate, minus debts. It does not include annuities, life insurance cash values, value of household equipment, social security or other pension rights, currency, or assets held in trust. However, these excluded items are all things that clearly increase in amount and value with age of the family head, up until the time he retires.

Empirical studies indicate that in recent years people whose children have grown up and left home have not saved much. There may be several reasons for this. These older people may not have shared the increases in income which younger and more mobile workers have received since World War II. Also, people's expenditures may well be dominated not by the necessities of life, but by other things such as vacations, entertainment, gadgets, tobacco, liquor and so on. Hence, a budget based on food and clothing, and such other prosaic items would not be realistic. Further, there is reason to believe that a person's wants become more elaborate and more expensive as he grows older. Finally, there is reason to believe that saving is a habit that is reinforced by successful achievements, and that past saving may raise one's aspirations to save in the future. If so, there would be an explanation for the "low" saving of the older couples whose children had left home, since many of them were forming their saving habits during the depression when it was almost impossible to save. This would also lead to an argument in favor of contractual saving commitments, even during times when wants are many and income is low, just to get the saving habit.

Saving for Retirement

One thing that is possible to figure with reasonable accuracy is how much it would cost to provide retirement income of any given size.   In our example, we ended up with an estimate of $145 per month needed to live on after retirement.   It is possible to buy an annuity for a lump sum which will pay this amount until the man dies, or until his wife dies, or until they both die.   The three types are successively more expensive because women live longer than men, and the chances of one of two people living for a long time are greater than the chances for either one alone.   If you wanted a retirement income without impairing your estate so that it would be left to the children, far more savings would be required.   Using rounded figures, since the rates vary and will undoubtedly be changed as life expectancies and interest rates change, we discover that to provide $145:

A. Indefinitely out of interest earnings, with capital left for estate, the couple would have to have $58,000 at age 65 if they could earn 3 per cent on it, or $43,500 if they could earn 4 per cent or $35,000 if they could earn 5 per cent.

B. Until the husband died, with nothing left after that, would cost about $24,000.

C. Until the wife died, with nothing left (or alternatively, half-rate for the wife if she outlives her husband), would cost $28,000.

D. Until both husband and wife died, with no estate, would cost $32,000.

E. Until the husband died plus $72 per month for the wife until she died, would cost about $28,000.

Since needed income would certainly drop if either the man or his wife died, some writers suggest one-third of the annuity be on the life of the husband, one-third on the wife, and one-third "joint or survivor" so that the survivor would always have two-thirds of the $145.

The reason companies can sell annuities that cost relatively little is, first, that the original sum is paid out as well as the interest earned, and, second, that interest is earned on the remaining amounts each year. For the individual, the annuity is a gamble, for if he dies early, he will not even get back what he paid, whereas if he lives a long time, he will get back far more than he paid in. The first of these possibilities bothers some people, so companies sell special policies that assure the holder or his heirs that he will get back all he paid. Of course the cost of this arrangement is great in terms of lower payments or a higher price for the policy by about 10 per cent. An annuitant exchanges an important risk of exhausting his money before he dies for an unimportant risk of dying early and leaving some money to the company.

The phenomenon of earned interest is helpful before retirement, too. You do not need to save $30,000 to have that much when you retire, since the savings of earlier years earn interest, and the interest earns interest. If you look in a set of mathematical tables under the heading "Amount of Annuity," you find that at a 3 per cent interest rate, $100 per year for 30 years accumulates to $4,757 rather than $3,000.[2]

The mathematics of compound interest with annual or monthly payments is complicated. Then there are the expenses of the company to be deducted too. At present interest rates, life expectancies, and company costs, one way to think of retirement is as follows.

Starting at age 35 and paying till 65, you would have to pay each month about one-half the amount you wanted paid to you each month after you retired, if the payments are to continue until you and your wife or husband are both dead. To retire on half salary, you would have to save a fourth of your income. If you are a man and the payments need only last so long as you live, a sixth of your income will do; if you are a woman, 20 per cent will suffice. (See Table 3.)

Of course, your income varies over your lifetime, and if you want to retire on half the salary you have reached just before retiring, you would have to save still more. On the other hand, since it is difficult to know just what your income will be, basing retirement plans on present income may be as good a rule as any.

TABLE 3

RATIO OF MONTHLY PAYMENT TO YOU WHEN YOU ARE RETIRED ON ANNUITY
WHILE PAYING TO MONTHLY ANNUITY PAYMENT, AS AFFECTED BY
STARTING AGE, RETIRING AGE, AND PAYMENT OPTION

		MONTHLY PAYMENT BY YOU AS PER CENT OF MONTHLY RETIREMENT BENEFIT IF BENEFIT LASTS UNTIL:		
Age When You Start Paying	*Age When You Retire*	*Man Dies (per cent)*	*Woman Dies (per cent)*	*Both Die (per cent)*
20	65	18	22	25
25	65	22	26	30
30	65	27	32	37
35	65	33	39	46
30	70	18	22	27

Note: Based on rates of Teacher's Insurance and Annuity Association, a partially subsidized organization, but based on 2 per cent interest accumulations and for a long-lived group of insured people. Table assumes husband and wife are same age. Upper right percentages can be interpreted as follows: if you start at age 20 and retire at 65, you can be assured of an income in the amount of four times your monthly payments to the company for as long as either of you live. If your payments to the company are one-eighth of your income, you retire on half-salary.

It is clear, then, that any reasonable amount of income after retirement requires setting aside substantial portions of your income. There are, of course, many qualifications to this. First, if you have more profitable ways to invest your money than at the rather low interest rates guaranteed in retirement annuity contracts, you need not save so much. Second, if you are under social security, or have a company pension scheme, the chances are that your benefits will be much larger, relative to your payments, than under individual retirement plans because of the lower costs and the partial subsidization by the government or the company. Third, there are ways of cutting the cost of living, and of consuming capital after you retire, for example, by living in your own home, doing the work on it, and letting it depreciate. Fourth, there may be sources of income which continue after you retire.   Finally, and most important, standards of living are flexible, and the frugal habits you develop struggling to save enough to provide for retirement may well reduce the amount you feel you need to spend when you retire. Indeed, you can go so far that you have lost the capacity to enjoy spending money.   Somewhere between the absurd miser who is found smothered in trash in a house cluttered with old junk and boxes of ten dollar bills, and the spendthrift who is the despair of his friends and relatives, there must be some reasonable level of saving.

Some Definitions

It is necessary to stop and ask what saving is anyway.   The example given dealt with income received and payments made over the lifetime of a family, but failed to look at the family's real economic position.   For instance, the purchase of a house might well have led to even larger payments on the mortgage. Some part of these payments are saving, because they repay a debt and increase the owner's equity in his house, but they represent cash payments at a time when other cash payments are also heavy.

But let us forget the money basis of the family finances, and look at the family's real economic position.   Take any one year and ask whether the family is better off at the end of the year than it was at the beginning.   Theoretically, we might find the answer by adding up the assets and subtracting the debts to find the family's "net worth," and then do this again at the end of the year to see how it has changed.   But this is very difficult, particularly if we want to include the value of the family's physical assets, or things so intangible as increased future earning power resulting from a year spent in going to college or learning a new skill.   In a period of inflation, current dollar values might increase, but we might not like to call this saving.

A typical balance sheet for a family might look like the following:

BALANCE SHEET, JOHN DOE AND FAMILY, JAN. 1, 19———

Assets	*Liabilities*
Monetary, fixed value	Monetary ....
Currency	Mortgage debt .
Bank deposits ..	Installment debt
U.S. savings	Other debts ....
bonds	Non-monetary ......
Negotiable but uncer-	Obligations to
tain or fluctuating	people outside
value	the family ...
Stocks and bonds	*Total Liabilities* ..$———
House	
Real estate	
Automobile	
Physical assets, not	
completely negoti-	
able	
Durable goods ..	
Clothes	
Household in-	
ventories	
Not negotiable	
Value of college	
education	
(aside from its	
effect on fu-	
ture income)..	
Value now of ex-	
pected future	
income	
Value of pre-	
sumptive rights	
to inheritances,	
aid from par-	
ents, etc.	

        Total Assets ....$———

Total assets, minus total liabilities, equals NET WORTH ....$———

This same procedure a year later will give another net worth figure, and the amount by which the latter is larger than the former tells how much the family has saved in the economists' sense of the term.

Why not just take total receipts and subtract total expenditures, and call the difference saving? The reason is simply that not all receipts are earned income, not all expenditures are for down-the-drain consumption, and there may well be income earned but not received or consumption not represented by payments.

The economist and the accountant make these distinctions by using different terms, and it will be useful if we learn them too:

Receipts: Money taken in for any reason, including gifts received, repayments of loans that had been made to others, receipts from sale of assets.

Revenue (or income): Money actually earned during the year. If we want to count intangibles such as the value of expected future earnings as assets, then increases in such values are also part of income in this real sense.

Expenditures: Money paid out for any reason, including gifts, purchases of assets, repayments of loans.

Expenses: The incurring of an obligation by actually consuming something. Depreciation on a car or house or durables is an expense but not an expenditure.

The definitions of revenues and expenses are clearly difficult because they depend on the extent to which we want to value intangibles in assessing net worth. If the definitions are consistent, revenue minus expenses will be equal to the change in net worth.

Both these methods of estimating saving are much too cumbersome and complicated. What most of us do is something like this. We eliminate the intangibles, except in interpreting the final figures. We find whether the fixed dollar assets (cash, bank accounts) have increased, and by how much. To this we add any amounts paid out for long-lasting assets, or to repay debts, for instance, repayments on mortgage principal, savings in life insurance as indicated by increased cash value of the policy (see Chapter 6), annuity payments by us or the employer, and purchases of durable goods. Then, we subtract receipts from the sale of assets, or in the form of gifts, and also make some estimate of depreciation on house, car, and durable goods.

This sounds worse than it is. Most of us do not buy or sell assets to any great extent. Unless there have been large purchases, we can take current purchases of durables as roughly equal to the depreciation on all of them.

Another way to look at the matter of saving is to categorize it into major types or forms:

Contractual saving: regular payments, sometimes partly for insurance, property taxes, and so on, but often largely saving.

Investments in physical assets: purchase of a home, or durable goods only a small part of the value of which will be consumed this year. On the other hand, most of these things cannot be sold easily and involve a level of consumption in the future that is predetermined by the depreciation rates of the assets involved.

Discretionary saving in liquid forms: accumulations of cash, bank accounts, and U.S. savings bonds.

Discretionary savings invested in assets: purchase of stock, real estate, money put into a farm or business, and so on.

An indication of the relative importance of these various forms of saving is given in Table 4, with some changes in definitions necessitated by the survey method. 1950 was a year of rather large purchases of durable goods, and such purchasing tends to make "discretionary saving" somewhat lower, but the important thing is the extent to which saving by ordinary consumers is contractual in form, even excluding social security payments.

The Investment of Savings

What can be said about the various forms in which saving is done and savings kept? Some of them are so important and complicated that whole chapters shall be devoted to them; others can be discussed briefly here. First, let us make a list of the places where savings are kept:

TABLE 4

Consumer Saving by Income Groups, 1950 [1]

Income after Federal Income Taxes	Per Cent of SU's	Contractual Saving [2]	"Discretionary" Saving [3]	Durable Goods Expenditures [4]	Total "Saving" [5]
$0–999	12.1	$16	$-116	$26	$-74
$1,000–1,999	20.0	76	-86	125	115
$2,000–2,999	21.9	117	-160	298	255
$3,000–3,999	21.3	228	-89	422	561
$4,000–4,999	18.0	300	-23	570	847
$5,000–7,499	9.5	436	112	854	1,402
$7,500–9,999	1.5	561	1,218	1,142	2,921
$10,000–	0.7	1,224	1,638	1,306	4,168
	100.0				

[1] Data from the 1951 Survey of Consumer Finances. These data exclude farmers, owners of businesses, and cases where any component of saving was not ascertained. They are, therefore, not precise estimates, but are presented for illustrative purposes. Needless to say these averages cover a tremendous diversity of individual behavior.

[2] Includes all life insurance premiums and payments on mortgage principal. Excludes social security payments.

[3] Discretionary saving equals increase in assets minus increase in debts (some of which are really contractual), plus purchase of home.

[4] Net of trade-in allowances. Includes cars, furniture, and major household appliances.

[5] Including net durable goods expenditures but without any deduction for depreciation of durables.

Social security

Company annuity and pension schemes

Private annuity schemes

Life insurance (cash value)

Own home

Automobiles

Durable goods and household equipment

Stocks and bonds

Businesses, farm, or other real estate

Credit unions

Postal savings, savings banks, Savings and Loan Associations, and U.S. savings bonds

Cash and checking accounts

Investment trusts

The best way to look at these various investments is to ask first what we want from them. What are the characteristics of a good investment? Which of these are most important? If we could have them all, these are the attributes most of us would like our investments to have:

Yield: They should pay a good interest return, or save us money, or gain in value over time.

Safety: They should return at least the amount we put into them.

Flexibility or marketability: We should be able to get our money out whenever we need it and without loss. We should be able to vary the amounts we pay into the investment. We should not have to keep working for the same company, or in the same town, in order to preserve our savings.

Inflation hedge: We should like the market value of the investment to go up with the price level.

Convenience: We may want an investment that does not require a great deal of our time and effort to decide about it or watch over it. On the other hand, we may want investments where we are partly paid for our management, so that we shall have a part time manager's job as well as an asset that earns money after we retire. Rental real estate is an example of this.

Tax status: We may be concerned both with the taxable nature of the interest or profit return, and with our ability to shift the income from one year to another in order to minimize our income taxes.

Let us look briefly at the list of investments, asking ourselves what advantages and disadvantages each one has. None of them, of course, will have all the qualities we want.

Social security comes as close to being the best of all possible investments as anything on the list.   It is not a pure investment, and only a few of us really have a choice whether to be covered or not.   It is worth while, however, to examine its provisions, particularly since they may influence what we want to do with the rest of our savings.

Social security is not a pure insurance and annuity scheme. The "yield" in terms of the relation between the amount you get in benefit payments, and the amount you and your employer pay into the system, is very high.   It is difficult to show this with any simple tables, because of the complex nature of the provisions.   There are payments to widows and dependents (insurance) and separate annuity provisions of different amounts for the wife and husband.   Furthermore, all the provisions are subject to change.   The payroll tax was increased to 4 per cent —that is, 2 per cent each by employer and employee—at the beginning of 1954, and is scheduled to increase to 5 per cent in 1960, 6 per cent in 1965, and 6½ per cent in 1970.   Benefits were increased 5–30 dollars per month in 1954, and the amount of income subject to tax raised from $3,600 to $4,200.   The benefits may well be increased further or the qualifications for coverage reduced.   At present you are fully covered if you have been working in a job covered by social security for a minimum of 6 quarter-years and more than half the quarters since 1950, or since you reached 21, or if you have put in a total of 40 quarters (10 years) in such employment.   You count the quarter year if you earned $50 or more in covered employment (or $100 from self-employment on which you paid a social security tax). Your widow and unmarried children under 18 receive benefits as survivors if you die when you are only "currently insured," that is, if you worked in covered employment for 6 of the 13 quarters immediately preceeding your death or retirement. The amount of benefits you or your survivors get depends on a complicated average monthly wage, not on the total amount you and your employer have paid into the system.[3]

A few examples will indicate what a bargain social security is.

If your average monthly wage is $350, the retirement benefits are $108.50 a month for you, plus $54.30 for your dependent wife or husband. The amount you would have to pay at age 65 for two such annuities purchased from a private company would be about $26,600. In order to qualify for coverage, you would have had to work for ten years and during that time you would have paid in $840 and your employer another $840. Some people get covered without working this long. If you had entered a social security covered job in 1950 at age 63 and worked for two years, you would have been covered. On the other hand, many people work for more than ten years and pay in two to three times the $1,680 we calculated above.

Taking the same kind of ratio as in Table 2, for example, the ratio of the monthly payments by you (and your employer) in proportion to the monthly payments you receive after retirement, we find in-payments of 4 per cent of $350 each month ($14), divided by benefit payments of $162.80 ($108.50 plus $54.30), or less than 9 per cent, compared with the ratios of 18–46 per cent in Table 2. Remember also that the ratios in Table 2 are based on the assumption that you pay in for at least 30 years.

On top of all this, there are substantial benefits to your survivors even if you die before retirement. The value of these benefits depends on the number and ages of your dependents, but for a man with a young wife and two children the value is equivalent to well over $45,000 worth of life insurance. (See Chapter 6.)

All this may make social security look so good that you may wonder why some people argue that it is inadequate. To some extent what is adequate is a matter of opinion. For most people, however, social security is probably inadequate as a total savings program. In addition, the payments are clearly inadequate in some situations, and there are a large number of people who are still unable to secure coverage by social security. Many workers do not have an average monthly wage of $350, and they receive less in benefits.

Company annuity and pension schemes, while not the bargain social security is, are frequently "subsidized" at least to the extent of the company paying some of the administrative costs. Your real salary is larger by the amount the company contributes to the scheme, and the amount the company pays for administrative costs—both amounts subject to income tax exemption. These schemes are automatic and compulsory, hence relatively painless ways of saving, just as social security is. They are as safe as the company and the trust company handling the pension fund. One serious difficulty with such plans is that as an employee you accrue rights to pensions that can be used only if you stay with the same company. Your opportunities to move to more remunerative jobs are restricted. If you move, the rights to annuity will be small or nonexistent.

The cost of private annuity schemes has already been indicated in Chapter 1. Most of them have an effective yield of 2–2½ per cent. They are automatic and quite safe, but inflexible, so that a young couple with a growing family might find the payments difficult to make because of the necessity for accumulating household equipment. Indeed, an adequate annuity with constant payments is quite likely to force the ordinary family to use installment plans or other forms of credit during certain periods. This amounts to lending money to the annuity company at 2½ per cent while borrowing money at the same time at 6 per cent or more.

Life insurance will be dealt with at some length in Chapter 6, but it can be stated here that insofar as it possesses a saving feature, it has much the same characteristics as a private annuity contract, with its automaticity, compulsory character, low interest yield, and high safety.

Investment in Houses, Cars, and Durable Goods

A very common and popular way to invest savings is to invest in a home. More than half the families in this country own their own home. More than half the non-farm families with homes have mortgage debts on them, so that they are still investing in their home by paying off the debt on it. In Chapter 8, the advantages and disadvantages of home ownership are more fully discussed. The "yield" on this investment is difficult to estimate since it involves direct satisfactions, usually involves better housing than rental quarters, allows the owner to earn income (tax-exempt) by doing his own repairs, upkeep, and so on. The risk of home-owning is also difficult to assess, since it depends on the likelihood that the owner will have to move when the housing market is depressed, or move too frequently to be able to write off the costs of selling and buying. The saving is, however, automatic if it is done by paying off the debt on the house. Some years ago, it was common to have mortgages where only the interest was paid, and payments on principal were made at will. This was a sensible arrangement for farmers with fluctuating incomes, but for many people it left too much to their own self-control and will power. The old melodrama about the mortgage coming due without any funds having been accumulated to pay it off was only too often a real life drama. Almost all mortgages now are "amortized," that is, the payments are calculated so that a constant amount per month, including interest, and sometimes taxes and insurance, will repay the debt in 15, or 20, or 25, or 30 years. There are a considerable number of people who either by neglect, or because they like the automatic and compulsory saving feature, keep a mortgage on their house while they have liquid savings in the bank, or in U.S. bonds or both. This amounts to lending money to the government or bank at less than 3 per cent, and at the same time borrowing it on the mortgage at the rate of 4½–6 per cent. There may be reasons why one wants a liquid reserve too, and there are some income tax complications for wealthier people, but there are certainly some people who are paying in terms of low yield for the compulsory saving involved in the mortgage. A house is an excellent hedge against inflation because payments do not increase but the value of the house does. In case of deflation, however, a house may become a serious burden, particularly if one is still paying off large fixed sums on the mortgage, or has to move at a time when it is difficult or impossible to sell it for a "reasonable" price.

It may seem absurd to say that people have savings "invested" in automobiles, particularly since they depreciate in value so rapidly, but two-thirds of the spending units in this country owned a car in early 1954, and included in these are nearly 8 per cent who owned two or more cars.[4] Because a car is an expensive piece of equipment, substantial sums of money are involved, and because a vast majority (62 per cent in 1953) buy on credit, they have a compulsory saving scheme insofar as their payments on the car pay off the debt faster than the value of the car depreciates.   In early 1953, one-third of all spending units owned a car worth $1,000 or more.   The relative importance of this asset compared with other assets of consumers declines rapidly with age as other assets are accumulated—the car being one of the first assets to be acquired.   In early 1953, cars accounted for a little over 5 per cent of all consumer assets (excluding life insurance cash values, retirement fund equities, value of social security rights, and household equipment), but even including those who own no cars, the proportion was 24 per cent for those in the 18–24 age group, 11 per cent in the 25–34 age group, 7 per cent, 5 per cent, and 3 per cent in the next three age groups, and less than 2 per cent for those 65 years old or over.   Of course, the actual purchase of a car may commit a person to a much higher level of consumption, particularly because of the rapid depreciation in the value of a car during the first few years of its life.

Durable goods and household equipment have the same general attributes as cars; their purchase may increase the family's level of consumption, but most of them last a long time and may even save money by eliminating laundry bills, food spoilage and so on. When they are bought on credit, the payments are generally greater than the depreciation rate, and hence are partly saving.   Purists would insist that the family determine how much money or time a household appliance will save and see whether it would pay for itself. Others suggest that since most people keep on buying durable goods all their lives that they should simply treat the expenditures as part of their consumption and neglect the growing stock of physical wealth. At any rate, the low liquid asset holdings and large debts of young families indicate that even if these purchases are really an investment, they lead to a shortage of cash and frequently a resort to credit.

Investments with Monetary Yields

Stocks and bonds can be purchased with a variety of attributes, but they have some things in common. There is somewhat more risk with most of them than with other investments, particularly in the case of common stock in smaller companies. The yields are usually higher to compensate for this but not always. Furthermore, there are so many different ones, and most people feel they know so little about them, that only some 10 per cent of the spending units in the country own any common stock, and many fewer than that own any nongovernment bonds. Stocks and bonds of the larger companies are sold in the big stock exchanges and are easily bought and sold, except that a stockholder may take a loss if he must sell at the wrong time.

Bonds of corporations generally provide for a fixed amount of interest that is paid before the stockholders get any dividends. The bonds are as safe as the company, and in case of failure, the common stockholders are the first to lose their invested capital. The stockholders' investments form a cushion that protects the bondholders. Bond yields are lower, of course. The actual interest yield is not the stated one unless you plan to buy the bond at "par." A $100 bond that pays 4 per cent a year or $4 may sell for $105, in which case the effective yield on your investment is less than 4 per cent. If you want to figure what the effective yield on a bond is, the simple rule is to do this. Take any premium you paid over par and divide it by the number of years till maturity of the bond. Subtract this amount from the annual interest payment (amount of the coupons) and divide by the amount you invested (paid for the bond).   In the case of a bond bought at less than par, simply *add* to each year's interest a fraction of the discount, since each year you earn not only the interest but an increase in the value of the bond—it is worth par when it matures.   Bonds are seldom advised for private investors.   They are difficult to evaluate, sold infrequently, and not easily marketable, except those of the large companies.   Another disadvantage is that they often come only in large denominations.

Furthermore, bonds are risky in the sense that you may not be able to cash them before maturity without a loss.   The Liberty Bonds sold during World War I were selling at 85 cents on the dollar in 1921 during a brief depression when many people wanted their money.   The reason was that the market interest rate had gone up and no one would buy a Liberty Bond except at a price that would assure him an equally high interest yield.   Since interest rate is more important the longer the term of the bond, the risk of fluctuations in market value of the bond is greater, the longer the term.   Consequently paid interest rates are generally higher for longer term bonds.   The loss from buying a bond at a low interest rate, when the market rate rises later, is not simply that you cannot sell it at par until maturity, but involves "opportunity cost" again.   If you had your funds in liquid form, you could have secured the higher market interest rate.   A simple rule is that if the interest rate rises by more than its own rate, that is if it rises from 4 per cent to 4.16 per cent, then you lose more from being tied to the low 4 per cent than you earn in interest.

Preferred stock is generally paid its stated dividends (including any which were missed in the past, in the case of "cumulative preferred") before any money is paid out to the common stockholders.   It is consequently somewhat safer than common stock, and again usually has a lower yield.

Common stock usually has no stated dividend yield, takes the brunt of the fluctuations in earnings, and theoretically provides the votes that elect the directors of the corporation. In actual practice, there are so many stockholders in most companies that the directors can assure their own re-election and determine who any new directors shall be. They can also determine the pricing and dividend policy of the corporation and their own salaries and bonuses. In practice, then, the stockholder does not run the company. The management of the corporation can legally do almost anything they want to with the stockholder's money, though in practice managements have been generally quite concerned with the welfare of their stockholders.

It should not take much thought to see that the amount of risk the stockholder takes in the form of fluctuation in earnings, as well as his average yield, depends not only on the type of business, but on the proportion of the assets provided by bondholders, preferred stockholders, and banks in the form of short-term credit. Let us look at two imaginary companies. (See diagram.)

COMPANY A

Assets: $100,000	Liabilities: 0	
	Bonds 0	
	Preferred stock 0	
	Common stock and surplus	$100,000

COMPANY B

Assets: $100,000	Liabilities:	
	Bank credit (3%) $10,000	
	Bonds (4%) 30,000	
	Preferred stock (5%) 10,000	
	Common stock and surplus	$50,000

Now suppose each of these companies makes 6 per cent on its total assets, or $6,000, before paying any interest charges or dividends. *Company A* will be able either to pay to the stockholders 6 per cent of their total investment or to increase the value of the stockholders' investment by this amount by reinvesting it in the business, or any combination of these.

Company B on the other hand will have to pay to the bank 3 per cent of $10,000 or $300, plus 4 per cent of $30,000 to the bondholders, or $1,200, plus 5 per cent of $10,000 to the preferred stockholders, or $500, a total of $2,000, leaving $4,000 for the common stockholders. But these stockholders only put $50,000 of their money into the business, in the form of original payments (plus past reinvested earnings), hence they are making 8 per cent on their investment instead of the 6 per cent they could make in *Company A*. This phenomenon is known as "leverage."

Leverage has another aspect, however. Suppose the companies each made only $2,000 one year. In *Company A* the stockholders would earn 2 per cent, but in *Company B* all the $2,000 would go in contractual interest charges and dividends on preferred stock, and the stockholders would earn nothing at all. On the other hand, if a very good year came along and the companies each made $10,000, the stockholders would earn 10 per cent in *Company A* but 16 per cent in *Company B* ($8,-000 after the fixed charges, on an investment of $50,000).

Consequently the amount of risk in any given stock depends not only on the nature of the business, but also on the amount of leverage. There are several other major considerations in judging a stock from the published records. The book value of the assets of the company, minus the claims of the bondholders and preferred stockholders, is one measure of the worth of the company and could be divided by the number of shares of stock to find "book value per share." But accounting is largely a historical process relying on historic costs, rigid policies about writing off the value of depreciating assets, adjustments by some companies for inflation, and a variety of inventory valuation policies, most of which understate the market value of the inventories.

Many years ago, it was common particularly for railroads and other public utilities to assume that replacement was enough. When the railroads in particular finally awoke to the reality of obsolescence, it was too late, and many of them had to be reorganized. The stockholders, who had been receiving what looked like profits (actually part of their share of the company being paid back to them), were left with no further equity in some of these railroads. At present, the opposite tendency is in vogue, that is, companies write off their equipment faster than it depreciates, even including obsolescence. It is difficult to tell without knowing a great deal about a company whether the amount on their books for net depreciated value of plant and equipment represents what it is really worth. It is probably true these days that the value is greatly understated. This is particularly the case because book values are in terms of prices paid for these assets, and after years of inflation it would cost much more to replace them. On the other hand the assets of a business that cannot sell its product may be worth very little.

As for inventories, it was once the case that most of them were valued at "cost or market value, whichever is lower," but when the Bureau of Internal Revenue allowed the "Last in, first out" method of inventory valuation, it became possible and usually advantageous to companies for tax reasons to use this valuation. Simply put, this involves valuing inventory at prices prevailing when the system was adopted, though if prices fell the inventory would be "written down." Since there has been a substantial increase in prices over the past twenty years, many companies now have inventories on their books at depression prices. All in all, however, if you take the book value of the assets, subtract the liabilities, and divide by the number of shares of stock outstanding, you generally have a conservative estimate of the value of the company's assets, per share of stock.

But the real value of a company is not what its equipment originally cost or is presently valued at, but what the company can earn in the future. If you want to use past reported earnings as a guide to this, however, you are again in difficulty, because among the expenses deducted in computing profits are depreciation on plant and equipment, and adjustments of inventory valuations.

Evaluation of past dividends paid and changes in the market value of the stock are somewhat better indicators. Stocks vary as to the proportion of earnings which are reinvested—presumably increasing the value of the stock—and the proportion which are paid out in dividends. If you want an investment for retirement income, a stock which plows back most of its profits will avoid income taxes and be preferable, provided the new investments are well chosen by the company.

This is not a book on investments. There are many such books. We have tried simply to indicate the nature of the problem.[5] It is complex enough to scare away most people in spite of the rather high yields. There is reason to believe that a program of purchasing a diversified array of stocks regularly without getting in and out of the market would, over a period of years, be reasonably safe and have high yield. Various studies have been made, using a variety of past periods. They all show that a saving program which each year invests half one's savings for the year in a broad array of common stocks, regardless of the level of stock prices, has better results than either putting it all in stock or all in fixed-value but low-yield investments.[6] What one is doing is reducing risk of purchasing stocks at the wrong time by buying steadily, and of course buying more shares when the prices are low since $100 will buy 5 shares when they are $20, and 10 shares when they are $10. One is also reducing the risk of buying the wrong stocks by buying a variety of them. Finally, the risk of suffering from long-run fluctuations in all stock prices is reduced by having some of your savings in things the value of which does not go up and down. The ordinary consumer might find it difficult to buy a variety of stock, because the broker's fees and complications increase if you buy one share at a time. A new institution has arisen in recent years to solve this problem: the so-called mutual fund or investment trust.

There are now a number of *investment trusts* or *mutual funds* which issue their own shares, invest the money in a broad range of stocks, accumulate the dividends and pay them to you, and charge a small commission for their services. They save money by buying and selling stocks in large lots, and also by knowing more about the specific companies, their management and potential profits than an individual could take time to find out. All in all, however, they probably provide a somewhat smaller average yield, together with the reduction in risk. The initial purchase cost is about 8 instead of the 1 to 6 per cent broker's fee if you purchase stocks directly, and the operating costs reduce your net yield by about six-tenths of 1 per cent each year. Of course, if all stock prices fall, the value of your shares in the investment trust will also fall. The trusts are regulated in some states and by the Federal Securities Act of 1933 and the Investment Act of 1940.

Whether because of the risk, or the amount of information required to select good stocks, the vast majority of the stock is owned by people with incomes of $10,000 and more.[7] Very few people out of the population have made use of the investment trusts, but the trusts can be counted on to grow in importance in the future.[8] A system for selling stocks on the installment plan was recently inaugurated, but is rather expensive unless the stock-buyer invests $300 or more every three months. Beginning in 1954, dividend income was partially exempted from federal income taxes, making the effective yield still higher.

Investment of savings in businesses, farms, or other real estate is uncommon except for farmers and those who are actively in the business. Some 6 per cent of the spending units of the country are farmers who own their own farms. Another 8 per cent own businesses, and some 14 per cent own real estate other than their own home. All these investments require knowing a good deal about the particular land, building, or business, and either direct participation or payments to someone else for managing the investment. There does seem to be some tendency for people to accumulate rental real estate and manage it long after they are retired from their regular job. Some 20 per cent of the people over 65 owned some income-earning real estate in early 1953, as compared with 12 per cent of all spending units. Another 3.5 per cent of all spending units get income from roomers in their own home. Most of these investments have some risk, and their yield is difficult to estimate, particularly since it depends on the ability of the individual to buy carefully at a good time and manage wisely. Some people regard a large house as a sort of business investment, because part of it could be rented out and managed by the wife, even while there were young children at home. Very shrewd investment in income-earning real estate, farms, or businesses can pay off, but the possibilities of losing your savings are also great. In particular, historical studies indicate that speculation in empty land is quite unlikely to pay off except for a few very lucky people who buy land just before it becomes ripe for development. The interest on your investment, which you could have earned elsewhere, can eat up an equivalent increase each year in the value of the land, and there is very little land that has increased in value by more than a few per cent per year over any extended period. The striking exceptions such as the corner of State and Madison Streets in Chicago make it all the more important to realize that they are exceptions, even for Chicago, the fastest growing city in history. One expert after studying land values in Chicago from 1833 to 1933 concluded that

. . . it would have been extremely difficult if not impossible to have selected investments (in land) that have yielded a net return of 5 or even 6 per cent per annum for the period covered by this study.[9]

Similar warnings are in order when it comes to small businesses, particularly small retail stores and restaurants. A very large proportion of these fail each year, and only a few of the others make any substantial profits, particularly if the effort of the proprietor and his family is taken into account. Unless the investor has something really new and better to sell, and can get the capital to get it started, it is probably better to buy an investment with proven earning potential. On the other hand, it is often nice to have investments which repay managing so that after retirement you will have something interesting and lucrative to do.

Savings accounts and postal savings are again low risk, low yield, but quite flexible and with no easy automatic features to help you save. U.S. savings bonds are less flexible, in that there is a penalty in the form of very low interest yield if you cash them before the first ten years are up. With rising interest rates at savings banks, there are places throughout the country where interest rates are higher than on government bonds. On the other hand, payroll saving plans where the employer sees to it that some fixed amount is deducted from your salary and invested in government bonds have again the advantage of automaticity, plus the feature which some people regard as an advantage, of deterrents to cashing the bonds and using the money. U.S. Savings Bonds of the Series A-F and J types are accrual bonds where the interest is paid when the bond matures, or is cashed. They can be held beyond maturity and still earn interest. This has income tax advantages for some people, since if you are on a cash basis as most people are, you only need declare the interest as income when you cash the bonds. If they are kept until an emergency, your other income may be so low that you pay no tax on the interest on the bonds. If you keep them until you retire, your other income will be low and you will have a double exemption because you are over 65.

Most saving accounts are insured up to $10,000 by the Federal Deposit Insurance Corporation and accounts in Savings and Loan Associations are insured to $10,000 by the Federal Savings and Loan Insurance Corporation. Both are government agencies. It pays to make sure your account is in an insured bank.

Some savings are kept in cash and checking accounts. Here there is perfect flexibility, no risk, but no yield. Indeed, in

some banks the checking account arrangements are so expensive
as to involve a substantial negative interest rate.   Some people
feel that checking accounts are bad because it is too easy to get
the money and use it without replacing it.   There are also
Christmas saving clubs or vacation saving plans which have
automatic saving features, and no interest yield.

Credit unions are a type of co-operative, often established in
conjunction with a co-operative or a labor union.   Members
invest in the unions.   They in turn make loans to members,
or invest the money in U.S. bonds or other credit unions or
federally insured saving and loan associations   They pay dividends to members in proportion to the amount invested by each
member.   Their income is not subject to taxation, though of
course the dividends are.   There are state laws governing their
operation, but there is also a Federal Credit Union Act of 1934
which provides for supervision by the Federal Security Agency
and some rules of operation for unions chartered under the act.
By 1950 there were some 4.5 million people in credit unions,
and these credit unions held about 10 per cent of the total consumer installment loans outstanding.[10]   Federal credit unions
are probably more strictly supervised than those operating under state law, but any credit union is safe so long as its management is adequate.   They are not insured.

In looking over the range of possible places to keep savings,
it seems clear that if you want either a very high degree of safety,
or an automatic compulsory saving scheme, then the yield is
likely to be low.   If you want *both* safety and automaticity,
then the yield will be still lower as with annuities or insurance.
This raises the basic question as to what you want.   When the
possibility of further inflation is added, the choice becomes even
more complex, and most of us tend to "diversify," that is, to
put some savings where it will provide an inflation hedge, some
in high-yield investments, some in a safe place, and so on.

There is a type of "investment' we have not mentioned which
is safe, profitable and proof against inflation, and that is investment in yourself or your family.[11]   Money and time spent in

increasing skills and knowledge will pay off in income-earning ability, the value of which goes up with the price level.

There are two important matters in connection with the law when it comes to investment of savings. This is not to say that there are not others, and for those with a great deal of money good legal advice is essential, but we shall only mention the two most important considerations here. First, there are differing legal forms of ownership, one of which involves two or more people owning as "joint tenants with rights of survivorship, but not as tenants in common." This means that either party can sell the asset, cash the interest or dividend checks, or otherwise dispose of it, but if one dies, the legal ownership reverts automatically to the other. This looks like a wonderful way to avoid a lot of legal problems and even reduce estate and inheritance taxes, but recent legal commentators are beginning to warn that it has a great many disadvantages.[12]

In the first place, the loophole has been plugged in the federal estate tax and in most state inheritance laws. Half of all assets in joint tenancy are considered as still owned by the husband at death and hence are part of the estate for tax purposes. Second, where the common bond between husband and wife does not hold, either joint owner can make life miserable for the other. Third, joint tenancy with rights of survivorship is frequently mixed up with tenancy in common, or tenancy in the entirety, either in the original title or by people who are handling such transactions as dividend checks. Some corporations insist on the names of both joint owners, in spite of the legal right of either to sign for both. Fourth, there are capital gains taxes to consider if the wife wants to sell any of the assets which have increased in value. This includes the house, since she is unlikely to want to buy another one that costs "at least as much" and will not get an exemption from capital gains tax. The present state of the law is such that the total asset is considered as owned by the survivor from the time the joint tenancy was established, hence the full capital gain from that time is payable if the asset is sold. On the other hand, assets held in the name of the deceased become those of the survivor at the market value at time of death for capital gains tax purposes, thus escaping any tax on the gain in value before that time. Finally, there are gift taxes, and putting assets in joint tenancy is considered as giving half of them to the other person, hence subject to gift tax. There is an exemption of $3,000 each year to a maximum of $30,000 from gift taxes, and a 50 per cent exemption of the rest in case the gift is to your wife, but there may still be a tax to pay, if, for instance, a house is purchased and put in joint tenancy. There will also be interest to pay on the tax and lawyers fees to straighten it all out if the records are not clear.

It remains true for small estates, that having all the assets in joint tenancy may avoid the expense and delay of probate, administrator and so on. It frequently takes more than two years to settle an estate even if it is simple, and an administrator as well as lawyers may have to be paid. On the other hand, for very large estates, lawyers sometimes suggest giving some assets to the wife, and paying the gift tax. The gift tax may not be as high as the estate tax, and the gift and tax deplete the estate further anyway. The new exemption of the first $50 of dividend income from taxes for husband and wife separately makes it wise either to divide ownership or to put the stock in joint tenancy.

Second, the income tax laws have a number of provisions that make the taxes different depending on the way the income is received. Money income can be received by individuals who are dependents of the head of the family, up to $600 a year tax free, and without loss of dependent status so long as the family still provides more than half the support of each dependent. Obviously, it pays to be sure that dependents do not go over these limits.

If you keep your accounts on a cash receipt basis, only income actually received is taxable. This means that an investment which does not actually pay cash returns but simply increases in value will delay the necessity for income taxes, perhaps until a time when you have no other income and would have little or no tax to pay, or are over 65 years of age so that you (and your wife) have double exemptions. Furthermore, if the increment in value is definable as a "capital gain," as in the case of increased market value of common stock, and if you owned the asset for more than six months, then the gain is taxable at a much lower rate even when finally "realized." Finally, if you are so fortunate as to be able to leave such investments to your dependents when you die, only estate and inheritance taxes are paid on them, and the dependents take them over at the current market value so that no income or capital gain tax is ever paid on the increased value before that time.

This does not exhaust the legal possibilities for reducing income taxes, though most of the others are either variants of the above, or are of minor importance to most people. J. K. Lasser Co. puts out a volume every year with many details on income taxes, and to those with complicated financial affairs, it can be quite useful.

There are frightening articles that appear occasionally in popular magazines about the horrors of not having every agreement in writing, or not having a will when you die, or not being insured against being sued because your golf ball hits someone. Some of the dangers are undoubtedly real, but a great many of them appear to be either improbable or applicable only to rather wealthy people.[13] One important problem arises when a widow is left with children, because many state laws provide that if there is no will, the children each receive some share of the estate. This may tie up substantial portions of the money in trust for the children when it is most needed to support the family and get them through school. An owned home usually goes to the widow outside this division, however, as do any life insurance benefits. It remains true that the law is expensive, time consuming, and not always equitable and that the law courts are to be avoided if possible. The old biblical injunction to settle matters with your neighbor out of court is still valid ethically, and in these days is also good economics. This does not mean that lawyers are to be avoided. Particularly where transactions involve valuable property or large sums of money, it is important to seek good legal advice. Legal advice is also important whenever you run afoul of the law for any reason. For those with no money and who have legal problems, there are many community Legal Aid Societies or other similar organizations set up to provide help.

The Use of Credit

Aside from mortgages on homes and farms, and business loans, consumer credit is a relatively recent phenomenon in this country, and still generally unacceptable in other capitalist countries like Germany. There are good reasons why a consumer might argue that the use of credit is justifiable and not simply an indication of bad planning or stupidity.

First, the pattern of expenditures over the life of the typical family, particularly if we add expenditures for mortgage payments, is such that when the family has young children and is accumulating durable goods and equipment, expenditures are likely to be larger than income. This does not mean that the family is consuming more than it earns, for a substantial portion of the expenditures are investments in physical assets, or repayments of debts incurred from such investments. The asset may well be cost saving (house) or income earning, rendering the debt "self-liquidating."

Second, there are emergencies for which it is difficult to provide adequate reserve funds: expensive illnesses, chances to make a good investment.

Third, as we have said before, you may want to use consumer credit in order to force yourself to save. Of course, it is far cheaper to save first and then buy the refrigerator—you even earn interest while you are saving—provided you can replenish your savings at least as fast as the refrigerator depreciates. But a few per cent interest may be a small enough price to pay to reinforce your will power and insure that you will end up with the item which you have paid for and still have your savings left intact.

Fourth, many people firmly believe that it is necessary to buy on credit in order to establish your credit in the community. There seems to be some truth in this. Lenders say that they tend to be suspicious of a man who has never used credit and first applies for it, because there is a chance that he is only doing so because he is in real trouble, and therefore is a bad credit risk. On the other hand, those who have successfully met the payments on past installment purchases are presumed to be able to do it again.

Fifth, people feel that they are more likely to get service and to have faulty mechanisms replaced if they have not finished paying for the item. Whether this is true or not is difficult to say, but certainly there are people who believe it is true, and such a comforting belief is worth something.

The other side of the coin is that consumer credit *is* costly. It is costly not only because of the interest charges, but because stores that sell on credit frequently charge more or have lower quality merchandise. Additionally you may not be able to take advantage of bargains or discount houses if you cannot pay cash.

In one of our studies we found a typical cash store doing a volume of $16,000,000 and making a net profit of $100,000 and a typical installment store doing a volume of $2,500,000 and making a net profit of $450,000.* In one store, I saw the test made on a watch that sold for $40 cash. It was also sold at $5 per week for ten weeks, a total price of $50. Then it was sold at $4 a week for 15 weeks, a total price of $60. The two payment offers greatly outsold the cash offer, but there was no measurable difference between the number of watches sold on the two time-payment prices. Installment selling and installment customers are much more satisfactory and profitable than cash selling and cash customers.[14]

It is also possible that credit might entice you into buying too much, and you might have trouble paying. Also, it may well be possible to "establish your credit" by buying on charge accounts that involve no interest charges, and that have similar advantages in terms of "better service" on faulty merchandise. It is frequently argued that cash-only stores have lower prices,

* P. 100. Remainder of quote will be found separately on p. 101.

but for many items there are no such stores, and the consumer is well advised to make use of the free credit involved in a charge account, particularly in view of the fact that he usually gets better service that way.　Stores regard their charge customers as their "regular" customers and treat them well.　Again, however, the problem of reinforcing one's will power arises, and some people do not like charge accounts because they make it too easy to over-spend.　Finally, if you use a life insurance loan to get cash to make a purchase, you pay a lower interest charge, but do not have the automatic payments compelling you to restore your savings.

What does consumer credit cost?　The charges are usually stated as a dollar amount, or even hidden in a series of monthly payments.　Sometimes they are stated as "3 per cent per month on the unpaid balance."　Let us work out one of these 3 per cent per month loans to see what it looks like.

TABLE 5

PAYMENTS AND BALANCES ON A LOAN OF $100 FOR A YEAR AT
3 PER CENT PER MONTH ON THE UNPAID BALANCE

	Payments	Cash Left to Use	Balance Owed on Principal
Jan. 1	. . .	$100.00	$100.00
Feb. 1	$10.07	89.93	92.93
Mar. 1	10.07	79.86	85.65
Apr. 1	10.07	69.79	78.15
May 1	10.07	59.72	70.42
June 1	10.07	49.65	62.46
July 1	10.07	39.58	54.27
Aug. 1	10.07	29.51	45.83
Sept. 1	10.07	19.44	37.13
Oct. 1	10.07	9.37	28.18
Nov. 1	10.07	*	18.95
Dec. 1	10.07	*	9.45
Jan. 1	10.07	*	—.34**

* You have already paid back more than $100 by this time.

** This company, it turns out, is charging you somewhat more than 3 per cent per month, 34¢ worth.

How shall we figure what this loan costs in annual interest rate, so we can compare it with other annual rates? There are several ways:

A. 3 per cent per month for twelve months is 36 per cent per year, isn't it?

B. Total payments are 12 times $10.07 or $120.84, of which $20.84 is interest charges. This is only 20.84 per cent of $100, but, of course, you did not have $100 for a year.

C. If we figure crudely that the average amount borrowed for the year was $50, then $20.84 is 41 per cent of that, though, of course, the company did not have half its principal back by the end of June together with interest (see Column 3 of Table 5).

D. If we figure how much we had to use during the year, it averages roughly $40, and $20 is 50 per cent of this.

E. There is a formula which gives a close approximation to the true interest rate:

$$\text{Rate} = \frac{\text{Total interest charges}}{\text{Half the amount borrowed}} \div \text{Number of years to pay}$$

$$\times \frac{\text{Number of payments}}{\substack{1 \text{ plus the} \\ \text{number of payments}}}$$

The first term is what we used in "C." above; the second does not apply here but is obviously intended to convert to an *annual* interest rate, and the last term is a correction factor for the discontinuous nature of the payments. In our example we have:

$$\left(\frac{\$20.84}{\$50} \div 1 \right) \times \frac{12}{13} \text{ or } 38.5$$

The best rule is probably to simply multiply the monthly rate by 12 if it is given, or apply the formula if it isn't. Our case is extreme for straight loans since 3 per cent per month is the maximum charge in most states, even for small unsecured loans. For installment credit the interest charges are much less, but they are usually thoroughly hidden in monthly payments along with some other charges so that it is difficult to ferret them out.

There is considerable variation, too, and stories are told of automobile dealers who have several different tables of installment charges, depending on the customer. Sometimes a "3 per cent" loan is 3 per cent of the original amount each month. This is about 6 per cent per month on the average remaining balance, or 72 per cent per year.

There is even something picturesquely known as "pack," illegal in interstate commerce and in a few states, whereby the finance company increases its monthly or weekly charges and rebates the increase to the dealer. What this means is that the "price" quoted by the dealer is misleading, because he is really charging you more by the amount of the rebate from the finance company. Most states have legal maximum interest rates for consumer loans, but legally buying something on installment is not borrowing but buying bit by bit; hence, it is not subject to these laws. Even in a few states where maximum interest charges on installment loans are specified, it is easy to get around them by calling part of the charge something else. The larger and more reputable lenders usually specify the rate of interest or the total carrying charges, and here so long as you are sure that the interest rate is on the remaining balance not on the original amount, the cost of borrowing is easy to determine. However, the extra charges may also include some rather expensive insurance, too.

Consumer credit is provided in many different ways. In recent years the largest total amount of consumer installment credit was granted and held by commercial banks—roughly 42 per cent of the total. Sales finance companies provided another 28 per cent of the total; retail outlets and dealers in cars and appliances provided another 14 per cent; and credit unions another 5 per cent. The rest came from other miscellaneous sources. In addition to installment credit, of course, there are charge accounts, single-payment loans, loans on life insurance policies. Charge accounts do not extend over long enough periods to allow much credit to an individual consumer at any one time. As we have noted, credit unions are a sort of co-operative bank where the members provide the funds for their own loans. They may be under state or federal control depending on their charter. Their interest rates vary from 6 to 12 per cent per year. Credit unions under the Federal Credit Union Act make loans to their members at a maximum interest rate of 1 per cent per month on the current unpaid balance. Credit unions usually allow you to pay off the loan faster than you agreed to, and many people like this feature. Other consumer loans attach a penalty if you want to pay faster.[15]

Beginning in 1954 the net cost to you of installment credit was reduced by allowing you to deduct the interest cost from income even if not separately itemized by the seller, up to 6 per cent. Of course, this only helps if you itemized deductions rather than taking the standard 10 per cent.

The Extent and Distribution of Consumer Debt

When a farmer borrows money to buy a tractor, he expects that the extra efficiency on his farm will enable him to pay off the loan. There is a wide range of loans which are self-liquidating this way. Even the mortgage on a house is gradually paid off out of the money you save through not having rent to pay. Whether installment credit is thus self-liquidating depends on the particular item purchased: a car to drive to work? automatic machines to eliminate need for domestic servants? or was it for an air conditioner or television? (and even television may keep you home in the evening). Excluding business debts some 62 per cent of the spending units in this country had debt in early 1953. If we subtract the 10 per cent whose debt was only a mortgage or other debt on their house, farm, or other real estate, we still have more than half the spending units with debts most of which are not self-liquidating but rather "dead weight debt." Table 6 shows several other interesting phenomenon. Debt on a home, farm, or other real estate is more likely the higher your income, with only 11 per cent of those with incomes under $1,000 having it, but 47 per cent of those with incomes of $10,000 and over. On the other hand, "personal debt" (all consumer debt except the clearly self-liquidating) is a middle-income phenomenon. Those with income between $4,000 and $4,999 are most frequently in debt, with 64 per cent (40 plus 24) reporting some personal debt in early 1954, as compared with 38 in the lowest income group and 44 per cent in the highest. (See Table 6.) Debt is clearly not primarily a low income or emergency phenomenon in America today.

TABLE 6

PROPORTIONS OF SPENDING UNITS IN EACH INCOME GROUP WHO HAVE
SPECIFIED TYPES OF DEBT, EARLY 1954

Income Class	Some Debt [1] (per cent)	Mortgage Debt [2] (per cent)	Personal Debt [3] Only (per cent)	Both Kinds (per cent)
Under $1,000	43	5	32	6
$1,000–1,999	50	6	39	5
$2,000–2,999	59	4	46	9
$3,000–3,999	64	7	44	13
$4,000–4,999	73	9	40	24
$5,000–7,499	73	12	29	32
$7,500–9,999	70	15	20	35
$10,000 or more	62	18	15	29
All spending units ..	63	9	36	18

Source: 1954 Survey of Consumer Finances.

[1] Excluding business debt of businesses owned by these people.
[2] Includes mortgage debt, land contracts, or other debt on houses, farms, farm operations, or other real estate.
[3] All debt except business and mortgage debt: includes installment credit, debt to individuals, medical debts, life insurance loans, and so on.

If we look only at those whose debt is 10 per cent of their income or more, the same pattern emerges. In all the income groups from $2,000 to $7,499, about a fourth of the spending units have personal debts amounting to 10 per cent of their income or more. In the lower income groups, fewer than a fifth had such debts, in spite of the fact that it takes less debt to amount to 10 per cent of your income when your income is lower.

Only 15 per cent of the spending units in early 1954 had personal debts that amounted to 20 per cent of income or more, and 1 of the 15 per cent could have paid off the debts out of their accumulated U.S. bonds and bank accounts. (See Table 7.) It is true that 26 per cent of the spending units had no liquid assets, but of these, 9 per cent had no personal debts either. The implications of these facts are clearly that the burden of this personal or non-self-liquidating debt is probably not serious in America today.

The reasons for this are not simply that consumers are sensible and wise in all their decisions. The lenders for their own protection try to make sure that their borrowers are able to repay the loan, and simply refuse to lend, or lend only a smaller part of the value of the item where the repayment potential is small. Many of the larger companies try to help borrowers budget their money. If they succeeded too well, they might drive themselves out of business, but partial success merely reduces the risks in their business.

It is also true that people less than 45 years old are more likely to look favorably on the use of consumer credit, and less likely to object to it for either moralistic or cost reasons. As the now young people grow older and have more experience with credit and less necessity to use it, they may become less favorably disposed toward it. It seems likely however that there is a historical trend toward greater acceptance of the idea of buying things on credit, in spite of the costs to the consumer.

Summary

Within any patterns that you may discover in the behavior of people as to saving, using up savings, or borrowing, there are tremendous differences between individuals that cannot be explained by their physical circumstances. People have different standards of living, and different patterns of wants. Some like to put their savings into a house and property, others keep very large sums in liquid forms. Some save a great deal out of very low incomes, others almost nothing out of very large incomes. When it comes to the use of credit, some use it all the time and continuously, and others "never touch the stuff." But all this bewildering variety of behavior adds up to a final

TABLE 7

PERSONAL DEBT IN RELATION TO LIQUID ASSETS AND INCOME

(EARLY 1954)

Personal Debt as Per Cent of Income	No Debt		Some Debt, But Less Than Liquid Assets	Debt Greater Than Liquid Assets		All Debt Asset Groups
	No Liquid Assets	Some Liquid Assets		No Liquid Assets	Some Liquid Assets	
0	9	37	...	...	...	46
1–4	...	...	10	3	1	14
5–9	...	...	4	4	3	11
10–19	...	...	3	4	7	11
20–39	...	...	1	4	5	10
40 or more.	...	...	*	2	3	5
All per cent groups ..	9	37	18	17	19	100

Source: 1954 Survey of Consumer Finances (percentages of all spending units).

The four numbers in the box tell us that only 14 per cent of all spending units had personal debts greater than their bonds and bank accounts *and* equal to 20 per cent or more of their previous year's earnings.

* Less than 0.5 per cent.

result which is that some total amount is spent by consumers as a whole, less than what they receive as income. Problems arise on the national level if this amount spent by consumers is too large or too small, and in the next chapter these problems will be considered.

SUGGESTED PROJECTS

1. Make some assumptions about your own future: marriage, children, the dates at which you will purchase a car, house and so on. From this make an estimate of the cost of living for yourself and your family over the next fifty years. Make some equally arbitrary

assumptions about probable income, perhaps using the U.S. Census data on median incomes by age and number of years of school completed (see tables and references in Chapter 11). Make a graph showing income and expenditures for each year as well as cumulative cash savings or deficit. Will you have enough cash for the down payment on the house?

2. Write a short paper on one of the following:

Advantages and disadvantages of joint tenancy.
Investment trusts versus buying your own stock.
Effective interest rates on various types of consumer credit.
Text-book principles on how to select stocks for investment.

3. Visit a car dealer, find out the installment charges and determine how much is paid for interest, how much for insurance and so on. Compute the interest rate, and compare the insurance charges with those of other auto insurance companies for the same car and age of owner.

FOOTNOTES TO CHAPTER 2

1 Special computations from the Survey of Consumer Finances, conducted annually for the Federal Reserve Board by Survey Research Center of the University of Michigan. Unless otherwise stated, references in this book to consumer behavior and attitudes and data on consumer incomes, assets, debts, and saving are from these surveys. For a more detailed description of the surveys, see Chapter 3; and see also "Methods of the Survey of Consumer Finances," *Federal Reserve Bulletin,* July 1950.

2 See *Mathematical Tables from the Handbook of Chemistry and Physics,* Cleveland, Ohio: Chemical Rubber Publishing Company, various dates.

3 *Social Security in the United States,* Federal Security Agency, Social Security Administration, U.S. Gov't Printing Office, Washington, D. C., 1953, esp. pp. 21–26. Look for a revised edition of this publication containing the 1954 changes.

4 See note 1 above.

5 Charles A. Dice and W. J. Eiteman, *The Stock Market,* 3rd ed., New York: McGraw Hill Book Co., 1952; for a cautious attitude, see Bernard J. Reis, "Investing in Stocks," *Consumer Reports,* Sept. 1953, pp. 405–408. For current information, see *Moody's Manuals* or *Standard & Poor's.* See also Julius Grodinsky, *Investments,* New York: The Ronald Press Company, 1953.

6 Wilford J. Eiteman and Frank P. Smith, *Common Stock Values and Yields,* Michigan Business Studies, Vol. XI, No. 3, Ann Arbor, Michigan: Bureau of Business Research, University of Michigan, 1953; William C. Greenough, *A New Approach to Retirement Income,* New York: Teachers Insurance and Annuity Association of America, 1951.

7 George Katona, John B. Lansing, and Peter E. deJanosi, "Stock Ownership Among American Families," *Michigan Business Review,* V: 12–16 (Jan., 1953), p. 16. See also Chapter 11, last section.

8 According to the National Association of Investment Companies, as reported in *The New York Times* of Jan. 17, 1955, p. 33, investment companies had nearly eight billion dollars in assets by the end of 1954, and 1,900,000 stockholders, of whom 3 per cent are institutions, foundations, and so forth. One of the earliest in the field was Massachusetts Investors Trust. See also: American Bankers Association, *Common Trust Funds,* 2nd ed., Washington, D. C., 1948; "How to Pick an Investment Trust," *Changing Times,* June 1953; *Johnson's Investment Company Charts,* Buffalo, N. Y.: Hugh A. Johnson (published yearly); Arthur Wiesenberger, *Investment Companies,* N. Y.: Wiesenberger & Co., 1953; or *Trusts and Estates,* 50 E. 42d St., New York (published monthly). The first three can often be used at brokers' offices.

9 Homer Hoyt, *One Hundred Years of Land Values in Chicago,* Chicago: The University of Chicago Press, 1933, p. 351.

10 Federal Security Agency, Social Security Administration, Bureau of Federal Credit Unions, *The Federal Credit Union Act* (as Amended to May 19, 1952), U.S. Gov't Printing Office, Washington, D. C., 1952; see also: "Credit Unions, Self-Help Credit," *Business Review,* Federal Reserve Bank of Philadelphia, March 1953, pp. 3–9.

11 Jacob O. Kamm, "Investment in Self," *Review of Economics and Statistics,* XXXIV: 179–188 (May, 1952).

12 Arthur K. Marshall, "Joint Tenancy, Taxwise and Otherwise," 40 *California Law Review* 501–525 (Winter, 1952); Emerson G. Spies, "Title to the Family Dwelling: Some Neglected Considerations," 40 *Virginia Law Review* 161–176 (Feb., 1954); Donald Kepner, "The Joint and Survivorship Bank Account—A Concept Without a Name," 41 *California Law Rev.* 591–637 (Winter, 1953–4); William J. Bowe, "Common Tax Traps," 26 *Rocky Mountain Law Review* 34–47 (Univ. of Colo.) (December, 1953); Mayo A. Shattuck and James F. Fau, *An Estate Planner's Handbook,* 2nd ed., Boston: Little, Brown & Co., 1953; "Should You and Your Wife Own Things Jointly?" *Changing Times,* June 1953.

13 Kenneth C. Masteller, *How to Avoid Financial Tangles,* Great Barrington, Massachusetts: American Institute for Economic Research, 1951. Most communities have legal aid societies for those who cannot afford a lawyer. Lawyers insist that most people wait too long before consulting a lawyer, just as they do with doctors.

14 Robert B. Barton, "The Role of Advertising in the Enlarged Utilization of Consumer Credit," in *Proceedings of the National Consumer Credit Conference for 1953,* New York University, Schools of Business, N.Y.U. Business Series No. 14, 1953, pp. 100, 101.

15 Maxwell Stewart, *Credit Unions—The People's Banks,* New York: Public Affairs Committee, 1941 (Public Affairs Pamphlet No. 50); American Association of Small Loan Companies, *Reference List of Small Loan Legislation,* Washington, D. C.: The Association, 1947 (?); Pollak Foundation, *Small Loan Laws in the U.S.,* 6th ed., Jaffrey, N. H.: Pollak Foundation, 1945; William T. Foster, *Loan Sharks and Their Victims,* New York: Public Affairs Committee, 1944 (Public Affairs Pamphlet No. 39).

chapter 3

Social Consequences
of Consumer Decisions
about Spending, Saving,
and Investing Money

The Adequacy of Individuals' Savings

In a relatively simple economy, old people tend to live with their children, and there are usually some productive jobs they can still handle, particularly in farming. Furthermore, wants are likely to be relatively simple and the need for money limited. In our economy today, more and more people are in occupations where they can no longer earn income after retirement, and must retire at 70 or 65 or even earlier. There has been some increase in expected length of life after that age too, chiefly for women who now live some five to six years longer than men, though the greatest gains in life expectancy (from 48 years in 1900 to 68 in 1950) have been through reduced infant mortality.[1] The movement to cities and concentration on specialized full-time jobs leaves most of us incapable of doing very much for ourselves. Hence there is greater need for money.

Furthermore, depressions, wars, inflation and developments in the fine art of getting people to spend their money, all make it difficult to save enough for an independent retirement. On the other hand, we have a very high standard of living compared with most of the rest of the world, so that insofar as we do not save enough, it can be argued that this is a matter of deficient will power, or "won't power," rather than deficient income.

But if any substantial group of older people reach retirement age without savings, either their children must take care of them or they must become a responsibility of the state (federal, state, or local) or some private charity. It was for this reason that the Social Security Act was passed. We have seen that the act is more than a forced saving scheme, since the benefits could never be covered by the contributions on an individual annuity-insurance basis, but it has been financed out of contributions so far because there are so many more people paying in than receiving. It has already taken a substantial load off the old-age relief rolls, and presumably also off the children of those who are receiving social security pensions.

In addition, we have developed a whole array of schemes for forcing ourselves to save: life insurance policies with savings features, company annuities and pension plans, amortized mortgages, consumer credit for buying durable goods, Christmas savings plans, payroll saving, and even the deduction of income taxes, social security, medical insurance, and so on, from our paycheck before we get the money. We have pointed out already that many of the voluntary types of these schemes are expensive, because of a low interest yield or high interest charges.

It can be seen that a saving plan *plus* will power is worth something.

One great social problem to which little attention has been paid is whether new products, advertising and consumer credit have managed, in spite of social security and other contractual saving devices, to get people to spend so much that they will find themselves with low savings and high wants, and therefore dissatisfied with what they have to live on after they retire. A detailed study of the facts and of people's aspirations about retirement might well show a great potential problem.[2] But whether the accumulation of savings is best from the point of view of all individuals is another problem.

Optimal Aggregate Saving

There is, given the situation and plans of government and business, one amount of consumer saving which is best. And it may not be the sum of the amounts of saving which are "best" for all the individuals as individuals. The "saving" that is important for the consumer is the increase in his estate, but the saving that must add to the proper amount for the economy is income that is not spent. These two are not the same. The consumer still saves—increases his net worth—when he spends on a house or on durable goods, but he keeps employment and output high by doing so. It may be almost a matter of indifference to him whether he rents or buys a house, and actually it might have very little effect on his economic position, but it will make a great deal of difference in the national housing market.

Economists have been aware for years that someone had to buy all the goods that were produced or a depression would ensue, and alternatively that someone had to produce more than he consumed if any resources were to be available for investment in productive capital. Too little saving would lead to inflation of prices as people tried to buy and consume more than was being produced and too much saving would lead to unemployment and deflation. But the nature of the problem was not thoroughly understood. The most serious inflations had been fed by expansions of the money supply and by wars, and the depressions seemed to be precipitated by bank failures and restrictions of credit. Speedy recovery from depressions was assumed to have come about by lower interest rates and digestion of previous expansions of capital.

It was not until the 1930's that even the economists began to see the nature of the problems systematically. The pioneering book was John Maynard Keynes' *General Theory of Employment, Interest and Money*,[3] but it was some time before the full implications of the new theory were spelled out, for reasons aptly described by one authority:

> The *General Theory* caught most economists under the age of 36 with the unexpected virulence of a disease first attacking and decimating an isolated tribe of South Sea Islanders. Economists beyond 50 turned out to be quite immune to the ailment. With time, most economists in-between began to run the fever, often without knowing or admitting their condition.[4]
> It is a badly written book poorly organized: any layman who, beguiled by the author's previous reputation, bought the book was cheated of his 5 shillings. . . . In it the Keynesian system stands out indistinctly, as if the author were hardly aware of its existence or cognizant of its properties; and certainly he is at his worst when expounding its relations to its predecessors. Flashes of insight and intuition intersperse tedious algebra. An awkward definition suddenly gives way to an unforgettable cadenza. When it finally is mastered, we find its analysis to be obvious and at the same time new. In short, it is a work of genius.[5]

Most explanations of Keynesian economics are either too simplified, or too complicated. Many of them are inaccurate or draw policy conclusions that really rest on further assumptions about specific situations. Many people assume that Keynesian economics provides a set of recommendations about how to preserve full employment or prevent inflation, and of course a great deal of the controversy among economists explicitly or impicitly has to do with such problems. But it is not this. It is a theoretical tool which enables us to analyze the problems of inflation and recession. The best explanation is to be found in Lawrence Klein's *The Keynesian Revolution*.[6]

Briefly put, the theory goes something like this. At any given time, with the amount of capital equipment and the labor force available, there is some total amount of goods and services that can be produced if all resources are fully employed. The ideal situation is one where all these goods and services are bought at prices that provide a "normal" level of profit, but without bidding up prices, or leaving unsold goods. Another way of saying the same thing is to point out that in any sale there is an expenditure by (cost to) one person, the buyer, and income to another (or group of others), the seller and his employees. Consequently, if everything is to be sold at prices to provide reasonable (same as previous) incomes, then incomes received in one period must be spent in the next period. If some people spend less than their income, others must spend more.

Still another way of saying the same thing is that the cost of producing things represents payments to the workers and suppliers of the producer (and profits to the stockholder). If the producer is to sell his goods without a loss, this is the amount that must be paid for them. For the economy as a whole, then, if all incomes are spent, all the products will be bought at prices high enough to cover costs. It is not necessary that each person and business spend exactly what it takes in, only that the totals be equal.

Spending less than one's income is what economists call saving, and spending more than income is done largely by those who are borrowing or using up bank accounts to invest in new capital equipment, or homes. Some people make decisions to invest, others make decisions to save, and what mechanism is there to assure that the two total amounts will be equal? Older economists assumed that the interest rate would do it. They thought it would rise when there was too much investment and not enough voluntary saving, and so encourage thrift and discourage investment, and vice versa. Others pointed to price movements which would change the import-export balance, or discourage saving by making accumulated dollar savings worth more.

It was clear by the later 1930's however, that if these equilibrating processes were working, they were working far too slowly for comfort. During World War II and afterward, it became clear that apparent self-interest would lead individuals and businessmen to actions which made the situation worse, this time in an inflationary direction.

Decisions to save mean that part of income is not spent; and since everyone's income is a cost to someone else, total costs will not be covered unless someone else dis-saves, whether for consumption or investment purposes. For the consumer, a most important fact is that this definition of saving is not the one which is relevant for his decisions as a consumer. From the consumer's point of view, it is the increase in net worth that counts, and he can increase his net worth either by not spending his income, or by spending it on a house, car, or durable goods only a small part of which are utilized the first year. Perhaps we should think of the consumer as deciding to save so much of his income (not spend on current consumption), and also as deciding to invest a certain amount in physical assets.

Businesses also save, by not paying out all their profits in dividends, and by charging depreciation allowances before computing their net profits. Also the government "saves" or "dissaves" by collecting more than it pays out, or vice versa. Finally, our international trade balance can be thought of as another institution known as the "rest of the world," which either "saves" (sells us more than it buys—an import surplus) or "dis-saves" (export surplus). Perhaps the best way to see how all these balance out is to look at the statistics for a recent year.

In 1953, the total value of goods and services produced in the United States was approximately $365 billion.[7] This includes some things like the value of food consumed on the farm, and the rental value of owned homes, and excludes others such as the value of housewives' services, but we shall not be concerned with either the specific details of the statistics, nor with their accuracy, except where absence of specific comment might be misleading. All these goods and services can be thought of as creating income for their producers. Let's see what happens to that income.

First the incorporated businesses of the country kept their records in such a way as to indicate that part of their income would have to be assigned to replacing the machinery that was used up in producing things that year. These "capital consumption allowances" were subtracted before corporate income was even stated, and they amounted to about $27 billion in 1953. In addition, the corporations held on to some $9 billion in profits which rather than passing on to the stockholders they kept in the business—increasing the value of the stock, of course. These two deductions by corporations left some $328 billion, but the governments (federal, state, and local) took money in taxes, and for social security, and as income of governmental enterprises. The government also pays out social security benefits and interest on its bonds, and government enterprises pay out wages, and so on. So for social security and government enterprises we will subtract only the net receipts of the government. All this amounts to a deduction of some $43 billion in 1953, most of it corporate income, excise and sales taxes. On top of this, the government took some $36 billion in personal income taxes, leaving the consumers with some $250 billion dollars. All this is a highly simplified picture of reality, of course. Included in the money left to "consumers" is the income of farmers and of unincorporated businesses. We have omitted the "rest of the world" which could either reduce or increase the total of incomes available, depending on whether we have an import or export surplus. Our international trade was roughly in balance in 1953.

Within each of the three "sectors" of the economy, government, corporations, and people, there are of course some who are spending more than their incomes and some who are spending less, but it is instructive as a first approximation to see whether the goods and services purchased in a given sector equal the available income.

If each sector were thus "in balance" we should expect to see corporations spending their depreciation allowances and undistributed profits, and no more, on replacement and ex-

pansion: $36 billion. Actually they spent far more than this;
in 1953 they spent $51 billion. If the government was to bal-
ance receipts and expenditures—which is not the same as a balanced budget, particularly because of social security—then government agencies should have spent $79 billion. Actually they
spent more than this by about $5 billion. Finally, the con-
sumers (including unincorporated businesses and farms) could
have spent $250 billion, but they saved, and spent only $230
billion.

Production of $365 billion in goods and services
implies incomes of:

$250 billion (after taxes) for consumers	+	$36 billion (after taxes and dividends, but before any depreciation charges) for businesses (9 billion undistributed profits plus 27 billion capital consumption allowances)	+	$79 billion (taxes and net social security receipts) for governments

Of which:

Consumers spent $230 billion	+	Businesses spent $51 billion	+	Governments spent $84 billion

So total spending equalled total value (cost) of production,
but only because the $20 billion saved by consumers was offset
by the $15 billion business spent over and above its own funds
and the $5 billion governments borrowed and spent in addition
to their tax receipts.

You will notice that the excess expenditures of government
and corporations exactly balance the savings of individuals.
This is not an accident, but results from definitions and accounting method. If business cannot sell everything, for instance,
this does not make total expenditures less than total incomes,

but results in involuntary "investment in inventories" by business. After the fact, saving is always equal to investment, but sometimes only at some cost, and the critical matter is whether if we could measure people's plans, they would also "wash out" like this without some uncomfortable readjustments.   Equilibrium exists only if *planned* voluntary saving equals *planned* voluntary investment plus the government deficit and net export surplus.

If the equality is preserved only by business cutting prices and losing money, or "investing" in unwanted inventories, then production and incomes and employment are likely to be curtailed.

In order to have simple tables where all investment is done by the business sector, the national income statistics put home construction in with business investment, and an estimate of rental value of homes, including those owned by their occupants, is included in business income.   They also treat expenditures on durable goods as consumption rather than investment.   Consumer investment in houses and durable goods has reached such levels, and is presumably so variable, that it is quite likely to be considered separately in the future, and even presented separately in the statistics.

One useful way to look at these problems is to think of businesses almost continually spending more money on capital equipment than they accumulate by depreciation allowances and undistributed profits.   In "normal times" the government has a balanced budget, and international exports are equal to imports (including as imports the billion dollars Americans spent abroad in 1953), so it is the consumers who make things balance by spending less than their income and lending the money, generally indirectly through banks or insurance companies, to business.

If people choose to spend more of their income, or invest it directly in houses or equipment, and businesses don't revise their investment plans, then people and businesses will be bidding resources away from one another.   If production can be expanded, the result is a useful stimulation to activity. If not, inflation results, and all sorts of dislocations occur. However, nothing can be counted on to induce people to act differently. Indeed, they may all decide to spend still more—the consumer before prices get any higher (or in view of the fact that inflation will make it easier to pay later), and producers because they have been making profits, if only on paper.

In wartime, the government comes in as another buyer on the market and can only get its war goods by inducing consumers and businesses to spend less. The alternative is for the government to bid the things away by constant inflation, or to pre-empt them.

If people actually save (do not spend) *more* than business or government needs to borrow, then some of the aggregate income paid out in producing goods and services does not come back through sale of those goods and services, and we have recession. Sometimes businesses can cause the same sort of trouble by reducing investment expenditures, or even cutting production and filling orders out of inventories. They pay out less income to their workers and suppliers, but still expect to sell the same amount of goods on the market.

Again, it is difficult to find automatic mechanisms that will induce people to adjust to such deflationary situations. The interest rate is institutionally determined in large measure, and moves too slowly and is too unimportant a factor in most decisions made by consumers or investors to have much effect. Changes in prices and wages are strongly resisted by various institutional or more direct pressures, and many economists argue that the influence of reductions in wages and prices, aside from some effects on the international trade balance, is likely to be important only if they fall continually, which is an unacceptable situation too. It would create continual paper losses for businesses, and redistributions of wealth in favor of people with fixed dollar assets. Keynes suggested that in practice it might be the level of employment that kept the saving and investing in balance, rather than any other mechanisms, and that it might be possible for this balance to be found at less than full employment for quite a long period of time.

In recent years, the pressures have been on the inflationary side, and a combination of government restraints plus the unusual capacity of American industry to expand production have prevented any serious difficulties. One way to think of inflationary pressures is in terms of demands for resources by business (or government) above what they can provide funds for themselves. In our economy, you will notice that a great deal of money is available for investment by business without ever being saved by consumers; it is taken out before the consumer ever sees his income. On top of this we have contractual saving devices such as amortized mortgages, life insurance, and social security all of which "force" the consumer to save substantial amounts in forms where he cannot get at it easily. In contrast, most underdeveloped countries have problems not only with business profits going abroad, and consumers striving to reach some decent level of current living, but also with lack of any extensive contractual saving devices.

On the other hand, depreciation allowances are fixed by the amount of capital now depreciating, and the institutional and legal rules and undistributed profits are determined somewhat by the level of profits and the customary division between dividends, wage increases, and reinvestment. This leaves personal saving as one balancing item that is not clearly determined but subject to large fluctuations in response to factors which may well not act to restore balance in the economy. Some two-thirds of the output of the country is bought by consumers, and as a consequence it is extremely important to know what the consumer is going to do with his money. Large fractions of income are spent for durable goods, many for replacement of items still in operating condition. The level of living is high enough for most people in this country so that they could save more if they wanted to. Finally, investment expenditures may well depend heavily on consumer spending to absorb the increased supply of goods that the investments make possible.

Still another way to look at the whole problem is this: There are three markets in which we want equilibrium: there is a market for money or loans, a market for goods and services, and a market for labor and other factors of production. The money market can be in equilibrium without either of the other two being in balance. People can save without lending, or they may borrow from a bank that creates the funds when no one is saving. Hence if the supply and demand for loans are equal, this does not mean that saving is equal in amount to investment of borrowed funds. The interest rate can "clear" the money market, but it cannot make voluntary saving equal to voluntary investment and it is the latter equality that assures us that the market for goods and services will be in balance.

The total goods and services produced by the economy will be voluntarily purchased provided all income is spent by someone. But as we shall soon see it is possible to have situations where everything is sold but where either there is a constantly falling or rising price level, or a "permanent" condition of underemployment of labor and resources. In other words, equilibrium in this market can exist without full employment.

The third market, that for labor and other factors of production, is the one we are most concerned with, since it affects our welfare most directly. Our standard of living depends on keeping our resources fully used, and if labor power is left unused, it cannot be used later instead. Some production possibilities are thus lost forever. A man cannot work twice as hard next year because he is unemployed this year. Indeed, he may be *less* productive in the future.

The most common question that arises is whether we could not keep everyone fully employed if we had more flexible prices to insure that the things they produced would be consumed. After all, you can always get people to buy things if you reduce the price.

Let us take an example of a very simple sort to see what the possibilities are here. Suppose that consumers wanted to save 20 per cent of their income and consume the rest, and that all income was paid out to them. They would then spend the equivalent of 80 per cent of the total value of goods and services produced. Suppose business investment needs comprised only 10 per cent of the full employment output. Let us see to what extent this "deflationary gap" of 10 per cent could be taken care of by reducing prices. The economy starts off producing $300 billion worth of goods and services. The consumers spend $240 billion, and investors spend $30 billion, but this adds up to only $270 billion. How can the goods be sold? Presumably by reducing their prices by 10 per cent. This makes book losses for business, but it sells the output. The economist might say to the businessman, "Yes, of course it looks like you lost money, but prices and wages and costs are all lower, and you can replace the stocks on the shelves for the $270 you took in."

So, spending $270, business produces the same full-employment output again. The consumers still spend 80 per cent of this, or $216, and the investors 10 per cent, or $27. But this is only $243 billion. The only way to sell all the goods is again to reduce all the prices by 10 per cent, counting on equivalent reductions in wages and costs to allow the shelves to be restocked for $243 billion. The next period, with $243 paid out in producing, consumers spend $194 and businesses $24, and another 10 per cent reduction in prices is necessary.

What this means is that if people save a constant fraction of their income which is more than others will invest, we can preserve full employment and constant real income only with constantly falling wages and prices. But this is an impossible situation that could only lead to trouble. Anyone who has physical assets suffers losses, at least on the books. Anyone with dollar assets has great gains because dollars are worth more. People will sooner or later see what is happening, and decide to wait till prices fall some more before they spend, and this would make matters worse. We have so many contractual arrangements in our society in dollar terms that the whole situation would be impossible and unfair.

In practice, then, wages and prices are unlikely to fall. What

happens in this situation? Unemployment develops, and the
total level of production of goods and services falls. Investment may fall too, but it cannot fall below zero. Saving falls,
probably faster, and can become negative. Bluntly put, real
incomes fall making people poor and wretched until they save
only the small amount that can be used in investment.

But it may take a substantial reduction in income and employment, since people also reduce their spending when their incomes fall. We have a circular process. Spending depends on
income for each person, but income depends on the spending
done by all. The diagram in Figure 1 may make clear what the
"underemployment equilibrium" looks like.

FIGURE 1

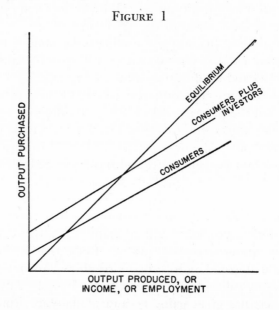

Because prices are not changing, income, output, and employment are all translatable into one another, and can be measured
—with different scales—along the horizontal axis. If we measure spending vertically, then the diagonal line represents possible points of equilibrium in the market for goods and services,
where the total output is bought by someone. The "CC" line

represents the amount of spending and consumption consumers will do at various levels of real income.   They do not get all the income, but whatever proportion they do get, we can plot the amount they spend.   We have not shown them consuming 80 per cent of income, since here we allow *real* income to fall, and they are unlikely to keep on saving that proportion as they get poorer and poorer.   The "Consumers plus Investors" line adds vertically the spending by business for investment at each level of income and output.   Where this line crosses the diagonal is an equilibrium in the sense that all goods produced are sold. But there is only one point along the horizontal axis which represents full employment, and there is no simple, automatic and completely effective method of being sure that the market for goods and services will be in equilibrium at full employment.

The consequences of a decrease in willingness to invest or consume can be seen by moving the lines down vertically on the chart.   The reduction in output is always greater than the reduction in the level of consumption or investment, for the reason that as the level of real output and employment falls, consumption and investment expenditures fall still more.   The angle between the "Consumers plus Investors" line and the diagonal indicates the degree to which shifts in the propensity to consume or invest will change the level of national output and employment.   If the angle is narrow, a small shift will cause a great change in employment.   Economists have taken great delight in working out the algebra and geometry of this, and refer to the relation between a permanent shift in consumption or investment and the consequent change in national output as the "multiplier."   The details are not important, but it is important to realize the problems.

We may summarize the problems as follows.   If prices and wages are not flexible downward, as they are not, then saving may be kept equal to investment (all goods sold) only at a level of output less than full employment.   Conversely, savings and investment may be kept equal only by continued increases in prices and wages.   In addition, since there is a continuous flow of new investment which increases our capacity to produce (output per man hour), people must consume more and more each year in order to keep full employment.   Fortunately there is some reason to believe that in the long run individual standards of living continue to rise, and the old Cracker Jack motto, "the more you eat the more you want," is even truer if you substitute "consume" for "eat."

There are of course some automatic forces that tend to mitigate the shorter run fluctuations in the economy.   Unemployment compensation and a backlog of savings allow people to continue to spend even when they are unemployed.   The fact that government expenditure is inflexible but that its revenue depends largely on the incomes of individuals and businesses means that reductions in employment reduce government taxes faster than the government purchases goods and services can be reduced, and people and businesses are left with a larger proportion of their incomes (after taxes).   Insofar as we have freer trade and there are some price changes, lower prices in depression reduce imports and increase exports, in a process known as "exporting depression" which is not well liked abroad.

On the other hand, there is some doubt that these would always be enough to keep us out of trouble.

Government Policy

There is a clear recognition on the part of both major political parties in this country that government has the responsibility for the maintenance of full employment without inflation. The Full Employment Act of 1945 established this responsibility and set up a Council of Economic Advisers to advise the president about the current economic situation and the possible necessity for government action.   They provide reports that the Congressional Joint Committee on the Economic Report submits to the President.

Basic political and economic differences exist, however, over particular policies.   In general they revolve around the degree

to which the role of the federal government is expanded or con-
tracted in the economy, and the degree to which tax increases
or reductions are concentrated on consumers or on business.
There are five major areas where the government can try to
have an influence:

> Consumer expenditures
> Business investment expenditures
> Import-export balance
> Government taxes
> Government expenditures.

Consumer expenditures have proven easier to restrict than to
encourage. Credit controls, minimum down payments on
homes, rationing, and sales of U.S. savings bonds to sop up excess
purchasing power helped a great deal in keeping prices down
during World War II and afterwards, though price controls and
the promise of equity by rationing also helped. On the other
hand, how would you go about encouraging consumers to spend
a larger part of their incomes? Easier credit terms, lower down
payments on houses and longer amortization periods on mortgages might help. Confidence of consumers that the government will not allow a real depression to develop might also help,
but the possibilities of manipulation of consumer demand seem
limited, particularly when expansion is desired.

Business investment expenditures have been restricted during
wartime by priority allocation of scarce materials, particularly
steel, and even after the war by informal restrictions on access
to funds for expansion. Here again, restriction seems easier
than stimulating expansion. Presumably investment is based
on expected profits, and these depend on expected sales. If the
consumers are not buying, it is difficult to see why anyone would
want to build new plants or buy new equipment, except to cut
costs. Special tax benefits for new investment have been suggested, and have been used in defense industries where particular expansions were desired. Businessmen speak a great deal
of the necessity for confidence and for freedom from undue in-

terference by government, but whether a friendly administration in Washington really stimulates investment by business is difficult to say.

The import-export balance affects the level of employment, since we can stimulate employment by exporting more than we import, or reduce inflationary pressures by letting goods flow in from abroad.   The rest of the world regards the former as "exporting unemployment," and the latter as "exporting inflation." They greatly fear the former, and are likely to take steps to prevent us from developing any substantial export surplus, for instance, by increasing their tariffs or putting quotas on their imports from the United States.   An American import surplus is usually of less concern abroad, and may even be desired, since it would stimulate business all over the world and perhaps help relieve the "dollar shortage."

Government taxes are easier to manipulate and less likely to lead to angry cries from abroad.   Reductions of taxes leave more money in the hands of consumers or businessmen, and they will presumably spend much of the increase, and those who benefit by a corresponding rise in their own income will in turn spend part of it, and so on.   Disagreements arise in the political arena as to whether business or consumer taxes should be changed.   Businesses have a tendency to prefer to invest only with their own funds, and to pay out some fairly constant amount of percentage of profits as dividends, so reductions in their taxes might lead to more investment, provided they can see some market for the additional output, or discover cost-saving technological improvements.   Insofar as the result is simply accumulation of corporate funds, or even higher dividend payments which go mainly to wealthy people and are likely to be saved, there is little stimulating effect.   When reductions in investment are desired, it is difficult to be convinced that increased corporate taxes would reduce investment so long as the corporations see profitable investment possibilities and can borrow money or sell more stock.   As for consumers, tax changes seem more likely to be effective, particularly those that affect the less wealthy or low income groups. However, problems of fairness between different groups in the country arise and make policy decisions very difficult.

Government expenditures are the most direct and "effective" device from the point of view of stimulating output or freeing resources for other uses. If stimulation is desired, public works expenditures on roads, schools, hospitals, and so on, directly increase employment and the purchase of materials, not to mention any additional spending by those who receive income from this. As economists put it, a dollar increase in government expenditures will increase national income by a dollar more than will a dollar reduction in government taxes.[7] There are of course political objections to increasing the scope of government, and to possible uses of resources when they might be more effectively used elsewhere, but from the point of view of effectiveness in stimulating employment or reducing inflation, changes in government expenditures are clearly the most direct method.

There is a real problem in forecasting business and consumer behavior, both in making government policy and in adjusting business policies. Much of the time and energy of forecasters is devoted to the problem of what the consumer is going to do with his money. It is no secret that estimates made in late 1945 that there would be six million unemployed by the spring of 1946 were based on what turned out to be wrong predictions about the behavior of consumers. In 1949 it was the business community that guessed wrong. In spite of widespread fears of depression, and production cut-backs by business in an effort to reduce inventories, the consumers kept right on buying and by midsummer some factories were running extra shifts. In 1950 consumers helped bid up prices when matters looked serious in Korea, but in 1951 and 1952 in spite of predictions of inflation, and higher incomes, they held back.[8] In 1953 they stopped worrying and started buying again.

Theories about Factors Affecting Aggregate Saving

Any prediction of behavior must be based on some theory about how decisions are made by the people, and economists have been trying to develop such theories. It is not necessary to explain all the differences between people in their saving-spending habits. The only crucial thing is to explain changes over time in the aggregate amounts people save. The fact that saving changes over the life cycle of the family is not important for predicting aggregate saving unless the rate of family formation is changing rather rapidly. The fact that some people find it easy to save, and others almost impossible does not require that we employ a clinical psychologist, because only *changes* in behavior are relevant.

Consequently the theories we shall survey briefly here are likely to seem overly simple, or might seem to concentrate on forces that are motivationally unimportant, whereas they are attempting to seize upon the factors that goad many consumers in the same direction.

The original Keynesian hypothesis was that saving depended almost entirely on income after taxes, everything else either washing out or else, as in the case of confidence, optimism and price expectations, being difficult to predict.

Keynesians soon began to elaborate on this simple hypothesis with guesses about lagged reactions to income changes; that is, with increases in income people might not raise their consumption immediately to its "equilibrium level," and with declines in income they would resist and restrict their consumption only very gradually.

As we have indicated, long before Keynes wrote, economists were assuming that the interest rate was a major factor affecting saving. The rational man was presumed to have made an adjustment between having his income now or later, taking into account that the interest rate would allow him more than a dollar to spend later for every dollar he saved now. If the interest rate rose, it would mean that he could get more in the future for every dollar he did not spend now, hence he would save more.

On closer examination, this theory did not seem to make quite so much sense. Unless a man's savings had been invested in fixed interest securities, an increased rate would increase the amount he would have to retire on by increasing the future value of what he had already saved. If he had some minimum amount he felt he needed for retirement, the higher the interest rate, the less he would have to save to get that amount.

During the 1930's a great deal of discussion revolved around the role of prices and the price level. Some people argued that if prices had been allowed to fall everywhere, not just in agricultural products, we would have gotten out of the depression more easily. The course of the argument could be summarized as follows:

CLASSICUS: When falling business leads to lower prices, less cash money will be needed for transaction purposes. The banks will find fewer loans asked for, and in order to stimulate business will offer loans at lower interest rates. This will induce some businessmen to borrow and invest and may also discourage consumers from saving so much, because the banks won't pay them so much interest on their accounts.

MODERNUS: But this doesn't convince me. Why should a businessman, who can't sell his product, borrow money and invest more just because the loan costs a little less in interest payments? The only investments where the interest costs are substantial are those requiring very large amounts of money over long periods, and here the uncertainty of the future is more important than interest costs. As for the consumers, they save for their old age and for emergencies, not for the interest they can get. The lower interest may even increase the amount of saving they need to do for their old age. Anyway, the interest rate cannot fall below some level which allows for the possibility that it may rise. Lender won't lend at a rate so low that they would lose money if the market interest rate rose— they will prefer to keep cash and lend it later. Finally, when prices fall, people lose money on inventories, and they expect further declines and so hold off from buying. This makes things worse.

CLASSICUS: Well, price changes have another effect too. They change the real value of people's past savings which are in fixed dollar forms like bonds and bank accounts. They can buy more goods and services with these savings. Therefore, they won't feel so much pressure to accumulate more savings, and will spend more of their current incomes, and business will pick up again.

MODERNUS: But this assumes that people have some fixed amount they want to save, in terms of goods and services their savings will buy. The motivation of savers is much more complicated than that, and their aspirations to save may very well change. Furthermore, to repeat, price declines will cause all sorts of other troubles: inventory losses, speculation on future declines, and so on.

CLASSICUS: Well, at least the level of assets held by consumers is important, because if everyone has some savings, those with income declines will be able to keep on buying things. When business is bad, more people have declines in income, and if more of them can use up assets to keep going, we have a built-in stability for the economy.

MODERNUS: But this isn't likely to be more than a minor factor, and in spite of savings, if people really get frightened about their future income and employment prospects, they'll cut spending as much as they can.

This discussion reveals disagreements about what motivates people to spend or save, and businessmen to invest, which clearly cannot be resolved by logic or intuition. As a consequence, more attention has been given lately to research into motivation—finding out how people behave under different and changing circumstances and trying to explain their behavior. Economists, psychologists and sociologists have been co-operating in a search for relevant theories and in the collection of more information about actual behavior of individuals. We shall discuss some of the more promising results, concentrating on consumer behavior although the general principles probably apply to businessmen as well.

The sociologists have a concept that refers to a "reference group," defined as the group that the individual tends to look up to and aspire to be like, and a theory that people's behavior is affected by their reference groups. This is not a specific theory like the one that says people will save less if the interest rate falls, and requires research to find out what relevant reference groups there are.

The social psychologists have a still more general type of theory which we may try to summarize briefly.

1. People do not make thoughtful, "rational" decisions all the time but live by habitual patterns which are only changed under stress, that is, only when the individual becomes conscious that his previous patterns of action will no longer be satisfactory.

2. At the infrequent times when individuals are actually making new choices, and even more so the rest of the time, they are remarkably impervious to factual information and almost always know less than they would have to to know if they were to act like the rational man of economic theory. It is difficult to see how a man's savings could be influenced by changes in the rate of interest, if he is completely unaware what the various rates are, or of the fact that they have been changing.

3. People have felt "needs," but these needs are primarily psychological and are related to reality only after the interposition of intervening variables such as "aspiration level" and "confidence in one's future." A car that is worn out and needs replacing in one man's eyes may be perfectly satisfactory transportation for someone else. Needs can be defined as a few rather basic things such as status, security, and so on. More specific desires are interpreted as means seen for achieving the more basic needs, but in any case the needs themselves and the specific paths seen to satisfying them are both attitudes of mind, often—particularly in a wealthy country like this—only vaguely related to such physical needs as shelter, sustenance, and warmth.

4. Insofar as these needs involve buying things, a man's ability to buy depends on his income and net worth, but what he perceives as his ability to pay for something is again affected by intervening variables such as confidence in his own and the country's future, and so on. These may change more rapidly than people's "real" economic situations, and change in the same way for large groups of people.

Given a general theory of this sort, it becomes important to find what sorts of things lead people to think they need to buy a great many things, and what leads to waves of optimism and pessimism for large groups of the population. Insofar as people start feeling a need for security, it is important to know what paths they will see for achieving that need. Some may try to earn more, some to spend less, others will take out insurance, or start a business on the side, or switch to a civil service job.

We need to know a great deal more about how people perceive the world they live in, what events are threatening, and which facts they are unlikely to know.[10]

Sources of Information about Consumer Motivation and Behavior

Three main sources of information about consumers have been used in an attempt to understand and predict their behavior. First, there have been aggregate statistics on debt, assets, purchases of various types of commodities and services, and more recently on total consumption, income, and saving. These are used to relate changes over time in, say, disposable income, to changes in consumer expenditures of various types, and to relate changes in profits to subsequent investment. Second, there have been small-scale studies relying on observation of selected groups, use of common sense, and even carrying out psychological experiments with individuals and groups. Third, there has been rapid development in recent years of the technique of surveying representative samples of the population, or of some defined group in the population, to find out their economic situation, knowledge, attitudes, and plans. Such cross-section data are useful in many ways. Changes in people's attitudes can be related to subsequent changes in behavior. Events that occur to all or to some can be related to changes in attitudes and behavior. Detailed analyses can be made of the circumstances under which people behave in certain ways. Finally, knowledge of their current situations and plans is directly useful in assessing the current outlook.

Aggregate data are available for the United States that have been systematically compiled since 1929. Earlier data are in somewhat less accurate and comprehensive form. Current data are published in the *Survey of Current Business,* a monthly publication of the Department of Commerce, and data for one year are generally published early in the following year—though they are subject to rather substantial revisions after that. As data from which we can infer something about consumer motivation and behavior, they have some serious drawbacks, however. The data on consumer investments in houses and durables are based on building permits and on manufacturers' production, both adjusted for sales not to consumers, and for unsold houses, or changes in dealers' inventories. What with varying mark-ups in prices, and difficulties with getting accurate information on what actually happens to the houses and durable goods, short-run changes in the data are likely to be difficult to interpret.

As for aggregate saving, the data include the profits of farmers and unincorporated businessmen, non-profit institutions, and trust funds. Since a substantial proportion of the saving is done by these groups, particularly the owners of unincorporated businesses, it becomes difficult to interpret these data in terms of the motivations of decision makers.[11] The things which cause business losses (which show up as dis-saving) for unincorporated businesses may be similar to those which cause people to spend more than their incomes, but the motivational significance is certainly different. Perhaps even more important than this is the fact that there is no way from the aggregate data to find out just what groups in the population are involved in any particular changes from one year to the next, and this is often a very effective way of inferring motivation.

Economists have, however, primarily used these aggregate statistics because they are available annually over a considerable period. If they are to be used, one of the most fruitful places to start is in the annual table, usually numbered Table 6, which reconciles two different aggregate saving estimates, one by the Department of Commerce as part of the national income statistics, and the other by the Securities Exchange Commission. The former is derived by estimating "disposable personal income" after income taxes, and subtracting from this an estimate of aggregate consumption expenditures.   Since both are subject to errors, the difference is nowhere near so reliable as other data in the national income statistics.   The S.E.C. estimate is more direct, estimating the changes in individual holdings of liquid assets, insurance and pension reserves, securities, and debts. Even here, it is rather difficult to estimate what proportion of bank accounts are personal, so accounts of farmers and unincorporated businessmen are left in.

Needless to say, use of any of these data requires awareness of the details of their creation and is better left to the experts. But it is also true that many people have used these data and drawn conclusions from them about the motivation of individual consumers when the behavior of the statistics may well have been dominated by other groups.   Chart 2 shows how some of these series look when plotted.

Of course, the great increases in gross national product and in disposable personal income are in large measure increases in prices.   If we ask about the real value of things, we can deflate all these series, but it is a difficult process, particularly in view of changes in quality.   They are generally published in deflated or "constant dollar" form, too.   It is clear that dollar saving has not kept pace with the increase in the price level since the war,

The bumps in "personal saving" from 1948–1950 are primarily changes in the inventories and debts of farmers and unincorporated businesses.   Perhaps most interesting of all is the conclusion which can be drawn that since World War II people have invested a great deal (in homes and durable goods) but on net balance saved very little in any other forms.

The second source of information about consumer behavior— small-scale studies, observation of small groups, experiments— has been a fruitful source of hypotheses.   The theory that people's aspiration levels are subject to rather rapid change as they achieve new levels has been tested in small-scale experiments.[12] The importance of certain motivations or behavior patterns discovered this way must, however, be tested by some other method.   Interesting consumer reactions may easily turn out to be important only to a very small segment of the population.

The third source of information is in surveys of representative samples of the population.   These have the advantages of securing details about the attitudes, actions, plans, and even expressed

CHART 2

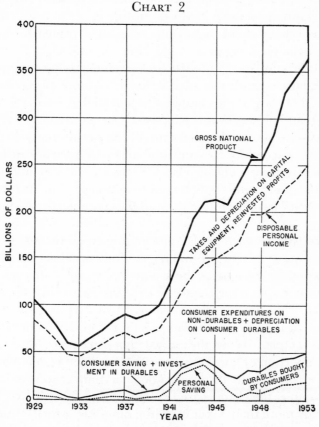

Source: U.S. Dept. of Commerce, Survey of Current Business, July, 1954, pp. 4–6.

reasons for actions of individuals plus the capacity for estimating the numerical and quantitative importance of factors affecting consumer behavior.[13]   To the casual observer, the most striking thing about surveys is the very small number of cases used to "represent" the whole population.   The fact is, how-

ever, that the size of the possible sampling errors which result
from not taking a complete census drops very rapidly at first as
you enlarge the sample, and then very slowly, so that even with
rather small samples the sampling error is (a) not so important
as other problems, and (b) could only be reduced further by
exorbitantly expensive increases in scale.

The reliability of survey data depends primarily on two
things: the methods used in securing the information and the
size of the sample taken.   Much more emphasis has been placed
on the latter than it merits, and much less emphasis on the former.   The larger the sample the less well trained the interviewers and the less time can be spent asking questions.   Careful
checks have shown that substantially more income will be reported for a family if more time and care is taken in asking
about extra sources of income, and about others in addition to
the head of the family who earned something.   Similar increases
in accuracy have been found by asking more detail on expenditures.

Emphasis has been placed on sampling errors because they are
relatively easy to estimate and the methods of reducing them are
well known.   So long as the sample is a "probability sample,"
that is, one where the chance of each individual in the population of being interviewed is known, then it is possible to compute what is known as the sampling error of any estimate made
from a sample.   When the estimate is a percentage, for example,
the proportion of families with incomes under $2,000, the sam-
pling error states that if you had taken a complete census instead
of a sample, the chances are two out of three that it would not
differ by more than X per cent (the sampling error).   Standard
practice is to assume that if the sample percentage differs by
more than two standard errors from some base figure, it would
differ even in a complete census, since the chance of a sample
estimate being different from a census estimate by more than
two standard errors is less than one in twenty.

When you want to compare two estimated percentages, you
must remember that they both have sampling errors, and the

errors may be in opposite directions so that they add. Hence the sampling error of a *difference* between two proportions is about 40 per cent greater.

Even if the reported data do not include estimates of sampling errors, it is possible to make some rather close estimates. All you need to know is the number of cases upon which the estimate is based, and the estimated percentage. The size of the sample is generally given, and if the percentage is the proportion of some subgroup you can usually estimate how many cases there were in that subgroup. For instance, if there was a sample of 3,000 people and the estimate was the proportion of farmers who had incomes under $2,000, this proportion will be based on about 270 cases since farmers are about 9 per cent of the population.

Knowing the percentage, and the number of cases, you can estimate what the sampling error would be for a pure random sample where everyone had the same chance of being interviewed. The formula is:

sampling error is the square root of: the percentage times [100 minus the percentage], all divided by the number of cases.

If the sample indicated that 45 per cent of farmers made less than $2,000 then the sampling error is

$$\sqrt{\frac{45 \times 55}{270}}, \quad \text{or } 3\%.$$

This means that there is less than one chance in twenty that a complete census would give an answer that differed by more than 6 per cent.

Table 8 gives some illustrative sampling errors of percentages. They depend on the true percentages as well as on the number of cases.

TABLE 8

RELATION BETWEEN SIZE OF A RANDOM SAMPLE AND THE SAMPLING
VARIABILITY OF AN ESTIMATED PERCENTAGE

PERCENTAGE ESTIMATED FROM THE SAMPLE WILL BE WITHIN
THIS RANGE ON EITHER SIDE OF THE TRUE PERCENTAGE 95%
OF THE TIME:

Size of Sample	If True Percentage Is 10 or 90%	If True Percentage Is 30 or 70%	If True Percentage Is 50%
25	12.0	18.3	20.0
100	6.0	9.2	10.0
500	2.7	4.1	4.5
1,000	1.9	2.9	3.2
2,500	1.2	1.8	2.0
5,000	.8	1.3	1.4
10,000	.6	.9	1.0
100,000	.2	.3	.3

(Add 50 per cent to these ranges, and you will be within this percentage of the truth 99 per cent of the time. For errors of differences between percentages, or of changes from one survey to another, add 40 per cent.)

For estimates of dollar amounts, such as average expenditures on durable goods by some subgroup of the population, or changes in such averages, the errors must be calculated individually since they depend on the distribution of amounts, particularly the variability between individuals and the presence of extreme amounts, but the general fact remains that the added accuracy is very small once the sample reaches 1,000 or 2,500. As a matter of fact, accuracy can be increased more effectively by more complicated sampling designs which, while still representative, are controlled to insure representation of various strata in the population and to take more interviews in the more crucial (variable) strata. It has also been found that small losses in accuracy per interview and great reductions in cost can be achieved by clustering two or three interviews in the same block.[14] In such complicated samples, the ordinary reader must rely upon accompanying estimates of sampling errors. It is useful to remember the general formula for the sampling error of a percentage estimated from a random sample from which Table 8 was derived.

For a sample of 100 and an estimate of 50 per cent, this works out as follows:

$$\sqrt{\frac{50 \times 50}{100}} = \sqrt{25} = 5\%$$

Hence if a man reports that 50 per cent of the people in his town own television sets, as against 40 per cent last year, and he has two samples of 100, we multiply the 5 per cent by 2 and then by 1.4 and discover that once in twenty times he could have found an increase of 14 per cent from one survey to the next even if there had actually been no change. Even if his respondents were not clustered geographically, he could not be sure that more people owned television sets.

For more complicated samples, the number of cases can be deceptive, since it may overstate the accuracy if there has been clustering of interviews, or understate it if there has been effective stratification of the sample. It is important to remember that the size of the population being sampled does *not* matter. It takes just as large a sample of New Yorkers to estimate their attitudes or incomes as it does of Americans to estimate their attitudes or incomes.

But whether we are dealing with dollar amounts or with attitudes, plans, family situations, and so on, there are more important problems than sampling errors. There are response errors, and errors by interviewers and coders. These are likely to increase with the size of the sample because of inadequate training, and the volume of work.[15] A major problem in getting information from individuals is to make sure they understand the question, and that the questions are about things on which the people could be expected to talk. Hypothetical questions about what people would do if something happened, such as an increase in income, are unlikely to be very closely related to what they might actually do. Questions about unimportant financial transactions some time ago lead to guesses, and to systematic biases due to a natural tendency for our memories to minimize the amount of change between the past and the present.

The potentialities of surveys in analysis of consumer behavior are enormous. The Surveys of Consumer Finances have already produced some important findings. An examination of the tables of the 1951 Survey of Consumer Finances, particularly in the September, 1951, *Federal Reserve Bulletin* article indicates (table numbers refer to this article):

1. There is tremendous variety in saving behavior. Some people save substantial amounts out of low incomes, others almost nothing out of high incomes. Clearly saving is not simply what is left after essential needs are satisfied. (See Table 3.)

2. Saving is tremendously concentrated. A large part of aggregate saving is accounted for by a relatively few high income people, many of whom are also businessmen. This may be a prosperity phenomenon. (Table 8.)

3. At all income levels except the lowest, business owners save more than other people, and they account for nearly half the aggregate noncorporate saving. (Table 16.)

4. Discussion of saving must specify what we do with purchases of durable goods, particularly in recent years. If we treat the purchases as consumption, as both the Survey and the aggregate statistics do, a third of the spending units spent more than their incomes (dis-saved) in 1950. If we treat the purchases as an investment of savings, then only a sixth of the spending units spent more than their incomes. The reader should remember that these data exclude social security contributions, and treat total life insurance premiums as saving. (Table 13.)

I have spent some time making more detailed analyses of these data, and would add the following general comments:

5. The number of people in the family has remarkably little influence on the amount of saving that is done. This is another indication of the degree to which saving is psychological rather than economic in its origin. People with larger families are

more likely to take on contractual commitments to save in the form of life insurance and mortgage payments.

6. The larger the city (including the metropolitan suburbs as part of the metropolis), the less people save. To some extent this represents differences in cost of living, but to a greater extent it is probably a matter of "standards of living." There are more ways to spend money, and more examples of other people spending theirs, when people live closely together. People, who live in the open country where there are no stores or movies near, save very large amounts.

7. Finally, looking at the typical life cycle of the family, there is a decline in the savings until the children leave home, after which they increase somewhat, but not so much as one might expect.

Comparison of changes in consumer attitudes through a series of surveys has indicated that there are shifts in these feelings which seem to result in subsequent shifts in purchasing-saving behavior.[9] Particularly in view of the fact that consumer investments in durables, houses, and additions and repairs to houses compete with liquid consumer saving—perhaps more than ordinary consumption expenditures do—it is not surprising that people's confidence in the future or attitudes about the present level of prices or business affects their decisions.

Understanding and prediction of consumer behavior, and even adequate statistical information about it, still leaves much for the future. It is clear that we need to make use of more than the customary economic variables, even when they include expectations about prices and sales and employment. From the consumer's point of view, it is interesting for him to know how important his decisions are, and at times how self-defeating.

There are three main agencies which survey businessmen to find out what their attitudes and investment plans are: McGraw-Hill Publications, published in *Business Week;* Dun and Bradstreet, published in *Dun's Review and Modern Industry;* and the U.S. Department of Commerce and Securities Exchange Commission, published in *Survey of Current Business.* None of them has a truly random representative sample, and they all rely on either mail questionnaires or rather simple questions which do not either assure that the question is understood or that the answer is clear.   However, they are still useful guides. The Dun and Bradstreet survey also includes tabulations for wholesalers and retailers, and is made four times a year.   The Commerce S.E.C. surveys are made quarterly, and the McGraw-Hill surveys annually, early in the year.[16]

In reading material that draws conclusions about his behavior, or about what people think or how they intend to vote, the consumer would do well to remember some of our comments about the available data.   It might be useful for us to list a few questions which should be asked about any statistical data:

A. Are they based on a census, a representative sample, or some sample which by quotas or other devices is quasi-representative?

B. Is it a sample or census of individuals, families, spending units (people who are related, live together, and pool their incomes for major items of expense), dwelling units, or what?   A representative sample of dwelling units that got information from those who were home at the first call might well be biased. It would certainly have too many women in it.

C. Is it possible to isolate relatively homogeneous groups in the population for separate study; that is, farmers, business owners, home-owners versus renters, and so on?

D. What was done about those who could not be contacted, or did not answer, and how many were there?   This is particularly critical when mail questionnaires are used.   Survey Research Center sent a mail questionnaire to a known group interviewed in the 1952 Survey of Consumer Finances.   The income distribution as estimated from the half who answered the mail inquiry is certainly not the same as the superior one estimated from the personal interview survey where the response rate was much higher, and information was available on which to estimate the incomes of the rest.

E. How was the information obtained?   Was there use of

nondirective questions in a personal interview allowing for full answers and explanations? Was there assurance that the question was understood? Was the purpose of the collector of the information known, and could his purpose influence the answer?

TABLE 9

ESTIMATES OF THE INCOME DISTRIBUTION IN 1951 FROM THE SURVEY OF CONSUMER FINANCES AND THE REPLIES TO A MAIL QUESTIONNAIRE

Income	Distribution of Original Sample	Distribution of Mail Replies
Less than $1,000	12.6%	8.1%
$1,000–1,999	15.3	11.2
$2,000–2,999	17.9	16.8
$3,000–3,999	17.9	19.2
$4,000–4,999	14.6	16.5
$5,000–7,499	14.4	18.2
$7,500–9,999	4.0	5.1
$10,000 and over	3.3	4.9

Source: Unpublished data from Survey Research Center.

F. Are the concepts used relevant, for example, in the definition of saving or income? How can you be sure all those who gave the information understood the terms and used them in the same way?

SUMMARY

Our decisions whether to spend our money, or buy houses and durable goods, or save it, all affect our present and future economic welfare as individuals. When we add up the behavior of millions of individuals, these same decisions, though in a different way, affect the welfare of everyone. Too much spending can lead to inflation, shortages, and perhaps price control. Too little spending can lead to unemployment and recession. The mechanisms by which business, government, consumers and the rest of the world interact are rather well understood. What is not so well developed are procedures for deciding what government policies are called for at any point in time. Improved ability to predict aggregate consumption and investment hinges upon better data, particularly of the type collected in attitude and intention surveys.

SUGGESTED PROJECTS

1. Find two speeches on the current economic outlook, preferably including one by a labor union leader. List the particular things predicted: investment, government deficit, sales of new homes, and so on. List next the areas where attempts to influence. consumer, business, or government decisions are suggested.

2. Find, for instance, in the *Public Opinion Quarterly* a report of a survey. See how many of the questions pertaining to adequacy of method you can answer about the survey. What possible problems of interpretation are suggested by this?

3. Find the most recent copy of the *Survey of Current Business* which contains the table comparing the Commerce and Securities Exchange Commission estimates of personal saving. Interpret the trends in saving over the past two years to determine which components have changed most and what they mean in terms of consumer or business decisions.

FOOTNOTES TO CHAPTER 3

1 See *Life Insurance Fact Book*, 1952, New York, Institute of Life Insurance, 1952 (issued yearly), pp. 91–93. Life expectancies are computed by the Office of Vital Statistics of the Federal Security Agency. For expectation of life at age 65 we used the 1937 Standard Annuity Table, male. Women live about six years longer than men.

2 See Jacob Tuckman and Irving Lorge, *Retirement and the Industrial Worker*, a Research Study of the Institute of Adult Education, New York: Bureau of Publications, Teachers College, Columbia University, 1953. (A study of I.L.G.W.U. members retired or about to retire.)

3 John Maynard Keynes, *The General Theory of Employment, Interest, and Money*, New York: Harcourt, Brace & Co., 1936.

4 Paul Samuelson, "Lord Keynes and the General Theory," *Econometrica*, 14: 187–200 (July, 1946), p. 187.

5 *Op. cit.*, p. 190.

6 Lawrence Klein, *The Keynesian Revolution*, New York: The Macmillan Company, 1947, esp. Chaps. 3–4.

7 *1954 National Income Supplement*, *Survey of Current Business*, Washington, D. C.: U.S. Gov't Printing Office, 1954. For current data, see the *Survey of Current Business*, especially each July issue.

8 Paul Samuelson, "The Simple Mathematics of Income Determination" in *Income, Employment and Public Policy*, essays in honor of Alvin Hansen, New York: W. W. Norton & Company, Inc., 1948.

9 George Katona and Eva Mueller, *Consumer Attitudes and Demand, 1950–1952*, Survey Research Center, University of Michigan, Ann Arbor, Michigan, 1953.

10 George Katona, *Psychological Analysis of Economic Behavior*, New York: McGraw Hill Book Co., 1951.

11 See my articles: "Individual Savings in 1947 and 1948," *American Econ. Review*, XL: 381–388 (June, 1950), and "The Structure of Aggregate Personal Saving," *Journal of Political Economy*, LIX: 528–534 (December, 1951).

12 For a survey of the literature, see Chapter 10 of *Personality and The Behavior Disorders*, 2 vols., ed. by J. McV. Hunt, New York: The Ronald Press Company, 1944.

13 See L. Klein, J. Lansing, G. Katona, and J. Morgan, *Contributions of Survey Methods to Economics*, New York: Columbia University Press, 1954.

14 William G. Cochran, *Sampling Techniques*, New York: John Wiley & Sons, Inc., 1953; and also Morris Hansen, William Hurwitz, and William Madow, *Sample Survey Methods and Theory*, Vol. I, New York: John Wiley & Sons, Inc., 1953.

15 See John Lansing and Leslie Kish, "Response Errors in Estimating the Value of Homes," *Journal of the American Statistical Association*, 49:520–538 (Sept., 1954).

16 See *Psychological Surveys in Business Forecasting*, Report of a seminar conducted by the Foundation for Research on Human Behavior, 1954, Ann Arbor, Michigan.

chapter 4

Budget Analysis, Planning, and Record Keeping

In Chapter 2, we discussed some basic ideas behind consumer decisions to spend, save, or invest. We noted that saving can either be in cash or other dollar forms, or can be invested in physical assets. In either case it results in an increase in the net worth of the family. If we choose to look at the situation broadly we can include in net worth even the expected future earnings, and can consider a college education as an investment rather than a consumption expenditure. We also observed that for a typical family, there is a pattern over the life cycle which is likely to involve different allocations of funds at different times, and to require extra saving at some periods so that higher consumption levels can be maintained at others.

We want to ask ourselves in this chapter whether analysis of the family situation and prospects, and the setting up of a budgeting and record keeping procedure, can help improve the consumer's allocation of his money. Many terms, like budgeting, are used in several ways. Let us, like Humpty Dumpty, use them to mean whatever we want, but assign them their meanings for this book at least.

By "planning," we mean looking ahead to guess what the

incomes and needs of the family are likely to be over the long pull, and setting up some sort of program to ensure that money is available when it is needed most.   Planning should at least establish some minimal level of saving, which would provide for an emergency fund and for retirement.

By "analysis," we mean assessing our past income and spending, particularly for the last year, to see whether we have saved anything and whether the allocation of our expenditures was, if not best, at least satisfactory.

By "budgeting," we mean setting up a somewhat more detailed plan for spending, saving and investing, generally for the next year and usually in terms of monthly or weekly expenditures for continual checking and control purposes.

By "record keeping," we mean the preservation of the facts of income and expenditures in such a way as to facilitate planning, analysis, budgeting, control of expenditures, and some other purposes such as income tax deductions, valuations for insurance, and so on.

Our definitions have implicitly listed the reasons why a consumer might want to keep records: He wants to answer questions like these:

Where has the money been going?

Have we been spending more than before?

Are we saving faster than our assets are depreciating, that is, is our net worth increasing?

Are certain categories of expenditures getting out of line with past levels or some norm?

Are the expenditures which are controllable getting larger, or is the increase owing to items we can do nothing about?

Some of these questions can be answered without any analysis or planning and with quite simple records.

Record Keeping and Control without Analysis or Planning

The simplest form of records will tell us whether we spent more last month than the month before; and the simplest form of control is that which uses past behavior as a base and tries to keep total expenditures from creeping upward. All that is necessary is to keep a record of receipts, and to add up our cash and bank balances on the first of each month. Cash balances at the beginning of a month plus receipts add up to available cash. Subtract from this the cash balances at the end of the month, and the rest must have been spent. Another way to look at it is that income not spent must show up somewhere, and for most people this means in their pockets or their bank accounts.

Successive checking will indicate whether total expenditures have been staying relatively constant. It will turn out rather soon, of course, that there are some irregular expenditures which throw expenditures for individual months out of line, and there are some expenditures which are mostly saving—mortgage payments, for example. The first are more bothersome than the second, because most expenditures that are really savings are fixed contractual items that stay the same month after month. At any rate, the next degree of complexity comes when you adjust your monthly expenditure estimate for irregular items, eliminating the ones that are savings, and spreading the others over several months. The best way to do the latter is to keep a cumulative record of excesses minus deficiencies around some initial base level of monthly expenditures.

The next step is to notice that many expenditures are not subject to control anyway. Rent payments, most utilities, installment payments, mortgage payments, insurance, taxes, and so on, cannot be adjusted downward except by major changes. Medical bills are not only uncontrollable, but irregular and cause even more difficulty. The simplest way out of this difficulty is to keep expenditure records on these "uncontrollable" items, subtract them each month from total expenditures, and keep watch on the undifferentiated total of "controllable" expenditures. This is not as difficult as keeping records on all expenditures, since we need records only on items that are either regular fixed payments, or large irregular ones.

Data from the 1954 Survey of Consumer Finances indicate that at most income levels except the highest and lowest, about a third of individual income goes to fixed payments: rent, mortgage payments, income taxes, installment debt payments, insurance, property taxes, social security, and annuity payments. Many of these are taken out of the paycheck automatically every month.   All of them are important in long-range planning, but for watching expenditures in the short-run, they merely confuse us.   Hence, each month, we can subtract them from our estimate of total expenditures to see what the other expenditures look like.

Let us turn from expenditures, and look at saving.   For people with very simple finances, the change in cash balances from one month to the next comprises their savings, but most of us soon develop more complicated financial arrangements so that, (a) some of our saving looks like expenditures (mortgage payments are partly saving, so are life insurance payments, and we may purchase U.S. savings bonds or other assets), and (b) we have physical assets which are depreciating so that all our accumulation of cash is not net saving, since some money will be needed to replace those things.   (We may also have cash receipts that are not income, for example, from cashing bonds.)   Nor are these things the same month after month.   Hence, if we want to analyze how we are getting along, a still further breakdown of our receipts and expenditures is needed.

Analysis of Recent Financial Progress

If we start out to analyze the increase in net worth of a family over, say, the past year, we can get into almost endless complexity, particularly if we start considering intangibles like future earning power, or the value of a college education.   On the other hand, we can be badly misled if we refuse to consider such tricky items as the depreciation on the car or the accrual of annuity or pension rights.

Theoretically, there are two different ways in which we could measure the increase in the family's net worth (that is, its savings).   One is to add up all the assets, subtract the debts and liabilities, and actually have an estimate of net worth on every

January 1. The change in this figure would be saving as the economist defines it. There are difficulties with this method in practice when it comes to valuing things without a fixed dollar value, such as houses, cars, and so on. Particularly in a period of inflation we may not want to count as "saving" a mere increase in the market prices of things we have no intention of selling. Nor would we want to subtract from our cash savings an item for a declining market value of our house. On the other hand, it's a lot easier to estimate liquid saving by comparing our bank balances on two January firsts than to keep track of a lot of individual deposits and withdrawals.

Another method of measuring saving is to keep track of where all our money goes when it is not for current consumption. We add our purchases of U.S. savings bonds, repayments on principal of debts, purchase of assets, and accumulations of cash, and subtract new borrowing and depreciation on our physical assets. This is not always easy, either. For instance, your mortgage payment involves a saving item: repayment of principal, which is slightly different every month. Rather than add all these, it's simpler to look at the amount remaining to be paid on principal at the beginning and end of the year. The difference is saving.

Needless to say, a combination approach that sometimes compares two balances, and sometimes adds a series of flows of money (or depreciation) is usually simpler. It may be more useful to make a list, roughly in order of complexity and conceptual difficulty, of the major items that compose an "increase in net worth" and to see how each can be estimated.

1. *Increase in currency and bank accounts.* There are no difficulties here except what to do about interest earned, and the only problem is that if you include it in saving, you must also add it to income; otherwise saving plus consumption will look larger than income. A purist might insist that you count interest earned but not yet paid or put on your account, but this is an unnecessary chore since even for income tax purposes you can count only cash receipts if you prefer.

2. *Change in debt.*   An increase in debt is a subtraction from saving, usually offset by the positive contribution of the item you purchased on credit.   With mortgage debt, it is usually quite easy to figure out how much debt you incurred when you bought the house—it is the total amount of the mortgage, not the monthly payments times the number of months to pay. The repayments are saving.   If the monthly bill does not state how much of the payment was for repayment on principal of the mortgage, it is easy enough to get a periodic check on the total amount remaining to be paid on principal.   Other types of debt are not so easy, since service charges, interest, insurance, and so on, are frequently combined with repayment of the debt in a single unanalyzed payment.   Furthermore, installment credit is usually used to buy something which depreciates, and depreciation is a subtraction from saving.   But depreciation is difficult to estimate, too.   One conservative procedure is to forget both the debt repayment and the depreciation, assuming that they offset one another.   This is conservative because most things we buy on credit are still worth something after they are all paid for.   On the other hand other things are depreciating too, and we may foresee such a long string of purchases that they might just as well be treated as consumption when they are purchased.   For an item as large as a car, however, we may want to include in our estimate of saving the repayment on principal over the year.

3. *Life insurance.*   As we shall see later, many life insurance policies are "package deals" that involve a contractual saving commitment, part of the premiums going to a reserve which accumulates to your account, and even earns interest.   Analysis of the premium into components is extremely difficult, and the value of the reserve is not a simple thing, since it is worth less if you take it in cash than if you leave it until the policy matures.   The annual increase in cash surrender value is usually printed on the policy or easily determined, and is close enough to true saving for all practical purposes.

4. *Annuities and social security.*   As we saw in an earlier

chapter, the contributions to social security have no relation to its value to you for several reasons.   Until you are covered, they are worth nothing.   When you are covered, their value does not increase as more money is put into it, except as the "average monthly wage" is affected.   Half the payments are made directly by your employer and are not counted as part of your income.   Finally, the benefits depend on the size of your family and the age at which you die.   The contributions you make are quite small anyway, and probably better neglected.   The value of social security benefits can be taken account of later when you make long-range plans for how much other saving is needed.

As for annuities, where you make regular payments until you retire and receive regular payments after that until you die, the increase in the value of the annuity to you consists of your payments during the year plus interest earned on the past accumulation of payments and interest.   There are two ways out of this one.   You can be conservative and count only your payments as saving, forgetting the interest.   Or you can take account of the effects of the annuity on how much *other* saving you need to do.   The second is particularly useful if your employer pays for part or all of the annuity (or pension) in which case you may not even know how much he is putting in, and need not count it as income anyway.   The difficulty, of course, is that you cannot make any simple estimate of how much you saved last year, but are limited to saying that in addition to what was necessary to provide for pension, annuity, social security, you also saved $_____ last year.

5. *Purchase of assets.*   These are of several main types which need separate consideration: fixed dollar value, variable value but interest earning, depreciating but cost saving, and just depreciating.   For fixed dollar assets like U.S. bonds we just add the purchase price to saving to offset the decrease in our cash.   The simplest way to treat interest earned is to wait until the bonds are actually cashed and then count the interest as income and saving for that year.   This is a compromise, but it is conservative and fits the method that most of us use for income tax

purposes. For "variable value but interest earning" assets like stock, bonds, real estate, businesses, and so on, the purchase can be treated as saving (assuming we bought wisely), and the earnings as income and saving, whether they are taken in cash or as increased value of the asset. Of course if they come in in cash they are automatically part of savings when we count the increase in cash.

The main depreciating but cost-saving purchase is a house. Houses really do depreciate even though in periods of inflation we tend to forget it. The purchase of a house is obviously not consumption during the year we buy it, but a shift of assets from one form to another.

Depreciating assets, like cars and durable goods become more troublesome the smaller and less durable they are. Shall we count the whole thing as an expenditure? Shall we count it all as a transfer of assets and subtract depreciation as part of our consumption?

6. *Depreciation.* The purchase of assets has raised a more general problem: the treatment of depreciation. Nearly everything we own gradually wears out or becomes too old fashioned for us, and to neglect this fact would amount to grossly overstating our saving. On the other hand, when the price level is going up all the time it seems as though it were our dollars which were depreciating, rather than the value of our physical assets. Indeed, the dollar value of our physical assets may go up rather than down. It is possible to argue, however, that we need to keep our concepts straight, and that we should distinguish (a) capital gains through increased value of things we own, from (b) depreciation on these things, which keeps the value from going up as fast as it would otherwise. Particularly since the future of prices is uncertain, and we do not intend to sell these things anyway, we may count the gradual using up of our investment in these things, and forget the "unrealized capital gains." If we take this point of view, we have settled another problem, too, and that is how to estimate depreciation. We should clearly estimate it as enough each year to "write off" our

original investment over the life of the asset (subtracting from investment what we expect to get for it when we turn it in on a new one). For instance, if I buy a car for $2,000 (net of trade-in) and intend to keep it for five years, at which time I think I will get $500 for it (barring further inflation), then it will cost me $1,500 over 5 years or $300 per year in depreciation. If there is inflation, this will not be enough to replace it at the new higher prices. If I sell before five years, it will probably cost me more than $300 a year since the heaviest depreciation in market values is during the first few years of a car's life. So, if I expect inflation, I may prefer to subtract enough from my estimate of my saving to accumulate a fund large enough to buy a new car at the inflated prices. If I have no idea how long I will keep the car, I may prefer to deduct the fall in market value of the car instead.

7. Finally, there may be other things that change the family's economic status or prospects. These are usually qualitative and difficult to assess. They are more important in long-range planning than in estimating last year's saving. Such things as changes in expected future earnings, or in the health of the family, or prospective inheritances can only be considered as part of a general situation. There isn't much point in assigning them dollar values and adding them.

At any rate, we can add some components together and come out with an estimate of how much we saved last year. Given the difficulty in dealing with purchases of physical assets which depreciate we may wish to keep a separate category for "investment in household equipment and durables, net of depreciation." Most of us will not have affairs so complicated that all these items will be involved, and we can always just "take account" of the items we don't want to bother measuring.

Long-Range Planning

Now, once we have estimated how much we saved last year, it is logical to ask, "Was that enough to save?" This is even more difficult to answer than the question, "How much did we save?" No one can tell anyone else how he should behave, but we can suggest a systematic approach, on the assumption that thoughtful decisions are less likely to lead to regret.

Why save? Presumably we save because we feel that the income we have available each year over our life will not be identical with the amount we need to spend; or stated somewhat differently, that if we spend all our income each year, we would be spending it for things that were not very important in some years, and we might not have enough money for things that were very important in other years. We have already discussed in some detail the likely patterning of needs and incomes over a typical life cycle. We noted that the major problem was the provision for retirement when, without planning, little or no income might be available. There are, of course other reasons for saving:

First, we may want to accumulate a liquid cash reserve to take care of emergencies. Second, we may want to accumulate funds for large expenditures (some of which may be asset purchases rather than consumption) such as down payment on a house, large durables, and so on. Finally, we might want to accumulate something to leave for our children, if we are in such fortunate economic circumstances.

Future needs are difficult to predict and, of course, further inflation might increase the number of dollars needed to fulfill future needs. Future income is also difficult to assess. One possible method of determining a "proper" amount of saving for retirement is to assume that you want to retire say, on, half salary, and that you will work until 65 at your present wage. Then it is easy to figure from social security and/or Table 3 how much you would need to save for this purpose. Your income may well go up, but so will your ideas about how much you need when you retire. You may prefer a higher yield, flexibility, and absence of compulsion of a personal saving program instead of an annuity. The amounts involved, however, are about the same, except that they can be distributed some-

	Cash Receipts and Expenditures		Saving Analysis of These Expenditures		
	last year	next year	last year	next year	
Wage and salary income	$4,000	$4,000			
Interest, dividends, and other income received	200	200			
Total income:	4,200	4,200			
Allocation to fixed commitments					
Income taxes	300	300	...	...	None of this
Life insurance and annuity payments	500	500	300	300	Saving part of insurance and annuity payments
Mortgage payments	1,000	1,000	500	500	Repayment on principal
Other debt repayments (installment payments)	100	100	60	60	Decrease in actual debt (excluding interest charges)
Other contractual saving (payroll saving, etc.)	100	100	100	100	All of this
Other contractual spending on consumption (rent, medical, insurance, etc.)	200	200	...	...	None of this
Total fixed commitments	$2,200	$2,200	$960	$960	Total contractual saving
Difference: Income minus total fixed commitments	2,000	2,000	−400	−400	Depreciation on house and durables (negative saving)

	Cash Receipts and Expenditures		Saving Analysis of These Expenditures		
	last year	next year	last year	next year	
			560	560	Total net contractual saving
Other saving (non-contractual in increased cash, purchase of assets, etc.)	350	440	350	440	Other saving, past and planned
Difference: Other expenditures last year, available for spending next year on things other than the above					
Total saving	$1,650	$1,560	$910	$1,000	Total saving

Long range plan indicates annual saving should be: $1,000

Net contractual saving is $ 560

Therefore minimum "other saving" should be $ 440

what differently in time, with less money being saved while children are in school, and so on.

We can now decide that in planning for the future we shall try to save about as much as we were able to save last year, or we can try to save some ideal amount based on an analysis of our future incomes and needs, or we can find some compromise between the two. Any plan which involves saving substantially more than last year will, of course, involve reducing expenditures on something. And some expenditures cannot be reduced, so it will involve reducing one or more of a limited number of expenditures. In working out an analysis of last year and a budget for next year, it is useful to take account both of saving, and of these fixed expenditures. Such an analysis might look like this (see Cash Receipts and Expenditures and Saving Analysis of These Expenditures).

This leaves $1,560 or $130 per month available to be spent on everything other than the items already accounted for. In allocating this, remember that parts of some expenditure categories are already included as fixed commitments, that is, the budget for medical expenditures should take into account the fact that medical insurance is already paid before the allocation of the $1,560 is made.

You will notice that estimated total saving, which is used to determine what additional saving should be planned, is figured after subtracting depreciation, while the calculation of income that remains to be allocated does not involve subtracting this $400 item. This is because the determination of the necessary amount of saving has already taken it into account.

There is no significance to the numbers used in this illustration, and it is quite true that there are a variety of circumstances that consumers encounter, but the figures should be useful in approaching budgeting. The consumer may allocate the remaining $130 a month to specific uses, or simply set up a system for checking to make sure that total non-fixed expenditures on consumption do not amount to more than that figure —or at least do not exceed it for several months in a row. In either case, only a relatively simple current record-keeping system is needed. Cash receipts and payments are shown rather than consumption and savings. Fortunately such computations involve a minimum of work.

Record Keeping

Simple records depend on two things: first, an initial planning that determines how much saving is needed in addition to any contractual commitments to save; and second, the assumption that in most cases expenditures represent consumption expenses, and receipts are income. In some cases this assumption is very close to the truth. We can treat the payment of last month's milk bill as this month's consumption without much error. This assumption does not always work, however, and then we must have some arrangement in the records to take care of it. Typical problem transactions involve receipts of gift money, or business travel expense funds, or the purchase or sale of an asset. The following outline of a possible set of monthly accounts suggests one possible method for keeping track of your money, and checking whether you are staying within some plan. It avoids requiring an elaborate procedure, but still allows you to keep track of the budget in real terms of income, consumption and saving.

RECORD FOR MARCH

Cash Balances March 1		$1,423.50
Plus: Receipts during March:		
Pay	$333.33	
Sale of assets	......	
Gifts	......	
Expense money	20.00	
Borrowing, or repayment of loans which had been made to others	......	
		353.33
Equals: Total cash available		1,776.83
Minus: Cash balances April 1		1,430.75
Equals: Total expenditures in March		346.08

Minus: Irrelevant transactions:

Purchase of assets (stocks, bonds, houses, durables)	$75.00
Spending of gift money	10.00
Use of expense money	10.00

Minus also: Fixed contractual payments:

Income taxes	25.00	
Life insurance and annuity payments	25.00	
Mortgage payments	75.00	
Other debt repayments	......	
Other contractual saving (payroll saving etc.)	......	
Other contractual spending on consumption (rent, medical insurance, etc.)	20.00	−215.00

Equals: Total expenditure on budgeted items: $131.08
(This is the item that in our numerical example was not supposed to be more than $130 a month.)

You will notice that this does not involve keeping records of your expenditures, except the fixed contractual ones, which are easy to remember anyway, and some infrequent ones which are generally large and easily recalled. The method makes adjustments for all the usual transactions that could make money expenditures unrepresentative of real consumption, or that could make receipts not representative of income. If most people's experience is any guide, this is as far as you should go at first in budgeting. The possible exception is that in looking at any one month's expenditures you might wish to recall unusual items that made your expenditures seem larger or smaller than "normal." Many people begin by using formidable budgeting systems, and after a few weeks or months decide that they get nothing out of them except a lot of work and the worry of trying to make them "come out." The outline above always "comes out" because any errors are hidden. The failure to remember that some expenditure was gift or expense money will make your budgeted expenditures look larger. Further, there is reason to believe that those who have kept books for a while find that they develop skills that reduce the effort required. By having a good set of records, they get some satisfaction out of knowing where their money goes. After this, you may want to go on to more detailed allocation of the expenditure on "budgeted items."

It is useful to know whether you saved more or less than the $1,000 total in the initial plan. It is easy to tell because the answer is the same as the answer to the question whether you spent less or more than $130 on the budgeted items. It is also useful to know in detail where the money went, particularly since some expenditures are much more subject to restraint and control than others.

The Allocation of Budgeted Expenditures

The allocation of expenditures has already been partly made in the fixed commitments that were deducted before arriving at the "budgeted expenditures," hence any further allocation has to keep this in mind. The world is full of advice and value judgments about how the individual should spend his money, from the religious ideal of stewardship to the hedonist's concepts of efficiency. The economists have spelled out what efficiency in allocation of expenditures involves, but in their desire to stay away from value judgments, they have said little beyond this about the subject. The economic theory simply states: given a family's values, attitudes, and physical situation, there is some distribution of expenditures that will make them better off, happier, and less subject to later regrets than any other. The characteristics of this distribution are simply that additional dollars are spent for each purpose until the *added* satisfaction derived is equal to or less than the satisfaction a dollar could bring if spent on some other purpose, including purposes later in time. It is assumed that added amounts spent in any one direction bring successively smaller increments of satisfaction as you approach saturation. Following the rule ultimately leads to an adjustment where no possible alteration would make the family better off.

All that is really being done here is to state explicitly the obvious criterion: Are there other uses of money more important than the chosen one?

In practice, there are two useful guides to use in allocating income to various expenditures. One is your own past experience, and it is probably the most important since people differ so widely in their patterns of living and in what they regard as important. A few decisions you have already made in the past —such as type of job, where you live, and whether you own your own home—will have a powerful influence on many of your present expenditures. Past experience is notably deficient, however, in items that are highly irregular from month to month. The other guide is the behavior of other people. The spending of others in similar circumstances is useful, but it is difficult to secure facts about it, except in personal conversations. Studies of expenditure based on interviews with samples of people are often difficult to apply to your own situation, but can be useful in setting broad general standards. For the most part, however, any deviations of your spending from "normal," which are obvious enough to show up in comparison with these budget studies, are likely to be obvious just from observation of your friends and neighbors. Data from the Surveys of Consumer Finances indicate that people in most income levels spend about 4 per cent of their income on insurance premiums, but as we shall see in Chapter 6, this is a completely inadequate amount at some stages of your life. These same studies indicate that at all income levels people have been spending about 8–10 per cent of their income (before taxes) on cars and large household items. Here again, it is obvious that there are times when it is reasonable to spend much more, and others when it is reasonable to spend much less. Most other expenditures are a varying proportion of income depending on the level of income. It is obvious that the proportion spent on food would be much larger for lower income families. Travel and recreation, gifts and entertainment tend to be more important at upper income levels.

The only regular source of information on how people allocate their expenditures is found in studies done by the Bureau of Labor Statistics. This bureau is responsible for the "cost of living" index, and this requires periodic re-examination of the proper weighting of various prices according to their importance in people's budgets. The 1952 revision in the index, for instance, is based on this allocation of items in the "market basket":

Food	30.1%
Housing	32.0
Clothing	9.7
Transportation	11.0
Other goods and services	17.2

Of course, the emphasis here is on workers' budgets and moderate income levels. Anyone in a higher income level who would spend so large a proportion of his total expenditures on food and clothing might find himself using his savings for other "necessities." [2]

There is another sort of "consumer budget" information that you may run across, and should not confuse with studies of actual expenditures. These "budgets" are set up by estimating some reasonable level of nutrition and style, and sometimes several levels appropriately labeled "emergency," "minimum," "moderate," and so on. Once the actual items included are determined, largely on the basis of dietary standards and of normative standards in other areas of consumption, then these amounts are multiplied by prevailing prices. The result is really a sort of cost of living index based on what people should or could consume rather than on what they do.[3]

At any rate, in areas where you think your past experience or the average experience of others provides some standard, you can attempt to control expenditures, and in others you can simply keep track of them. More important than whether you can set standards, is whether the expenditures are actually controllable or not. Regular uncontrollable (fixed) expenditures were presumably already subtracted in arriving at the budgeted expenditure limit, but there are others that are not constant from month to month, and others that are extremely irregular and unpredictable. Such things as medical expenses can vary widely from month to month, and are probably not controllable in any direct fashion anyway. Other items are more easily predictable, but still not controllable: property taxes, fire and auto insurance, moving expenses, and others. In budgeting, and still more in record keeping, it is useful to treat these as a group. For the records, the expenditures on them can be subtracted from the "total expenditures on budgeted items" to arrive at another figure that can be watched from month to month, and might be called "controllable budgeted expenditures." Setting some allowance for the uncontrollable ones is difficult, but will allow the $130 to be divided between the uncontrollable and controllable groups. Budget studies seem to show medical expenditures running near 4 to 5 per cent of income, or about $15 a month for the family cited. Many of its other uncontrollable expenditures can be predicted on the basis of past experience.

It is also true that many of the fixed commitments are not really fixed in the long run, and at critical times in your life, you will be more easily able to change them. Or you may be forced to change them, as when you move and are able to decide how big a house you will buy or rent. Furthermore, since houses and durables are treated as assets that depreciate, their purchase has been considered as an investment outside the expenditure budget. The amount invested is important because the amount of depreciation in the future will depend on the amount of depreciating assets you own. Furthermore, entirely aside from your economic position and saving, it is necessary to consider your cash position, or the purchase of durables may lead to problems. The important thing is that some decisions will involve changing the whole budget plan. The purchase of any major durable will increase depreciation and reduce automatic saving, and therefore require an increase in "other necessary saving" which you must deduct before other allocations are made. If you buy on credit, there is an automatic saving added, and also a larger automatic expenditure. The former reduces the amount of "other necessary saving," while the latter increases fixed expenditures and reduces the available "dis-

posable income." It may be useful to have a separate budgeting for expenditures on durables.

Moving, changes in income, and so on will also involve re-
planning. On the other hand, for month-to-month analysis, we
can usually stick to approximately the same budget without difficulty, and it can be useful in indicating whether certain types
of expenditures are "drifting" upward.

One final elaboration might be the separation of the "controllable" expenditures into two parts, the irregular items like
clothing and vacations, and the relatively stable items like food,
utilities, household operation, transportation, personal care,
and so on. The latter group can be watched from month to
month, whereas for the former it is necessary to watch the cumulative trend over several months and ask whether the excesses
and "deficiencies" are averaging out.

Anyone who has tried keeping track of his expenditures will
tell you that it is primarily useful as information on where the
money has been going rather than as a control device. Large
fluctuations can occur from month to month even in items like
food (if you have visiting relatives or friends). There are even
arguments against attempting such control on the grounds that
it concentrates your attention on little things like the fuel bill
when the real problem involves big choices such as how you
spend your vacations, or where you live. It also may tend to
emphasize negative aspects of the problem of allocation of
money rather than the positive aspects of careful choices. And
of course, rigid application may worsen these choices if, for instance, you always spend the surplus in one category, even when
you are running over the budget in others. On the other hand,
record keeping and some attention to "standards" can force you
to make choices consciously that might otherwise be made un-
consciously and (generally) less well. It might also be added
that financial records are increasingly important for tax purposes.

Very little information is available on what people actually
do about budgeting. There is evidence that they rely on con-

tractual saving plans and on installment credit to help them budget the payment for (and depreciation of) durables. Some small-scale investigations by Survey Research Center have indicated (on a non-random sample of middle and upper-middle income people) that few people do more than make use of their check book as a record of expenditures or keep a crude recording of income. No great social problems arise from this, except perhaps the failure to save for retirement which we have already discussed. Those with complicated affairs are gradually being forced into more detailed record keeping in order to comply with the income tax laws.

SUMMARY

We have suggested a method of approaching the problem of handling money systematically. If records are kept in such a way that you are able to see real results before you get discouraged or confused, there will be an outline for future budgets. The steps are: first, to use a simple system for finding out how much you are spending and saving; second, to work out a long range plan to determine how much you feel you should save; third, to analyze your present contractual saving to see how much saving your plan requires in addition to the contractual saving (taking into account depreciation); fourth, to set up a system for current records to be sure that your noncontractual spending does not go beyond the limits implied in your figure for "minimum other saving." Beyond this, detailed records on current expenditures will allow you to set up standards, and if you wish, budget these expenditures in detail if you can tolerate the paper work, and if you will not be discouraged when your estimates of expenditures based on income minus changes in cash balances do not agree perfectly with the sum of expenditures recorded directly.

Record keeping, analysis, planning, and budgeting can be fun and can lead to more carefully considered expenditures provided you start slowly and easily, acquire habits that make it less "work," and develop satisfactions that provide the motivation to continue. Finally, record keeping is a waste of time unless you also attempt some analysis and planning. A set of expenditure records that never separate saving, investing in durables, and current spending is not very useful. We have left the details to you, since you will be more enthusiastic about a system that you build gradually to suit your own needs and temperament.

SUGGESTED PROJECTS

1. Secure a copy of *Your Income Tax,* an annual government publication that sells for 25¢. Read through the sections on itemized deductions and make a list of the types of information that would be useful to have in your records if you decided to itemize your deductions.

2. With the same booklet and a copy of Schedule D "Gains and Losses from Sales or Exchanges of Property," make a list of the information that would be useful if you ever sold any property, such as a house, or stocks.

3. Make a list of your assets and liabilities, concentrating on those with a market value. See whether you can piece together an estimate for a year ago. Has your net worth increased? If so, where were the savings "invested"? Did they show up in increased bank account, or greater potential future earning power, or what?

4. Make a set of categories into which your expenditures seem to fall and estimate how much you have been spending on each. Keep records for a month and check to see how close you were. Were the "miscellaneous" categories larger than you expected?

5. Work through a budget analysis for yourself, figuring out how much saving there is in your contractual commitments and how much hidden spending through depreciation. How much other saving should you do to offset the depreciation and still be able to supplement your contractual saving? How much does this imply is left over to be budgeted after the contractual commitments are paid?

6. How would you handle the problems involved in each of the following transactions (in keeping records, or analyzing them):

a. Aunt Ella gives you $50 for Christmas, which you spend in February and March.

b. You go on a business trip, paying your expenses on the trip, and are reimbursed the next month.

c. You buy a car, trading in your old one for $400, and paying $1,400 cash.

d. You cash a U.S. savings bond which matured.

e. You get a bonus in your job around Christmas time, which varies from nothing in bad years to $150 in good years.

f. You find that your budget for medical expenditures has not been used up or exceeded for several years.

g. You lend someone $100.

h. You sell a house for $15,000 for which you paid $10,000, then buy another which cost $19,000. The new mortgage payments are higher.

FOOTNOTES TO CHAPTER 4

1 Bureau of Labor Statistics Expenditure studies appear in the *Monthly Labor Review*. Most recent separate publication is *Family Income, Expenditures, and Savings in 10 Cities*, Bulletin 1065, 1952. For a fuller elaboration of methods but older data, see *Family Spending and Saving in Wartime*, U.S. Bureau of Labor Statistics, Bulletin No. 822, Washington, D. C., 1945. For some comparisons of 1941 and 1944, see *How Families Use their Incomes*, U.S. Dept. of Agriculture, Misc. Pub. No. 653, (no date). The last Survey of Consumer Finances to present data on saving was the 1951 Survey, see "1951 Survey of Consumer Finances, Part IV, Distribution of Consumer Saving in 1950," *Federal Reserve Bulletin*, September, 1951. See also "Methods of the Survey of Consumer Finances," *Federal Reserve Bulletin*, July, 1950.

2 There are a number of booklets on how to set up a budget, some with prepared forms, but none, in the author's opinion, as good as the one you develop yourself and elaborate as suits your taste. See: *Guiding Family Spending*, U.S. Dept. of Agriculture, Misc. Pub. No. 661, Washington, D. C., 1949; Z. C. Dickinson, *Consumer Accounts and Budgets*, Edwards Letter Shop, Ann Arbor, 1948; Women's Division, Institute of Life Insurance, *A Discussion of Family Money* (How budgets work and what they do), New York Institute of Life Insurance, 1952; E. C. Harwood and Helen Fowle, *How to Make Your Budget Balance*, Great Barrington, Massachusetts, American Institute for Economic Research, 1940; U.S. Dept. of Agriculture, *Managing Farm Finances* (by Harold C. Larsen and Neil W. Johnson), Misc. Pub. No. 652, Washington, D.C., 1948.

3 U.S. Bureau of Labor Statistics, *Workers' Budgets in the United States, City Families and Single Persons, 1946 and 1947*, Bulletin No. 927, Washington, D. C., 1948, especially pp. 3–30 by L. S. Kellogg and Dorothy S. Brady, "The City Worker's Family Budget, General Description of Purpose and Methods"; see also publications of the Heller Committee for Research in Social Economics, University of California, Berkeley, California.

chapter 5

Detailed Purchase Decisions

There is a story about a man who was always telling everyone how much he liked children.   One day he came home to find several of them putting their handprints in a newly laid sidewalk in front of his home.   He proceeded to spank the ones he could catch, and when someone reminded him by saying, "I thought you liked children," he replied, "I do like them, in the abstract, but not in the concrete."

Consumer decisions, to turn a bad pun into a worse analogy, are theoretically made in full knowledge of all the relevant facts, shrewd appraisal of the future, and careful use of the rules of optimal decisions.   In practice, ("in the concrete") matters are not that easy, but let us look first at what consumers *might* do.   The first rule of optimal decisions was spelled out in the last chapter, where we noted that in deciding whether to spend money satisfying one need, we had to be sure that there was not some other more important need that could be satisfied with the money.   This is the sort of rule we presumably apply in fixing the amounts in various budget categories, and in deciding what specific items we should buy within each category.   In application, this rule is complicated by the fact that many decisions are for the most part predetermined by other decisions we have already made.   Sometimes this is a physical matter; if I own a car, I will be required to buy gas.

Sometimes it is social-psychological; if I work with people who eat lunch in expensive restaurants, I am likely to do so also. Furthermore, needs change, and not uncontrollably or unpredictably. (See Chapter 12.)

A second rule is that in satisfying any particular need we try to use money as efficiently as possible. But what is efficiency? It is clearly not efficient to spend half a day shopping to save 20 cents on a purchase. On the other hand, if I am buying a new car, it might well pay to spend some time reading up on technical reports and shopping around for good trade-in offers. One way of looking at this problem is to say that one important "thing" we need is leisure, so that unless shopping or looking for technical information are recreation for us, we need to value our shopping time and count that as part of the cost, if only in lost leisure time. It is sometimes difficult for someone like a housewife, who is not earning a money wage, to think of her time as worth money, and its proper allocation as a problem in economics. But everyone's time is worth something. We can say nothing very useful about such allocation, aside from stating the principle, since there is a tremendous diversity of ways of spending time, particularly for a housewife, and wide differences in what things people (a) consider important be done well, and (b) dislike most to do.

Turning to decisions which actually require purchases or the allocation of money, we see the consumer faced with several problems.

Is the purchase important, either because of the amount of money involved, or because you want to be sure to get the right style or quality? If so, then some effort put into securing market information may be worth while.

Is information available as to what variety of styles, models and quality grades are on the market, and at what prices? Does it require elaborate technical knowledge to interpret quality differences? Can price information be secured by phone or newspapers, or must you spend the time and energy visiting stores to find out? A housewife with a good memory for past prices can frequently make use of the food advertisements in the newspapers both in deciding which store to patronize and in adjusting menus to take advantage of low prices. Particularly with standard merchandise the telephone as an instrument for shopping is an efficient device frequently overlooked. This may even be true for services where the amount of money is large. I recently spent a few minutes a day for several days on the phone and received bids that started at $365 and ended at $220 for repairing a car. By insisting on second-hand parts—it was an old car anyway—and not being in a hurry, I saved some money, even though it took a little longer to get the car repaired.

Is information likely to prove worth while? Are there likely to be any differences in quality that aren't reflected in price? Do you always "get what you pay for"? The most useful clue in answering this question is whether other people generally shop around a great deal for the item. If they do, bargains are not likely to be frequent. The obverse is not always true, however. Sometimes people do not shop because there are no great differences in values obtainable. It is more likely, however, that if most people assume there is no use shopping, or find it emotionally difficult to do so, there may be great differences in price or quality not correlated with each other. This is particularly true where tastes or styles are important and where personal selling or door-to-door selling is stressed, or where unimportant accessories or special features are stressed rather than price or efficiency of the item.

For instance, it would be difficult for a store to sell a vacuum cleaner for $175 when other brands were selling for $70, however fancy it was. It would be too easy for people to visit a few other stores. But it is apparently not difficult for door-to-door salesmen to sell such a fancy item to housewives who rely on their word that other vacuum cleaners cost even more (which is true) and that all the attachments "go with it," and that it is convenient at only a few dollars a week to pay for it, and that it is unhealthy to have all that dust in the house, and so on.

Other areas where people tend not to shop around, and where prices consequently do not always reflect quality, are insurance, medical and dental care, all sorts of professional services, and small jobs by the building trades, for instance, painting or plumbing, and repair services.

On the other hand, there are some things for which people shop a great deal. Good taste and style may be such personal matters or depend so much on individual judgment that from your own point of view great differences in values still exist. What is the money value to a woman of being sure to get a dress she really likes?

Some purchase decisions are so important, and the necessity for technical information and understanding so great, that we have reserved separate chapters for them (insurance, medical care, housing and "other major expenditures"). For the others, the variety of technical information is so great that all we can usefully do is say something about sources of information for the consumer.

Sources of Consumer Information

It is likely that most of us receive our major source of information from conversations with our friends and neighbors. This is perfectly sensible because we can evaluate the information in terms of the similarity of tastes, and probability that the other person is a critical judge. There are two major disadvantages to this, however. First it is not always true that we know someone who has recently bought one of each brand of whatever it is we are considering buying. Second, particularly with large durable goods, people have a tendency to like a new thing and overlook its faults. Others have a tendency to cavil at minor adjustment problems which are not important. The tendency of people to forget the negative aspects is a real problem to the seeker of full information. I once quizzed the owner of a brand of refrigerator that I knew from sad personal experience was deficient in some major respects. The conversation went as follows:

How do you like your refrigerator?

Fine.

Never had any trouble with it?

No.

Can you keep ice cream in the freezer part?

Yes.

But does not everything else freeze when you do it?

Well, yes, that is rather a problem.

What about the crisper drawers—do they work?

Well, not very well. We just took them out and we use vegetable bags instead.

You should be able to picture from this conversation how misled someone would be who simply asked for an evaluation without knowing what specific questions to ask.

On another occasion I asked a housewife how she liked her clothes dryer, and of course she thought it was wonderful. Probing revealed, however, that it did not have an outside vent, but blew all the moisture into the house, steaming up the windows and walls and generally creating a nuisance.

Perhaps the most concentrated source of information directly relevant to consumer decisions can be found in the publications of product testing organizations like Consumers Union and Consumers Research. Consumers Union has far outstripped its rivals and has a circulation large enough to be able to afford rather extensive product testing. In addition, its monthly magazine, *Consumer Reports,* has a number of other types of information, including discussions of current economic controversies, articles on health and medicine, notes on how to do things around the house, letters from readers, ratings of movies, and scientific information of a general nature that is likely to be useful.

In view of the fact that earlier issues of the House Un-American Activities Committee's *List of Subversive Organizations* contained the name of Consumers Union, it should be added that in 1953 the Committee formally cleared Consumers Union of any guilt and removed its name from the list.[1]

However the consumer must still evaluate the information he

receives. Most of the information is designed to allow him to choose the proper brand of some product. Since the tests are based on samples of these products, they should assist the consumer in drawing an inference that one brand is better or worse than others. This requires proof that the variation in test results is a difference between brands, and not between items. In mass production processes, it is often an easy inference that if one item is not right, the others are equally bad. But this is not always so. There might be considerably more variation between different boxes of the same brand of canned peas than between the average quality of the different brands, in which case the use of brand name in purchasing would be useless. It is not always possible to tell from the reports whether the data allow a valid inference that one brand is likely to be better than another, though great improvements have been made in recent years in both testing and reporting of results.

Whether or not the test tells anything about brands, there is a second question whether the qualities tested are important to you. The usual tests on refrigerators would not have revealed either of the two troubles mentioned in the conversation reported earlier. It is often easy to test for consumption of electricity, shock hazard, and other mechanical features, but these may not be the most important to you. One apartment washing machine was rated as unacceptable because of its excessive wear on clothes, but it was the only one that spun the clothes dry, a rather important feature for people who do washing in limited space and hang it up in their apartments. A finding that automatic dishwashers stain stainless steel, fade colored glaze on dishes, and make a great deal of noise may be more important than facts concerning their water consumption.

All in all, however, consumer product-testing organizations are valuable sources of information with the undeniable advantage that they are primarily interested in the consumer and his welfare, and not in selling him something or justifying their own choices.[2]

It is all too easy for other publications which accept advertising from manufacturers to mention only their good points in articles—particularly, in the case of new products—without looking for disadvantages or bad points.   The ratings in *Consumer Reports* are generally in terms of several quality levels, and within these, the "best buys" are mentioned so the reader can tell whether an item is being primarily recommended because of its high quality or because of its low price.   Even where all possible brands are not tested, the criteria used in testing can sometimes be helpful.   For instance, the difficulty in adjusting the cutting bar of lawn mowers was used by testers as one criterion, and this could be roughly judged by looking at the machines in the store.

"Testing agency" reports are perhaps most useful for new models or entirely new products, where spotting of defects or of particularly good new models or items is most helpful.   Occasionally, a new item comes out that is outstanding in almost every way, but if none of your friends happen to buy one and tell you about it, you would not be able to tell from the advertisements that this time the producers were not exaggerating.

There are other sources of information that are useful, and they vary a great deal from time to time.   U.S. government pamphlets offer information in a wide variety of fields.   They are not generally informative about specific brands, but are useful in establishing criteria.   The Department of Agriculture's *Farmers' Bulletins* and other publications, particularly those of the Bureau of Human Nutrition and Home Economics, are frequently useful.   The Women's Bureau of the Department of Labor and the Bureau of Standards of the Commerce Department occasionally publish something useful for consumers.   The variety of information, and of government bureaus is very great, however, and the easiest way to keep informed is to be placed on mailing lists so the Government Printing Office will send regular notices of the latest publications.   If your interests are very broad, you can subscribe to, or check at the library for, the *Monthly Catalogue of Government Publications.*

Many magazines have articles and sections devoted to informing consumers.   Aside from such features as Mary Sheridan's monthly "Your Money's Worth" in the *Progressive,* most of them have to do with praising new products somewhat uncritically.   Professor Ray G. Price of the University of Minnesota compiles and revises a selected list of magazine articles of interest to consumers.   The magazines most frequently referred to in his latest list, in order of the number of articles mentioned are:

MORE THAN TEN ARTICLES MENTIONED
Better Homes and Gardens
Consumer Reports
Good Housekeeping
Changing Times

NINE TO THREE ARTICLES MENTIONED
American Home
Reader's Digest
Coronet
Today's Health (Hygeia)
Consumers Research Bulletin

TWO ARTICLES MENTIONED
Woman's Home Companion
Parents Magazine
Colliers
McCalls
American Mercury

ONE ARTICLE MENTIONED
Saturday Evening Post
Journal of Home Economics
Ladies Home Journal
New Republic
Science Digest

Mail order catalogues often reveal, if you compare their "good," "better," and "best" qualities, the main dimensions of quality and the things to look for.   And, of course, newspapers are often an excellent source of current market information, both in the want ad section, and in notices of sales by stores.

When it comes to durable goods, the people who service them —provided they do not also sell certain brands—are often a good source of information about the things that go wrong. One of the most important pieces of information, particularly in avoiding very bad mistakes, is the range of prices a particular type of item is selling for.   An examination of the frauds commonly perpetrated on consumers reveals that most of them involve building up in the consumers' minds the illusion that something is worth more than it really is.   From this point of view, mail order catalogues are also useful.   As we noted before, if you ask pertinent questions, the experience of your friends may well be the most valuable of all. Particularly in the case of new products, it often pays to wait until some friend has "tested" it first.

But of course, information comes from a variety of sources, and an inquisitive person who enjoys that sort of thing can make use of facts that would slip past others. For example, you see an ad for a new set of dishes guaranteed not to fade in automatic dishwashers. The conclusion is not necessarily that these dishes are better, but almost certainly that there exists some problem of dishes fading in dishwashers. The same sort of oblique inference can be drawn from extensive advertisements of things to stop water seepage in basements, that is, that basements are often a problem. Often, where there are competing products, you will notice that each advertises the features that are actually the advantage of the other. Electric stoves are advertised as fast, and gas stoves as cool.

Some years ago a great deal of attention was given to grade labeling, and some of the things you buy still have grade labels, but the importance of the grading system is not great because the labels are confusing and difficult to remember.[3] Trade associations such as the American Gas Association and Underwriters Laboratories put their seal of approval on appliances that meet minimum standards. Where they have such obvious reasons to insist on safety standards—as with gas or electric appliances—such approval is worth looking for. Canned fruits and vegetables are sometimes grade-labeled but it is doubtful that it is worth learning what the different labeling systems mean. A little experimentation will generally tell what locally available brands are like. Finally, even salesmen can be a source of information, particularly if (a) you ask them enough questions, and (b) you ask enough different salesmen. If you are buying fire insurance on your house, you may find most of the agents saying that all companies have the same rates, but one of them may point out that some mutual companies pay dividends. If you talk to enough appliance dealers, you may find something about the faults of competing lines.

In recent years it has seemed almost a rule that anything new, however widely hailed, had certain drawbacks at least in its initial stages. Automatic washing machines used more hot water, or did not wash as well. Dryers steamed up the house until you vented them outdoors, and shrank things and "removed" the starch. Aerator faucets did not let so much water through, and hence tended to allow the garbage disposer to clog. Ball-point pens smudged and stopped. Plastic toys had a low life expectancy. Nylon shirts were hot when it was warm and icy when it was cool. Even the new wonder drugs turned out to have some drawbacks.

At any rate, it can be concluded that useful information is difficult to find, transitory in its relevance, tricky to use, and harder still to remember unless you are really interested. If you get the habit of being inquisitive and noting useful facts, then being an informed consumer is both easy and enjoyable. If you do not enjoy it, and if you do not have the mechanical bent necessary for interpreting much of the information, then the whole process of being informed is a chore and you may prefer to rely on someone else's judgment, or even to depend on the reliability (at least the low expectancy of being badly cheated) of famous brands or "reputable" dealers. But both the store of facts, and the ability to use them will accumulate as you learn to make "informed decisions." I once knew a fellow who was so interested in wise buying that he checked on the thermal expansion co-efficient of fuel oil, and came to the conclusion that the lower summer price was no bargain because you got more oil per gallon in the winter when it was cold. I have never checked on his facts, never having purchased fuel oil. I know other people who can remember prices of things for months and are never fooled when a store advertises a sale on something at the same price it has been charging for months. Some of our friends wander from supermarket to supermarket looking for bargains, and others shop in a local delicatessen where they claim they save money by not buying so much.

So, if you like searching for evidence and analyzing it, it is worth doing; if not, you can purchase leisure by making decisions somewhat less well.

Shopping

Most of the books on how to get more for your money devote a great deal of attention to the advantages of shopping around, both as a method of finding information about quality and as a method of finding the lowest price.[4] As we have pointed out before, time is worth money too; and even on a purely economic basis, shopping may or may not be worth it. If there are added satisfactions from bargains for some people, they may prefer to shop partly as recreation. Other people may dislike crowds and shopping so intensely that few possible bargains would be worth it.

There are also "sample houses" and "discount houses." The former sell remnants and samples and, if legitimate, often at low prices. The latter were established as a result of resale price maintenance laws and attempts by manufacturers to maintain a uniform retail price regardless of the differences in distribution costs among different retailers. The legal status of resale price maintenance is still in doubt, but so long as high mark-ups and uniform retail prices are kept, there are bound to be some retailers who would prefer to sell more at a lower profit per unit.

More prevalent than discount houses are sales of various sorts by regular retailers. Some, such as the January "white sales" of sheets, are traditional and can be counted on. In many other lines there are sales during slack periods, or at the end of a season. Sometimes there are "special purchase" sales where a new line of merchandise is brought in for the purpose, and the line may or may not be a bargain.

Rather than deal with a changing situation as to the periods of sales, it is more important for us to ask why these sales exist. Understanding the economics of sales will enable us to make better use of them.

Why should a retailer have a sale? Presumably for one of these reasons:

1. To get rid of things that wouldn't sell because of bad styling, overpricing, and lack of consumer interest.

2. To regularize sales over the year and keep the store busy during the slack seasons.

3. To clear out most of the seasonal items at the end of a season rather than store them until the next year because styles might change by next year.

4. To entice customers into the store hoping that they will buy something else. It may be only one customer who will get the advertised bargain. In its extreme form this is called "baiting."

5. To maintain profitably high prices for those who do not shop or wait for sales, and make a little extra at low mark-ups on those who are more careful buyers. (A form of price discrimination.)

Of course, some "sales" are not sales at all, but advertising, and involve no real bargains. In almost any town there are some stores that "go out of business" regularly, once or twice a year, and others where the prices are marked up and then down again for a "sale," but anyone who talks with his neighbors, and keeps his eyes open, will soon spot them.

If the first reason is behind the sale, the only problem is to make sure you are buying something you really want and know is worth the price. The second type of sale is likely to offer only small mark-downs, but legitimate ones. The third type, end-of-season sales, often provides substantial reductions, particularly in style goods where you run the risk of finding the article out of style by the next season. The fourth type is all right, provided you do not buy something else you did not need in the process. Rebuilt sewing machines and vacuum cleaners seem to be the most usual "bait" in these traps. The most interesting interpretation of sales is the last one, the system of splitting the market into "shoppers" and "nonshoppers." This is similar to what theaters do with first run movies, except that there may be some satisfaction in seeing a new movie early, whereas waiting for the sales, and planning ahead on things you will need, may cost nothing at all. From the point of view of the manufacturer even discount houses make sense, so long as there are not too many of them. Those who can afford to pay are charged the full price, and others who cannot, or will not, are offered a lower price which covers costs but adds somewhat less per unit to profit. The difficulty with this system from the consumer's point of view is that those who can afford to wait for the sales are often those who could best afford to pay the higher prices. There is a sort of perversity whereby poorer people who have to live "hand-to-mouth" and buy things only when they have to have them, do not (or cannot) take advantage of bargains. How much of this is psychological is difficult to say. Some of it must be, for casual observation indicates that the poorer people almost never buy bus tokens with the saving of a few cents, but pay the full price one fare at a time. On the other hand a recent study by Survey Research Center indicates that low income people are as likely as others to get their large durables on sale or at a discount.[5]

Just as the 1920's were the times of muckraking in politics, the 1930's can be considered the era of muckraking in consumer economics. Great attention was paid to all sorts of frauds, adulteration of products, the wastes of advertising, and the wastes of emulating the consumption habits of your neighbors. Such books as *"100,000,000 Guinea Pigs; Eat, Drink and Be Wary;* and *Your Money's Worth* made fascinating reading, even if they spoiled your appetite.[6] Many of the problems then so important have been reduced by government action, or consumer sophistication, but others have taken their place. The basic fact is that so long as people are gullible, there will be people to take advantage of the fact. The devising of new and legal methods of getting people's money seems always to keep ahead of the activities of the law and the consumer organizations.

One is struck by the tremendous pressures of advertising and the efforts made to find what motivates consumers so that they can be induced to buy particular products. One of the consumer's best defenses is to read the professional materials of the advertising and selling people—the books on how to sell, the trade journals—to see what new and ingenious devices are being developed to sell him something. It is tempting to believe that if some of this money were spent finding what consumers want in a product and attempting to produce it, both the manufacturer and consumer would be better off, but in practice a great deal of the "research" in marketing seems directed solely toward selling the consumer what is produced.

Outwitting Yourself

A prevalent notion is that you can save money by buying in large quantities, and by stocking up when prices are low. The marketing experts have an opposite theory that if you can get things, particularly food, into people's homes, they will be used up faster. Of course, both ideas are partly true. If, however, you are likely to use more of something when you have it around, careful decision-making involves deciding whether you want to use more of it. For example, it is almost certain that if you have more items like canned peaches on the shelf, you will use them rather than bothering to make desserts. Whether this is good or bad depends on whether you are trying to save money on the food budget, or think that the peaches are good for the family and not worth economizing on.

It is clearly possible to outwit yourself by stocking up on healthy but inexpensive foods, and buying the expensive things only as they are needed. Use of a home freezer leads, for many people, to stocking up on rather expensive items like meats and fruits, and it is quite likely that the net result is not money saving but better eating.

A similar phenomenon is the purchase of something that is a bargain, but which is not exactly the style or color you wanted, or is something which you might not have bought otherwise.

I have heard a great deal of regret expressed by people who bought something of this sort and had to use it for many years, never satisfied with it but not willing to part with it because of the amount of money involved.

A third aspect of "bargains" is the difficulty in assessing quality. A number of writers of "how to save money" booklets stress the advantages of private brands. Sometimes these are really bargains, particularly when a large manufacturer sells part of his output through a mail order house or a large department store without the manufacturer's label on the items. On the other hand, there is frequently a real difference in quality. My wife insists that there is a real difference between various brands of flour and shortening. Vitamin drops may have the same vitamin content, but differences in taste or in quality control in the manufacturing process.

The Service Trades and Professional Services

In the case of appliance repair and other services, the consumer is hard put to know whether he is spending his money wisely or not. No system has ever been developed for securing and pooling consumer information locally on the prices and quality of such services. In spite of difficulties in measuring quality, I am convinced that such pooling could be done on a more formal basis than the casual conversational methods people now use. One complaint about a service man may be a fluke, or a mistaken impression, but a series of complaints by different people over a period of time would lead to some presumption that something was wrong.

As in manufacturing, economic theory says that the sellers of services who provide the best quality for the lowest price will drive the others out of business. Observation of the scene, however, seems to indicate that the service outfits that charge high prices and plow their profit back into large buildings and fancy equipment expand at the expense of the ones that concentrate on service. To some extent the equipment allows better service, and the extra capacity often allows for speedier service. On the other hand, extra capacity also leads to a tendency to sell repairs and replacements that are unnecessary. Every so often some magazine will send out an agent with a car or a television set with some simple defect, and see how many repair places will sell him a lot of unnecessary parts and adjustments. What appears fraudulent might be only inefficiency and inability to diagnose the trouble. I once took 21 radio tubes to five different places to be tested. Not one was rated OK by all five, and not one was rated bad by all five. At least some of this must have been unreliability of the test rather than dishonesty of the testers. Even the selling of unnecessary parts may be inefficiency rather than fraud. It may be difficult to be sure whether the part is good, or it may be faster and cheaper to replace the part than to test it. However, I have seen new batteries sold to car owners when they had a short circuit in the electrical system that could have been discovered easily. I once found myself charged $15 for a replacement part when the only thing wrong was a corroded $2 electrical switch attached to it. In this mechanical age, apparently, a certain amount of mechanical know-how is a valuable thing. It is hard to resist drawing the conclusion that many people pay more for repairs, and pay for some things they do not really need, because, feeling that they do not know anything about quality of service, they patronize the larger organizations with the more impressive buildings and equipment, assured that they will at least be responsible. On the other hand, an unimpressive location does not insure low prices or good service.

In the purchase of professional services of doctors, lawyers, and dentists, the consumer is even more at a loss because of the great difficulty in assessing quality and price. Indeed, the "ethics" of many professions make it difficult to find out how much individuals are charging, to secure "bids," or to go to various individuals for small services in order to evaluate their abilities. Here, too, the result seems to be a concentration of business on a few well-known people who raise their charges, perhaps as much in self-defense as for any other reason. The result is a wide variety of prices for services and a situation where some "shopping" or investigation by the consumer is likely to pay off far more than it would in buying most merchandise. Of course, some service trades, notably the barbers, have standardized their charges leaving the consumer with no way out short of cutting his own hair.

Advertising, Selling, Social Customs, and the Consumer

It is all very well to talk about consumer shopping and methods of getting information as though the consumers were interested in finding out what was available and were making rational decisions that would get them the most satisfaction for their dollars. The truth of the matter is that only a few act in such a way. To a large extent, people rely on habit. This can even be regarded as rational, since finding new facts is involved, and making up our minds each time consumes time and energy. This is why most people have rather standard patterns for what they eat for breakfast. A certain amount of flexibility in choices of foods will save money since prices fluctuate, but many foods require getting accustomed to them. Few people who were not brought up on hominy, sorghum molasses, or salt pork are likely to care for them. The only danger in relying on habit is that there is failure to sense that it is time for a change, or to realize that habit patterns were not well selected. For instance, some patterns of food consumption are not well balanced nutritionally.

We also are greatly influenced by social custom or convention as to how we spend our money. Most of us do not like to admit it, but a careful inspection of what we and our neighbors do usually reveals a number of things, particularly with regard to dress, housing, marriage and burial arrangements, which are done according to conventions. We must all conform to some extent, but it is frequently possible to free considerable amounts of money for other uses by refusing to conform.

Into this picture comes the seller, who wants to sell what he can make. He will make use of customs and conventions if he

can, and try to establish new ones—"Everyone is doing it." He
will try to make it a habit for the customer to think of, or buy,
his product, if only by drumming its name into the customer's
ear. Try counting the number of times a product's name is
mentioned in an ordinary commercial.

But the real problem of the seller is not to rely on habits or
customs that exist, but to create new ones. This raises an interesting problem of evaluation. Suppose a seller creates a
product, then goes out and somehow convinces people that they
need it and should buy it. Is this a misuse of resources, because
the people did not want it in the first place, or a creative act
because a latent want or need of consumers was uncovered and
satisfied, or a neutral act since the consumer really does not
know what he wants anyway and was merely diverted from one
product to another? Is the creation of new wants necessary so
that people will spend most of their money and keep business
good and employment high? Does the stimulation of desires
make people unhappy because it raises their aspirations too
fast? There is not any simple answer to these questions so far as
I know.

From your point of view as a consumer, however, there is the
possibility of trying to understand a little about the mechanisms
used in "creating wants." This might help you avoid being
convinced by advertising that you need something that appeals
to your weaknesses. Occasional reading in the advertisers'
journals and in textbooks on marketing and selling will reveal
what is going on in the sellers' minds, and help you guard
against the tricks.

What does advertising do? It tries to tell you that a product
is available and offers you information about it. It tries to convince you that some particular product is different from, better
than, or cheaper than, others. Most important, it tries to con-
nect the product with some need or desire: the desire to be
modern and up to date, the desire to do everything you can for
your children, the desire to avoid embarrassment, to get a bargain, and so on. Sometimes, as in the "B.O." ads, or a more

recent case where parents were told their children would be social outcasts if they did not have television, there is some rebellion against the techniques, but generally the ads are more subtle and only insinuate the ideas. It is hard to resist the feeling that when consumers are really bilked, it is because some of their less laudable motives have been used: greed (special deals, bargains where some "normal" price has been established), pride (distinguished men), or guilt (the fancy funeral because we could have treated him better while he lived).

Critics have been in rebellion against what they regarded as bad taste in advertising. A recent study seems to show that advertising used to be much worse than it is now, but on the other hand, the modern consumer finds it more difficult to avoid seeing or listening to the constant bids for his money.

Wrily, the older hands may suggest that modern advertising is in peril of foundering in a slough of good taste, of inhibition, from which it will be impossible to extract it. This seems a pessimistic view. Advertising, after all, is the mirror of man, and man has never been in serious danger of becoming bogged down in grace.[7]

The Social Scene

Since it is difficult to state or discover just what peoples' tastes and preferences are, it is difficult to say whether or not they are spending their money efficiently. The consequences of inefficient allocation of money are primarily visited upon the consumer himself, and only in extreme cases does society interfere with free choices. In the case of harmful or habit forming drugs, the government prohibits or greatly restricts sale. In the case of some articles regarded as luxuries—such as tobacco, alcoholic beverages, luggage, cosmetics, and furs—high excise taxes have been applied, partly to discourage consumption but probably largely because of the impression that the tax would not affect sales much, would hit largely those who could afford to pay it, and would not injure anyone.

There are some other less obvious interferences with consumer choices by the government. Home ownership is favored by several provisions of the income tax laws and by subsidized low rent housing. Saving through life insurance is encouraged by the methods of determining taxable earned interest for income taxes. Consumption of healthful foods by children is encouraged through subsidized school lunch programs. And of course some things which people would not, or could not, provide for themselves are socially provided: parks, schools, sewer and water systems, and others.

For the most part, however, people are allowed to have their own preferences and make their own mistakes. Indeed, the freedom to spend one's money as one chooses is regarded by many as one of the fundamental characteristics and advantages of a democracy. Even in providing information and guides to consumer choices, the government has limited itself to the more general kinds of information rather than taking the chance of interfering with private enterprise.

One consequence of free consumer choice has been a natural tendency to prefer variety and special services, and an equally natural tendency of sellers to provide these. The result has been a rapid diversification of products. The use of trade names and widespread, effective advertising has led in many areas to what the economists call "monopolistic competition." What happens is that when a particular field seems profitable, competitors enter, but since each seller has a group of customers who will stick with him even if his prices are a little higher, few of the competitors go out of business. The final result is too many producers, or too many stores, all operating at less than "capacity" as an engineer would define it, and all forced to charge enough to cover the higher costs per unit which result from this.

This situation is clearly not monopoly, for there are many sellers. Anyone can go into the business with a product that is similar to the ones being sold, or in the case of retail stores, supply a location and line of goods similar to those presently in existence. Nor is it competition, since the more efficient businesses cannot drive the others to bankruptcy and secure their customers.   Each is protected by the fact that he is not selling exactly the same product or service, and has some customers whose preferences he supplies.   In a sense, there is "too much competition," and in another sense too little.   The importance of this problem was recognized in Great Britain during World War II, when in order to free manufacturing capacity, furniture and some clothing items were standardized and produced in fewer factories, freeing the others for war production.

Perhaps the most striking thing about this is that it is the consumer who brings the high costs upon himself by being unwilling to shift to the business that offers a better bargain, and by demanding variety, special services, and convenience.   It is all very well to point out that fewer filling stations could handle all the business, but so long as consumers will tend to go to the most convenient one, it will pay to start new ones.   The retail trades give the best example of this general problem.

Co-operatives and Buying Clubs

In spite of their undoubted successes in England, Sweden, and some farm communities of the United States, co-operatives have never made any substantial impact here.   A co-operative is essentially a buying club which follows certain general principles established by the weavers of Rochdale, England, who founded the first co-operative.[8]   Prevailing prices were charged, and dividends were paid to members in proportion to their purchases.   Every member had one vote regardless of his original subscription to the operating funds, or the amount of his purchases.   Co-operatives since then have gone into manufacturing too, but not on a large scale.

Co-operatives were seen as a method of fighting monopolistic exploitation of consumers, as a method of improving the efficiency of retailing, as a method of getting better quality merchandise and more information about quality to the consumer, and as a method of achieving better community co-operation through the experience of working together.   Farmers' co-operatives in this country found that they could get their machinery and supplies cheaper and that they could market their products better through co-operatives, some of which built and operated grain elevators. The California Fruit Growers Exchange is a co-operative that has increased efficiency in marketing citrus fruits.

City consumer co-operatives, however, have traditionally gone into food retailing, where they have found that they were adding one more retail outlet where one of the difficulties already was "too much competition." The consequence was increased distribution costs. The other difficulty was that the large food chains had a superior method both of improving efficiency and of driving down the prices of suppliers. In a few notable instances, such as the Harvard Co-operative Society, enough volume was secured and efficient management hired so that substantial rebates were and are paid every year. The Harvard "Co-op" concentrates on books, clothing, appliances, and other high mark-up items, rather than on food.

On the other hand, co-operatives have started Credit Unions which have been successful and of great use to their members. They also have done a great deal to disseminate product information to their members and to encourage careful buying. Their members are generally people with interest in their community and will be found active in many other community enterprises. If they could abandon the field of food distribution, and concentrate on consumer information—particularly about the local service trades, and the location of discount houses—and sell only high mark-up items, they could be still more useful. If the resale price maintenance laws remain, the co-operative is perhaps one of the best methods of securing for its members discounts that otherwise would go only to people with "connections." In so far as they either help break up resale price maintenance, or introduce competition among local service trades, they benefit not only their own members but the whole community.

SUMMARY

In making detailed choices how to spend your money, you, as a consumer, must receive information regarding both the variety of things available and the reasonability of prices. Some things have stated fixed prices, but there are also sales, discounts, variable trade-in allowances, and so on. Others have no stated prices. Other things, particularly services, vary so widely in quality and are so difficult to specify that no simple price information is meaningful.

Depending on your own personality and interests, some shopping is bound to be worth while, and some a waste of time, except as a recreation. Sources of information have varied relevance, accuracy, and availability that differ from product to product, and from time to time. Even though products change, know-how about securing and using information, along with personal enthusiasm for doing so, are likely to be cumulative.

SUGGESTED PROJECTS

1. Go through the library files of newspapers in your home town, or some selected city for the past two or three years, making a list of the advertised sales, recording the dates, types of things on sale, and degree to which the sale is widespread or confined to a few stores. How predictable is the pattern? Are the advertised markdowns similar in amount from year to year?

2. Make a list of standard grocery items, for instance, grade A large eggs, creamery butter, bananas, round steak, pork loin, and so on. Price these items in a large number of stores of different sizes, including a co-operative if there is one, indicating apparent differences in quality. Then select two or three supermarkets that appear to be competing, and price the same list each week for about eight weeks. How much did you save by shopping in the supermarkets? Is there any consistency in the differences between supermarkets? What sort of strategy in deciding where to shop would seem best?

3. Select one appliance, say a table model television set or automatic washing machine. See how much you can find out about the mechanical problems of the appliance, the characteristics of different brands, and the prices and possibilities of discounts or "special

deals." Among others, talk to dealers, repair men, recent purchasers if you know any, and read the advertisements and the reports of testing agencies.

4. Go through the recent issues of some of the magazines that carry articles of interest to consumers. Select five articles, preferably on the same general subject. Write a critical appraisal of them, as to adequacy and relevance of factual information. Also evaluate the degree to which value judgments vary, mentioning the factors over which some people might disagree.

FOOTNOTES TO CHAPTER 5

1 See the *1953 Annual Report* of the House Committee on Un-American Activities, Washington, D. C.: U.S. Gov't Printing Office.

2 Eugene R. Beem, "Consumer-Financed Testing and Rating Agencies," *Journal of Marketing*, January 1952, pp. 272–285; Alfred R. Oxenfeldt, "Consumer Knowledge: Its Measurement and Extent," *Review of Economics and Statistics*, XXXII: 300–314 (November 1950); Calla Van Syckle, *Practices Followed by Consumers in Buying "Large Expenditures" Items of Clothing, Furniture, and Equipment,* Lansing, Michigan: Michigan State College Agricultural Experiment Station, Department of Home Management, Technical Bulletin 224, June 1951.

3 With the ending of compulsory grade labeling of meat in 1953, the labels "prime, choice, good, commercial, utility, cutter, and canner" will only appear if packers choose to continue to use them. Aside from this, and the A, B, and C grades used with some canned foods, there are few grade labels in use. See: Helen Dallas and Maxine Enlow, *Read Your Labels*, New York: Public Affairs Committee, 1942 (Public Affairs Pamphlet No. 51 revised); see also: *Using Standards and Labels*, Consumer Education Series, Unit No. 6, American Association of Secondary School Principals, Washington, D. C., 1947; see also: Jules Labarthe, Jr., "Fabric Facts versus New Names," *Journal of Home Economics*, 44: 419–422 (June, 1952); for an example of the complexity of the problem of defining standards, see U.S. Department of Health, Education, and Welfare, Food and Drug Administration, *Canned Vegetables and Vegetable Products*, definitions and standards under the Federal Food Drug, and Cosmetics Act, Washington, D. C.: U.S. Gov't Printing Office, reprinted March, 1954, from Service and Regulatory Announcements.

4 See, for instance, Sidney Margolius, *How to Buy More for Your Money*, Garden City, New York: Doubleday & Company, Inc., 1947.

5 George Katona and Eva Mueller, "How Purchase Decisions Are Made—A Study of Deliberation by Consumers," *Consumer Behavior*, Lincoln Clark ed., New York University Press, 1954.

6 F. J. Schlink, *Eat, Drink, and Be Wary*, New York: Covici-Friede, 1935; Stuart Chase and F. J. Schlink, *Your Money's Worth*, New York: The Macmillan Company, 1934; Arthur Kallet and F. J. Schlink, *100,000,000 Guinea Pigs*, New York: Vanguard Press, 1933; Roger W. Riis and John Patric, *Repairmen Will Get You If You Don't Watch Out*, New York: Doubleday & Company, Inc., 1942; for a recent summary and restatement of the problems, see Leland J. Gordon, *Economics for Consumers*, 3rd ed., New York and Cincinnati: American Book Company, 1953.

7 Ernest S. Turner, *The Shocking History of Advertising*, New York: E. P. Dutton & Co., Inc., 1953, p. 340.

8 Marquis Childs, *Sweden, the Middle Way*, rev. ed., New Haven, Connecticut: Yale University Press, 1947; U.S. Department of Labor, *Organization and Management of Consumers' Cooperatives*, Bulletin 1024, Washington, D. C.: U.S. Gov't Printing Office, 1951. There are many books on co-operatives, almost all polemical or poetical, but with an incomplete economic analysis.

chapter 6

Risks and Insurance

It is commonplace knowledge that all of us are exposed to risks of all sorts. Some risks have declined with the "growth of civilization" and medical progress, such as the chance of typhoid or malaria. Others have increased, like the probability of being hit by an automobile. Still others have become more serious, such as death of the wage earner. This is because of the greater need for money income in raising children—income that can be earned only by working at a job away from home.

We need at the outset to make a distinction between risk and uncertainty. Some unfortunate events occur with sufficient regularity so that for a large group one can predict rather accurately which groups will suffer, and which, proportionally, will not suffer such events. These are risks, and death is an example of a risk. For an individual, it is not possible to specify the probability that he will die next year with any great accuracy— he may be healthier than others, or engaged in a more dangerous occupation. But the differences between individuals cancel out in large groups. In addition one can predict more accurately for a numerical percentage of a group even though the chances are the same for everyone in the group. The cancelling out of differences has its analogy in "diversification" in investment portfolios where one avoids any large losses by not having any

substantial amount invested in any one place. The reduction
in variability even if there were no differences in probabilities
can be shown simply by a coin-tossing example. If you toss a
coin 100 times, you expect 50 heads, but once in twenty times
you will get more than 60 or fewer than 40. If you toss the
coin 10,000 times, however, you will get 49–51 per cent heads
95 per cent of the time. With 10,000 tosses, the chance of
getting less than 4,000 heads or more than 6,000 is infinitesimal
and could happen only with a biased coin.

Uncertainty, on the other hand, refers to risks where it is impossible to state the probability of occurrence even for a large
group. A striking example is unemployment where individual
differences do not cancel out, and the chances of a depression
are difficult to assess. What is called unemployment insurance
is a form of government guarantee of funds to tide you over
during short periods of unemployment, with a contributory
element added to avoid having it look like a dole, or charity.

Major Consumer Risks

What risks are important to the ordinary consumer? Let us
list some of the more important ones:

1. Death of the wage earner
2. Total or partial disability of wage earner
3. Death of wife
4. Death of child
5. Disability of wife
6. Disability of child
7. Illness (with or without loss of wages) or accidents in family
8. Fire or other damage to house
9. Theft of items in house
10. Fire or other damage to car
11. Theft of car
12. Suit for damages done by your car
13. Suit for damages to someone on your property

Even this gruesome list is probably incomplete and includes
more items that are insurable risks than items that are not, such
as mental illness. Probably all the items in the list are risks.

They differ from the risk of missing the bus in the morning because the loss involved is important financially. The concept of "amount at risk" is important, even if it is difficult sometimes to put a financial value on the loss resulting from some of these events.

Why Insurance?

It is an interesting fact that people like to take some risks, although, at the same time, they are avoiding loss by insuring against others. What reason is there for trying to avoid some losses? The economist would say it is because of the declining "marginal utility of money," that is, because the increase in satisfaction from having an additional $1,000 in cash is not as great as the decrease in satisfaction from having $1,000 in cash taken away. Economists used to use this as an argument against gambling, pointing out that even in a fair bet such as "heads you pay $10, tails I pay you $10," the psychic value (negative) of the loss is greater than the psychic value of the gain. Of course, people do gamble, and economists have recently tried to explain this on the grounds that a large increase in income can change your whole pattern of possibilities, and hence there are ranges within which the marginal utility of money increases.[1] Other people have pointed out that people enjoy the thrill if the possible loss is small, and that gambling is a method of getting sums large enough to purchase important durables or clothes with an average expense not much greater than small loan charges. The average expense is the income of those who run the gambling game.

Insurance is taken out against the very large losses, the ones so disastrous that it seems rather academic to talk about the marginal utility of money. Insuring involves taking a small loss (the cost of the insurance) in order to avoid a much larger loss (or rather provide compensation for it). If someone offered to play roulette with you with a wheel with 20 pockets, and you pay 5¢ a game and get $1.00 if the ball falls in the first pocket, you would know that if you played long enough you would

break even—the mathematical expectation is one-twentieth of
$1.00 or 5¢. Since insurance companies have expenses of op-
eration, you cannot buy insurance except by paying more than
the mathematical expectation. Hence, in the long run, you
come out a little behind. But this is irrelevant because you are
not playing a game, but avoiding an uncompensated disaster.
If someone offered to flip a coin and, if it were heads, to double
your year's income with an added $1,000 to boot, and if it were
tails, to take all your income for a year, you would be likely to
turn him down, even though you would have an *average* gain of
$500 per game if you played enough games. One wrong flip
would ruin you.

What does insurance do? Briefly, it eliminates risk by pooling the risks of various people.* The insurance company is not
bearing the risk for them, it is eliminating risk altogether by
averaging it out over a large group. Sometimes those who have
more money in the bank than they could possibly lose by wreck-
ing their car carry no auto collision insurance and talk about
"self-insurance." This is incorrect. There is no such thing
as self-insurance, because there is no pooling of risks. There is
only self-taking of a risk because it does not seem like a disaster
if it occurs. There is nothing wrong with doing this, particularly in view of the costs of insurance, but it is not self-insurance.

It is probably true that most consumers do not think of insurance in either mathematical or economic terms. Life insurance is not generally bought, but is sold to people by agents.
Auto and fire insurance are almost always forced upon us by
the institutional arrangements under which we live. There
is nothing wrong with this. Auto liability insurance, which
insures against suit from someone whose property or person
you damage with your car, is required by law in some states.
It is essential in most states if you have an accident. Fire and
general damage insurance on the home is required in most
mortgage contracts. Medical insurance schemes are almost
automatic in many companies. Automobile installment pur-

* See the glossary of terms at the end of this chapter.

chase contracts generally include a charge for insurance on the car and frequently on the life of the purchaser as well.

When Is Insurance Worth While?

There are several questions that need to be answered in deciding whether insurance is worth taking out:

1. Is there an insurable interest? That is, is there a loss which needs to be compensated?

2. Is the loss so large that you cannot bear it without serious disruption and sacrifice?

3. Do the rates you pay on available insurance represent some reasonable approximation to the probabilities you face times the amount of compensation?

The last item requires some explanation: Sometimes rates are so low that even as a gambling scheme the insurance would be worth it. This is particularly true of G.I. life insurance where the government pays all the administrative costs and even the insurance payments for death in combat. It is also true of some group insurance schemes where an employer is subsidizing the scheme. For the most part, however, the rates include a "loading" to cover the expenses of the insurance company, and these expenses are not negligible. They vary from 15 to 60 per cent of the premiums. The amount of "loading" depends a little on the profits of the insurance company, but much more on such things as:

a. Selling costs (agents' fees, etc.).

b. Lapse rate (which means selling costs are not spread out over such a long period since many policies are not renewed).

c. Uncertainties as to probabilities, or past bad experience of the company, or moral risks, and consequent caution by actuaries in setting rates.

d. Where savings schemes are involved too, the interest earned on the investments of the company.

e. General operating expenses and efficiency.

f. The company's mortality experience resulting from its selection of clients.

g. High interest guarantees on older policies.

In addition, the rates can reflect the fact that the probabilities used by the insurance company in setting its rates are different from the ones you face.

a. The company may have bad selection of clients, as when people who expect to have children or illnesses are more likely to take out medical insurance. The company will then have to assume that if you apply for insurance, you too are more likely than the average man to get sick.

b. They may include in one rate a wide range of conditions, and you may have much lower chances of loss than most of those in the group that includes you. Group life insurance often has identical rates over wide ranges of ages, and, of course, this is a better bargain for those at the top of the age range, because they are more likely to "cash in." Also, if you have more money, you are more likely to be sued; hence, liability insurance whose rates are set for rich and poor alike is a better bargain for you if you are rich.

c. Finally, the probability of loss or the amount you lose may depend on whether you are insured or not, in which case the insurance company rates do not represent the situation if you are not insured. Personal liability insurance may be an example. People may be more likely to sue you if they know you are insured. You yourself may be more careless about locking up if your things are insured against theft. A doctor may be tempted to charge more if you have medical insurance.

It is *not* true as you may think that the value of being insured depends on the likelihood of the disastrous event happening to you. The critical question is whether the event is sufficiently disastrous to be worth insuring against, and whether the chances of it happening to you are reasonably well reflected in the probabilities used by the insurance company in setting its rates.

In general, insurance which is sold individually with high agents' fees to a small group so that adverse risk selection is easily possible, for an event which is difficult to define and/or depends on the consumers' own initiative to avoid or minimize, is not likely to be any bargain. But all these points will be clearer if we discuss specific types of insurance. Let us start with the most important one—life insurance.

Life Insurance—Consumer Needs

What is at risk? The joke books have many variations on
the idea that when you're dead you don't need money any more.
The answer, of course, is that you have others depending on you
for their support. They are counting on you to continue living and earning money. In addition, in our society, it is often
quite expensive to die, particularly after a long illness, and to
be buried. Many people feel an obligation to leave enough
money to cover these expenses. In lower income groups where
other savings are inadequate, it is common to have some insurance on each member of the family, referred to as "burial insurance." Finally, there are ways in which a family depends on
one of its members not for money but for real services, the loss
of which would leave the family much worse off, and perhaps
require monetary outlays to replace. The obvious example of
this is a housewife, particularly while there are pre-school children.

Clearly, the most important single case is the wage earner
with a wife and other dependents; so let us look at his situation.
How much is at risk here? One possible answer is his total
possible future earnings which would be lost if he died—this
after subtracting what would be required to support him, including support in his retirement. Such a figure is difficult to
estimate, of course, because of uncertainty about the future: his
future earnings, the cost of living, possible changes in social
security laws, or in annuity rates, and so on. It also requires
dealing with time, because a dollar ten years from now is not
the same as a dollar now. If you have 75¢ now, you can invest
it at 3 per cent and have a dollar in ten years. This means that
the present value of the loss is not the total amount, but its
"present value," that is, all the future earnings and amounts
necessary for the worker himself each "discounted back" to the
present. Seventy-five dollars now will make up for a loss of
$100 ten years from now, if you invest it in the meantime.

It is not easy to convert values to the same point in time, because not only does money earn interest, but the interest of the past earns interest—a phenomenon called "compound interest." For example, if you buy a savings bond for $75 and get $100 ten years later, you have earned $25 in interest. But 2.9 per cent of $75 for ten years is only $22 in simple interest; the other $3 is interest on the interest.

The solution is to find a set of tables which will tell you the "present value" of $1 for any number of years hence, and at any of a number of reasonable interest rates. Such tables are easily available.[2] But, of course, the appropriate rate of interest is also difficult to determine.

But is this the amount at risk anyway? Why insure the man's potential contribution to his family? Why not simply ask how much is needed to take care of the man's dependents and call that the "amount at risk"? Since most people cannot afford enough insurance to cover the total amount at risk anyway, let us look at this definition of amount at risk, which will give us a smaller amount.

To take an extreme case, suppose a man has excellent earning prospects, but his only dependent is his wife who could easily return to earning her own living, and they have an accumulation of savings sufficient to ease the transition. Here, on our second definition, there is nothing at risk, and no insurance is needed. The argument is even more obvious in the case of a single person with no one counting on him or her for support.

What about the family man? He presumably wants to provide support for his wife and for the children until they leave home. The definition of a minimum support is difficult here. Does he assume that the wife will take a part-time job as soon as the children are in school, and a full-time job when they leave home? Can she get such jobs? Can the children work their way through school? What standard of living is really minimum? What other savings or sources of funds (such as social security) are available? In general, about all that can be said is that, if there are young, dependent children and a wife, the total amount at risk on almost any set of assumptions you want

to make will be enormous, even discounting future needs on the
assumptions that interest can be earned on the unspent balance
of any funds made available at the time the husband dies.

More important than the absolute amount of insurance
needed at any point in time is the *changed* amounts needed
as time passes.   Thinking in terms of the life cycle of the typical
family, you will remember that the needs of the family reached
a peak when the children were growing up, and declined rather
rapidly when they left home.   When we cumulate this pattern
of yearly future needs back to the present, however, in spite of
any discounting, it will almost always turn out that the cumu-
lated amount is at a maximum at the time when the obligations
for care of dependents are incurred, that is, marriage, or concep-
tion of children.   And as time passes, the total amount at risk
drops rapidly, particularly as the children leave home, and it
drops even more rapidly if you assume that the wife will work.
The amount drops, too, because a family with any saving plan
at all will accumulate other reserves that can take care of part
of the needs.   In addition, the family accumulates household
equipment that can be consumed without replacement, reducing the money outlays necessary.   •

We should not concentrate on the needs of dependents to
the exclusion of the fact that we are insuring against loss of
earnings to provide for these needs.   When the head of the
family retires, then, regardless of the needs of his dependents,
there is no point in his carrying insurance if there is no stream
of future earnings that ceases with his life.   Some retirement annuities are set up so that they cease when the man dies,
but they can be converted easily so that some portion of the
annuity lasts until both the man and his wife die.   Once this
is done, there is no need for insurance any more.   Insurance
is very expensive then, too, since the probability of dying is
great.   During the life of a family, the total future earnings
that would be lost if the wage earner should die becomes
smaller, of course, since he has fewer years of employment ahead

of him.   Hence, even if the "need" did not drop, the insurable interest would.

All this may seem like a very hard-hearted and "scientific" analysis which does not treat the psychological reactions of people whose standards of living may increase steadily through time.   A housewife who has lived comfortably, reared a family of children, and seen them off on their own is not likely to be happy if forced to go to work, even if she can find a job.   Since, as we shall see, many insurance policies involve a large element of pure saving, some people start insurance policies for their children even though the children do not have any dependents, and are not earning income, primarily in order to get them in the habit of carrying insurance, because they feel their children should "get the habit."   But no matter how many other considerations we bring in, or how we define "need," the striking fact is that for most families there is a tremendous amount at risk during the few years immediately following the birth of the children, and a rapid drop after this particularly during the period when the children leave home.   Indeed, the amount may also drop rapidly after they leave home if the accumulation of other reserves is speeded up—what with the children gone, and income probably higher than before.   In addition, if there was any need for insurance on the wife, it was temporary, and also ends after the children leave home.

Life Insurance—What It Provides

We have seen that life insurance theoretically fulfills certain needs of the individual, and that they are likely to vary rather widely from one year to the next.   What policies do insurance companies offer, and how do they fit these needs?

The first thing that strikes us when we start examining insurance policies is that it is almost impossible to buy pure insurance.   Most types of policies involve a saving program as well.   What is pure insurance?   If we look at a table showing the estimated proportion of people in a particular age group who die each year (the Commissioners Standard Ordinary, 1941), we note that out of 100,000 men aged twenty, we could expect 243 to die within the year. If an insurance company collected $2.43 from each man, they would have $243,000, enough to pay $1,000 to the survivors of each of the men who died. If they charged enough more than this so they could cover their operating expenses, they would be in the business of issuing pure (one-year term) insurance. For these same 100,000, or rather the 99,757 of them remaining, the rate would have to be higher for the next year, because 2.51 per 1,000 men among them will die. As we saw earlier, there is no risk for the insurance company provided they have enough customers, have estimated the mortality table properly, and do not have an "adverse selection" of risks, that is, a group of unusually unhealthy policyholders. They need enough customers to avoid the pure random chance of an unusually large percentage of deaths, but even with as few as 10,000 policyholders of all ages, this variability becomes quite small. The risk is further reduced for most companies because they are mutual companies: their premium rates are set high, and the excess after covering operating expenses is returned to the policyholders as a dividend at the end of the year. Of course, the dividend will change to take care of any variations. In addition, all insurance companies accumulate reserves.

Some writers make a big point of the fact that the companies are using an out-of-date mortality table. Since fewer people die than the number estimated in each age bracket, they argue, the rates are higher than they need be. Actually, this is irrelevant, because the rates include a "loading" to cover expenses and profit anyway, and because the companies can set their own standards of selection and refuse all but the most healthy clients. It is also misleading, because the mutual companies return the extra charge as a dividend, and the stock companies have had to reduce their charges to compete with them.

Probabilities of dying—mortality tables—have been computed by those selling insurance as a necessary adjunct to their business. The first published table was the "Northampton Table" based on data over a period of 40 years in Northampton, England, and published in 1783. The one most widely published and used in this country is the 1941 Commissioners Standard Ordinary (often called CSO) Mortality Table, based on the experience of a number of the larger U.S. companies between 1930 and 1940, and increased by a small safety factor. On the other hand, the 1937 Standard Annuity Male (1932–1936), which is used in computing rates for annuities, assumes a longer life. It shows 29 people dying per 1,000 at age 65 instead of the CSO's 40. (See Chart 3.)

But rather than look at the mortality tables used, or the risk selection, or even as we shall see later the stated interest rate on savings, the simplest way to answer the question whether the "loading" of the insurance company is large, that is, whether the rates depart very far from a "fair bet," is to look at the proportion of the premiums and other income of the companies which goes to cover their expenses, and for stock companies, their profits as well. According to *Life Insurance Fact Book, 1953,* published yearly by the Institute of Life Insurance, the costs of all life insurance companies taken together, including taxes and dividends to stockholders of the stock companies, amounted to some 19.2 per cent of income of the companies.[3] Because this income to the companies includes both premiums and the interest earned on money you have loaned to the company (and which they have invested elsewhere), this means that 19 per cent of the money you turn over to the insurance company goes to cover its operating expenses. In addition, another 5.6 per cent goes to "additions to special reserves and surplus funds"—called in one company report, "general and investment contingency reserves"—which may ultimately go to the insured in future dividends but are a present cost.

As we said, it is difficult to find policies that are pure insurance. The reasons are rather simple: First, the company that sold only pure insurance would never have any very large amount of investment funds; second, pure insurance can be

CHART 3

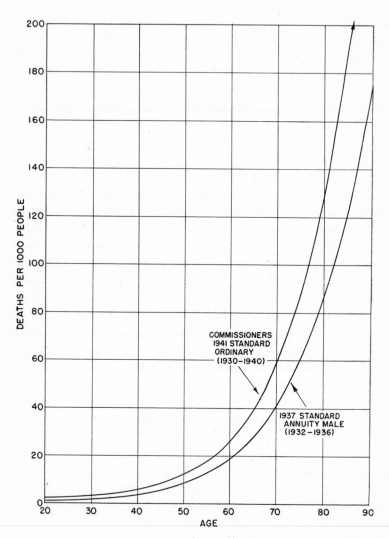

COMMISSIONERS
1941 STANDARD
ORDINARY
(1930-1940)

1937 STANDARD
ANNUITY MALE
(1932-1936)

DEATHS PER 1000 PEOPLE

AGE

Source: Life Insurance Fact Book, 1954, New
York: Institute of Life Insurance, 1954, pp.
98–99.

dropped at any time, and because the costs of insurance grow rapidly, particularly after you are 50 years old, people are tempted to drop it; third, insurance is sold by agents who must be paid, and it is expensive to have a high lapse rate; and finally, policies that involve additional saving features not only reduce lapses, but provide contractual saving devices which many people need if they are to save.   Let us describe the main types of policies to see what is involved.

Term insurance: One-year term insurance, which is almost impossible to obtain, is pure insurance.   It is sometimes called "temporary insurance" or "more costly" or even "of no value if the need for insurance is lasting," but these terms are either meaningless or incorrect.   Insurance is insurance, and its cost is roughly the same in any policy except for small differences in the amount of expenses "loaded" on.   Term insurance is generally sold as 5-year, 10-year, or 20-year term insurance, meaning that the premiums per year are constant over that period. Five-year term is often sold in a policy that provides for renewal until age 65, at the end of each five years, without another medical examination but at a higher rate.   The level premium for each period is possible because it more than covers the cost of the insurance during the first few years, building up a reserve which, together with any interest it earns, covers the extra cost of the later years over and above the premium, and reduces the cost of insurance because the company has less "at risk"—the reserve helping to pay the face value if the man dies.   By cost of insurance we mean the amount that must be taken from each policyholder's account to pay the death benefits to those in his age group who die, and to help cover the expenses of the insurance company.

Ordinary Life (or "straight life"): This is the most common type of life insurance, accounting for some $60 billion dollars of insurance (face value) in force in 1950 out of a total of $234 billion dollars, or more than 25 per cent.[4]   The plan calls for a constant premium each year over the life of the insured, though in mutual companies the amount of dividend is low in the early years to cover the agents' fees and to discourage dropping the policy by increasing the dividend each year. As we shall see in more detail later, the payments in early years are greater than the cost of the insurance, and they accumulate a reserve which (a) reduces the amount the company has at risk and therefore the amount of pure insurance, and (b) earns interest to help cover the cost of the insurance and to continue the increase in the reserve. From the point of view of the consumer, the plan is a combination of a declining amount of pure insurance through time, and an accumulation of savings. Particularly since 1948, companies have a system where the cash surrender value of the policy, if you cancel it, is less than the value of the reserve, and the amount you can borrow on it is also less than the reserve. The main purpose again is to discourage cancelling of policies, but it makes it even more difficult for the consumer to know just where he stands. It is possible to borrow up to the "loan value" at any time, paying 4.5–6 per cent interest depending on the policy, or to borrow from a bank using the insurance policy as security for the loan. Some people refer to this as paying interest on your own money in order to use it, but it must be remembered as a partial justification that the company is allowing interest to accumulate to your account as though they still had the full amount of the reserve invested.

Chart 4 shows the amount of insurance actually involved each year with a $1,000 ordinary life insurance policy, the cost per $1,000 worth of insurance, and the cost of the amount of insurance actually involved. You will notice that the amount of insurance drops steadily and rather rapidly.

Limited-payment life: Limited-payment life insurance policies have higher premiums, and become "paid-up" at the end of some fixed period, usually twenty years. After that you pay no more premiums, but the policy remains "in force" until you die, and then the face amount is paid to your dependents. At the point where the policy is "paid up" the reserve is large enough so that (a) the amount of insurance is rather small, and

CHART 4

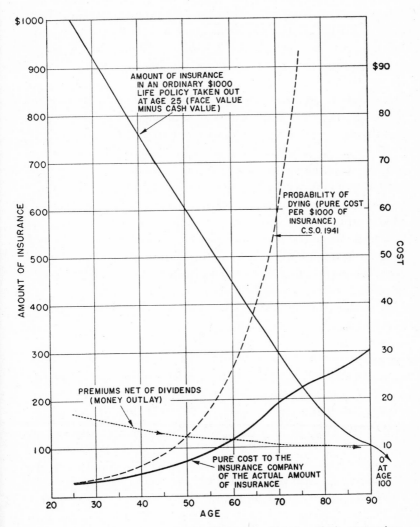

AMOUNT OF INSURANCE
IN AN ORDINARY $1000
LIFE POLICY TAKEN OUT
AT AGE 25 (FACE VALUE
MINUS CASH VALUE)

PROBABILITY OF
DYING (PURE COST
PER $1000 OF
INSURANCE)
C.S.O. 1941

PREMIUMS NET OF DIVIDENDS
(MONEY OUTLAY)

PURE COST TO THE
INSURANCE COMPANY
OF THE ACTUAL AMOUNT
OF INSURANCE

AMOUNT OF INSURANCE

COST

AGE

Source: Northwestern Mutual; author's computations.

(b) the interest on the reserve is enough to pay the cost of the insurance including the "loading" and increase the reserve for the next year.   For a 20-year policy taken out at age 25, premiums cease at 45 at which time the cash surrender value is some $616—and the reserve somewhat larger than that—so that the amount of insurance is really less than $400 on a $1,000 policy, and continues to drop.   This type of policy accounts for even more policies than "straight life," though not quite so much face value of insurance in force.   In 1950 there was some $58 billion dollars face value of this type policy in force, or slightly less than 25 per cent of the total insurance in force.

Endowment policies: These policies mature either at the end of a stated period, or at some age, such as 65.   When they mature, the reserve is actually equal to the face value of the policy, so you can take the money in cash, or convert it into an annuity. You no longer have any insurance.   Since the reserve in a 20-year endowment policy must be $1,000 at the end of the period, not merely a little over $600 as with limited-payment life insurance, the premiums are correspondingly higher, and the amount of pure insurance drops still more rapidly.

Retirement income policies: These policies have still higher premiums, and a reserve which reduces the amount of pure insurance to zero before maturity, sometimes in less than 15 years. At maturity they have accumulated a reserve sufficient to pay, on a "$1,000 policy," $10 per month for the life of the insured.

Family income policies: These policies are relatively recent. They provide for $10 a month from time of death until the end of 20 years after the policy was taken out, plus $1,000 at the end of that time.   Consequently, the amount paid to your survivors is very large if you die the year after you take out the policy; it amounts to $120 per year for twenty years plus $1,000 at the end of the twenty years, a total of $3,400 which even discounted at 2.5 per cent has a present value of $2,500 (or at 2 per cent a value of $2,650).   The amount of insurance drops rapidly as the period during which the $10 a month would have been payable elapses, and as the policy builds up a cash value.   (See

Table 10.) After the first twenty years, the policy is exactly like an ordinary life policy taken out at the initial age, and the premiums, which were higher to cover the additional insurance, drop to those of such an ordinary life policy. The higher premiums during the first twenty years simply paid for a decreasing term insurance policy.

TABLE 10

ESTIMATED NET PREMIUMS, CASH VALUE AND AMOUNT OF INSURANCE FOR A $1,000 FAMILY INCOME POLICY, TWENTY-YEAR PLAN

TAKEN OUT AT AGE 25 (NORTHWESTERN MUTUAL RATES)

Age	Premium, Net of Estimated Dividend	Cash Value	Amount of Pure Insurance Discounting Future Payments at:	
			2½ Per Cent	2 Per Cent
25	$25	$ 0	$2,480	$2,658
30	18	56	2,120	2,247
35	17	135	1,696	1,776
40	16	212	1,227	1,267

AT AGE 45 AND AFTER, IDENTICAL WITH A $1,000 ORDINARY LIFE POLICY TAKEN AT 25:

45	$12	$303	$697	$697
50	11	386	614	614
55	10	470	530	530
60	9	551	449	449
65	8	628	372	372
100	...(paid up)	1,000	0	0

Source: Mr. Clinton Purdy, Northwestern Mutual agent. Dividends are based on 1953 schedule which can change. Two and one-half per cent discounting added for comparison purposes.

Mortgage Protection Policies (also called Income Protection Plans): These are sold as a method of insuring that if you die your house will be left free of debt for your dependents, but they are essentially nothing but a decreasing amount of term insurance. They frequently call for some amount per month for the remainder of a period starting when the policy is taken out, for example, $100 per month from the time of death until the end of 20 years from the original date of the policy, but this can be translated into a lump-sum amount of insurance at any time. These policies are generally sold as an addition to some other policy, but at least one company, Occidental of California, sells a large variety of decreasing term policies in different amounts and for different duration periods. (See Table 11.)

From the point of view of the needs of the typical family for a maximum amount of protection when there are young children, and a declining amount from then on, a straight decreasing term policy is ideal. It allows you to carry a lot of insurance at a rather low premium, and to have it decline steadily and automatically. All this assumes, of course, that you can take care of your saving program some other way.

TABLE 11

PREMIUM AND INITIAL AMOUNT ("COMMUTED VALUE") OF PROTECTION FOR $100 PER MONTH INCOME PROTECTION POLICIES WRITTEN TO RUN FOR VARYING NUMBERS OF YEARS:

Number of Years Protection (From time of taking out policy)	Present Value of Insurance the First Year	Present Value of Insurance at Beginning of Second Year	Annual Premium Cost if Taken Out at:	
			Age 20	Age 30
50	$34,490	$34,140	$152.00	—
40	30,530	30,080	105.80	$180.20
30	25,460	24,880	83.00	115.10
20	18,960	18,220	61.20	73.90
10	10,640	9,690	40.70	44.60

Rates: Occidental of California. Present values, using 2½ per cent rate.

There are a bewildering variety of other types of policies, but all of them are variants on the ones we have discussed, consisting of varying amounts of pure insurance, and varying amounts put each year into a saving program. There are also many special "riders" or special provisions for which extra charges are made. The most common one is entitled "waiver of premium" and simply says that if you are unable to work you need not pay the premiums during that period. It is nothing but a very small amount of disability insurance sufficient to pay your premiums if you are unable to work. Such a provision seems unnecessary if the disability is temporary, and if the disability is permanent there is no point in keeping the insurance anyway.

There are also *methods of selling* policies other than through the individual insurance agent, most important of which is a group insurance. Group insurance is generally handled by employers, usually without physical examinations, and with premiums deducted from paychecks. Since the selling and collection procedure is so simplified, administrative economies are made, and, in addition, many employers partially subsidize such schemes. The rates often do not go up with age, or go up only when you reach another broad age bracket; hence, those at the top of the age brackets generally have a better bargain. But, group policies are usually a bargain for everyone covered.

At the other end of the scale are small "industrial insurance" policies sold door to door, and with premiums collected door to door each week or month. These policies have very high premium rates because of the expensive method of selling and collecting, the high lapse rate, and the somewhat worse mortality experience. Such policies are frequently taken on everyone's life in the family except the wage earner, who of course is the only one who should be insured. The agents are not so well informed as regular life insurance salesmen, and the policies are not flexible enough for the varying incomes of many of the people who take them out.

There are also companies or fraternal associations which sell insurance to limited groups, such as the Teachers Insurance and Annuity Association, often at favorable rates. In New York, Connecticut, and Massachusetts the savings banks sell life insurance over the counter at very low rates but only to residents of those states.

There are some special policies sold only to groups with very good life expectancy, for example, desk workers, and only in large amounts. If you fit into one of these groups, you can frequently benefit by the lower premiums of a special policy.

It should not be forgotten that there are provisions for dependents of those covered by social security. Payments are made to a widow caring for a child or to a single child under 18, even if the worker was only currently insured and had not worked enough to be "covered"—that is, half the quarter-years since 1950, or 40 quarter-years. The scheme is not insurance in the usual sense, because the benefits depend on various circumstances which reflect need, and on the average monthly wage. The payroll taxes pay for this and for old age benefits, so it is impossible to tell what "premiums" are being collected for the use of survivors' benefits. The amounts paid if a worker had an average monthly wage of $350 or more are:

	Monthly Payment
Widow (or dependent widower) at age 65, or one child alone, or dependent parent	$81.40
Widow and one child under 18	162.80
Widow and two children under 18	200.00
Widow and three children under 18	200.00

If you look at a typical example, it is apparent that these provisions can take the place of a substantial amount of insurance. Assume a case where a man earning $350 a month is fully covered, and has a wife and two children aged 1 and 3. If he dies, his family gets $200.00 a month for the next 16 years, $162.80 a month for two years, nothing until the wife is 65, and $81.40 a month until the wife dies. The payments while one or both of the dependent children are under 18 amount to some $48,207, which even discounted to a present value at 2.5 per cent, is now worth about $39,000. If the wife is 35 years old, her old age payments will not start for 30 years, but they are equivalent to an annuity which would be worth about $15,000 at that time, or, again discounted at 2.5 per cent is now worth $7,250. Consequently, the 2 per cent of $4,200 which is taken in social security contributions ($84 a year) plus the equal amount contributed by the employer, pays for some $46,000 worth of insurance in this case, in addition to the retirement benefits in case the worker does not die.

This is not intended as a full treatment of social security. It was pointed out earlier that the retirement provisions amounted to the equivalent of a large amount of savings. The details depend on individual circumstances and are subject to change by Congress, so everyone must check the details which apply to his own situation.[5] The only important thing to remember is that there are substantial and important life insurance aspects of the social security law.

Comparing costs of various types of policies is difficult because most companies are mutual companies that pay dividends. These dividends vary from year to year but are generally larger each year of the policy. One way to compare companies is to look at the total premiums minus dividends for the first twenty years using historical dividend data. Approximate rates on such a basis are given in Table 12.[6]

TABLE 12

NET COST OF VARIOUS TYPES OF LIFE INSURANCE POLICIES

Type of Policy	Premiums Minus Dividends for 20 Years, $1,000 Face Value (Divide by 20 to Get Average Annual Net Premium) Taken Out at Age:			
	20	25	30	35
5-year Term Insurance Renewed Three Times	$101	$117	$147	$202
Ordinary Life (Paid Up at 85) .	297	337	388	453
20-Payment Life	511	561	618	686
Family Income (After 20 Years, Same Premiums as Ordinary Life)	337	384	449	541
Retirement Income (at age 65) .	—	609	738	913
20-year Endowment	903	911	923	944
One-year Renewable Term	119	134	162	212
Decreasing Term ("Income protection") Insurance of $1,896 at Beginning; Nothing after 20 Years	122	133	148	176

Aside from small differences in the degree of participation in dividends and the amount of expenses loaded on different types

CHART 5

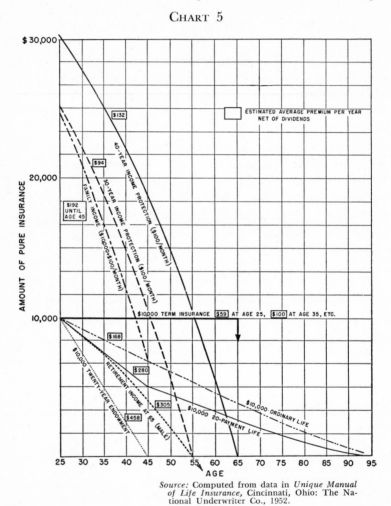

Source: Computed from data in *Unique Manual of Life Insurance,* Cincinnati, Ohio: The National Underwriter Co., 1952.

of policies, the cost of the insurance is about the same. The vast differences in the net premiums result from differences in the actual amount of insurance involved, and differences in the rate of accumulation of a reserve of savings. The actual amount of insurance involved at various stages for some of the major types of policies is shown in Chart 5, for policies with $1,000 face value.

These rates, and the mortality tables, are based on the assumption that some people will be excluded from insurance for medical reasons. The insurance companies have a Medical Information Bureau, a sort of central file, which keeps a record on anyone who has ever applied for insurance. In addition, almost all policy application forms ask whether you have ever been refused insurance and for what reason. If you are turned down by one company, the others are also likely to refuse you, and insurance experts advise seeing a doctor *before* applying for insurance, in order to cure temporary defects. If the doctor's opinion is that the companies would refuse you, there are policies which do not require medical examination. Even with these policies, experts advise taking out the insurance in reasonably small amounts at first in order to avoid being refused. Most companies also avoid possible large losses to themselves by reinsuring some of their policies with other companies. There are also some special policies for high-risk people, but the premiums are usually very high.

Life Insurance Policies—General Principles

Any life insurance policy can be analyzed quite simply into its components as follows:

FIGURE 2

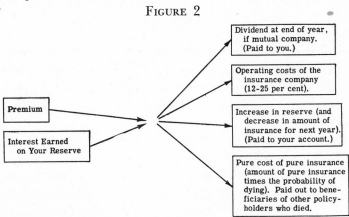

Each year you contribute two sums to the insurance company, one is the cash premium minus any rebate, and the second is the interest earned and credited to your policy reserve, even though you never see it and do not even have to declare it as income for tax purposes.

These two contributions do two things for you: They pay for the cost of insurance, and they increase the reserve which the company invests for you.

The cost of insurance each year is the product of the probability that you will die this year times the amount of pure insurance, plus a charge to cover the expenses of the insurance company. The amount of pure insurance, sometimes called the amount at risk, is what the company pays you if you die *minus* the value of your reserve. If you have a policy reserve of $400 in a $1,000 face value policy, then $400 of the $1,000 the company pays you when you die is your own money. Remember, insurance is the elimination of risk by pooling, and in this case you are only eliminating $600 worth and are bearing $400 worth because you have that much saved.

Another way to think of the cost of insurance is that it is the amount the company has to pay out to the survivors of those who die over and above what is in their reserves. The company must therefore charge that amount against the accounts of the policyholders in that age group.

The amount of insurance is thus the face value of the policy minus the reserve. Until 1948 the cash surrender value of the policy, and the amount you could borrow on it, were almost as large as the reserve, but since then they are considerably less for the first 10–20 years. We have, however, used cash values in most of our charts to represent the policyholder's savings, because that figure is more easily available, and because it ultimately has to accumulate to the same figure as the reserve, that is, the face value of the policy. Chart 5 indicates for some of the more common policies the way in which the amount of insurance decreases each year. For the family income policy, of course, it is more than twice the "face value," but drops rapidly; and for term insurance, of course, it never drops at all.

Since most of these policies involve both a saving plan, where interest is accrued, and an insurance plan, with a different amount of insurance each year, it is difficult to talk about the cost of insurance. The over-all value of the policy depends on the cost of the pure insurance and the amount of interest earned on your savings, and it is difficult to separate them. One can look at the over-all experience of the company. Its mortality experience, the yield it nets on its investments, the loading necessary to cover its operating expenses, and profits if it is not a mutual company, combine to determine the company's efficiency from the consumer's point of view.

The rate at which interest is accrued on policy reserves is predetermined and printed right on each policy, so differences in mortality experience, investment yields, or operating expenses are taken care of by differences in premiums, or in premiums *and* dividend rates if the company is a mutual one. Some years ago, policies were written calling for 4 per cent guaranteed interest, and many of them even provide for an annuity option whereby the death benefit can be turned into an annuity on the life of the beneficiary, again earning 4 per cent, but this time not on the reserve but on the whole face value of the policy, or what remains of it each year. Currently, policies only accumulate at 2.5 per cent, but the dividends are lower for everyone in order to pay the guaranteed 4 per cent on the older policies. The older policies get lower dividends than if the rate of earnings on investments had never dropped, but the newer policies take part of the burden. In stock companies, there is no dividend, so the company, and of course the newer policyholders take the full brunt of being forced to guarantee 4 per cent on reserves which are invested but only earning 3 per cent.

One can ask, what proportion of the premium (net of dividends) is saving by the consumer, and what proportion pays for insurance? But this is a meaningless question since the consumer is also implicitly contributing the interest earned on his reserve by leaving it there as saving. The amount of saving depends on three things which change continually from year to year: The amount of insurance keeps falling rather steadily, the cost per dollar of this insurance rises more and more rapidly, and the amount of interest earned on the policy reserve increases rather steadily as the reserve increases in size. In addition, in some mutual companies the dividends increase each year, so that the net premium continually falls. The product of the falling amount of insurance and the increasing cost per dollar's worth is a gradually increasing annual cost for pure insurance in the case of an ordinary life policy. But the contribution of the policyholder also increases because of the increasing reserve which earns interest. The net result is a rather constant amount of saving. If we take the saving as equal to the increase in cash reserve, it is roughly equal to the annual net premium after the first few years, for an ordinary life policy. Table 13 shows the ratio of the increase in cash surrender value (saving) to net premiums for various policies and various ages.

TABLE 13a

RATIO OF INCREASE IN CASH VALUE TO ANNUAL PREMIUMS * FOR AN ORDINARY LIFE INSURANCE POLICY

Attained Age of Policyholder	*(Treating Increase in Cash Value as Saving)* Age at which Policy Was Taken Out			
	20	25	30	35
25–29	82%	47% *	—	—
30–34	89	85	51% *	—
35–39	96	90	84	55% *
40–44	102	96	89	82
45–49	102	101	93	86
50–54	102	101	95	87
55–59	108	101	93	87
60–64	105	98	90	83

* Average ratios for Travelers Insurance Company, a stock company, so dividends did not have to be deducted. Basic data from *Unique Manual 1952*. Ratios are low for the first few years because of agents' fees.

Not only does the mixed character of most insurance policies make it impossible to tell whether there are differences in the cost of the pure insurance in different types of policies, but since they could only be different by rather small amounts, it seems obvious that the type of policy chosen depends on what pattern of insurance one needs. The difficulty is that the only way to secure a declining amount of insurance each year, aside from taking out a lot of small-term insurance policies and dropping them one by one or taking a decreasing term (income protection) policy, is to take policies which involve substantial saving features. Aside from family income and income protection policies, one characteristic of all other insurance policies is that *if* the amount of insurance declines, it is because the reserve has increased by the same amount, and the reserve increases only because you have saved and lent this amount of money to the insurance company.

TABLE 13b

RATIO OF INCREASE IN CASH VALUE TO ANNUAL PREMIUMS FOR
VARIOUS TYPES OF POLICY TAKEN OUT AT AGE 25

Attained age of policyholder	Ordinary Life (per cent)	20-Payment Life (per cent)	20-Year Endowment (per cent)
30–35	85	97	102
35–40	90	108	113
40–45	96	121 *	133 *

* These policies are paid-up at the end of this period; hence, the ratio never gets any higher. Same source as above. *Conclusion:* The errors resulting from assuming that your premiums are equal to your saving are negligible except for the first few years or term insurance policies.

Now if the typical family has maximum demands on its income, and particularly on its cash because it is investing in housing and durable goods in the years when the children are growing up; and if, as we have said, the maximum amount is at risk once the obligations to a wife and children are assumed, then most families are unlikely to be in a position to decrease the amount of insurance they carry by saving the full amount of this decrease every year. Indeed, it is quite unlikely that they can carry enough insurance if any substantial saving feature at all is added to it. The solution may be decreasing term insurance or a series of term insurance policies, though the insurance agent is sure to attempt to discourage it.

The family income policy comes close to meeting what is likely to be the need for insurance without quite so much contractual saving, though there is still a substantial amount of saving in a family income policy. It seems clear that decreasing term policies—"income protection policies"—are the ideal way to get a lot of pure insurance and still have a declining amount as time passes.

Insofar as combinations of insurance policies make it possible, there are people who argue that the thing to do is stick to pure insurance (some form of term insurance) and do your own saving. U.S. savings bonds have a higher yield, even after income taxes, than most insurance policies now available pay on their reserves. In addition they are at least as safe, and far more flexible and liquid. You can cash U.S. savings bonds of the main types with no loss except a slightly lower interest yield; whereas if you give up an insurance policy, you do not even get all the reserve back; and if you borrow on the policy, you must pay 2.5 per cent interest even net of the 2.5 per cent credited on the reserve. It is easy to think of situations where temporary unemployment, illness, or other financial pressure would make it extremely difficult to continue a large fixed payment every month and require using some accumulated savings. Furthermore, with any sort of care you can invest your money quite safely and earn substantially more than U.S. savings bonds pay. For instance, open-ended investment trusts, which invest your money in a wide variety of carefully selected stocks for a small handling charge, earn 3.5 per cent and more. For people in upper income brackets, there are certain tax advantages from saving in the form of life insurance: You can have a policy that converts to an annuity even if you do not die, and the income from the annuity is taxed as though an amount equal to your total net premiums were your own money being paid back to you (and hence not income) when in fact some part of these premiums was a payment for insurance. Since, in addition, annuity payments are taxable in a complicated way so that only the last few payments are considered income *in toto,* you avoid most of the income tax by even taking this income when you have little other income and double exemptions because you are over 65 years old. On the other hand, some of this can be achieved by other means, such as holding on to discount bonds or stocks in rapidly developing companies.

The decision what kind of insurance policy to take is one more example of a choice between an inflexible commitment that will force you to save but pay a low yield and a more flexible arrangement that has a higher yield and more adaptability but requires that you be able to save without compulsion. It is easy to visualize a family with children with the following situation:

BORROWING	LENDING
Mortgage 4.5%	Savings bonds 2.9%
Installment credit 6–20%	Annuity or other retirement plan 2.5%
Insurance loan 5%	Insurance reserve 2.5%

It appears that this family is borrowing substantial sums of money at high interest rates, and at the same time lending substantial sums at low interest rates—hardly a good way to get rich! There are even some combination mortgage and life insurance policies that are advertised as 4.5 per cent interest on the mortgage, but which involve also a life insurance policy with a cash value. In the latter years of such a deal, the cash value of the policy is greater than the amount you presumably still owe on the mortgage. You are paying 4.5 per cent interest on the latter, and being paid 2.5 per cent on the former, and here the lending and borrowing involve the same company! This is one more of the many cases where "package" contracts have expensive features which make them far less economical than the separate pieces, and frequently involve some features that you do not need.

In summation, you the consumer must decide how much pure insurance you want, and how much of your saving you want to invest in the low-yield, inflexible, but automatic form of a life insurance reserve fund.   You need to ask yourself whether you can count on being able to meet the premiums and never borrow on the policy.   On the other hand, you need to ask yourself whether, if you used up your savings in an emergency, you would replenish them unless you had to, to avoid paying interest, as in a policy loan.   It may require a combination of insurance policies, some to be dropped after a time, in order to get what you want.[7]   Decreasing term insurance seems to be the most adaptable to the needs of the typical family, since it can be arranged to decline over a period of any length that suits your needs.

Shopping for Life Insurance—Comparisons Between Companies

Three things make it difficult to compare the costs of insurance offered by different companies: the variety of special provisions in policies, the different dividend rates of mutual companies, and the mixture of pure insurance with saving plans which involve interest rates.   The over-all efficiency of a company depends on three things: its actual mortality experience which may differ from the tables, the rate of interest it earns on its investments, and its operating expenses which depend largely on lapse rates because of the large agents' fees.   However, most insurance companies also sell annuities and other types of insurance such as medical and disability.   Furthermore, the proportion of their business that is group insurance may differ, or the average size of policy may differ.   Also, the way in which operating expenses are charged to various types of policies can differ.

If we give up trying to compare one company with another in general, and concentrate on a specific type of policy with provisions as similar as possible from one company to the next, we find published data that help us, but may also deceive us. Available books take a policy, say an ordinary life policy taken out at age 25, and compute for the next twenty years the total premiums. Then they subtract the total dividends if the company is a mutual company and not a stock company, and subtract the cash value at the end of twenty years, and provide an estimate of net cost over twenty years. But this net cost does not account for the interest earned on your savings. This would not matter in comparing companies if they all accumulated the same amount of reserve and paid the same rate of interest, but they do not. For many practical purposes, these net cost figures are close enough, but it is always possible for a company to show a low net cost by building up the cash value faster, for example, by paying lower dividends in the earlier years of the policy. It does not help to look separately at the premiums minus dividends, and at the stated interest rate at which the reserve is increased, since the latter is a fiction in mutual companies, set low and offset by higher dividends, in order to leave the company an adjustable amount in case their actuaries were not quite correct.

For term insurance, where there is almost no reserve, and hence no problem of interest rate, the net premiums are sufficient for comparison. Further, because the main differences between companies are in their mortality experience, their investment yields, their operating costs, and the amount of older high-interest policies they are saddled-with, many people compare net premiums of companies on ordinary life policies and are satisfied with that. Such comparisons are published and made available by the Massachusetts Savings Banks, because their life insurance is the cheapest of any generally available in that state, and by Northwestern Mutual which usually looks best of any of the legal reserve life insurance companies. They are also published in journals like the *Life Insurance Courant,* and annually in the *Unique Manual of Life Insurance.*

G.I. insurance, for those who have it, is a bargain even more than group insurance or some of the old policies with high interest guarantee. The complete overhead costs are covered by the government, as well as payments for death in combat. A free "waiver of premiums" provision gives you free insurance while you are disabled for as long as you are disabled, on the term policy. The rates are based on a conservative mortality table, but, by law, surpluses must be distributed as dividends, and dividends have been very large. On G.I. policies with reserves, you can borrow the full amount of the reserve at 4 per cent interest. Also, some people have G.I. insurance who are excluded by some private companies, particularly negroes and people in certain risky occupations.

Because it is such cheap insurance, there is every reason to keep a maximum of it, which you can only do by keeping it in the form of term insurance. There have been repeated extensions of the period you are allowed to keep these policies as term policies without converting, and extensions are likely to continue. Some of the annuity options—for the way in which payments are to be made to beneficiaries—are also bargains.

Insurance agents have in general refrained from inducing veterans to drop G.I. and take private insurance. As a matter of fact, the agents have a gentlemen's agreement not to induce people to drop policies in another company to take one in theirs, an operation known in the trade as "twisting."

Insurance is also sold by mail, sometimes by companies that are not licensed to have agents in your state and hence not subject to control by your state insurance commission. If you had to sue to collect from them, it might require going to another state and hiring a lawyer there, an expensive procedure.

Insurance companies are regulated by the states, and are generally conservatively run. Hence, any company that is registered with the state insurance commissioner to do business in your state is probably honest, legitimate, and safe. There is a story of one insurance company which had a provision that the death benefit would not be paid unless the insured appeared in the head office in person within six months of death, but such shenanigans are unlikely today, particularly since the Federal Trade Commission now also has some jurisdiction over the insurance business. In addition, most companies are mutual companies so that any extra profits must go to increase the policyholders' dividends.

It is a striking fact that in no area of consumer choices is there more detailed published information than in life insurance. Not only are all the facts available about the rates and experience of the various companies, but there are a number of books on how to buy life insurance.[8] A large number of the books, however, do not explain the principles involved. Some which do, like Gilbert's *Insurance and Your Security,* are well worth reading even if his judgments seem a little harsh toward the insurance companies.

The most important thing to remember about insurance is that some policies involve a combination of pure insurance with a saving program. It is obvious that over most people's lives the need for insurance decreases, because the potential loss of future earnings is less and because the needs of dependents will exist over a smaller number of remaining years, and because you also accumulate savings which can partially take care of dependents. On the other hand, your accumulated savings need to increase in order to provide for retirement. The over-all problem is to get a combination of insurance and savings programs that will meet your needs. All this is made more difficult by the fact that the need for savings may vary depending on what happens to social security provisions, your family situation, and attitudes and aspirations and living standards of the family.

What Consumers Actually Do about Life Insurance

Roughly eighty per cent of the spending units in the United States carry life insurance, over half of them paying more than $100 a year in premiums. Aside from the lowest income group, the median proportion of money income put into premiums stayed between 2.6 and 3.3 per cent, being somewhat lower for spending units with lower incomes.[9] Professional and managerial people carry more insurance in proportion to income, and so also do married people, of course. Young doctors, in particular, having so much invested in their own training, frequently carry very large amounts of insurance, often with special provisions to keep the premiums low for the first few years. In other words, the policies are almost pure term insurance at the beginning and gradually take on more and more savings through added premiums.

On the other hand, it seems clear that a great many people are under-insured, even on the most limited estimates of the needs of their dependents. In early 1950, 23 per cent of the spending units had no insurance at all, and half the rest had less than $3,200 in face value.[10] Even among families with children under 18 years old, 16 per cent were not insured at all, and less than half of those insured had $5,000 or more in face value of insurance.[11] Even for those with $5–10,000 it is difficult to resist the value judgment that for those with children more insurance would be worth while.

Looking at types of policies, we have the following distribution as of 1950: [12]

TABLE 13c

	Per Cent of Policies	Per Cent of Total Face Value
Ordinary Insurance		
Straight life (ordinary life)	9	24
Limited payment life	12	16
Endowment	7	9
Retirement income with insurance	1	4
Regular term	1	3
Family income and other combination policies	2	7
Extended term, reduced paid-up, etc. ...	1	1
	33	64
Group Insurance		
(Practically all term)	14	22
Industrial Insurance		
Straight life	9	2
Limited payment life	28	9
Endowment	10	3
All other	6	*
	53	14
	100	100

* Less than 1%

Source: Institute of Life Insurance.

This table, of course, understates the amount of pure insurance in term policies, because the amount in the other policies, particularly endowment and limited payment life is much smaller than the face value.

In spite of the arguments against it, industrial insurance is still an important part of total insurance. In addition, there are still people taking out endowment policies on their children, primarily as a forced saving scheme to accumulate money for a college education, again in spite of the obvious fact that there is no point in carrying insurance on dependents.

Life Insurance and the Total Economy

In any "industry" so extensive as life insurance, the maintenance of competition is clearly important. Life insurance policies have been made quite complex, and are generally sold by individual agents on a personal basis, so that it is unlikely that very much price competition can exist. In the 1930's the insurance companies were charged with agreeing on rates and other contract conditions, but in view of the rather close regulation by the various states of the insurance companies, and the fact that most of them are mutual companies anyway, it seems likely that the rates would be rather similar anyway.[13] More recently, the federal government's anti-trust laws have been interpreted to cover insurance. (See Chapter 10.)

The development of group term insurance, and of savings bank life insurance in New York, Massachusetts, and Connecticut, as well as the widespread G.I. insurance, may gradually make people aware of the costs of private insurance, and might even lead them to shop around more for insurance. There are enough differences between companies in the per cent of total income going to cover their expenses to indicate that such shopping would help the consumers. One major company in 1952, for instance, had expenses of only 11 per cent of total income (net of investment expenses). This compares with an over-all average expense of 19 per cent. The same company put 2.7 per cent into "special reserves and surplus funds" rather than the 6.5 per cent over-all average. Although state regulatory agencies can control the investments, and the actuarial soundness of companies, it is doubtful that they can insure efficiency in their operations.

The mixing of life insurance and savings plans has had two important consequences. First, in an endeavor to sell more of the combination policies, insurance companies have gradually restricted the amount and types of term insurance they have made available and have provided higher agents' fees for selling the combination policies. This has led to concentration on the selling of combination policies, sometimes to people who can not afford them, or who get much less pure insurance than they need. The ordinary life insurance agent will go through a series of arguments somewhat as follows: "Term insurance is temporary insurance," he will say, "and more expensive." To prove this, he will compare it with an ordinary life policy. For the ordinary life policy he will add up for ten or twenty years the premiums minus dividends, then subtract the cash value at the end of the period. He will compare this with term insurance for the same face amount, and it will look much cheaper. If you are sophisticated enough to point out to him that he has neglected the fact that you are lending money to the insurance company, and ask him what rate of interest you are earning on that money, he will not point to the 2 or 2.5 per cent stated on the policy, but will do the following: For each year, subtract the cost of a $1,000 term insurance policy from the cost of a $1,000 face value straight life policy. If this is the amount of money you are lending to the insurance company, the agent will argue, and if it accumulates to the cash value of the policy, it is earning about 4.5 per cent interest. What the agent has not admitted, and perhaps not noticed himself, is that it is unfair to compare $1,000 in straight life insurance with $1,000 in term insurance, for the former is not that much pure insurance. The only fair comparison is to subtract from the ordinary life premium the premium for an amount of term insurance equal to the actual amount of insurance you have with an ordinary life policy. Such a procedure will indicate that you are earning about 2.5 per cent on your money or less. The important thing is not that the consumer is confused, but the fact that he frequently ends up with the wrong type of insurance.

The second important consequence of the selling of insurance-saving mixtures is that the companies have become an extremely important channel whereby savings are channeled into investments. Aside from the difficulty we have already mentioned that, having guaranteed high interest rates to policyholders in the past, insurance companies are forced to pay much lower yields on newer policies in order to make up the difference, there is the more important problem that, in order to insure safety of the policyholders' money, state regulatory agencies have insisted that the insurance companies invest only in high grade bonds, government bonds, mortgages, and an extremely small amount of high grade stocks. Thus, a major flow of saving is restricted to users who are large, well established, and willing to tie themselves to a guaranteed interest rate. Most new investments should be financed with "equity capital," for instance, by the sale of common stock. Some states, notably New York, have recently liberalized the restrictions on stock investments by insurance companies. Another consequence of these limitations on investment policy is a low rate of return to the insurance companies, a rate which had gone below 3 per cent in the 1940's and was only 3.36 per cent in 1953. With the tremendous amounts involved, it seems as though the safety of diversification would allow more investments in stocks.

In addition, the tremendous amounts of money invested have raised the problem whether the life insurance companies could not exert control over a great deal of American industry. Similar questions have been raised about the banking system, but so far no one has provided any convincing demonstration that such power had been used. Life insurance companies do not "vote" the stock they hold.

What improvements can be suggested? It seems to me that the placing of some part of everyone's savings in equity investments, diversified perhaps by the use of open-ended trusts, would increase the earnings on their savings and provide for business more of the equity capital most economists think is so scarce. So long as insurance contracts guarantee minimum interest rates over long periods, it would be difficult to let insurance companies go too heavily into stocks. The alternatives would seem to be either separation of savings from insurance plans, or elimination of interest guarantees. Both of these are unlikely, so the consumer will have to make the best of the situation, and the economy will have to develop other methods of allowing new enterprises to get funds.

Disability Insurance

From the point of view of the amount at risk, a possible disability of the wage earner and consequent loss of earnings from accident or illness is more important than death. The amount at risk is larger because the former wage earner also must be supported for the rest of his life, and there may be medical bills. (We shall discuss medical insurance in the next chapter.) There are serious difficulties with disability insurance that do not exist to the same degree with life insurance:

A. There is not an adequate body of experience as to incidence rates.

B. The amounts payable depend on the length of the disability period, or the life of the permanently disabled, and can become extremely large, whereas with life insurance the total amount is fixed. Actuaries do not like small chances of very large payments and tend to write in provisions limiting the total amount payable.

C. The definition of disability is not clear. When is a man completely unable to work? What about other sorts of work? Not only does this make the work of the actuary difficult, but it raises questions of "moral risk." Whether it is really moral, psychological, or what, is hard to say, but it is a problem. During the depression when the amounts payable for disability were

greater than many people could earn even if they could find a
job, the insurance companies had difficulties. As a result, they
have raised rates and left themselves more leeway. They are
also more careful about refusing to insure bad risks. A recent
handbook intended for insurance agents warns them:

> In connection with moral hazards, there is need for careful ap-
> praisal of motives, needs, and insurable values. Particularly when
> special forms are requested, attention should be given to speculation
> and overinsurance. A person is overinsured when the amount of
> disability indemnity provided by his accident and health insurance
> exceeds his earned income. Voluntary applicants—those who apply
> for insurance without being solicited by an agent—should be
> checked carefully for an ulterior motive.[14]

D. There tends to be a high lapse rate, and this intensifies
an already adverse selection of risks. When only a small proportion of the population is insured, in spite of all restrictions,
it is likely that those more likely to need the insurance apply for
it, and those least likely to need it either do not take it, or let
it lapse sooner. In addition, the courts have been rather gen-
erous in their interpretation of what disabilities were meant to
be included in the contracts, and some authorities feel that disabled people have lived longer than the actuaries expected,
partly because of the economic security resulting from their
disability payments.

The net result of all this is that the insurance companies who
still handle disability insurance are extremely cautious, have
put all sorts of limitations on the policies, and have raised the
rates to allow a more substantial safety margin. Many policies
are no longer "non-cancellable," which means that the company
can terminate the policy or refuse to renew it if, as is often the
case, a few illnesses indicate that permanent disability is likely
to come. Many policies have special provision for greatly reduced benefits if the insured person is not actually confined to
the house, and, of course, the agents are a great deal more careful in refusing to insure anyone likely to become disabled.
One authority has concluded:

. . . casualty companies do not, except in small amounts and under special safeguards, write insurance on the disability hazard, but on a selected and minor part of it—that of accident. . . .

. . . the unsold disability business is largely business the companies do not want.[15]

In view of all this, it is doubtful that you would be well advised to take out a disability insurance policy, even if you could find a non-cancellable one. The risk remains a problem, however.

Accident and health insurance as well as disability insurance have been sold by mail in recent years, and the Federal Trade Commission is investigating these mail solicitations for deception and fraud. The complexity as to possible coverage and exclusions is so great, however, that the consumer can still be "taken in" by a statement which is completely accurate and legally honest.

Household Insurance

There are two general types of household risks important enough to be insured against: One is damage to your home and possessions by fire, wind, and so forth; the other, personal liability for injury to people on your premises. The former is quite common, most mortgages requiring it. It is generally sold by agents, and very little shopping is done by the consumer. The consumer who decides to look around is likely to be fooled in many states by the fact that the premiums charged are fixed by the state, and seem to be identical for all companies. If he persists, however, he will discover that there are some mutual companies which pay dividends as high as 25 per cent of the total premium, or more. He will also discover that on a three-year contract, he can save another 16⅔ per cent by paying all at once for three years.

Unless the mutual company is quite large, the consumer might want to be sure that his policy is "not assessable." A mutual company is essentially a co-operative, and its members are responsible for its debts. There have been cases of farmers losing their farms to pay the debts of insurance companies that have failed.

As we have pointed out before, insurance companies not licensed to sell insurance in your state can still sell by mail, but are not subject to any regulation by your state insurance commissioner, and cannot be sued except in their home state.

Finally, there is in some policies a "coinsurance clause" that states that if you insure your house for less than 80 per cent of its true market value, then the insurance company will pay only a portion of the total damage equal to the proportion of 80 per cent of the value which is insured. For instance, if you insure a $10,000 home for $6,000 on the assumption that in most cases only part of the home would be destroyed anyway; and if you have a fire that does $1,000 damage, the insurance company would only pay 6,000/8,000ths or 75 per cent of the damage. Such a clause is particularly important in times of rising prices, when you might become underinsured simply because your house is worth more. Some companies write insurance without the coinsurance clause, and some offer a policy *with* such a clause at a lower rate. A consumer who wants to be insured against total loss anyway, may want to choose the latter, but carry an amount of insurance equal to the full present value of the house. If you insure for 80 per cent of the value, then the company will pay in full for any damage amounting to less than 80 per cent.

Finally, records of the original cost of the house and the items in it are useful in establishing claims.

The other main type of household insurance is for personal liability of members of the family against damage suits. Legally you can be sued for damages only if (a) you or someone in the family is guilty of negligence, (b) the damaged person was not guilty of contributory negligence (not taking proper precautions), and (c) even though he was negligent, you had a "last clear chance" to prevent the accident. However, some courts have ruled that children under seven are not capable of contributory negligence, and there is even some doubt about children between seven and fourteen years old.[16]   Some states have "guest laws" which state that, where there is no negligence, you are not responsible for medical bills arising from accidents on your property, but many individuals feel there is some moral responsibility anyway.

There are clearly some difficulties with insurance in this area: The amount for which you are likely to be sued is not independent of your income and wealth, consequently such insurance is more of a bargain for wealthier people.   Furthermore, for a private householder, it seems unlikely that his neighbors or friends would sue him unless he did something malicious; and what is worse, it seems possible that the very existence of insurance might make the householder less careful, and his visitors more prone to sue if they knew it.   Furthermore, since such insurance is not common, it is likely that those most likely to need it purchase it, and the rates are based on this situation. On the other hand, where there are assets such as an owned home that can be lost in a lawsuit, the amount at risk is quite large and the probabilities small so that the premiums are not large.   A policy for three years for $10,000 for each accident for bodily injury, and $10,000 for each accident for property damage, and $250 medical payments for each person (even where no negligence is involved), costs about $25, with dividends as high as 25 per cent.   The rates for "fire and extended coverage" insurance are about $6.50 per $1,000 for three years, minus dividends, though they vary and are higher particularly where there is no organized fire department.

Automobile Insurance

Automobile insurance falls into four main categories: liability for damage to others' property; liability for injury to other people; loss of, or damage to, your car except by collision or upset; and damage to your car by collision or upset.   There are also provisions for medical payments arising from accidents in which you are involved regardless of who is at fault, emergency road service, and other minor provisions.

The most important of these from the point of view of amount at risk is of course liability for personal injury to others, where people have been sued for forty thousand dollars and more. The amount at stake is possibly your life savings, car, and house. In Massachusetts this insurance is compulsory, and in other states you can lose your driver's license if you injure someone and do not have such insurance. The same general rules about negligence apply as with household liability insurance, but one observer notes:

All in all, there can be no question that the most careful driver may find himself liable for accidental injuries inflicted, even on persons who have themselves not been too diligent in avoiding injury.[16]

If you compare the premiums, it costs very little more to carry $40,000 rather than $20,000 liability insurance, and the extra coverage seems clearly worth it. Insurance against liability for damage to others' property, and against loss by theft, hail, or other damage to your car is quite inexpensive and generally accepted as necessary by most car owners. Collision insurance, on the other hand, is quite expensive and raises several problems of the type we have run across with other kinds of insurance: The rates cover a wide variety of probabilities depending on the amount of driving done and the temperament of the driver. In addition, small damages are easily handled by the individual but are expensive for an insurance company to investigate and to pay. Consequently, most collision insurance is sold as "deductible" for a certain amount, meaning that any damage below that amount is repaired at the individual's expense, and only amounts above that are paid by the company.

For instance, if you have $100 deductible collision insurance, and are in an accident where no one else with insurance was to blame, and your car costs $150 to repair, the company will pay you $50.

But even a deductible policy may not be a good idea for someone who does not drive much, particularly if his driving is mostly slow, in-town driving, or for someone who is more careful than most, or for someone who can take the risk himself and save the inevitable "loading" of about half the premiums that goes to cover the expenses of the insurance company. Particularly if you have an older car which is not worth much anyway, the total amount at risk even if the car is completely demolished is quite small, and could be borne. A general difficulty for the insurance companies arises from the habit of repair garages of charging more when the insurance company is paying the bill. This means that the amounts at stake are greater if you are insured than if you are not, again making the insurance expensive. Finally, those who take collision insurance probably expect to use it, and the rates are adjusted for this fact.

There are substantial differences between rates charged by various companies, sometimes because they have less "loading," and sometimes because they are more careful in selecting those they are willing to insure. Insurance is generally included in any installment payment scheme, primarily to insure that the creditor will get his money. Unless you insist on taking out your insurance separately, you are likely to find yourself with a more expensive insurance policy this way; and the dealer is likely to try to induce you to take insurance and installment loan all in one package.

Since the agent's fee is an important part of costs, particularly if there is a large turnover, at least one company—the State Farm Mutual Automobile Insurance Company—charges this fee at the beginning, and can charge lower rates from then on, thereby reducing their turnover and providing a better bargain for those willing to stay with one company. There are also differences in the way various companies categorize different risk groups, and you may find yourself in a high rate group in one company and a low rate one with another, so it frequently pays to shop around.

Claims are frequently made that one company is better than another at paying claims without arguing or lawsuits. It is difficult to prove this one way or another. Companies that do

not belong to the insurance association may be involved in more
lawsuits, but they may also make fewer arrangements with other
insurance companies that are detrimental to the auto owners—
for instance, by settling a case out of court for enough to cover
the insurance company's obligation under a deductible collision policy, but not enough to cover the owner's costs.   Also,
a company that is stricter about invalid claims or excessive
garage repair bills may be able to provide better rates.   Certainly you should not take the word of an agent for one insurance company about the payment practices of competing insurance companies.

There are, of course, many other types of insurance, such as
that against theft of personal possessions while travelling.   As
in all insurance, the consumer must ask himself the same questions we listed at the beginning of this chapter, particularly:

Do the rates reflect the amounts of loss and probabilities I
face?

Do these amounts and probabilities change if I am insured?

How much of the premiums go into the operating expenses
or profits of the insurance company?

Aside from life insurance and group insurance, and the Blue
Cross and Blue Shield medical insurance discussed in the next
chapter, almost any type of insurance sold by individual agents
will have agents' fees and company expenses that absorb approximately half your premiums.[17]   Hence, as a simple gambling device, most insurance is a worse deal than the race track
or a bingo game.   You can save the 50 per cent by bearing your
own risks, and probably only the unbearable large risks should
be insured against.   This is not meant as a criticism of insurance companies, which are bound to desire a reasonable profit,
and which have substantial expenses from the type of personal
solicitation necessary, the high lapse rate, and the necessity for
many small complicated bookkeeping transactions.

The Government and Consumer Risks and Insurance

For the most part, the government has been concerned merely with the honesty and safety of insurance companies. State regulations have generally been effective here. The Federal Trade Commission and the Anti-Trust Division of the U.S. government do have some jurisdiction over insurance companies now. The provisions for dependents in the social security law were presumably based on the theory that people would not of their own initiative carry enough insurance to keep their dependents off the relief rolls. At the other end of the scale, there have been varying laws in the states aimed at preventing people from risking their money by gambling. The objections to gambling may have been partly moral objections to excesses which leave dependents with no support, and to the vice and corruption which seem to accompany many gambling schemes. On the other hand, some states have found it extremely profitable to license race tracks, supervise their bookies, and take a percentage of the bets. This situation is a potential source of corruption because of the power of the state over the profits of the race track operators, and there is continual pressure for extending the length of the "racing season."

Many, it seems, can be taken in by "bargains" in insurance, and in addition to state laws, the federal government protects the consumer when the U.S. mails are used. In general, however, the consumer is left to his own devices, and if he is underinsured, or over-insured, or wrongly insured, this is his own business.

SUMMARY

We all face risks of many sorts. Not all of them can be insured against, and for many of them, insurance is so expensive that it may pay to bear the risk yourself. Combining a clear recognition of a few simple principles with a willingness to look up easily available facts should enable you to come much closer to having the right amount of the right types of insurance with the right companies than most people do. There are no simple substitutes for comparing companies' premium charges, or for analyzing how much insurance you need, or for separating the pure insurance aspects of any policy from all the other provisions.

Finally, both the insurance needs of a family, and its need for compulsory saving programs combined with insurance depend on the willingness to bear risks, the ability to save without compulsion, the degree of flexibility in living standards, and willingness and ability to adjust to new situations.

SUGGESTED PROJECTS

1. Pick a type of life insurance most companies carry, for example, straight life. Call up a number of insurance agents and find out what the premiums and net premiums (after dividends) are for their company for that policy at your age. Then get the *Unique Manual* from the library and look up the 20-year net cost figures. What range of prices did you find, and do premiums, premiums minus dividends for twenty years, and premiums minus dividends for twenty years minus cash value at the end of twenty years all give the same ranking of companies?

2. Try to buy either term or decreasing term insurance and make a list of the arguments used by the agents against these policies. Analyze the arguments.

3. Shop around for auto insurance for your car (or your father's if you are a student), getting separately the premiums for the various categories of insurance. What methods are used to divert attention from cost differences, for example, special provisions? Does your ranking of companies agree with one made for a different car and different age of insured owner, and different size of family?

4. Respond to some insurance advertisements by companies in other states, preferably for disability or personal liability insurance. Find out all you can about the policy. See if you can get a copy of it. Check in the *Spectator* for benefit-premium ratios for this and other companies.

5. Work out in a specific example the comparison between carrying a straight life insurance policy versus carrying term insurance for the same amount of insurance each year (face value minus cash value) and putting the difference in premiums into U.S. savings bonds. Assume a 20 per cent (marginal) income tax is paid on the

interest of each bond when it matures, or, if you prefer, assume they are not cashed until you die and 20 per cent of the interest is paid in taxes then. Plot the cumulative amount of savings over the next 40 years or more under each plan.

A Glossary of Some Important Words Used in the Insurance Business

Face value: The amount payable to your beneficiary if you die.

Cash value: The amount of your own money which you can regain if you cancel your policy, generally equal to loan value.

Loan value: The amount (of your own money) you can borrow back, generally at a predetermined interest rate of 5–6 per cent.

Policy reserve: Amount of your savings held and invested by the insurance company.

Insurance: The elimination of risk by pooling. The amount of insurance in a policy—the amount the company has at risk—is the face value minus the reserve.

Dividends: A return of part of your premiums at the end of the year, by a mutual company. May be used to reduce the next premium, increase the amount of insurance, or increase the reserve.

Loading: The added charges above the cost of insurance necessary to cover the costs of the insurance company.

Lapse rate: The proportion of policies allowed to lapse each year.

Mortality table: A table showing the proportion in each age group who are expected to die each year, generally based on actual experience of insurance companies, for example, 1941 CSO, Commissioners Standard Ordinary.

Annuity table: A similar table with longer life expectancies used for determining annuity rates. For women, you generally use the data for a man five years younger.

Group insurance: A single policy which covers a whole group, generally without medical examination and with a single payment to the insurance company.

Renewable term insurance: Term insurance is renewable at higher rates for successive periods, but renewable term means without medical examination on renewal.

Non-cancellable: A policy that states that the company cannot refuse to continue the insurance. Particularly important in disability insurance.

Self-insurance: There is no such thing. You can bear the risk yourself, but it takes a group to eliminate risk by pooling.

Adverse selection: A tendency for those with higher chances of collecting to take out insurance.

Contingent beneficiary: A second person named to receive the face value in case the first one named is also dead. Frequently the children are so named.

Contributory negligence: Any want of ordinary care on the part of the person injured which contributed to the injury as a proximate cause thereof, and which the injury would not have occurred. You are not liable for damages if the other fellow did not take reasonable precautions.

Participating: A policy in a mutual company that receives dividends. Even in mutual companies, some policies are not participating.

Whole life policy: A general term for a policy where the insurance remains in force until the insured dies, including ordinary life and limited payment life.

Moral risk: The possibility that the insured will not use insurance as it was intended, for example by pretending disability.

Paid-up life insurance: Insurance where the reserve is so large relative to the face value that accrued interest on the reserve can pay for the cost of insurance and continue the accumulation of the reserve. No premiums need be paid after this time.

"Twisting": Inducing an individual or individuals to drop insurance in another company and to take out a new policy with one the agent represents.

Guaranteed interest rate: A fiction in a mutual company, since it is frequently made low enough to allow substantial dividends which are themselves partly interest too. However, in all companies, older policies have such high guarantees that they cannot be covered by investment yields, even by reduction of dividends in mutual companies.

Re-insurance: A practice of spreading the risk better by reinsuring some policies with another insurance company, when a company feels that it has too much insurance on one person or type of risk.

Industrial insurance: Small policies sold door to door, usually with weekly premiums and high premiums for the amount of insurance.

Family income policy: A combination of decreasing term insurance and an ordinary life policy designed to take care (crudely) of the needs of a family with young children.

Term insurance: Pure insurance, with almost no saving features except in policies that maintain a stable premium over ten or twenty years.

Income protection policy (mortgage protection): Decreasing term insurance.

Annuity policy: Sometimes used to refer to an insurance policy that turns into an annuity later. Strictly speaking an annuity involves paying into the company over a period of years until a specified date, then receiving a specified amount per month from the company from then until you die.

FOOTNOTES TO CHAPTER 6

[1] Frederick Mosteller and Philip Nogee, "An Experimental Measurement of Utility," *Journal of Political Economy,* LIX: 371–404 (Oct., 1951); and Milton Friedman and L. J. Savage, "The Utility Analysis of Choices Involving Risk," *Journal of Political Economy,* LVI: 279–304 (Aug., 1948).

[2] Mathematical Tables from the *Handbook of Chemistry and Physics,* Cleveland, Ohio: Chemical Rubber Publishing Company (many editions and dates).

[3] Institute of Life Insurance, *Life Insurance Fact Book, 1953* (published in New York annually), p. 47. Our estimate was derived by subtracting the increase in policy reserves as per cent of income from the 38 per cent of income reported as additions to policy reserves not paid in benefit payments. In earlier years this figure was published separately.

[4] *Ibid.,* p. 9, or 1954 edition, p. 9.

[5] U.S. Federal Security Agency, *Social Security in the United States,* Washington, D. C.: U.S. Gov't Printing Office, 1953, p. 24.

[6] Rates as of 1952 for the Metropolitan Life Insurance Company, from the 1952 *Unique Manual of Life Insurance,* Cincinnati, Ohio: The National Underwriter Company, 1952, pp. 455–465, except for the 1-year term and decreasing term which are from Occidental Insurance Co., of California, a stock company, *ibid.,* p. 631.

[7] See particularly, Clyde S. Casady, *A Buyer's Guide to Life Insurance,* Boston, Massachusetts: Savings Bank Life Insurance Council, 1946.

[8] Philip Gordis, *How to Buy Insurance,* New York: W. W. Norton & Company, Inc., 1947; E. Albert Gilbert, *Insurance and Your Security,* New York: Rinehart & Company, Inc., 1948; Maxwell S. Stewart, *How to Buy Life Insurance,* New York: Public Affairs Committee, 1941 (Public Affairs Pamphlet No. 62).

The above primarily take the consumer's point of view, and Gilbert in particular is critical of some insurance company practices. For the agents' and companies' point of view, see: Joseph B. Maclean, *Life Insurance,* 7th ed., New York: McGraw Hill Book Co., 1951.

[9] *Life Insurance Ownership Among American Families, 1954,* Survey Research Center, Institute for Social Research, University of Michigan, Ann Arbor, p. 41. (Special tabulations prepared for the Institute of Life Insurance from data collected in the 1954 Survey of Consumer Finances conducted for the Federal Reserve Board.) These tabulations have been issued annually.

[10] *Life Insurance Ownership Among American Families, 1950* (see note 9 above), p. 5.

11 *Ibid.,* p. 4.

12 Institute of Life Insurance, *Life Insurance Fact Book, 1953* (published in New York annually), adapted from p. 9.

13 U.S. Temporary National Economic Committee, Monograph No. 28, *A Study of Legal Reserve Life Insurance Companies,* Washington: U.S. Gov't Printing Office, 1940.

14 *Handbook of Accident and Health Insurance,* rev. ed., Cincinnati, Ohio: The National Underwriter Company, 1952, p. 39. See also: Robert W. Osler, "What You Should Know about Accident and Illness Insurance," *Better Homes and Gardens,* Dec. 1953, pp. 6, 9, 162.

15 Clarence A. Kulp, *Casualty Insurance,* rev. ed., New York: The Ronald Press Company, 1942, p. 367.

16 Philip Gordis, *How to Buy Insurance,* New York: W. W. Norton & Company, Inc., 1947, pp. 58–9; see also Charles T. McCormick, *Handbook on the Law of Damages,* St. Paul, Minnesota: West Publishing Co., 1935, pp. 261–3.

17 See, for example, *The Spectator,* annual statistical issue, Philadelphia: The Spectator Company, November 1952, pp. 40, 41, 54, 93; Spectator, *1952 Accident Insurance Register,* Philadelphia: The Spectator Company, 1952, *passim.;* Spectator, *Financial and Underwriting Analysis of Fire and Casualty Insurance Companies as of January 1, 1951,* Philadelphia: The Spectator Company, 1951; Spectator, *Handy Chart of Casualty, Surety and Miscellaneous Insurance Companies, for Five Years Ended, January 1, 1952,* Philadelphia: The Spectator Company, 1952.

chapter 7

Medical Care

‖‖

THE CONSUMER'S PROBLEM

Another major type of consumer expenditure is medical care. Medical care is important not so much because of the amount spent but because of the erratic nature of the costs and the tremendous importance of the quality of service bought.

Avoiding Illness and Accidents

The consumer makes choices that help him avoid the need for medical care; he makes other choices that affect how much the care costs and how adequate it is; and, finally, he has to decide how to deal with the small chance of large, unpredictable medical costs. First, look briefly at cost avoidance. Given the great and increasing costs of medical care, to say nothing of the possible loss of earnings, it doesn't take much imagination to see that anything that can help avoid illness or accidents is likely to be worth while, if it does not cost too much.

There are some methods of avoiding illness that are either so difficult to do on an individual basis, or so important, that it has become a function of the government to do them or to insist that individuals do them. Contagious diseases, particularly those that can be eliminated or reduced in intensity by vaccination or inoculation, have been controlled by general and, in

194

most cases, compulsory use of such means without charge to the consumer. The U.S. Public Health Service concerns itself with epidemics, importation of diseases, research at the National Institutes of Health, and other medical problems. In recent years, the role of state and local governments in prevention of illness has been made more important by new possibilities such as the use of sodium fluoride in water to reduce tooth decay. New problems include the necessity for control over rapidly growing developments outside the service areas of existing water, sewage, or garbage collection systems. There is reason to believe that some of these problems are accumulating faster than they can be dealt with adequately, particularly in areas with many individual septic tanks and individual sources of water. There are still many densely settled areas in this country without any general sewage, water, or garbage collection and disposal systems, and frequently with inadequate control over the individual systems. Raw sewage and inadequately treated sewage is still being dumped into many a river or bay. Raw garbage is still fed to pigs in a few places, with consequent increased danger of hookworm, trichinosis, and other ailments.

There are also private voluntary organizations that do some preventive work. They provide free chest X-rays to find tuberculosis cases, conduct research, and provide free or subsidized treatment. But regardless what governments or voluntary organizations may do, the individual is still primarily responsible for his own health. This is not a book on how to stay healthy and we shall restrict ourselves to outlining the types of choices the consumer makes that affect his health. They can be roughly classified as safety, healthy living, preventive medicine, and mental hygiene. There are books on these topics, and a continuous stream of advice in the current periodicals. Some of the information is useful, but a great deal appears to be either common sense, or so technical as to be difficult to apply.

Safety, like God, Country, Mother, and Peace is something everyone is for, and we are all exhorted to seek. Aside from some home-accident surveys, little is known about the relative importance of various types of accidents, though it is easy to tell from the newspapers that automobile and boating accidents are only too common.[1]   A good many of the automobile accidents apparently arise from excessive speed and from taking chances, such as passing on hills and curves, or driving while sleepy.   Many of the drownings in boat accidents could be eliminated by having life preservers or by hanging on to the boat instead of striking out for shore.   My own brief experience as a life guard indicated that swimming out too far, particularly in pursuit of beach balls which were always just out of reach, was a common cause of trouble.   Swimming where there is no life guard also means taking chances.   And of course people *will* insist on smoking in bed.   Beyond these rather obvious things, the actions that cause accidents seem to be so varied that no simple set of standard rules for action can be applied.

Inaction sometimes causes accidents by allowing conditions to persist that can cause trouble.   Striking examples are: leaving cisterns uncovered into which children can fall, or abandoning ice boxes in which they can lock themselves, or misplacing poisons they can sample.   Nearly every house has at least a few of the following: sharp corners and edges, loose scatter rugs, slippery floors, dimly lit or tricky stairways, frayed lamp cords, overloaded electric circuits, slippery bathtub, rickety ladder, and a host of other danger spots.   A quick survey of one's home for things of this sort is often useful, though it is all too easy to allow such hazards to remain without doing anything about them.   In industrial and public buildings, much more care has been taken to reduce safety hazards, partly because of the existence of a merit rating under some state workmen's compensation laws and the threat of lawsuit, and partly because of the obvious costs to all concerned.   Some of the lessons learned about power machinery do not seem to be used in most home workshops, however, where guards on power saws, for example, are frequently not used.

The second type of decision whereby consumers can reduce their need for medical care involves what we called "healthy living." Here again, most of what we can say seems obvious. Our only excuse is that the obvious is frequently forgotten. In spite of repeated evidence of the dangers, people with heart trouble seem to persist in shoveling snow too energetically, or living too active a life. The Greek philosophers' emphasis on the golden mean, everything in moderation, seems particularly apt here. Even when we come to more technical matters such as nutrition, reasonable variety and moderation plus some attention to making sure one gets "protective foods," such as milk, eggs, and fresh vegetables, will go a long way. It turns out, for instance, that the color of vegetables is a rather good guide to the type of vitamins they contain, and a good variety of colors will generally insure a good variety of vitamins. Counting calories and vitamins in detail is probably reserved for those on diets and those who use this as a form of recreation. Nutrition is a very complicated science where progress is being made continually. An example of the tricky nature of the problems is this. It has been observed that people in sunny countries like Puerto Rico have rather good teeth in spite of the fact that they drink almost no milk and get little calcium elsewhere. It turns out that vitamin D, the "sunshine vitamin" is necessary for the absorption of calcium and if it is abundant, a little calcium goes a long way.[2] A great deal of attention has been given to the advantages of cooking foods rapidly and with a minimum of water, but very little to the differing nutritive contents of apparently identical foods.[3]

Furthermore, there is a great deal of advice on nutrition from faddists, and many writers succumb to the temptation to draw conclusions from medical research when it is still quite inconclusive. Whether the suggestion be to chew your food more, take a particular type of exercise, or eat yogurt or wheat germ, it is likely to be good in moderation and dangerous if overdone. A more useful group of "reformers" has been concerned with the use of chemicals in food products, and the potential dangers to health from these chemicals.

Recent "experimentation" with the effect of smoking on cancer of the throat even caused some of the doctors working on the project to stop smoking, but like many such experiments it was not "controlled" and hence not conclusive. There is still some chance that the results could be explained differently, for instance, smokers were more tense, or had different diets, or drank more coffee, or more alcohol, and so on. Until we know more than we now know, moderation and variety in diet seem to be enough.

There is some evidence that the human body is quite adaptable and can stand deficiencies of various sorts for substantial periods, hence there is no need for every meal to be a balanced one. Indeed, the consumer can save himself money by eating what is inexpensive rather than sticking rigidly to a particular pattern of foods. The housewife who insists on lettuce every week in the face of its tremendous fluctuations in price and quality (usually in opposite directions) is simply paying for her own inflexibility, not for better diet. Another example concerns proteins, made up of varying combinations of 22 simpler materials called amino acids. The body can create its own supply of more than half of these by transforming other acids of the amino family. The others come in various foods, with meat, poultry, fish, eggs, milk and cheese containing a wider variety of amino acids than other foods do. However, cheaper sources can be combined with small amounts of these more expensive food sources, since the "high-grade" proteins combine with the less complete proteins and make the latter more useful than if eaten alone.[4] In other words, there is a lot to be said for macaroni and cheese, or meat stew.

But matters are made much more complicated by the fact that there are great differences in the nutritive content of foods, particularly vitamins like ascorbic acid, resulting from different climatic conditions where the foods are grown, different storing and cooking methods, and how ripe they were when picked. All these things interact in the most bewildering way: vitamin content of tomatoes and peppers is greater the riper they are, but green beans and onions start to lose vitamins as they get ripe. Canning sometimes causes less vitamin loss than freezing, but then the canned vegetables may lose more in storage. The ordinary consumer cannot know where his vegetables are grown, nor what the animals he eats were fed, nor how long and under what conditions the food has been stored or shipped. About all he can do is pick vegetables that look fresh and colorful, and cook them fast in a minimum of water.

The third area is called "preventive medicine," and involves such things as early diagnosis and treatment, vaccination, and, when the water does not contain sodium fluoride, treatment of children's teeth. Many types of illness, and particularly mental illness, are extremely difficult or impossible to cure if allowed to go too far before treatment is started. On the other hand, a great number of illnesses practically cure themselves. It is possible to spend a great deal of money and waste a lot of the doctor's time merely to discover that you have "caught" something that is "going around," and will run its course in a few days. This is particularly true with children, both because of the number of things they "catch," and the greater concern of parents with their children's health. Fortunately, there are excellent and inexpensive books on child care that can help parents decide what is serious and what is not.[5] Parents are also aided in some states by state-financed "well-baby clinics" that give vaccinations for nominal charges, offer periodic check-ups, and provide school health programs. Knowledge of some of the symptoms of cancer, polio, and other diseases is useful, provided one does not use them except as imperfect indicators and guides to action.

Probably the most important area of all where consumer choices affect the amount of illness they will have is mental hygiene. Mental illness is already the leading cause of disability in terms of days lost. It is extremely expensive to treat, and frequently impossible to cure. For those without money for such fantastically expensive treatments as visits to a private psychiatrist, there remain only a few counseling agencies and the state mental hospitals. State mental hospitals are notoriously understaffed, underequipped, and underfinanced. They are in no position to do much more than keep their patients from harming themselves and others. There are exceptions to this, of course, but the consequences of mental illness are so great that early diagnosis and cure are important. Maintaining mental health in the first place is well worth a good deal of attention. Even minimal psychiatric treatment involves weekly visits and costs running over $1,000 a year.

How does one make sure that he stays mentally healthy? There are many frightening books in the field of mental health; others full of stories; and still others dealing with extreme cases. What the ordinary consumer needs, however, is common-sense methods of self-assessment and self-treatment, with the help of his family if possible.[6] In addition, it is imperative to know something about the major factors that seem to be causing mental illness.[7] Aside from such physical symptoms as tics or sleeplessness, which may have physical causes, there are two important warning signals: One is reacting in ways and to an extent all out of proportion to the original stimulus. All of us carry over conflicts from one situation to another, like the father whose spanking of his son arises as much from the strain of a hard day at the office as from the action of the boy. But if we do it all the time or in extreme forms, something is wrong. The other is lack of adaptability and perspective, insisting on continuing a course that has not been successful and is not likely to be.

The conclusion of many observers, Karen Horney is particular, is that much of the mental illness of today comes from the conflicting pressures that are on us, and on major conflicts between the values advocated by the church, the state, and the economic system. Indeed, only an amazing capacity for compartmentalized thinking could account for the fact that there are as many sane people as there are. The conflict, for instance, between modern warfare and Christian ethics is serious. The gulf between the demands of war on the one hand, using conscripted men to rain indiscriminate death upon the enemy and psychological warfare to increase hatred at home and fear abroad—and the standards of the sixth commandment and the Sermon on the Mount on the other, cannot be exaggerated. A young man of today who takes the following seriously will have to struggle against tremendous social pressures.

Ye have heard that it hath been said, An eye for an eye, and a tooth for a tooth: But I say unto you, That ye resist not evil: but whosoever shall smite thee on thy right cheek, turn to him the other also. And if any man will sue thee at the law, and take away thy coat, let him have thy cloke also. And whosoever shall compel thee to go a mile, go with him twain. . . . I say unto you, Love your enemies, bless them that curse you, do good to them that hate you, and pray for them which despitefully use you, and persecute you; That ye may be the children of your Father which is in heaven: for he maketh his sun to rise on the evil and on the good, and sendeth rain on the just and on the unjust. For if ye love them which love you, what reward have ye? Do not even the publicans the same? (Matthew 5: 38–47)

Conflicts also arise between the values of generosity and those of wealth and power. Tremendous emphasis is placed on financial or professional success. By definition success cannot be achieved by all, since all cannot be the best. The resulting levels of aspiration are out of proportion to possible achievement, and anxiety and frustration are frequently the consequence. A person can reduce the danger of mental illness and avoid the tremendous costs, monetary and otherwise, by remembering: to face conflicts, decide what is really most important in life, strike a balance where one is possible, keep a broad perspective and sense of humor.

There are no easy standards for measuring whether consumers spend an adequate amount of time and money avoiding illness. Doctors and dentists are convinced that most people do not come in frequently enough for a "check-up." Public health officials feel that people allow serious medical conditions to develop because of the initial cost barrier in going to a doctor or hospital. Writers of novels seem to believe that many wealthy people make the opposite mistake and merely make high in-

comes for the doctors willing to take their imagined ills seriously.   Where individual initiative obviously falls short, governments may sometimes intrude, for instance, by insisting on
pure drinking water, or subsidizing healthy lunches for school
children.

There is such a shortage of medical personnel and facilities
today, relative to the need and ability to pay for them, that
preventive medicine (early diagnosis and treatment) is difficult
and underemphasized.   Try going to a doctor and asking for
a general check-up.   Unless you have some obvious symptoms
of trouble, you will be lucky to get more than an examination
for blood pressure, urine sugar, heart beat and respiration.
There are some clinics that specialize in complete "check-ups,"
but they are few and far between.   Indeed, there is a problem
in strategy here, too.   Is it best use of resources to examine ten
thousand cases to find two people with cancer or tuberculosis?
Or would the same resources be better used to provide medical
care for known cases who cannot afford adequate treatment?

Buying Medical Care

No matter how careful he has been in trying to avoid it, the
consumer is likely at some time or other to have a need for
medical care.   Medical services are provided by an alarmingly
great number of different specialists, any one of which is needed
so infrequently by an individual consumer that he is unlikely
to have the time or inclination to look around for a "best buy,"
even if he had the ability to judge.   He will be referred to
specialists on the advice of his family doctor or the general practitioner he happens to go to.   In turn, they may call in still
other specialists.   His dentist may refer him to an oral surgeon
for extractions.   His minister may refer him to a psychiatrist
or marriage counselor.   In most cases these referrals will be
suggested at a time when he is anxious to get well, and in circumstances where about all he can do is to find out ahead of
time what it is going to cost.   A doctor or specialist who refuses
to discuss costs is violating one of the rules of the American

Medical Association, and should be suspected of excessive charges. In addition, knowing the amount of charges will take some of the sting out of the bill when it arrives. On the other hand, if the patient thinks the fees excessive or the doctor guilty of malpractice, he can go to the Grievance Committee of the local chapter of the American Medical Association. Most of such matters are subject to so much qualitative interpretation, however, that he is unlikely to get much satisfaction from a body of fellow-doctors except in the most extreme cases.[8]

One conclusion seems to follow from this, and that is that the selection of a regular or family doctor is more important than it seems. Most general practitioners in an area will have about the same charges and be capable of handling the usual run of illnesses, but they may differ on more important matters such as the degree to which they have the patient's finances in mind and try to save him money, their ability to refer their patients to the proper specialists, and their wisdom in deciding when the services of a specialist are called for.

There has recently been formed an American College of General Practitioners, membership in which will require higher standards than those required for a general medical license and will indicate that the doctor who belongs is keeping up to date on recent developments. There is also a new system of accrediting hospitals by a Joint Commission on the Accreditation of Hospitals. Even now most good hospitals insist on keeping records indicating whether tissues removed in an operation turned out to be normal or not. If a surgeon has a record of having removed a large number of normal appendixes, one would not want his advice on whether or not the appendix needed removing. Since the ordinary patient is unlikely to have access to the hospital records, he must depend on his own doctor to steer him to the proper surgeon.

Whether it is the general practitioner or specialist, the patient wants careful diagnosis, reasonable fees, and a clear statement of the probabilities (a) that the diagnosis is right, and (b) that the suggested treatment will effect cure. Refusal to discuss any of these problems, hasty and cursory examinations, or poor office records are warning indications.

Clearly medical care is an area where it is difficult to shop around, and one result of this situation is that most people who can afford it tend to demand medical care from the one or two best (or best known) doctors in an area. This is hard on these popular doctors whose propensity to die of heart attacks at ages as low as 45 is well known. These doctors raise their charges or reduce their service (refusing to make home calls, letting nurses and assistants do much of the work, and sometimes getting less careful) partly in self-defense. Other doctors may have difficulty getting started, even though their ability is as great or greater. This means that the consumer who shops around a little bit may get better quality medical care at less cost.

Referrals to a series of specialists are expensive in time lost as well as money, and wherever there are group clinics where the specialists are all in one place and the patient is routed through systematically, there are likely to be savings in both time and money. Further there may well be better care since the various doctors check up on one another more closely.

Finally, all this is made still more complicated by the medical practice of adjusting charges to the patient's ability to pay, particularly in the case of the larger bills.

Meeting the Cost of Medical Care

Budget studies and aggregate statistics seem to indicate an average expenditure of about 4–6 per cent of income for medical care. Since both standards of care and the costs increase with income, an individual could use this as a rough average expectation, unless his income were very low, in which case he might have to use a larger percentage. This crude average can be refined by taking into account such obviously important factors as the number of people in the family and their ages. Children go to the doctor more frequently, but almost always for minor things. Old people are more likely to have serious illnesses. Also, families differ as to their general state of health;

some are seemingly never ill and others apparently inherit a propensity for illness. Hence the best prediction is the family's own experience—adjusted for increasing numbers of children or advancing age.

But all this omits the most important problem, which is the unpredictable and uncontrollable expenses of major illnesses that may involve costs so great as to wipe out the savings of a lifetime. The regular, small expenses can be budgeted. The occasional larger expense can be handled out of reserve funds. But the infrequent, major expenses is another matter, particularly when a wage earner is involved and temporary or permanent disability ensues. Exact statistics on the incidence of illness (and accidental disability) are simply not available. Some people become ill or even disabled without ever going to a hospital. The distinction between medical disability and unemployment because of age is not always easy to make. Statistics on admissions to hospitals record the illnesses only of those who either get charity or can afford the costs. It is interesting to note that the rate of admissions to hospitals per thousand people is considerably higher in Saskatchewan, Canada, where they have a universal prepaid (and subsidized) hospitalization scheme, than it is in Michigan. Furthermore, the rate of admissions rose rather significantly in Saskatchewan after the introduction of the Saskatchewan Hospital Services Plan.

The Saskatchewan plan involves a special tax plus use of some general tax funds to pay for hospitalization of anyone who needs it.[9] This removes the cost barrier to a large extent (individuals still must pay for the doctor except in the Swift Current region where a pilot experiment with a complete coverage scheme is under way.)[10] There were some limitations on admission because of shortages of hospital space, and, on the other hand, perhaps a few people stayed in the hospital because the plan does not pay for hospital treatments of "outpatients," who come for treatment and then go home, but the data from Saskatchewan are still better as indicators of incidence than those from anywhere else. They show that only a fourth of the people who went to the hospital stayed more than 10 days, but this quarter accounted for nearly two-thirds of the "hospital days." Nearly a third of the total hospital days, and therefore of the total hospital costs, were accounted for by the 5 per cent of the patients who stayed more than 30 days in the hospital. (Table 14.)

TABLE 14

THE RISK OF ILLNESS AS INDICATED BY HOSPITALIZATION IN SASKATCHEWAN, 1952.

Length of Stay in the Hospital in Days	Per Cent of Cases	Per Cent of Hospital Days
1–10	74.3	35.2
11–20	16.0	21.6
21–30	4.7	10.9
31–60	3.5	13.6
61 or more	1.5	18.7
	100.0%	100.0%

Source: Annual Report, Saskatchewan Hospital Services Plan, 1952, Department of Public Health, Regina, Saskatchewan, Canada, 1953, p. 18, Table XVIII. 92–94 per cent of the population is covered by a plan financed by a personal hospitalization tax plus other tax revenues (largely from a sales tax). No limitation is placed on number of days stay in the hospital and the complete bill is paid.

What does this mean? It means that the cost of medical care is not a simple expense but an insurance problem, because it involves small chances of extremely large costs. One useful way to think of the risk of illness is in terms of alternative types of insurance that are possible. The cost to you of an insurance plan that covered only the first thirty days in the hospital, excluding the infrequent but very large bills, is just as great as the cost of a "deductible" plan where you pay for the first ten days yourself, and *all* hospital bills beyond that are covered by the insurance. The latter plan is clearly preferable as insurance, though such insurance is not generally available. In recent years, "deductible" catastrophe medical insurance policies were introduced, but the temptation to put restrictions in them has been great. One authority notes:

> Some are destroying the purpose of catastrophe insurance by use of elaborate methods for increasing the deductible and limiting the period of time during which medical bills must be insured. Both of these methods serve to reduce the coverage so it can be offered at a ridiculously low premium rate, and still bear the title of catastrophe medical insurance.[11]

These are mainly individual, rather than group, plans, hence have high expense "loadings," that is, half or more of your premiums go for insurance company expenses and profits. One possibility, suggested by the President's Commission on the Health Needs of the Nation, is to have the government reinsure private health insurance plans for the very large payments they might be called on to make. Whether this would ultimately help the consumer get better medical insurance is hard to say. When we think of including all medical bills, not just hospitalization, other problems arise. With the rapid increase in very expensive methods of treatment, many of dubious efficacy, the problem of predicting maximum amounts that could be needed for medical care becomes more and more difficult.

Such "deductible" policies are opposed for two almost opposite reasons. First, it would be difficult for an insurance company to sell a policy that paid nothing in nearly three-quarters of the cases. Second, from the point of view of those interested in public health, the initial cost barrier of going to the hospital would remain. It might still induce people to postpone medical care rather than secure early diagnosis and treatment.

Even though the range of choice of hospital insurance policies is limited, being familiar with the size distribution of hospital bills allows the consumer to judge the merits of the available policies. Many of the apparently cheaper policies or those with apparently greater coverages of extra services like X-ray, will turn out to have narrower limits on the number of days paid for. If it is insurance against the big risks you want, then such a limitation is quite important and unwelcome. Of course, here as in any other insurance, the ratio of amounts paid the hospitals by the insurance company to premium receipts of the company will show how much of your money is going for benefits and how much for the expenses and profit of the insurance company. This proportion going for insurance company expenses and profits varies from almost nothing in some plans where an employer covers the administrative costs, to 45 per cent or more in individual policies issued by insurance companies. Individual policies are more expensive for several reasons: higher selling costs, no administrative economies, adverse selection, and higher lapse rates. For similar reasons, it is a safe general rule that Blue Cross will be better insurance than any private company plan. The average "loading" for expenses of Blue Cross plans is about 15 per cent. The variety of coverage is so great that comparison of specific provisions is usually not fruitful, though there may occasionally be other plans more suited to an individual's needs than Blue Cross. Blue Cross plans are generally organized on a state basis, but they are joined in a national federation and have reciprocal arrangements with other states so that the member can go to the nearest hospital when ill.

For a plan covering the whole family, charges under Blue Cross plans vary from $19 to $67 per year, depending on what the individual plan covers. Associated with these plans are Blue Shield medical-surgical insurance plans that cost from $24 to $62 per year for a family. Rates for couples or single people are lower, of course. The "loadings" under various medical insurance plans are given in Table 15. Since these plans do not cover all medical costs, one possible budgeting method is to allow 6 per cent of income for medical care, part going into insurance and the rest into a reserve fund if current bills do not exhaust it.

The value of any medical insurance policy is also affected by the fact that the rates are not finely adjusted to actuarial costs but often involve a type of income redistribution among policy holders.   Many plans have the same rates regardless of age, though they may refuse insurance after 65.   Canadian experience shows that the frequency of illness and length of stay in

TABLE 15

PER CENT OF NET PREMIUMS NOT USED FOR BENEFITS IN MEDICAL INSURANCE PLANS

Type of Policy	Per Cent "Loading"
Commercial Companies (1951)	
Group Insurance	
Hospital, surgical, medical	11.1
All other *	18.9
Individual insurance	
Hospital, surgical, medical	47.7
All other *	57.6
Independent plans	
Industrial	7.3
Non-industrial (consumer, community wide, private group clinics)	15.9
Blue Cross—Blue Shield	
Blue Cross—hospitalization	10.2
Blue shield—medical-surgical	20.3
Workmen's Compensation	
Private companies	55
Competitive state funds	48
Exclusive state funds	16

Source: Building America's Health, U.S. President's Commission on the Health Needs of the Nation, Vol. IV: "Financing a Health Program for America," pp. 215, 349, 355–59.
* Cash disability, death, dismemberment, etc.

the hospital increase with age, after an initial drop during the first five or ten years of life.   (See Table 16.)   Also there are differences between men and women, owing largely to hospitalization for childbirth.   Hence medical insurance is a "better buy" for older people and for married women.   Again, while

Blue Cross has different rates for single people, married couples, and families, the third rate applies regardless of the number of children, and is therefore a bargain for large and growing families. In looking at competing policies, it is particularly important to be sure that you can keep the policy as you grow older. Any insurance company that accepted only younger people, refusing to continue to insure them when they got older, could offer better rates. But this would leave them without insurance when they were older and more likely to need it.

TABLE 16

THE RELATION OF AGE AND SEX TO THE NEED FOR HOSPITAL CARE, 1952

Age of Patient	Number of Discharged Cases Per 1,000 Beneficiaries [1]		Patient Days Per 1,000 Beneficiaries [2]	
	Male	Female	Male	Female
0–1	331	251	2,911	2,229
1–4	175	145	1,167	902
5–14	139	134	962	868
15–24	122	302	966	2,200
25–44	107	332	963	2,794
45–64	166	239	2,274	3,295
65–69	251	285	4,572	5,119
70 or over	392	387	8,553	8,521

Source: Annual Report, Saskatchewan Hospital Services Plan, 1952, Department of Public Health, Regina, Saskatchewan, Canada, 1953, pp. 12–13, Tables XI and XII.

[1] Excluding newborn babies. Hospitals count people when they leave the hospital, because then they know cost and length of stay.
[2] Number of cases times average stay. Excludes newborn babies.

There is an even more important problem, particularly with insurance that covers doctors' bills, arising from the possibility that the charges may be increased for those who are insured. In this case, the insurance becomes much less advantageous, since either the rates must reflect the higher charges made for treating those who are insured, or if the payments are fixed in amount, the patient pays the doctor an additional charge. It is easy to see how doctors, and even hospitals, accustomed to charging according to ability to pay, would be tempted to raise rates to those who are insured. Great efforts are made by Blue Cross to insure standardized hospital charges, and in some states doctors agree to accept the standard Blue Shield payments as full payment for services to any patient whose income is below some amount, such as $2,000. Unless the individual falls in this low income bracket, he is better protected if he can rely on his doctor or surgeon not to take advantage of his insured status. Since the type of bills paid by Blue Shield and other medical-surgical insurance plans are primarily the large bills where the doctor uses his own discretion anyway, and since there is no way of keeping your insurance status secret—it must be stated upon admission to the hospital—this problem is particularly important with medical-surgical insurance, and for higher income people who are most likely to be charged more.

What do consumers actually do about illness and disability? We have already seen that the big risk is that of temporary or permanent disability of the wage earner, and that insurance with adequate coverage of this risk is not available. For that part of the disability risk that can be insured, "loadings" of 40 per cent or more are common because of the usual costs and the "moral risk" problem.[12] The next largest risk is extended hospitalization. By July, 1953, more than 87 million people or 57 per cent of the population were covered by hospitalization insurance of some sort, and the number has been growing rapidly every year.[13] More than 74 million had some form of surgical insurance. The difficulty in interpreting these figures arises from the fact that there are so many different plans with different degrees of coverage. Data are fragmentary, but even Blue Cross, which generally has more extensive coverage than private plans, has been estimated to cover about 75 per cent of the hospital bill in most cases, and Blue Shield 50–60 per cent of the physician's bill.[14] About a third of the people covered by Blue Cross plans get full benefits for more than 30 days in the hospital; the rest get them for 30 days or less. Only 8 per cent of the subscribers and dependents are covered for more than 90 days.[15]

The conclusion of the Senate Committee cited above was:

> Conversely, by the highest of the above estimates, voluntary insurance plans do not cover about 80 per cent of that portion of the Nation's medical bill generally regarded as the minimum that is potentially insurable.[16]

The quotation refers to all insurable medical costs, of course, and not just hospitalization.   The ill may, however, find placement in charity clinics, receive allotments for work injuries under state workmen's compensation, and, in the case of veterans, secure free medical care.   In Rhode Island, California, New Jersey and New York, workers covered by unemployment compensation may also receive cash payments when they cannot work because of sickness.   Private foundations or governments provide special assistance in the case of cancer, poliomyelitis, mental illness, tuberculosis, or venereal diseases.   Social security provides disability benefits.   But in spite of all this the individual is still primarily responsible for his own medical care. There are no adequate data on how people handle their medical costs, but there is reason to believe that most people make no provision for them aside from the medical insurance that they usually secure through their employer.   If an employee cannot take care of the bills out of current income or reserve funds, he delays payment or borrows.   In early 1954 there were some 19 per cent of the spending units in this country who owed money to doctors, dentists or hospitals, though half of them owed less than $50.[17]   There were undoubtedly others who had borrowed from other sources to pay medical bills.   The rate of rejections by the Army because of medical conditions that could have been eliminated by early diagnosis and treatment is frequently cited as an indication that many people also simply fail to secure adequate and timely medical care.

In both the type of medical service received and the method of payment chosen, the consumer has a rather complicated array of choices, some of which depend on where he works, or on his income. The Senate Committee report referred to above, and a Federal Security Agency publication, *Guide to Health Organization in the United States,* furnish an excellent description of this complicated situation.[18]

MEDICAL CARE—SOCIETY'S PROBLEM

Care for Everyone?

Underlying all the arguments and discussions about medical care is a general assumption that society has some responsibility in ensuring that people have some care. This belief is stated persuasively in the introduction to the first volume of the report of the President's Commission on the Health Needs of the Nation:

For the state, health is the wellspring of a nation's strength, its provision and protection one of the first obligations. Failure to safeguard health, whether through ignorance, neglect, or the lack of means, exposes the individual to suffering, incapacity, or death. National neglect of proper measures for the preservation of health exposes the country to weakness and destruction. The goal of optimum physical, mental, and social efficiency and well-being justifies all prudent efforts for its attainment—whether these be social measures necessary for the promotion of health; application of technical skills in the prevention of disease, diagnosis, treatment and rehabilitation; training of specialized personnel; expansion of facilities; or the organization necessary to make health services available to all.

When the very life of a man, or the lives of his family, may depend on his receiving adequate medical services, society must make every effort to provide them. When this man knows that such health boons exist, available to some and denied to him, a free society will find the way to comply with the demand that he will surely make. And democracy requires that the same high quality service be made available to all men equally.[19]

The Commission formulated the following principles to be used as a guide in approaching our health problem: [20]

1. Access to the means for the attainment and preservation of health is a basic human right.

2. Effort of the individual himself is a vitally important factor in attaining and maintaining health.

3. The physician-patient relationship is so fundamental to health that everyone should have a personal physician.

4. The physician should have access to proper facilities and equipment, affiliation on some basis with a hospital, and the help of trained personnel in order to fulfill his part in providing comprehensive health services.

5. Comprehensive health service includes the positive promotion of health, the prevention of disease, the diagnosis and treatment of disease, the rehabilitation of the disabled—all supported by constantly improving education of personnel and a continuous program of research.

6. Comprehensive health service is the concern of society and is best insured when all elements of society participate in providing it.

7. Responsibility for health is a joint one, with the individual citizen and local, State, Federal governments each having major contributions to make toward its fuller realization.

8. The American people desire and deserve comprehensive health service of the highest quality and in our dynamic expanding economy the means can be found to provide it.

9. The same high quality of health services should be available to all people equally.

10. A health program must take into account the progress and experience of the past, the realities of the present, and must be flexible enough to cope with future changes.

In other words, medical care can be regarded as a service which is in some measure the responsibility of society. There are several reasons for this. The health of the population is one of the basic resources of society, and from a purely pragmatic point of view it is worth while applying some other resources in the form of medical care, sanitation, and so on, to keep human capital from deteriorating and even to improve it. Secondly, from a humanitarian viewpoint, society has long felt responsible not to let people die if they can be kept alive. Given this responsibility, some minimal medical care is likely to be provided, even if the person cannot pay for it. But it is likely to be more efficient, as well as nicer, to insist that people have somewhat earlier and better medical care than this, so that they will be productive and efficient citizens and able to provide for their families. Indeed, in many countries of the world today where tremendous emphasis is being placed on industrial investment programs, investment in the health and education of the human capital might pay off even more handsomely. For our own country, once we set some minimum standards of care we feel everyone should have, the problem becomes a "simple" one of how it is to be paid for without impairing the independence and high standards of the medical profession.

A great many misleading statements are made on both sides of the problem. The statement of the President's Commission overlooks the fact that there may well be types of treatment so unproven and so expensive that one would hesitate to insist that everyone with the same particular symptoms be given that treatment. Statements that people should, and can afford to, take care of their own medical care needs are irrelevant if they will not in fact do so without some further inducement or compulsion. How much freedom of choice should society allow in an area of behavior where the results affect society as well as the individual, and where society may be committed to expenditures resulting directly from individual neglect of health? We have already seen that under social security the federal government is committed to pay amounts worth as much as $46,000 to the survivors of an insured worker. Certainly, then, the government has some interest in seeing to it that the worker takes care of his health.

How is it possible to increase the amount and quality of medical care people receive? As in most other economic problems, we can first separate problems of demand from those of supply. Let us look first at the problem of how to increase the demand, then at the problem of how to increase the supply. We are assuming that additional expenditure for medical care is a good use of resources for most of us. We are certainly in no great danger of putting too much of our resources into medical care. As a nation we spend about as much for alcohol, tobacco, and smoking supplies as for medical care. So long as there is some chance that a life can be saved, we are unlikely to cavil at the cost of trying.

Increasing the Demand for Medical Care

There are four general methods that have been suggested for increasing the demand for medical care. First, some say, educate people and convince them that it is to their own advantage to ask for the best medical care. Second, prepayment plans and other methods are urged for helping consumers to budget their medical costs and to insure against the risk of large costs. Third, it is possible to subsidize medical care so that it is less expensive, even going so far as to provide it free (socialized medicine). Fourth, the state may use compulsory means to insure individual health, or insist on universal insurance so that there will be no economic barriers to medical care when it is needed.

It is a difficult problem in social psychology whether people can be motivated by educational or propaganda means to take care of their own medical needs. There is also an economic problem since even if people were all sold on the idea, and all wanted insurance to cover the very large bills, there would be some who could not afford to pay for their own medical care. The distinction between being unwilling to pay and being unable to pay is a difficult one to make. If people are unwilling to pay, society must either allow medical care to remain inadequate, provide it on a subsidized basis, or compel the people to pay for it. In the latter case, where people are genuinely unable to pay, society must either allow inadequate care or provide it on a subsidized basis.

Insofar as cost barriers and the difficulty of budgeting for unpredictable costs are the problem, prepayment schemes are clearly one of the most important means of being sure that people will demand adequate medical care and be able to pay for it. Most of the discussions of the problem of medical care in this country have centered around the question whether such insurance-prepayment schemes should be voluntary or compulsory.

It has generally been assumed that the government could not, or should not, coerce people into securing adequate medical care, or into joining a private prepayment scheme. It has also been assumed that socialized medicine is not wanted.

The question whether there should be compulsory medical insurance is not simply a question about compulsion. There are three major dimensions to be considered in the discussion: the degree of compulsion, the effects of any plan on the distribution of the burden of the costs of medical care (who will pay?), and the amount and type of government interference or control over the hospitals and the medical profession. A typical argument over compulsory medical insurance is likely to run like this:

Pro: Some people cannot possibly pay for their own medical care. It would be simpler to have them included in a compulsory prepayment plan but with no payments to make, than have the confusing and inequitable array of charity clinics and welfare medical payments we now have. Some can pay but will not and are not getting adequate medical care. Some want to pay but no adequate insurance is available to them to cover the really big expenses. Those who cannot get into a group plan also must pay very high rates for the inadequate insurance that is available. Besides with a universal compulsory scheme the rates can be adjusted to ability to pay.

Con: Voluntary insurance is growing rapidly, and can do most of the job. For the very poor, welfare departments or charities can enlist them in voluntary insurance schemes and pay the fees or provide free medical care. Compulsory insurance will involve governmental interference with the medical profession, bureaucracy, and inefficiency. As for adjusting charges to income, there are more effective ways to redistribute income than this.

Pro, rebuttal: Extensive voluntary insurance will raise the same problems: interference with the medical profession, group bargaining in the fixing of their incomes, and maintenance of clerical bureaucracy and red tape. The likely difference is that doctors will be better represented than patients in the voluntary plans. The rates will continually rise. Then people will either drop the insurance or there will be a redistribution of income from patients to doctors. A universal insurance scheme is bound to have lower over-

head costs because there are no selling costs.   Everyone is effectively
protected as in a group insurance scheme.   There could be no adverse selection or lapse rate problems.

Con, rebuttal: There is still a basic problem of freedom from government interference, both with individual choices and with the
standards of the medical professions.

There is clearly no simple answer to the question: "Which
is best, the present situation or compulsory medical insurance?"
Either scheme involves problems.   The concern here is with
sorting out the arguments and making clear the implications.
For instance, look at the effect on the distribution of income
inherent in the idea that compulsory insurance rates could be
adjusted to income.   What might easily happen is that the
rates would be zero for some of the people who are now charity
patients, about as high as the actual average expenditures for
upper-middle income groups, and perhaps more than actual
expenditures for some lower-middle income groups.   In other
words, it is possible that some people who are now getting free
care would be forced to start paying for care.   Some who had
been getting no care would be forced to get it and to pay for it.
And of course the costs would be spread so that they fell on
everyone, not just those who were ill.   Depending on the actual
schedule of rates, various redistributive possibilities exist.

In general, it seems clear that both economic and other problems are bound to arise with the great extension of medical insurance *whether voluntary or not.*   When most of the income
of a hospital or doctor comes from the insurance payments, the
insurance officials are in a position to determine the incomes
of most of the medical profession and allied technicians.   If
the doctors dominate the organization, consumer interests may
well be neglected.   What means are there for insuring that
hospitals will be run efficiently, or determining what a fair
salary for hospital personnel is?   An interesting approach to
this problem was taken in Saskatchewan where the payments
to hospitals are originally equal to their operating costs, but
computed as somewhat more than 100 per cent of their over-

head costs, and somewhat less than 100 per cent of their variable
(and controllable) costs. This means that if their variable costs
increase relative to the others, their receipts will not increase
proportionately, and they will be under pressure to economize.

While a compulsory insurance scheme might have better consumer representation, it might create more interference with
medical standards. So far there has been enough of an open
market for medical services so that some idea of what is fair
remuneration to doctors and hospitals can be gained.

There is the impression that most doctors have rather strong
emotional feelings that any scheme which involves the government would be very bad for them.[21] They have visions of government inspectors checking their records, inquiring whether
a particular prescription or a particular test was really necessary,
checking patients to make sure they actually got the treatment,
and generally requiring the poor doctor to file endless forms in
great detail and seven copies. The doctor's freedom to charge
more for patients who can pay or who take up a great deal of
time, and to provide free services to others who are not so well
off, would be reduced. Whether such fears are justified, and
whether the problems would be worse than under "private" prepayment schemes, once they cover most of the population, is
hard to say.

To add to the confusion, the influence of the producers of
medicines and medical supplies and equipment must be considered. They have an extremely profitable, but recently hazardous, business because of the rapid rate of technological progress, particularly in antibiotics. They spend great sums of
money on their own research, which is primarily of a practical
sort. They seem to be greatly concerned with the possibility
that if the government gets involved in the field of medicine, the
acceptance of new medicines might be determined by government officials rather than doctors and hospitals, and perhaps
even more important, that purchasing and distribution might
be done on a bulk basis without the tremendous mark-ups that
are now possible. If medicines were all purchased in bulk by

hospitals they might be able to force down the prices even faster and further than competition between the pharmaceutical houses has done.   Retail druggists would be still more seriously affected.   Consequently doctors and druggists are flooded with polemic literature against "socialized medicine," much of it from the makers of medical supplies or from the American Medical Association, whose journal is supported by advertisements from these same sources.

On the other hand, the Federal Security Agency, concerned with the nation's health, and the rather chaotic combination of charity payments, and of free or partially subsidized clinics some of which have a "means test" to exclude those who presumably can pay, has generally favored some sort of compulsory prepayment scheme.   It is difficult to get the flavor of the arguments and the degree to which emotion is involved without reading some of the polemic literature.   A good recent example appeared in a professional economic journal.[22]

All this may appear inconclusive, and it is, because these problems are not simple, and predicting what the results of alternative solutions would be is a hazardous business.   Furthermore, the argument as to whether medical insurance should be voluntary or compulsory concentrates on two possible approaches and frequently leaves large areas of medical care out of consideration altogether, such as dental care, optical treatment, mental hygiene, preventive medicine, and so on.

Most people who like to keep their arguments straight insist that compulsory medical insurance is not socialized medicine. They say that "socialized medicine" is a term which should be reserved for a system of subsidizing the costs of medical care out of tax funds.   The British scheme is socialized medicine. But what about the Saskatchewan scheme which is financed partly by a per-capita tax and partly by other means, primarily a sales tax?   Should the public health services and state health departments in this country which provide all sorts of free medical services be included in the definition?   What about the Hill-Burton Act and other means whereby hospital construction is financed from government funds, thus allowing somewhat lower hospital charges? What about the Veterans Administration and various degrees of free medical care for veterans? Even subsidized medical education, and subsidized medical research will increase the supply and quality of medicine and reduce its cost. As in many other areas, there is already some "socialization." The problem is really one of degree, and of organizational arrangements. One recent estimate is that the consumer, directly or through insurance plans, now pays something less than two-thirds of the total amount spent on medical care (including hospital construction); the rest involves direct or indirect government contributions.[23]

It is not even true that the adequacy of medical care and the amount of governmental subsidy are necessarily related. It is conceivable that the government could insist that people get adequate medical care and allow them to work out their own payment methods, just as Massachusetts now insists that residents carry liability insurance if they drive an automobile. On the other hand, in discussions of government subsidy in the field of medicine it is common to find statements about how much the program would cost. The inference is that the government cannot afford to spend so much money. Any such discussion of the costs of "socialized medicine" is irrelevant and misleading for two reasons. First, where the medical care would have been secured anyway, the same cost would exist but be paid by individuals or private insurance schemes. Second, medical care is only a cost in the same sense that building a factory is a cost. It creates and maintains human capital that, in most cases, is productive. And where the people involved are already too old to be productive in the usual sense, most societies feel a moral commitment to provide the same sort of care as for the productive workers. Many of the arguments that support free public education could be used in the field of health as well.

What makes the problem less clear is that medical care is not simple, routine, and unchanging. There are a variety of services, some of unproven worth, many of them very expensive, and a number of them bordering on the luxurious. Who is to decide whether a person most of whose teeth are bad should have several thousand dollars worth of dental work done, or have his teeth extracted and a set of plates ("false teeth") made? Are private rooms in hospitals necessary to recovery? When is hospital treatment rather than home treatment essential to recovery? In Great Britain, it is still customary to have children born at home, and some feel that it is safer in view of the serious epidemics like infant diarrhea. In this country most women would not consider having a baby outside a hospital.

Whichever plan of medical care one may prefer, problems still remain concerning the present system of medical payment that need to be solved.

First, there is the cost barrier to medical care that keeps some people from securing adequate care, and, more importantly, from securing early diagnosis and treatment. Many hesitate to pay the costs for chest X-rays and other types of tests until serious symptoms develop. Indeed, if an individual goes to a clinic and asks for a check-up, the doctor is unlikely to suggest expensive tests unless he suspects there is something wrong. Postponement of necessary treatment is probably most important in fields like dentistry, optometry, and mental illness. There was a substantial increase in the frequency of visits to doctors in Great Britain once the cost barrier was removed even with the shortage of practitioners and the long waiting periods for patients in the doctors' offices.[24] There was also a great surge in demand for dental care in Britain that could not conceivably have been malingering.

Second, there is reason to argue that the present system is chaotic and inequitable, involving both a differential burden of costs on different people, and the amounts paid to the various people and institutions providing the services. Some states have cash sickness payments, and all have workmen's compensation at different levels of inadequacy. Charity clinics differ widely as to whom they will accept. People who are completely indigent and rely on charity frequently get better care than those who do not qualify for free or subsidized care but who feel they cannot afford the "full" charges. Extra high charges for wealthier patients may seem fair enough, à la Robin Hood, but this is a rather odd way to redistribute income, since only the rich people with serious illnesses are hit. The dual system involving private practitioners and specialists has led to a concentration of patients on a few doctors who make very large incomes and are literally "worked to death." The temptations toward fee-splitting become great. The relative incomes of specialists versus general practitioners is perhaps somewhat out of line, and certainly the peonage of internship puts a heavy burden on those who would like to enter the profession, all of which tend to limit the profession to those with wealthy parents, extreme tenacity or dedication.

We have been discussing the demand for medical care and the problems involved in paying for care. The other side of the coin must reflect the availabilities of supply. There are important problems here and they would become even more important if we succeeded in increasing the demand for medical care. Let us look at the "medical industry."

The Supply of Medical Care

It is difficult to summarize a situation as complicated as our present arrangements for supplying medical services. The job has already been admirably done in the five-volume report of the President's Commission on the Health Needs of the Nation entitled *Building America's Health*. Some quotations from their findings may give a rough impression of the situation:

Physicians, dentists, nurses, and auxiliary medical workers are the indispensable and irreplaceable core at the center of the provision and distribution of medical care. . . The personal skills of the health worker, accumulated over as long and grueling an educational process as we know in America today, are still the pivotal factors in the promotion of health and the prevention of disease. There is no substitute for the skilled surgeon, the precise dentist, the trained and resourceful nurse. . .

With the increasing demand by the people for more complete health services, there has arisen an almost equal pressure for more health personnel. Even though some of the health professions have doubled and tripled their ranks in the past few decades, they have failed to keep pace with this surging demand. . .

We see no prospect for a great increase in the number of health workers in the near future. The lengthening of the training period for our health professionals, an indispensable element in raising the quality of medical care, makes this expansion process a slow one. . . No matter what is done, we can expect continuing shortages in the next few years. . .

There are not enough general physicians, and most of those we have are so busy that they cannot give the patient the time and sympathetic care the old family doctor used to give in a home visit. . . In fact, with the possible exception of surgery, there seems to be no area of specialization in which the supply of physicians meets even the present demand.

It has been suggested by some that the physician shortage is largely a matter of distribution, that it can be solved, for example, by transplanting physicians from well-doctored Manhattan to under-doctored Mississippi. This proposal overlooks a number of important facts. First, our society is not one in which people can be moved about without regard to their own wishes. Second, even in the areas with a relatively better supply of physicians, numerous vacancies exist. . . Third, we have received impressive evidence of the fact that medical students, upon completion of their training, tend to return to the area and kind of community in which they were brought up. Fourth, it is our carefully weighed conclusion that the growth of prepayment plans and the extension of preventive medicine will increase the demand for physicians to a point higher than the present or predicted total supply, even if an ideal distribution were possible.[25]

An interesting sidelight on the problem of geographic distribution of physicians, which varies from 175 per 100,000 people in the metropolitan areas to 50 in the rural areas, is that it is much more difficult to become a doctor if you live in an area that needs doctors badly.[26] One-third of the states do not have four-year medical schools. Fifty of the 80 medical schools impose residence limitations on admission of medical students.

In 35 schools, less than 15 per cent of the freshman class come from out-of-state.[27]   Since people tend to go back to their home community or somewhere near it to practice, such limitations on medical education will make it difficult to improve the geographic distribution of doctors.

But the real difficulty is the *expense* of training doctors at all. The cost of a medical education is several times the tuition paid. The rest comes from state funds, other university funds, private endowments, and grants provided through the Public Health Service and other federal agencies for research, construction, teaching, fellowships, and training.

As for dentists, even though almost 11 million people in the United States are now drinking fluoridated water, and such systems have been approved for another 17 million people, the President's Commission concluded that this would not significantly affect the number of dentists required during the years immediately ahead.   Dental schools have problems similar to medical schools, with tuition and fees from students covering only about a third of the cost of their education.

In the case of hospitals, the federal government (under the Hill-Burton Act) has helped to finance almost a third of all non-federal hospital construction in the years 1948–1951, but

even with this aid, new construction for short-term patients is just keeping pace with the population increase, while the construction of beds for long-term patients is actually falling behind.[28]

As in the case of doctors and dentists, the demand for hospitals is as much a result of rising standards of living as well as of an increasing population.   Indeed, in the case of hospitals, prepayment plans have been a major reason for increased demand:

Many prepayment health plans which have the financial means to encourage the growth of out-patient services make it almost mandatory for a patient to assume a horizontal position before receiving medical care in a hospital.   Their policy of payment exclusively for in-patient services has forced excessive use of hospital beds and, in many areas, impeded medical progress.[29]

Questions have also been raised whether better co-ordination and more efficiency are not possible, particularly in the use of specialized services in the laboratories, such as the X-ray, and other diagnostic and therapeutic equipment. The overlapping functions of governmental and private agencies have led to suggestions for simplification and co-ordination.[30] One of the most obvious possibilities is group practice, where physicians of different specialties co-operate to render a more complete and balanced health service. Dentists may even be included. The early history of the American Medical Association contains some unpleasant instances of opposition to group practice wherever it involved any prepayment scheme, including even denial of membership in the county medical society. This opposition still exists in some degree, showing up in charges that soliciting memberships in such a group scheme is in violation of the association's ban on advertising medical services. There is also a tendency for specialists to stay in the group long enough to build a practice, then to leave and try to take their patients with them. Apparently there have also been difficulties in arriving at equitable financial arrangements among the various doctors, some groups being set up "primarily to enrich a central controlling group at the expense of the other physicians who become mere employees." [31]

Perhaps more important to the consumer than the need for expansion of medical schools and for increases in efficiency in the use of the specialists' time is the problem of standards of medical care. The field has been aptly described as a self-regulating monopoly, since the doctors through their professional associations accredit the schools and set the standards for admission to the profession. Specialists have "boards" that accredit new specialists only after they have served an apprenticeship under a specialist plus their internship as a general practitioner.

The associations have been accused of making it overly difficult to get a medical education in order to restrict entry into the profession and maintain high doctor's incomes. On the other hand, they have, as they insist, been concerned with maintaining higher standards. Since the American Medical Association lost its anti-trust case in 1943, the associations have not tried to stop formation of co-operative prepayment clinics. In almost every community, they have established grievance committees to hear complaints of excessive fees, refusal to attend a patient in need, or other malpractices.[32]

The most commonly denounced practices are:

1. Fee-splitting: secret division of a fee between two physicians, usually between a referring physician and a specialist, since the latter finds it easier to charge large fees.

2. Payment of rebates to physicians who refer patients for technical services, including laboratory services or appliances.

3. "Ghost surgery" where the patient is led to believe that his physician performs the operation but where it is actually done by someone else, as in the famous novel, *Arch of Triumph*.

4. Increasing fees when the patient has an insurance policy which pays part.

5. Unnecessary surgery.

Opinions differ as to the importance of these but no one has produced any evidence that they are widespread. The reason for the objection to the first two is that it is likely to affect the quality and validity of the doctor's advice. He may be tempted to suggest surgery or medicines that are not necessary, or to refer the patient to the specialist who best splits his fee rather than send him to the most competent one.

Standards for hospitals are also important, and recently there was formed a Joint Commission on Hospital Accreditation, composed of representatives of the American Medical Association, the American Hospital Association, the American College of Physicians, the American College of Surgeons, and the Canadian Medical Association.

But far more serious than any of these problems of standards are the problems picturesquely entitled "quacks and nostrums." In spite of efforts by the profesional associations, the Federal Trade Commission, the Food and Drug Administration, the Public Health Service, and the local health departments, there continues to be a problem with people who sell medicines or devices that are useless or even harmful. The old travelling Indian medicine man may even have had some tribal remedies which had some effect, but the modern medicine man frequently has nothing but promises couched so as not to commit him. There always seem to be enough gullible people looking for a cheap cure to keep it profitable enough to promise one.

There are also a number of types of healers outside the regular medical profession: osteopaths, chiropractors, chiropodists, faith healers, and others. They usually do not have a medical education, though they may try to make you think that they do. They should not be relied on for anything beyond relief for minor aches and pains—certainly not for diagnosis or advice on treatment.

There are, of course, many publicly provided health services such as control of water supplies, milk pasteurization, food and drug safety, immunization, and communicable diseases. Largely as a result of such services, infectious diseases are no longer the problem they once were. In some southern states, however, where such services are not so well provided, disease rates are still relatively high.

Local health departments vary a great deal, and there is much they can still do to improve sanitation, particularly with respect to the disposal of garbage and the extinction of rats.[33]

An important part of the supply of medical care would seem to be medical research, particularly in view of its recent successes in the field of antibiotics. Much of medical research is actually a public service, its funds deriving from government grants. In 1951, the different governments provided 42 per cent of medical research funds; industry, 33 per cent; private philanthropy, 14 per cent; and hospitals and medical schools, 11 per cent.[34] The main arm of government research is at the National Institutes of Health at Bethesda, Maryland, but the Public Health Service also gives research grants-in-aid to medical schools, universities, and hospitals and clinics, as well as fellowships and other grants related to research. The President's Commission remarks that the amount spent on medical research is less than the amount spent on monuments and tombstones. Government-aided research is frequently more long-range and basic, whereas industry research, particularly by pharmaceutical houses, is likely to be "target research."

SUMMARY

In summary, a great deal is being done in the field of medicine, but it is rather easy to make a case that much more should be done. Voluntary organizations such as the National Tuberculosis Association, the American Social Hygiene Association, the American Heart Association, the American Cancer Society, the National Foundation for Infantile Paralysis, the National Society for Crippled Children and Adults do some research but spend most of their funds on remedial aid to individuals in need. In spite of some public health services and aid from these organizations, the individual is primarily responsible for seeing to it that he gets medical care for himself. He can take out health insurance that will cover some of the risk, but he still faces uninsurable risks of huge medical bills for long-run disability, or mental illness.

And finally, in thinking about the broader problems of medical care, the ordinary consumer will be hard put to it to sift the arguments he hears and make his own decision. The literature is full of erroneous or irrelevant statistics, emotional reactions, qualitative judgments about "adequacy," "ability to afford," "equitable," and so on. The only safe way through the maze is to keep in mind the basic distinctions we have tried to make, and to know something about the author of anything you read. What particular axe is the author grinding? The insurance companies are interested in getting into medical insurance as a profitable business; hence, oppose any sort of universal compulsory insurance plan. On the other hand, life insurance companies are interested in anything that increases life expectancies, since it reduces their payments. The pharmaceutical houses and retail druggists are likely to oppose anything that threatens their profitable markets or makes competition any more intense than it already is. The professional associations are concerned with the incomes of their members, professional standards, and freedom from outside controls. The Public Health Service is interested in adequate medical care for everyone, and the advancement of preventive medicine. Many individual writers are concerned with the distribution of income, or in exposing frauds even if they exaggerate their importance in the process. A generally reliable and useful source are the Public Affairs pamphlets.[35] Most important to remember is that there are real problems behind all the arguments. These problems are not simply the result of the avarice of suppliers or medical service, or the desire of bureaucrats to control medicine, or the unwillingness of consumers to pay for medical care. Medical care is becoming increasingly expensive, and the risks are such that individuals find it difficult, if not impossible, to handle them alone. Finally, the cost of training medical personnel and building facilities are so great that no good method of financing has been worked out.

SUGGESTED PROJECTS

1. Visit a hospital and make arrangements to talk to the business manager. Ask him what they do about people who cannot pay, and what proportion of their income comes from Blue Cross, from welfare departments, and from insurance companies.

2. Interview the county health officer. Ask him about sewer and water problems in the county. What does he do? What free medical services are offered in the community?

3. Write a review of one of the footnote references by de Castro, Serbein, Spock, Horney, or J. J. B. Morgan.

4. Investigate one of the medical insurance plans you see advertised. Try to secure a copy of the policy, or get the Blue Cross-Blue Shield provisions and compare each one with that of the other policy. Pay particular attention to inclusion or exclusion of services or needs not named specifically, and to the maximum number of days allowed in the hospital.

FOOTNOTES TO CHAPTER 7

1 University of Michigan, School of Public Health, *Home Injuries* (Investigation and Application of Home Injury Survey Data in Development of Preventive Procedures, a study supported by a research grant from the National Institutes of Health, U.S. Public Health Service), Ann Arbor, Michigan, 1953.

2 See, for instance, Josué de Castro, *Geography of Hunger*, London: Victor Gollancz, 1952.

3 U.S. Department of Agriculture, *Factors Affecting the Nutritive Value of Foods*, Misc. Pub. No. 664, Washington, D. C.: U.S. Gov't Printing Office, December 1948; see also: G. Adams and S. C. Smith, *The Vitamin Content and the Preservation of Foods*, U.S. Dept. of Agriculture, Misc. Pub. No. 536, Washington, D. C.: U.S. Gov't Printing Office, 1944; and L. E. Booker, E. R. Harzler, and E. M. Heuston, *A Computation of the Vitamin Values of Foods in Relation to Processing and Other Variants*, Washington, D. C.: U.S. Dept. of Agriculture, Circular 638, May 1942; U.S. Dept. of Agriculture, *Principles of Nutrition and Nutritive Value of Food*, Misc. Pub. No. 546 (by Henry C. Sherman), Washington, D. C.: U.S. Gov't Printing Office, 1944; U.S. Dept. of Agriculture, *Tables of Food Composition in Terms of Eleven Nutrients*. (Prepared by the Bureau of Human Nutrition and Home Economics in cooperation with the National Research Council), Misc. Pub. No. 572, Washington D. C.: U.S. Gov't Printing Office, 1945; U.S. Dept. of Agriculture, *Vitamin and Mineral Content of Certain Foods as Affected by Home Preparation*, Misc. Pub. No. 628, Washington, D. C.: U.S. Gov't Printing Office, Jan. 1948; U.S. Dept. of Agriculture, *Composition of Foods, Raw, Processed, Prepared*, Agriculture Handbook No. 8, Washington, D. C.: U.S. Gov't Printing Office, June 1950 (supersedes Misc. Pub. No. 572).

4 U.S. Dept. of Agriculture, Bureau of Human Nutrition and Home Economics, *Nutrition, Up to Date, Up to You*, Washington, D. C.: U.S.D.A., 1950 (with added sections on buying and storing).

5 Benjamin Spock,*The Pocket Book of Baby and Child Care*, New York: Pocket Books, Inc., 1946.

6 J. J. B. Morgan, *How to Keep a Sound Mind*, New York: The Macmillan Company, 1946; and Karen Horney, *Self Analysis*, New York: W. W. Norton & Company, Inc., 1942.

7 Karen Horney, *The Neurotic Personality of Our Time*, New York: W. W. Norton & Company, Inc., 1937.

8 Sidney Shalett, "Can We Trust All Our Doctors?" *Ladies Home Journal*, LXX: 53, 192–8 (March, 1953); see also *U.S. News and World Report*, interviews with Dr. Paul R. Hawley, Director of the American College of Surgeons, Feb. 20, 1953, pp. 48–55, and with Dr. R. B. Robins, President of the American Academy of General Practice, April 13, 1953, pp. 44–51; and Greer Williams, "Unjustified Surgery," *Harpers*, 208:35–41 (Feb., 1954).

9 Dominion of Canada, Province of Saskatchewan, Department of Public Health, *Annual Report of the Saskatchewan Hospital Services Plan, 1952*, Regina, Saskatchewan, Canada: The Province of Saskatchewan, 1953.

10 A. D. Kelly, "The Swift Current Experiment," *Canadian Medical Association Journal*, 58:505–511.

11 Speech by A. M. Wilson of Liberty Mutual, reported in *Eastern Underwriter*, Jan. 22, 1954, p. 37; see also Oscar N. Serbein, *Paying for Medical Care in the*

United States, New York: Columbia University Press, 1953, esp. Part VIII, Chap. XXX.

[12] Edwin J. Faulkner, *Accident and Health Insurance,* New York: McGraw Hill Book Co., 1940, p. 263.

[13] Odin W. Anderson, *National Family Survey of Medical Costs and Voluntary Health Insurance,* New York: Health Information Foundation, 1954; see also The Health Insurance Council, *Annual Survey of Accident and Health Coverage in the United States* (as of December 31, 1951), New York: The Council, 1952.

[14] U.S. Senate, Committee on Labor and Public Welfare, *Health Insurance Plans in the United States,* Three parts, Washington, D. C.: 82nd Congress, 1st Session; U.S. Gov't Printing Office, 1951, Part 1, p. 76; see also Odin W. Anderson, *op. cit.*

[15] *Ibid.,* Part 2, p. 11.

[16] *Ibid.,* Part 1, p. 1.

[17] 1954 Survey of Consumer Finances, *Federal Reserve Bulletin,* July 1954; see also Odin W. Anderson, *op. cit.*

[18] U.S. Federal Security Agency, Public Health Service, *Guide to Health Organization in the United States* (by Joseph W. Mountin and Evelyn Flook), Washington, D. C.: U.S. Gov't Printing Office, 1952; see also Serbein, *op. cit.,* note 11 above.

[19] U.S. President's Commission on the Health Needs of the Nation, *Building America's Health:* Vol. I, Findings and Recommendations; Vol. II, America's Health Status, Needs and Resources; Vol. III, America's Health Status, Needs and Resources, A Statistical Appendix; Vol. IV, Financing a Health Program for America; Vol. V, The People Speak—Excerpts from Regional Public Hearings on Health. Washington, D. C.: U.S. Gov't Printing Office, 1953, Vol. I, p. 1.

[20] *Ibid.,* Vol. I, p. 3.

[21] For example, William W. Bauer, M.D., *Santa Claus, M.D.,* Indianapolis, Indiana: The Bobbs-Merrill Company, Inc., 1950.

[22] R. R. Campbell and W. G. Campbell, "Compulsory Health Insurance: The Economic Issues," *Quarterly Journal of Economics,* LXVI:1–24 (Feb., 1952); I. S. Falk, "The Economic Issues of Compulsory Health Insurance: Comment," *Q.J.E.,* LXVI:572–585 (November, 1952); D. Netzer, "Further Comment," *Q.J.E.,* LXVI: 586–591 (November, 1952); R. R. Campbell and W. G. Campbell, "Reply," *Q.J.E.,* LXVII:125–134 (Feb., 1953).

[23] *Building America's Health,* Vol. IV, p. 151.

[24] Great Britain, *Report of the Ministry of Health* for the year ended 31st Dec. 1952, Part 1, Sec. 1, London: Her Majesty's Stationery Office, Sept. 1953 (Cmd. 8933), p. 50.

[25] *Building America's Health,* Vol. I, pp. 11–13.

[26] *Ibid.,* Vol. II, p. 118.

[27] *Ibid.,* Vol. I, p. 13.

[28] *Ibid.,* Vol. I, p. 26.

[29] *Ibid.,* Vol. I, p. 26.

[30] Vlado A. Getting, "Unmet Needs in Public Health Services," in *Building America's Health,* Vol. IV, pp. 83–89, see also Part I, p. 28.

[31] *Building America's Health,* Vol. I, p. 34.

[32] Alice Lake, "The Doctors Clean House," *American Magazine,* August 1951, pp. 18–19, 89–93.

[33] Albert Maisel, *Your Neighbor's Health Is Your Business.* New York: Public Affairs Committee, 1952 (Public Affairs Pamphlet No. 180).

[34] *Building America's Health,* Vol. I, p. 39.

[35] See, for instance, such Public Affairs Pamphlets as: No. 27, by Beulah Amidon, *Who Can Afford Health?* 1941; No. 101, by Louis H. Pink, *The Story of Blue Cross; on the Road to Better Health,* 1945; No. 104, by C. E. A. Winslow, *Health Care for Americans,* 1945; No. 152, by Oscar Ewing and George Lull, *How Shall We Pay for Health Care?* 1949; No. 172, by Kathleen Doyle, *When Mental Illness Strikes Your Family,* 1951; No. 176, by Herbert Yahraes, *Something Can Be Done About Chronic Illness,* 1951; No. 186, by Albert Deutsch, *What We Can Do About the Drug Menace,* 1952; No. 187, by Lucy Freeman, *It's Your Hospital and Your Life,* 1952.

The above pamphlets are published by Public Affairs Committee, New York, N. Y.

The following organizations and companies are often useful sources of information provided you remember their particular interests: American Cancer Society, 350 Madison Avenue, New York 17; American Dental Association, 222 East Superior Street, Chicago 11; American Federation of Organizations for the Hard of Hearing, 1537 Thirty-fifth St. NW, Washington 7, D. C.; American Heart Association, 1790 Broadway, New York 19; American Hospital Association, 18 East Division Street, Chicago (Blue Cross); American Medical Association, 535 North Dearborn St. Chicago 10; American National Red Cross, Eighteenth and E Streets NW, Washington 13; American Public Health Association, 1790 Broadway, New York 19; American Social Hygiene Association, 1790 Broadway, New York 19; Boy Scouts of America, 2 Park Avenue, New York 16 (Handbook and merit badge handbooks on life saving, first aid, and public health); Household Finance Corporation, 919 Michigan Avenue, Chicago 11; John Hancock Mutual Life Insurance Company, Life Conservation Service, Boston 16; Metropolitan Life Insurance Company, Welfare Division, 1 Madison Ave., New York 10; National Committee for Mental Hygiene, 1790 Broadway, New York 19; National Education Association, 1201 Sixteenth Street NW, Washington 6, D. C.; National Foundation for Infantile Paralysis; National Research Council (Publications office), 2101 Constitution Avenue, Washington 25, D. C.; National Safety Council, 20 N. Wacker Drive, Chicago; National Society for Crippled Children and Adults, 129 East 52nd St., New York 20; National Society for the Prevention of Blindness, 1790 Broadway, New York 19; National Tuberculosis Association, 1790 Broadway, New York 19; The Nutrition Foundation, Inc., Chrysler Building, New York 17; Public Affairs Committee, 30 Rockefeller Plaza, New York 20; United States, Departments of Commerce, Agriculture (Bureau of Human Nutrition and Home Economics, *etc.*), the new Department of Health, Education, and Welfare, and others. For a relatively complete listing, see Federal Security Agency, Public Health Service, *Guide to Health Organization in the United States,* Public Health Service Pub. No. 196 (1951), pp. 4ff. In particular see Food and Drug Administration, Public Health Service, Children's Bureau (Soc. Sec. Adm.), Bureau of Human Nutrition and Home Economics, Dept. of Agriculture, and Women's Bureau, Dept. of Labor.

chapter 8

Housing

||||||||||||||||||||||||||||||||||||||||||||||||||||||||||||||||||||||||||||||||||||||||||||||||||||||||||||||

INTRODUCTION

Housing is a major item of consumer expenditures, accounting for about a fourth of total expenditures in the middle income groups.   Even more important, however, is the fact that a few major decisions are made about housing which affect not only direct housing expenditures but many other expenditures over long periods of time.   Theoretically, it is not difficult to move, nor very expensive, but in practice you do not move if you can help it.   Hence, when you select a place to live (particularly if you buy a home), you buy a neighborhood, a standard of living, and even a pattern of living unless you are extremely individualistic or have no children.   Remarks have been made about the difficulty of keeping up with neighbors, or about the grievances that arise because some have dogs or children and others have flower beds and nice lawns, or because some like open sweeps of lawn and others like fences and privacy.   The plight of a poor family whose daughter associates with girls who have wardrobes of cashmere sweaters is no laughing matter.

A great deal of research has been done by sociologists, and much has been written by them as well as by architects, urban redevelopment experts, and reformers of all sorts.[1]   Much of the writing is strongly emotional and loaded with implicit and explicit value judgments. Partly as a result of the strong emotional content and partly because of the inherent difficulty of doing research in this area, much of the research is faulty and many of the available statistics are either inaccurate or misleading.[2]

Furthermore, until recently, little attention has been paid to the economic aspects of the housing of people, except for the great attention given to the housing construction industry and its notorious inefficiency. As a matter of fact, however, many of the problems are economic. At least they need to be interpreted in light of the economics of the situation. Many of the difficulties a home-buyer faces arise from the nature of the market for houses, which is hardly an ideal economic market for setting a "normal" price. Most transactions are secret; hence people do not have much information about house prices on which to base their decisions as to homes offered to them.

The realtors in many cities have an association which not only pools information on the properties currently listed for sale but also reports actual sale prices. Hence, any realtor can tell you at what prices houses have been selling.

Houses are all different—there are wide ranges of styles, ages, and equipment—but only a few of them will be on the market at any one time even in the middle of a housing boom. Technical advice and information can usually be obtained only from people with something to gain or lose from your decision— hardly an unbiased source. Most people buy only a few times in their lifetime and hence have little chance to profit from experience. Finally, the home is a symbol full of emotional content and significance, and people can easily be led by their emotions to decisions they will regret.

Following our usual procedure, we shall first discuss the consumer's problems in satisfying his own housing needs, and then look at the larger social scene and the problems concerning housing and community which the consumer can help solve as a voter.

CONSUMER DECISIONS ABOUT HOUSING

Rent, Buy, or Build?

Theoretically, the consumer in deciding whether to rent, buy, or build, takes account of the state of the housing market, the comparative costs, the chances of his having to move, his ability to do repairs and maintenance himself, and the importance of owning a home; and then makes his decision. But most of these are difficult to assess.

Take the most apparently factual of all, the comparative costs of owning versus renting. Monthly rentals plus cost of utilities for housing of various types are not too difficult to discover, though there are great disparities. But how much would a house cost you to buy or to build, and to keep up? Even for an older house where the previous owner has kept records, it is not easy. For instance, taxes may have been anywhere from ½ to 3½ per cent of the value of the house, but reassessment is possible, particularly after a sale. Repairs and maintenance can be allowed to accumulate, and the house may be infested by termites or carpenter ants, or rats or cockroaches. Depreciation is often taken to be about 2 per cent per year, but in periods of inflation and housing shortages you may even make money on a house! Insurance and utilities are important items, and they can be estimated with some accuracy, at least for an old house, though even here the cost depends to some extent on the user and his activities. An old person who closes off some rooms and does very little washing and cooking may have abnormally low bills. Finally, and perhaps most important, is the cost of the money you invest in the house, or borrow for it. Some writers, and a good many salesmen completely neglect to mention the fact that if you rented, you could earn interest on the money you would have invested in a house. In fact, a good many people look at the payments on the mortgage as the cost of the house. This overlooks not only a lot of other regular costs that must be paid in cash but also depreciation and the "opportunity cost" of your own down payment and accumulated payments on principal.

But what rate should you assume you could earn on this money? Even if you take as a minimum the 3 per cent you could earn on perfectly safe government bonds (and investment in a house is not necessarily safe, as we shall see), a man with $10,000 of his own money in a house could have earned $300, or $25 a month on it. On the money you borrow to buy a house, there is a direct outlay cost of 4½ per cent to 6 per cent. Of course, the amount you pay off on the principal of the mortgage each year is not a cost but saving invested in the house. It is possible then that the costs not included in the mortgage payments may be offset by the part of the payments which are not costs, so that, by accident, the mortgage payments are equal to the real cost of the house. But in most cases where the monthly charges are advertised as the cost of the house, they are probably less than its real cost.

If having a house built is being considered, estimates of cost are even more difficult. There is also a temptation to forget that the cost of the house itself is only about 80 per cent of the total cost, the rest being the cost of the land and fees and landscaping. Additional special assessments for streets, sidewalks, and so forth may also be likely.

In any case, there will also be appliances and furniture and other items which seem "necessary." Most moves involve changes in housing standards, and when you buy a home, you generally buy more expensive and larger quarters than you would have rented. To some extent this is natural, because a home will be owned for many years and you are tempted to buy one which will handle your peak demands. And after all this discussion, it may turn out that in order to get the type of housing you want in the neighborhood you want, you will have to buy a house.

Indeed, historically speaking, there is a sort of inverse or perverse relation: In the depression when houses were extremely cheap and a good investment, they were relatively more expensive to own than to rent—rents were extremely low.   In recent years, when prices of houses have been extremely high, rents have been even higher.   People have therefore been induced to buy at very high prices which may or may not prevail over the next twenty years.   All of which simply means that the relative costs of owning and renting may lead to one decision, and guesses about the long-range future prices of houses may lead to a different one.   In recent years, a combination of shortages of rental property and selling by banks and other investment holders of homes they had been renting has led to a substantial increase in the proportion of families who own their own homes, from 44 per cent in 1940 to 55 per cent in 1950.[3] As an example of the treacherous nature of statistical generalizations, however, it might pay to pause and examine the question of home ownership.   The figures just quoted are the percentage of dwelling units owned by someone living in them.   It is possible to ask other questions and get other answers:

What proportion of families own their own home?

What proportion of spending units own their own home?   Just because people live together does not mean that they are not separate households with separate finances (and probably desires for separate housing).

What proportion of non-farm spending units own their own home?

These questions can be answered easily after referring to Table 17, for early 1954.

By combining items 1 through 9 of Table 17 in various ways you can easily find that in early 1954:

59 per cent of homes were owned by someone who lived in them $(1 + 2) \div (1 + 2 + 4 + 7 + 8)$

57 per cent of families owned their own home $(1 + 7) \div (1 + 2 + 3 + 4 + 5 + 7 + 8)$

51 per cent of spending units owned their own home $(1 + 7) \div (1 + 2 + 3 + 4 + 5 + 6 + 7 + 8 + 9) = (1 + 7)$

56 per cent of non-farm families owned their own home $(1) \div (1 + 2 + 3 + 4 + 5)$

50 per cent of non-farm spending units owned their own home $(1) \div (1 + 2 + 3 + 4 + 5 + 6)$

75 per cent of farm families owned their own home $(7) \div (7 + 8)$

TABLE 17

HOME OWNERSHIP BY FARM AND NON-FARM STATUS AND SPENDING
UNIT COMPOSITION, EARLY 1954

(PERCENTAGE DISTRIBUTION OF ALL SPENDING UNITS)

Non-Farm	*Per Cent of Spending Units*
Home Owners	
1. Non-farm primary spending units who own their homes	46.1
Renters	
2. Non-farm primary spending units who rent	30.5
3. Non-farm unrelated secondary spending units who rent (roomers and boarders)	2.5
Neither	
4. Non-farm primaries (house furnished by relatives, etc.)	2.8
5. Non-farm unrelated secondaries (housing furnished by employer, etc.)	0.9
6. Non-farm related secondaries (children living with parents or *vice versa,* but keeping separate finances)	9.6
Farm	
Owners	
7. Farm operators, primaries who own farm	5.3
Renters	
8. Farm operaors, primaries who rent farm (or are on shares)	1.8
Neither	
9. Farm operator related secondaries, plus a few primaries with farm furnished by relatives	0.5
	100.0

Source: 1954 Survey of Consumer Finances (Federal Reserve Board, Washington
D. C., or Survey Research Center, University of Michigan. See Preface.)

Both from the point of view of the standard of living, and of
the future demand for housing, the important problems are:
What proportions of those individuals or spending units who
would like separate dwelling units have them, and secondly,
what proportion own their own homes? When we talk of families, we fail to note "doubling-up" of families. Even spending

units may contain dependents who would rather be independent and live alone. One of the ways in which a rising standard of living has manifested itself in this country has been undoubling and the setting up of separate households. Whether increases in the proportion who own their own homes represent an increase in the standard of living is more difficult to say.

The values and owners' equities in non-farm homes in early 1954 are given in Table 18, and the pattern of ownership over the family life cycle in Table 19.

TABLE 18

Value of Owner-Occupied Non-Farm Homes, and Owners' Equity, in Early 1954 [1]

(PERCENTAGE DISTRIBUTION OF ALL NON-FARM HOMEOWNING FAMILIES)

Value or Owners' Equity (dollars)	By Value of Home	By Owners' Equity in Home [2]
Under 2,500	7	15
2,500–4,999	12	19
5,000–7,499	18	24
7,500–9,999	16	13
10,000–12,499	18	12
12,500–19,999	20	11
20,000 or over	9	6
	100	100

[1] *Source:* 1954 Survey of Consumer Finances. Unascertained cases were assigned on the basis of age, income, and other information about the spending unit.

[2] Value minus mortgage debt. Table reads: "15 per cent of all non-farm home-owning families had less than $2,500 of their own money invested in their house."

To return to the problem of comparison of owning versus renting, there are a series of rules of thumb often suggested:

Fire insurance will be equal to $\frac{1}{4}$ to $\frac{1}{2}$ per cent each year of the value of the house.

Maintenance will be $2\frac{1}{2}$ per cent of value each year.

Taxes will be $2\frac{1}{2}$ per cent each year.

These rules are crude, and the estimate for taxes is almost certainly far too high for most communities. In the 1949 and

TABLE 19

HOME OWNERSHIP OVER THE FAMILY LIFE CYCLE

(PERCENTAGE DISTRIBUTION OF ALL NON-FARM SPENDING UNITS IN EACH LIFE-CYCLE GROUP)

	Young, (Under 45) Single	Young, Married, No Children	Young, Married, Youngest Child Under 6	Young, Married, Youngest Child 6 or Over	45 or Older, Married, Children	45 or Older, Married No Children at Home	45 or Older, Single
Own their own home	8	38	46	66	69	71	46
Rent	32	51	48	30	27	25	35
Live with relatives or in quarters furnished free by relatives, employer, or welfare agency	60	11	6	4	4	4	19
	100	100	100	100	100	100	100

Source: 1954 Survey of Consumer Finances.

241

1954 Surveys of Consumer Finances, people were asked what their house was worth and how much they paid in property taxes, and the median tax was less than 1 per cent of house value for most groups in the first survey and slightly over 1 per cent in the second.[4] The official tax rate is a meaningless figure to use because it is applied against an assessed valuation of the property which may be anywhere from 10 to 95 per cent of the market value, and can easily be changed as soon as you purchase the house. The rates are higher in large cities where more services are provided—police, fire department, libraries, and so forth—and lower in the country.

Fire insurance varies little but is lower where you are protected by a regular fire department.

And, of course, the cost of maintenance depends on many things including the construction details and the degree to which you have the time and mechanical ability to do things yourself.

In view of the difficulties in estimating individual costs, some people advocate simpler rules such as:

Do not spend more than three times your annual income on a house.

Figure what you can spend for housing per year, for example, 25 per cent of your annual income, and pay no more than ten times that for a house, because the annual cost is about 10 per cent of the purchase price. (Others say a house is worth 100 times the monthly rent you could get for it, which would figure out to an annual cost of 12 per cent of the purchase price.

Figure the cost of owning a home by adding interest, amortization, and taxes plus an additional 50 per cent of this figure to cover other costs. This is frequently done for you in pamphlet tables.

The author of the last estimate, pointing out that a good deal of advertising directed toward potential buyers says that the mortgage payments and taxes "cover everything," charges the ad writers with "deliberate gross misrepresentation." [5]

The relative cost of owning or renting is only one of a number of considerations, of course. Most of these considerations are favorable to one decision or the other, so let us list them in the form of arguments for renting or for owning a home.

In favor of renting:

A. It is easier to move if you want better or smaller quarters, or if you have to move to be nearer a new place of employment, or if you find the neighborhood deteriorating. The only costs are moving costs, and there are fewer emotional ties. Willingness to move may affect your economic position and your ability to take a better job. According to census mobility studies, 20 per cent of the people move every year in this country, 6 per cent to a different county or state. Young people are especially likely to move, with 38 per cent of those between 20 and 25 moving every year. According to the 1954 Survey of Consumer Finances, nearly half the non-farm home owners bought their homes less than seven years ago, while more than three-quarters of the renters had moved at least once in the past seven years. The 5 per cent brokers fee and other costs of buying and selling houses can become important costs if you move very many times. If the housing market is depressed when you have to move, you may find it difficult to sell. Of course, it may also be cheaper to buy in the town where you move, but this is no help if you take such a loss in selling your old house that you cannot make a down payment on another one.

In a one-company town, home ownership can prove extremely bad. Caliente, California depended on steam locomotives, and Iron Mountain, Michigan on the production of Ford station wagon bodies made of wood. In both cases home owners found themselves without a job and with their life savings tied up in a home they could not sell for any reasonable price.[6]

B. It is easier to budget and to control expenses if you rent, because you know what will have to be paid. You will not be led into housing you find you cannot afford when all the extras and hidden expenses start coming in. No emergencies like the need for a new furnace or hot water heater will force you to borrow.

(Arguments A and B are primarily the basis for strong arguments that home ownership has been oversold and is particularly dangerous for wage earners.[7])

C. You need not be concerned about upkeep, repairs, and so forth. These take time as well as money, and you might better spend the time making money at something you like and are good at.

D. It is cheaper than owning most of the time, and during the temporary periods when it is not, houses are extremely expensive and likely to be a bad long-term investment. If renting were really expensive, then it would be profitable for investors to get into the rental business; but they have shown no great tendency to do so. Renting is also cheaper because you can adjust your quarters to your needs, and hence need not have over-capacity before and after the period of your peak family needs, with its consequent costs. It may also be cheaper because you are less likely to have more housing than you need and, hence, to over-balance your expenditures in favor of housing.

E. As for arguments that owning a home gives you credit standing, this assumes that you are foolish enough to need credit with all its expenses and do not have any reserve funds. If you can save without a mortgage to force you, you will have more reserve funds. This will not only establish your credit, but will probably make it unnecessary to use credit.

In favor of owning:

A. You can stabilize your costs, and will not get caught in an inflation with rising rents at the very time when it is expensive to buy a house.

B. A house is a safe investment and an ideal way to reduce the need for cash expenditures after you retire. It provides a type of visible security for your wife and children.

C. There are tax advantages (if your deductions are more than 10 per cent of income so that it pays to fill out the long form) because property taxes and mortgage interest are deductible. Also, there is no tax on the imputed interest on your own investment in the house, whereas if you rented and invested the money in stocks or bonds, you would pay taxes on the interest or dividends you received. Some states have homestead exemptions which mean lower property taxes on owner-occupied homes than on rented ones, so that owning is somewhat more likely to be cheaper than renting in those states.

D. You have an incentive and an automatic system for saving through amortized mortgage. This is the most inviolate of all contractual saving forms, because it is almost impossible to stop making the payments, and you cannot borrow on the principal so easily as on the cash value of your life insurance.

E. It gives you better credit status and standing in the community.

F. You can usually get a better environment, because the better sections of town are made up predominantly of home owners and you will not be likely to find a house for rent there.

G. You are free from the authority of a landlord and can do what you please with your property.

H. You can save a good deal of money by doing things yourself around the house, and these things can become a form of recreation. You may stay home and do gardening instead of playing golf, or taking expensive vacations. You can time your repairs and additions to suit your needs and pocketbook rather than the landlord's! You may even design and do the improvements yourself—a profitable form of self-expression.

I. Particularly if you build rather than buy, you can get the type of house you really want, designed for future expansion or for the particular needs of your family.

J. In answer to the argument about the rental business being unprofitable, this may not be because renting is cheaper than owning, but because of the managerial costs and the fact that renters are just more careless about doing simple things to protect the property.

What can we conclude from all this? Once again, one man's meat is another's poison. The man with a job that is unlikely to require that he move his place of employment to another town, and who likes to do things around the house, and who can pick a good house and neighborhood, may decide to buy and never regret it. A man with an unsteady job and no mechanical ability may buy a house that is too expensive for his present income or too small for his future family needs. All sorts of possibilities exist, and perhaps our main conclusion should be that a consumer needs to consider all these things, and to be careful that he is not being unduly influenced by emotional feelings rather than by considerations of more mundane sorts.

The prices of houses have been rising since 1940, and particularly since the war. More than a third of all the houses, and over two-thirds of the new houses purchased in 1952 and 1953, cost $12,500 or more. Of the existing stock of houses, non-farm owners in early 1954 estimated in 9 per cent of the cases surveyed that their house was worth $20,000 or more, and at the other end in only 19 per cent of the cases that it was worth less than $5,000. (See Table 18.)

More than half the non-farm home owners have debts on their houses, and 19 per cent have debts greater than half the value of the house. It is largely the young people who have purchased homes more recently or had less time to accumulate assets, who have the most debt.

TABLE 20

RELATION OF AGE TO DEBT AS PER CENT OF HOUSE VALUE
(PER CENT OF NON-FARM HOME OWNERS WITHIN EACH AGE GROUP)

			Age		
	Less Than 35	35–44	45–54	55–64	65 and Over
Per cent with debt equal to 50% or more of value of house	48	30	12	7	3
Per cent with no debt on their house	18	28	56	70	78

Source: 1954 Survey of Consumer Finances.

Expenditures on the house, however, are not limited to the initial purchase. According to the 1954 Survey of Consumer Finances 40 per cent of non-farm home owners reported some additions or repairs to the house in 1953, and some 17 per cent reported spending $500 or more on additions or repairs. Recent purchasers, with the exception of those who bought just a year or two previously, were just as likely as others to have such expenditures, and those who had recently purchased were almost as likely to have spent large amounts.

We noted that an important argument in favor of buying a home was that it provided an automatic method of saving. This has been a rather recent development. Before the 1930's many owners had first mortgages that did not specify any repayment on principal so long as the interest was paid regularly. As a result of the difficulties with foreclosures during the depression, it has finally become accepted practice to use only amortized mortgage loans in financing house purchases. In an amortized mortgage, a standard monthly charge is computed that will pay interest on the remaining balance, and pay off larger and larger amounts of this balance as time goes by so that it is completely paid off at the end of 15, 20, or 30 years. In the early years most of the payment is interest, and at the end, it is mostly repayment of principal.

Since the payments on principal are really saving—increasing the owner's equity in the house—the amortized mortgage becomes one more contractual saving device. In addition, since most people can think of the monthly payments as rent, the saving seems painless. Since there is no easy way to stop payments or to borrow more, this savings fund is practically inviolate. For added convenience, banks often arrange to pay all the taxes and the fire insurance premiums as well, and sometimes other utility charges, out of their single monthly charge to you.

In recent years, salesmen of building materials have been advocating a device known as the "open-end mortgage," whereby a man who wants to make an addition to his house can merely continue the same mortgage payments for an added period, or pay more per month.   This is not so bad as the earlier system where no payments were made on principal.   So long as the additions actually increase the value of the house, the amount of contractual saving is merely increased.

TABLE 21

INTEREST RATE ON NEW MORTGAGES FOR VARIOUS PRICE-INCOME GROUPS

Interest Rate on Mortgage (per cent)	Low Price, Low Income [1] (per cent)	Medium Price, Medium Income (per cent)	High Price, High Income (per cent)	Low and Medium Price, High Income (per cent)	All [2] (per cent)
Under 4	...	3	...	3	2
4–4¼	26	35	19	26	28
4½–4¾	12	34	46	41	33
5–5¾	26	22	30	24	26
6 and over	36	6	5	6	11
	100	100	100	100	100

Source: Survey Research Center, *Relevant Considerations in Recent House Purchases,* (pursuant to a contract with the Housing and Home Finance Agency) Ann Arbor, Michigan; Institute for Social Research, University of Michigan, June, 1951, Table V-11, eliminating those with no mortgage, and distributing unascertained cases. This monograph is out of print, but will be reprinted with additions in 1955, by the Housing and Home Finance Agency.

[1] "Medium income" is $3,000 to $4,999. "Medium house price" is $7,500 to $14,999.

[2] Includes 27 per cent of the sample in other price-income combinations, and 4 per cent where price or income was not ascertained.

Hence, buying a house involves contractual saving payments. But for the majority who must borrow on a mortgage in order to buy a house it is the actual outlays including the total mortgage payment each month that determine how much they can afford to pay for a house.   In other words, there is a rather arbitrary institutional arrangement forcing you to save considerably more than the amount by which the house depreciates, and also to pay an interest charge which is rather high, given the type of risk involved, and likely to be higher the less you can afford to pay it.   Table 21, derived from a sample survey of recent home purchasers, illustrates the latter phenomenon.

The very high interest charges are concentrated in the low-price, low-income groups. It is probably income rather than the price of the house which affects the interest rate charged, because those in middle and high income groups who bought low-priced houses did not pay such high interest rates. Of course, F.H.A.-guaranteed or G.I. loans specify a maximum interest rate of 4½ per cent.

Several factors probably cause this perverse relation of costs to income: One is the risk element which is greater for lower income people, and for mortgages which are a larger part of the value of the house—which lower income people often have to have. The other, however, is probably the degree of competition. People with higher incomes can afford to look around and to go to banks or other lenders that take only the very safe loans, and charge lower interest rates. Interest charges are generally higher in smaller cities, too, probably reflecting less competition in areas served by only a few financial institutions. In the metropolitan areas, only 6 per cent of the mortgages were for 6 per cent or more. In cities of 50,000 or more, 8 per cent were for 6 per cent interest or more, and in cities of 2,500 to 49,999, some 22 per cent were high-interest mortgages of 6 per cent or more. An added 1 per cent interest on a mortgage debt of $10,000 is $100 a year or more than $8 a month, so the interest rate is important.

Even more important in affecting the monthly payments you have to make is the length of the period over which the mortgage is to be paid off. Table 22 shows how the monthly payment of interest and on principal is affected by the interest rate and the number of years over which the mortgage runs. Sometimes authors add 30–60 per cent to these amounts to indicate about how much you will really need to operate such a house and make up a table showing "amount of loan which income for housing will finance."

One of the advantages of F.H.A. insured mortgages is that they generally provide for a maximum interest rate (currently 4½ per cent plus ½ per cent for the insurance). They also

allow the mortgage to be as much as 90 per cent of the appraised
value of an existing house or 95 per cent of the value of a new
house up to $6,000, and 75 per cent of the remaining value up
to $20,000.　These terms are much more generous than most
banks would allow without the F.H.A. guarantee.

TABLE 22

MONTHLY PAYMENTS ON INTEREST AND PRINCIPAL FOR EACH $1,000 ORIGINAL
MORTGAGE FOR DIFFERENT INTEREST RATES AND LENGTH OF PAYMENT PERIODS

Years to Pay	Interest Rate						
	3%	4%	4½%	5%	5½%	6%	7%
5	$17.97	$18.42	$18.65	$18.88	$19.11	$19.34	$19.81
10	9.66	10.13	10.37	10.61	10.86	11.11	11.62
15	6.91	7.40	7.65	7.91	8.18	8.44	8.99
20	5.55	6.06	6.33	6.60	6.88	7.17	7.76
25	4.75	5.28	5.56	5.85	6.15	6.45	7.07
30	4.22	4.78	5.07	5.38	5.69	6.00	6.66
35	3.85	4.43	4.74	5.05	5.37	5.71	6.40
40	3.58	4.18	4.50	4.83	5.16	5.51	6.22
45	3.37	4.00	4.33	4.66	5.01	5.37	6.10
50	3.22	3.86	4.20	4.54	4.90	5.27	6.02

Source: 5–25 years: *Monthly Payment Direct Reduction Loan Amortization Schedules*, 3rd ed., Boston: Financial Publishing Company, 1939.
30–50 years: *Direct Reduction Loan Amortization Schedules for Loans With
Quarterly, Semiannual, and Annual Payments*, 2nd ed., Boston: Financial Publishing Company, 1949.
Conversion of these quarterly payments to monthly payments involves a slight
error because of the shift from quarterly to monthly computation of interest.
Note: The largest reductions in monthly charges come from extending the payment period from 5 to 30 years.　After this the effect is quite small both because
of the larger total amount of interest charges and because an additional five years
is a smaller proportionate extension of time.

F.H.A. insured mortgages have other advantages, particularly
in areas where the local building codes are weak.　For instance,
the F.H.A. will insist on checking construction details, location,
and so forth and will refuse to guarantee where the house is
badly built or a risky investment because of location.　Indeed,
some critics charge that the F.H.A. has been too conservative,
making it difficult to introduce new architectural styles, or insisting on uniform provisions such as sidewalks, or painted

rather than varnished outside doors, even when circumstances do not require it. Also, in many cases F.H.A. applications have taken months in the processing and have led to delays which are frequently costly in house building. Finally, for several years the F.H.A. actually insisted on racially restrictive covenants, but under popular protest changed the policy.[8]

Actually, recent research tends to show that while entry of a different racial group into a neighborhood causes a few frightened people to sell at lower prices, most sales are at a higher price than in other comparable districts.[9] If anything, the shoe is on the other foot, and the minority group is forced to pay high prices for housing. In general it is probably true that the value of a community to the individual is a result of how well he gets along with the rest of the community and the extent to which he can develop common interests with his neighbors. There is reason to believe that this depends as much on the economic status, occupations, and personalities of people as on their religious or ethnic backgrounds.

There have been, from time to time, co-operatives which have attempted to organize consumers to buy land, lay out its uses, and have houses built co-operatively in order to save money and to have a better community.[10] Unfortunately, many of these co-operatives have been financial failures, and the members have lost a good deal of money. Others have succeeded because the adequate financial resources of the members allowed them to pay the costs. A few have succeeded in providing housing *and* savings for their members. It is my opinion that, if there are some members willing to devote the necessary time and energy to organization and management, and if there is adequate financing, co-operatives can succeed in this field and achieve a better final result than individual or even speculative builders.

Before leaving the question of buying, building, or renting, we should note a few of the legal incidentals that are involved, some of which merely lead to fees that add to the expenses, others of which can lead to substantial financial losses for the buyer.   Particularly in the older areas of the eastern United States there are many legal tangles over the title to land.   Theoretically, it is necessary to be able to trace a chain of valid purchases all the way back to the original land grant.   As a first precaution, it is essential that you are certain that someone else does not have possible title to the land rather than the person from whom you are buying it.   There are companies that will search the records and write up the title history of a plot of land, and some that will insure you against loss if the title proves bad. *The law is such that, if you build a house on a piece of land that proves to belong to someone else, that party also owns the house.*   At any rate, the necessary searching, recording of deed, and so forth involve fees which, while not large compared with the cost of a house, often come at a time when cash is scarce. There are legal proceedings that can be used to clear up title to the land, or you can fail to pay the taxes, let the state or local government auction the land at a tax sale.   Then, when you buy it back, you have a clear title to it.

The other major legal complication arises from what are called mechanics' lien laws.   These laws were passed to protect building craftsmen from unscrupulous contractors who refused to pay them.   In practice, however, they make the owner responsible for the debts of the contractor who built his house for him.   Mere payment of the contractor does not discharge the owner's obligations to the various suppliers of labor and materials until each of them signs a "waiver of lien," or until some period of time fixed by law for the filing of claims has expired.   A contractor may make a series of mistakes and gradually get so far in debt that he is paying for one house with the money of the purchasers of subsequent ones.   If the contractor finally gives up and leaves town, the last buyer who had a house built by this contractor will find that in order to keep his house, he may have to pay for it twice.   The various craftsmen were not paid for the work they did on *his* house, and these debts are assessable not only against the contractor, who may be bankrupt, but against the property itself.   Many "how to" books

suggest insisting on signed waivers of lien before paying the contractor, but the building process is complex enough that only
the honesty and solvency of the contractor are any real guarantee.

What Kind of Housing?

An assessment of the consumer's choice problem in this area
is difficult for several reasons.

First, there is very little freedom of choice really present.
Less than one person in twenty buys a house in any one year.
Only one in a hundred buys a new house, and most of these
are designed and built by speculative builders. Even the very
few who have a house built are subject to the customs of the
times (carports and breezeways, picture windows, and so forth),
the resistance of builders to anything new, and the delight of
architects in the new and striking (however useless). Satirical
articles are already beginning to appear, and more can be expected, poking fun at fireplaces which throw the automatic heating system out of balance or *vice versa*, picture windows with
drapes to keep the "solar heat" from fading the furniture and
rugs, "efficient kitchens" with no room for the husband or
children, the "open-plan" allowing the noise of dishwasher, and
other appliances and the odors of cooking to wander through
the house, extra bays and angles which add to the cost but not
the space, carports which end up as porches, and so forth.[11]

Second, the needs of home buyers are widely different. Some
like quiet; others, large cocktail parties. Some have children.
Some want a separate living room for the children, or hobby
space, or many bedrooms, or a large lot with room for a garden.
Many of the things buyers feel they need are not for the simple
provision of shelter, cooking, eating, and sleeping space.

Third, there has been very little research on what people
want in housing, and since this is a place where people's wants
are capable of expansion and change, most people cannot visualize what they would like beyond the next few improvements.
On the other hand, most people want more housing than they

can afford. A study during the period 1949–1951 showed that nearly half the houses bought in metropolitan areas were bought with the purchaser putting up less than 6 per cent of the price of the house.[12] Furthermore, the same study showed that as incomes increased during this period, the per cent of new houses with more than 1,000 square feet of floor space increased from 35 per cent in the latter part of 1949 to 54 per cent in early 1951. More revealing of what the buyers wanted is noted in a survey conducted by the Survey Research Center in 1950. (See note 7.) The report of this study concluded that:

1. Many people want more living space than they are getting. In particular they felt that they needed more bedrooms and more adequate dining space.

2. The arrangement of houses were not always suitable; people wanted more than one place to eat, and a provision for a more formal atmosphere for occasional dinners. This same dissatisfaction with either kitchen or living room for eating appears in a British study.[13]

3. Arrangement for more privacy for bedrooms and bath and either basements or more adequate substitutes for them were desired.

4. The prices of houses were felt to be too high.

5. Though the location of dwellings was not a major subject of investigation in this study, it was found to be a very important consideration for many buyers. Nearness to schools, public transportation, shopping districts, and place of work were mentioned as important, but equally important appeared to be the kind of neighborhood in which the dwelling was located.

6. People also desired larger lots.

7. 74 per cent wanted one-story houses, and only 60 per cent got them.

This study makes an interesting application of normative standards to check the adequacy of the number of bedrooms. It assumes that a family needs a second bedroom for a third adult or a child, a third bedroom if there are children of two sexes, or three or more children. If these standards are reasonable, 78 per cent of the families with four or more children or with extra adults and children did not have enough bedrooms. Over-all, 17 per cent did not have enough bedrooms *in houses they had just purchased.*

An interesting confirmation of our earlier statement that most people buy a better house than they would rent is the fact that 60 per cent of the buyers said it cost more to live in the new house than before they moved, and only 20 per cent said that it cost less.

Other studies of more limited groups seemed to show that the major and most prevalent cause of dissatisfaction is lack of adequate space.[14]   Other complaints seemed to be widely distributed and the result of unique situations of the individuals or of specific features of a housing project. A study by Svend Riemer based on 300 mail questionnaires in Seattle indicated that crowding was the main variable, though younger people and "status groups" were also concerned about equipment.[15]

A study with a more adequate personal interview was done by the Women's City Club of New York City in 1947 as a follow-up of a previous study in 1936.   The 1936 study had been done in slum areas, and had found that two-thirds of the people wanted to stay where they were in order to be with friends or because they were used to it.   In 1947 people in housing projects with vastly improved housing conditions were interviewed, and over half of them wanted to move where they would have conditions which would be still better for their children.   They also gave other reasons which indicated a tremendous advance in their aspirations.   The housing projects had many modern improvements, but there were complaints about child care, location of playgrounds, need for better storage, especially for baby carriages, indoor play space for children, and better drying space for clothes.   All except the last of these, where the project was actually less convenient than the slums with their pulley lines for clothes, indicated advanced standards:

Minimum standards of safety, health and sanitation have been afforded.   But these advances have in turn raised her values, have widened her horizons, and have stimulated her to look ahead to further improvements in her living conditions, whether or not they are immediately obtainable.[16]

Another study in publicly aided housing projects, where both tenants and managers were interviewd, some in 1942 and others in 1945, again indicated that the primary source of dissatisfaction was overcrowding.[17]   Just as in the British study (note 13), there were desires for individual back yards, individual entrances and porches, and more storage space, and there were strong feelings, particularly in families with children, that a combination living-dining space was bad.   Drying space was a major problem, particularly since the community laundries were so far away.   Kitchens were clearly too small, because 89 per cent used them for dining and 82 per cent for ironing clothes.   An interesting example of the necessity for open personal interviews occurred in this study.   A large number of people objected to asphalt tile floors, and some had even covered them with felt floor coverings.   It turned out that the objection arose because of the dark color which showed every speck of dust, and not to asphalt tile in general.

The British study referred to in the footnote above found the British housewives with simpler and less ambitious desires for improvement in their housing than the Americans, presumably because housing in Britain is so primitive compared with American standards.   While dissatisfied with some features, the British are able to get along with others which seem quite impossible to us.   Their desires are for better-placed fireplaces rather than central heat, inside toilets rather than extra powder rooms or gadgets.

To a great many people . . . the idea that they might either like or dislike their home is a novel one.   They take their home for granted, and they just live there with little further thought.   It is a closely interwoven part of their background, and they would normally as soon think of analyzing their own motives in going to a pub or clipping a troublesome child on the ear, as of sitting down and thinking whether and why they were not satisfied with their homes. . . .[18]

In view of the pervasive finding that most people need more space, it seems clear that in recent years they have been accepting houses that were too small but insisting on modern heating, plumbing, kitchen cabinets, and costly details.   Some would argue that a basement is really a luxury appendage, because one can get additional bedrooms or other living space for the same cost in a basementless house.[19] The other frequent problem —clothes drying space—is not so serious because it can be solved by an automatic dryer. One private housing development of basementless houses, which I have seen, insists that the houses be equipped with clothes dryers. In this way, passers-by will not see, framed in the picture window, the wash hanging in the living room to dry.

Another way to approach the problem of what kind of housing to buy is to look at the books and pamphlets written—mostly by architects—on optimum layout for houses.[20] Of course, some minimum standards are obvious: not more than $1\frac{1}{2}$ people per room, central heat, daylight in every room, and adequate storage space. Other suggestions are not so immediately ob· vious. A famous article by Harrison, Whitney, and Woodward once listed some useful ones, classifying them "essentials" or "desirables": [21]

Essentials:

1. Living room not reached by a passage through any other major room.
2. Living room used for dining not separated from kitchen by any other major room.
3. Kitchen convenient to dining space.
4. Chamber (bedroom) not reached by passage through any other major room except living room or dining space.
5. Bathroom reached from all chambers (bedrooms) without passage through other rooms.
6. Bath accessible from all rooms without passage through a chamber (bedroom).

Desirables:

1. Living room not the only passage to other major rooms.
2. Kitchen accessible for service directly to entrance without passage through other rooms.
3. Bath and bedroom hall located so that it may be isolated.
4. Bath access from bedroom not across apartment entrance circulation.
5. Hall or foyer giving direct access to all major rooms.
6. Circulation direct and compact.

An additional problem has arisen with newer housing designs which save space by using the living room as a hall and passageway. A living room with entrances in three corners, particularly if it is the only way to get from kitchen to bedrooms, will take a lot of traffic and will be difficult to arrange into convenient furniture groupings. The saving of space can be illusory, too, because a living room that can be shut off from the rest of the house can also be used as a guest room.

In northern climates, small entrance rooms or vestibules have proven useful to keep drafts, snow, and overshoes out of living rooms. Unless modern laundry and kitchen appliances become a lot less noisy than they now are, architects will soon be advocating some method of shutting their noise and heat from the living room and perhaps even from the kitchen.

A good many other standards have been stated by various writers, but they turn out upon examination to be not minimum standards but luxuries, which are not found in most houses anyway, and certainly not in trains and public buildings. Recently, writers have begun to take a dim view of such "standards." [22]

In judging quality of an existing house, apart from the floor plan and layout, there is an old government publication called *How to Judge a House,* which is still useful, and articles appear intermittently in such publications as *Consumer Reports* (August, 1952), and *Better Homes and Gardens.*[23] One authority, in discussing wood versus brick or stone houses said:

A frame house may require slightly greater average expenditures on maintenance, but hardly out of proportion to the difference in the original cost as compared to a brick house. For all practical purposes, therefore, even the rate of depreciation might be the same.[24]

He goes on to say that it is not depreciation as such but obsolescence which is important:

The obsolescence which would probably be the chief factor in the ultimate depreciation may occur gradually, or it might take place at any moment for reasons unrelated to the specific property and outside the control of the individual property owner.[25]

Of course, the original design of the house has much to do with its obsolescence; but as we shall see in the next section, the main determinant is the community in which the house is located.

The most difficult thing about deciding what kind of housing you want arises from the fact that the size and activities of your family change from year to year. Most families go through a "life cycle" with constantly changing housing needs.[26] There is likely to be a period of 10–15 years, before the children leave home, when the need for space is greatest, but housing to be "adequate" during this period would be extravagant both before and afterward. There seem to be emotional and physical obstacles to selling a house that has been lived in for many years. The physical obstacles arise from the imperfect market, difficulty of selling and buying a more appropriate house, and possibly a depressed market for houses, which is hoped to be temporary. The emotional obstacles come because people put so much thought and energy into making their houses suitable for their own purposes, and because they get used to whatever disadvantages and inconveniences their houses have. It is hard to avoid the feeling for which there is no empirical evidence, that there are a great many older people living in houses that are much to big for them and even dangerous to their health because of the work they entail. At the same time there are people living doubled up with relatives or in houses much too small for their families. If the older people could only move to the apartments and small houses, a substantial amount of housing would probably be made available.

Buying or renting a house that suits your needs seems in most cases to be a matter of getting what you want at a minimum cost. When, however, there is a choice between a modern, convenient, one-floor house and a less expensive house of more traditional design, many of us face a difficult choice. Owing largely to the traditionalism of the building industry, it is generally possible to get more space in a traditional two-story house and a house with a basement than in a one-floor house that costs the same amount.

What are the offsetting advantages of the one-floor house? First, since there is a trend to one-floor houses, it may have a lower rate of obsolescence. Second, if it is really more convenient, it may save the cost of a weekly cleaning lady at $8 a day, one day a week, or $416 a year. Over twenty years, even discounted at 5 per cent, this is more than $5,000 saved. My own experience is that a well laid-out one floor house actually saves a great deal of energy that goes, in an ordinary two-story house, into climbing stairs and carrying things up and down them. Particularly with children who require frequent attention the stairs can be a real annoyance. They are also a safety hazard. Of course, those who live in traditional houses get along fine, and can find advantages to their own arrangements.

Choice of Community

Far more important than the decision whether to own or to rent, or the decisions about what kind of housing, is the choice of the community where you live. This choice will affect the cost of living. It determines the amount of time and energy spent going to work, to school, and to the stores. More important, the community will affect your standard of living and that of your children. It is likely to affect the quality of their schooling, and their basic attitudes—toward minority races, for example. The community will also largely determine the cost of housing itself. Taxes vary. Further, they are likely to go up if the community does not have all the services you most want. The cost of services and even of food sometimes vary. Many of the service trades, including, particularly, the professional ones, like doctors, dentists, and lawyers, gauge their clients' ability to pay largely by where they live.

Most important of all, perhaps, is the impact of the community on the rate at which your house depreciates in value. It is possible in a physical sense to keep a house "as good as new" by proper upkeep, repairs, and occasional modernization; yet, in some areas, old houses are worthless, and, in others, they are worth more than they were a hundred years ago. The basic reason for this is that the value of a house depends on what is going on around it, what others do with their land and houses. It is no exaggeration to say that zoning, police powers, and the law of easements are all inadequate except in the most extreme cases. If your neighbor puts a noisy air conditioner in his window and it happens to be near your bedroom window, or if he piles junk in his back yard, the law courts are not likely to provide redress.

It is easily possible that a truck route will be planned to go past your house, or an airport will be built nearby, or the area will be turned into a factory section, an area of shops, or doctors' offices. Unless there are unusually good zoning laws and an unusually stern zoning board to refuse changes, you can do nothing but sit and watch the value of your property decline. Of course, if you are either wise or lucky, you may find a school being built nearby (but not too near), or a shopping district, or a bus line routed to stop at your corner, or a park or playground built nearby, and discover that your property values are enhanced. Even the type of houses built on the formerly empty lots nearby, or the way in which your neighbors keep up their property, will affect the value of your investment.[27]

Zoning laws were, of course, passed and used in recognition of the fact that not only could uses of one piece of property affect the value of others, but that also all property would be worth more if the uses were properly spaced and regulated. These laws left a great deal to be desired however.

Naturally enough, zoning ordinances and practice were uneven in quality from city to city. In general, the major weaknesses were (a) the overzoning of relatively high-income uses; (b) the failure to prohibit residential construction in commercial and industrial districts; (c) the fact that a large majority of the zoning ordinances were not based on any comprehensive land-use plan for the municipality; (d) in later years, too easy variations and exceptions by zoning boards of appeal; and (e) in metropolitan areas, the separatism and unrelatedness of ordinances applied to economically and socially interdependent but politically independent areas.[28]

At present a great deal of development is taking place outside the city limits of most cities, and here there are frequently no zoning laws at all. It is a gamble to buy in an undeveloped neighborhood unless there is strict zoning and you know the developer and his plans. A good clue is the size of the lots. The larger they are, the more likely the developer is to be concerned with developing a nice pleasant community. Provisions for playgrounds, schools, and so forth are another clue.

There are several other legal arrangements which may aid the property-owner, however. There are "laws of nuisance" under which one can prevent his neighbor from piling junk or garbage on the front lawn, or doing something which can unequivocably be called a nuisance or danger to life or health. But the type of person who would do that sort of thing is likely to be a bad neighbor anyway, and the law only prevents the more obvious and clearly defined types of nuisances. There are laws by which someone who wishes to cut across a corner of your property, or shut off some of your light or air, can purchase an "easement" from you to obtain this right. On the other hand there is a legal provision known as "presumptive easement" whereby, if you allow people to do anything of this sort for a given number of years without protesting or charging them, they can then do it forever without paying. There is a quaint old street on Beacon Hill in Boston known as Louisburg Square, which is owned by the property owners along it. They retain their rights to it and to its future conversion in any way they see fit, by blocking it off once a year with signs indicating that it is private property.

Finally, property owners can protect their property by agreeing with one another and signing "covenants" restricting the future use of the property. Unfortunately, restrictive covenants have all too often been designed to keep out minority races or restrict architectural styles to those of the prevailing period. Some of the more ingenious ones have set up minimum sizes of lots, prohibited things likely to become a nuisance, such as the raising of chickens. Some have even put minimum construction costs on houses to be built, with escalator adjustments for possible future increases in prices. That is, if the cost of building houses doubles, the minimum house value for new houses built in the area is also doubled. Whether or not it is actually a good thing to have the type of one-class neighborhood envisaged by most of these arrangements is difficult to say. It is probably true that what most of us want is congenial neighbors with somewhat similar interests, and it is almost impossible to draw up a legal document to specify this. On the other hand, in spite of our democratic ideals, it has been noted that, when people with different incomes and occupations are thrown together in housing projects, they frequently object to one another as neighbors.

Both covenants and zoning or other ordinances frequently turn out to have lacked foresight. Industrial uses of land were once considered the most noxious. The modern factory with almost no noise, no smoke, treatment of its wastes, landscaped grounds, and a shrubbery-enclosed parking lot is probably nicer to have near your home—particularly if you work in that factory—than a gas station or a bar or a bowling alley.

Legal devices are a weak reed, at best, upon which to lean. There is always, however, the possibility of co-operative action by property owners. One of the most striking instances of the power of such co-operative action is the preservation of Beacon Hill in Boston as a fashionable area over many years while all the other once-fashionable areas were becoming slums or areas of doctors' offices and businesses.[29] It is true that Beacon Hill was close to Boston Common and to the center of Boston, but so were several other fashionable areas. My own casual observation leads me to feel, however, that, ordinarily, it is extremely difficult to get property owners together soon enough to do much good. Our population is tremendously mobile. If the 20 per cent who move every year in this country were a random selection each year, less than a third of the original residents would remain in an area after five years. The situation is not quite this bad, because moving is concentrated somewhat among younger people and those with occupations which require it, but it is still serious. Furthermore, while a threat of a noisy highway going through nearby may arouse the people to co-operative protest, the need for sidewalks or playgrounds to keep their children off the street is less dramatic and inspiring.

The individual is left one final defense, and that is to select his neighborhood shrewdly so as to minimize the need for any legal or other actions. A study of the growth of cities will show certain patterns developing: some areas built early and with cheap houses destined for slums, other areas taken over largely for industrial or commercial uses, others a mixture of all sorts of things. Some developments are so important and inevitable that no combination of zoning and covenants will stop them. Industry is almost certain to take over much of the area near railroads and main highways. Areas very close to the center of town will ultimately become business districts or, worse, cheap rooming-house districts. Areas partially built up as residential areas and then arrested by depression or something else for many years are in danger of becoming blighted areas unless the original houses were very well built and are well cared for. Beyond this type of generalization, those who have studied urban development do not agree among themselves whether there are any standard patterns of development. Even debatable generalizations, however, are useful to study because of the empirical material used for them.[30]

Most cities of any size have a planning agency, which has been watching these trends of development and trying to make them more reasonable and consistent. They are generally glad to talk with people and to guide their decisions. The zoning board, city engineer, telephone company, and public utilities usually know a great deal about what has been happening. Real estate agents have their own interests in mind, of course, and their own ideas about what makes a good neighborhood, but suitably translated are another source of information. Whatever the source of information, the following questions need to be asked:

What is the situation regarding public transportation, schools, churches, parks, and playgrounds?

What is the situation regarding water, sewer, streets, sidewalks, zoning regulations, and police and fire protection?

Do most people own their own homes? Are they people who are likely to move away or will they stay here?

Does the zoning board have a record for firmness and integrity? Have they been "tightening up" zoning by reducing uses of property that spoil the community, or have they allowed a considerable number of "variations" or spot zonings that have permitted new businesses in residential areas, and so forth?

Is the community predominantly made up of younger or of older people? There is some evidence that communities themselves go through a sort of life cycle—being made up initially of younger people with children, then by people with older children (mostly the same people), and, finally, largely by older people with no children. Aside from the age of the houses and obsolescence of the plumbing, lot size, and so forth, there is the problem of lack of common interests with neighbors. Parents of children may find that they need to worry about the noise their children make, their damage to lawns, the lack of playmates, the shortage of baby-sitters, and general differences in interests among the adults.

Are there houses of many different ages and styles? This may make the community interesting but is more likely to lead to "eyesores" here and there in a few years.

Are there many empty lots in spite of the fact that the existing houses are already old? This may be a symptom of what is often called "arrested development." It may lead either to absorption by commercial and industrial uses, or development again of a community with "eyesores."

Is the community in the path of an outward spread of industry from the center of town—along some railroad, highway, river, and so forth?

Are there specific nuisances: odors from factories, water or sewer seepage, traffic, noise, airports, and so forth? Often the present inhabitants are a good source of information about this.

Is the community "homogeneous"? It is generally argued that the more so, the better. If this means homogeneity of interests, occupations, or educational backgrounds, there may be some truth to this. If it means restriction to certain racial groups or narrow income levels, it may well not be true and may reflect a type of snobbishness among the people in the community which would prove most undesirable. How much difference, and of what kinds, is optimal for a good neighborhood, is difficult to say, but living only with people with the same occupation and income seems likely to be as boring as would living among people with whom one had nothing in common. Some people suggest visiting the community between 4 and 6 PM on a weekday to observe the fathers and children coming home.

Finally, can you afford the neighbors? In terms of peace of mind, it is probably better to be slightly better off than your neighbors, and it is certainly dangerous to think that you can live cheaply in a wealthy neighborhood. Even if the parents can resist the temptation to take up golf, skiing, yachting, and giving lavish parties, the children are likely to feel the pressure to conform.

What do consumers typically do in choosing a community? We have very little empirical evidence here. We do know that people regard the community as a major factor in choosing a house, and because there are so few houses up for sale at any one time, their choice of a house is likely to be primarily a choice of a community. However, many people buy a house after a rather short period of looking around, often because they are moving in from out of town and need a place for their family to live.

On the other hand, people even get used to slum communities and do not like to leave them.[31] And even when they do not like the community, they do little about it.

To an extent unbelievable to those who have not investigated it, many people are passive-minded, letting things be done to them, hardly thinking of what they could get done, if they would cooperate with their neighbors and fellow citizens.[32]

Summary

In his choices whether to buy a house and in which community the consumer is constrained by circumstance to make decisions in ways adverse to long-range economic trends, buying in inflation and renting in depression. He does not have stability of income or location to permit him to buy a house in the depression, and renting is relatively cheaper then anyway. He

is forced to buy during an inflation.   He finds it difficult to get
accurate and unbiased information about houses, house prices,
or communities.   He is constrained by society and the building
codes to put his money into fireplaces, trim, landscaping, and
archaic plumbing and construction methods.   If he has a family, his housing needs vary over his lifetime, but he finds it
physically and emotionally difficult to move to suitable quarters
each time his family changes.   He does not feel adequate to
judge architecture; yet, he has an uneasy feeling about what is
described as newest and best in the field.   If his income is low
and uncertain, he may be unwilling to put enough into rent to
secure "decent" quarters, but may find it only too easy to buy
more of a house than he can easily manage.   Most important of
all, he is concerned about his neighborhood and city but can
do very little to control what happens to them.   He has a feeling that housing costs too much, that slums are a menace to be
eliminated, that cities need better layout and planning, but does
not see what can be done about it.

HOUSING AND THE COMMUNITY AS SOCIAL PROBLEMS

Introduction: The Problems

As in the case of medical care, inadequate housing is regarded
as a public problem because what others do affect us too.   It
is generally recognized that inadequate housing can affect the
health and productivity of people, and that concentrations of
bad housing can help produce crime and delinquency, though
the evidence is not always conclusive.   There is also some feeling that there should be some minimum level of decency in
housing below which people should not have to live.   There
are differences of opinion as to what this level is.   The advocates of public housing have standards which include not only
adequate protection from the elements and rudimentary possibilities for sanitation, but such "extras" as inside toilets, hot
and cold running water, privacy, and such "amenities," to use
the British term, as playgrounds, storage space, clothes drying
space, and so forth.

Even if we accept some minimum standards of housing and communities, there can be a difference of opinion as to how they are to be achieved, whether by compulsion, economic inducements, education, or what. Should one work on the supply side to eliminate sub-standard conditions and increase the supply or reduce the price of adequate housing, or should one by education and income redistribution ensure that demand with funds to pay is present? Since the various methods usually involve different costs written into the government budgets, and different amounts of redistribution of income, a great deal of the argument has to do not with the realities of the problem or the decision as to what is essential, but on the relative degree of government interference and the degree to which poorer people are indirectly subsidized by the provision of low rent or cheap housing. The more one is willing to induce people to move to better quarters by such bribes as subsidized low rents, the more indirect and less oppressive the interference of the government, some feel. But others argue that the exercise of police powers to enforce minimum housing standards is less noxious than to have government competing with private house builders and owners of rental real estate for customers.

To add to the confusion, not only are we talking both about inadequate housing as such, and of concentrations of inadequate housing in slums and blighted areas, but we are also concerned about some problems of urban communities which arise because of their layout even where the physical housing of people is adequate. We shall first look at housing, then at the problems of slum clearance, urban redevelopment, and city planning.

Housing as a National Problem

The over-all statistics about housing show substantial progress over the last 60 years and indicate that bad housing involves a rather small proportion of the total houses. This does not mean that it is not a problem, of course. The 1950 Census of Housing reveals the following: [33]

Since 1890 there has been an increase in population of 16 per cent every ten years, and an increase in the number of occupied dwelling units of 22 per cent every ten years. This has meant an increase in the amount of housing per person which reduced the average number of people per dwelling unit from 5 to 3½. A substantial building boom was showing its effects already by 1950, with one-fifth of the houses standing in 1950 having been built in 1940 or later. There were 55 per cent more home owners in 1950 than in 1940. The homes showed substantial improvements in that the proportion with

	increased from: in 1940	to: in 1950
Private flush toilet	60%	71%
Bathtub or shower	56	69
Electric lights	79	84
Mechanical refrigeration	44	80
Radio	83	96

On the other hand there were signs that some problems remained:

Six and two-tenths per cent of the dwelling units still had more than 1½ people per room in 1950, indicating overcrowding. If we set a standard that says that an adequate dwelling should not be dilapidated and should have hot and cold running water, a bathtub or shower, and an inside flush toilet not shared with anyone, only 64 per cent of the dwelling units met the standard in 1950, so that one could still say that one-third of the nation was ill-housed. The proportion of married couples sharing dwellings with other people was 6.8 per cent in 1940 and still 6.6 per cent in 1950 indicating some doubling up, though not so much as the 9 per cent in 1947. Finally, as compared with 28 per cent in 1890, 44 per cent of the 1950 home owners had a mortgage on their home. Table 17, from the 1954 Survey of Consumer Finances, indicates, in addition to the general ownership picture, that if we include single persons living with relatives, we have some 10 per cent of the spending units of the country living with relatives (related secondaries). In addition to this there are another 3 per cent who are roomers and boarders in the homes of strangers (unrelated secondaries).

Clearly, it is possible to be either proud or concerned, depending on how one looks at the facts. A comparison with the per cent of people in England with mechanical refrigerators or central heat, for instance, makes us look well-off indeed. It is also probably true that some people are willing to spend more on housing than others within the same income levels. In 1952 the average renting family paid less than $50 a month, excluding utilities, for rent.

Table 23 shows for each family income group the median rent paid by the non-farm renters in that group, and the median house value for non-farm home owners. Family income is used because, if two related spending units live together, their combined income is a better indicator of what they could spend on housing than the income of either one alone. What the table clearly shows is that renters in most income groups are spending less for housing than home owners. This can be seen as follows: Allow 4½ per cent of house value as interest on the investment in a home—whether paid on a mortgage or foregone because money is invested in the house instead of an income earning asset—plus 1 per cent for property taxes, 1 per cent for depreciation, and one-half per cent for upkeep and repairs. These add to 7 per cent of the value of the house, and are a rock-bottom estimate of costs that does not even allow for heat and other utilities, which are included in many rent payments. In the income group $4,000–4,999, the median house is worth $9,060, and for this house minimum costs are $634 per year or $53 per month. The median renter in this income group pays $48 per month, probably plus a few minor utilities. Other tabulations show that only 13 per cent of the non-farm renters put 30 per cent or more of their income after taxes into rent.

In spite of everything we might say about how some people could afford decent housing if they would stop smoking or drinking or wasting their money, the fact remains that there are some rather tight limits on the amount of money a family can

safely spend on housing, and there are some people with incomes too low to afford what most of us regard as decent housing.

TABLE 23

MEDIAN RENT PAID BY RENTERS AND MEDIAN VALUE OF HOMES OWNED BY
HOME OWNERS IN EACH FAMILY INCOME LEVEL IN EARLY 1954 [1]

(NON-FARM)

| Family Income | Median Rent | | Median House Value [2] |
	Monthly	Annual	
Less than $1,000	$26	$312	$4,850
$1,000–1,999	32	384	4,150
2,000–2,999	35	425	6,000
3,000–3,999	43	516	7,370
4,000–4,999	48	576	9,060
5,000–7,499	57	684	10,775
7,500–9,999	75	900	12,225
10,000 or more	99	1,188	16,975
All Incomes	$46	$552	$8,950 [3]

[1] Data from 1954 Survey of Consumer Finances. Income is for the whole
family, including related secondary spending units, for the entire previous year,
1953.

[2] These medians are interpolated from bracket data; hence, subject to additional small errors of interpolation.

[3] This is a median correctly estimated from detailed data, though still subject
to sampling and response errors.

Inadequate housing has attracted the most attention when it
has been concentrated in slums or blighted areas in cities,
partly because it is more noticeable there, and partly, perhaps,
because the closer people are together, the more things like personal cleanliness and adequate sewage disposal become important. The statistics, however, indicate that the proportion of
homes that are below standard is much higher in farm areas
than anywhere else. (See Table 24.)

It is also possible to argue that housing is a problem because
of the lack of rental housing in sufficient quantity to take care
of those who prefer to rent. Certainly many people have been

"forced" to buy a home since the war. Each year some 38 per cent of the young people between the ages of 20 and 24 move, and there is some scattered evidence that most families do most of their moving during the first ten years after the family is formed.[34] This is the stage in life where families have the least free cash to invest in a house and can least afford possible capital losses if they have to move and to sell the house. The amount of rental housing managed by banks and large financial institutions has remained small except in the large cities, and there mostly it has been in the form of large apartment buildings. It is possible that the management of rental properties is so complicated and depends so much on personal relations with tenants that large-scale rental real estate is uneconomic.[35] It is certainly reasonable to believe that a man who owns his own home will be more careful with it and will do a great deal to keep it in repair without calling for expensive outside help.

TABLE 24

PERCENTAGE OF HOMES WITH HOT WATER, PRIVATE TOILET, AND BATH,
AND NOT DILAPIDATED

By Region of the Country		By Place (Urban-Rural)	
Northeast	78%	Urban	78%
North central	61	Rural non-farm	45
South	45	Rural farm	23
West	78		

Source: 1950 Census of Housing, U.S. Summary, Table 7, Bureau of the Census, U.S. Department of Commerce, Washington, U.S. Gov't Printing Office, 1953.

Whether rented or owned, there is a strong belief in this country that housing costs too much. The blame has usually been placed on the house-construction industry with its inefficiencies, monopolies, and various restrictions on progress. It is also true, however, that the cost of the land and improvements is substantial, and that the taxes and interest charges are a substantial part of the costs of owning a house. Let us look at interest, taxes, land costs, and then the cost of house building.

You have seen that monthly mortgage payments depend not only on the amount borrowed, but also on the interest rate, and the duration of the repayment period. In the past twenty years, the federal government's and the Federal Reserve System's interest rate policy, coupled with the insuring of home loans by the Federal Housing Authority and the Veterans' Administration, has led to some reductions in the interest rate paid on loans. There has also been a tendency in recent years to use more long-period mortgages of 25 or 30 years. This reduces the monthly payments by reducing the consumer's forced saving rather than cutting the real costs of housing. In Connecticut, Chester Bowles managed to get through a "non-subsidized" housing program where, by using the state's credit, the interest charged on mortgage loans made by the state, including administrative costs and fees, was reduced to 1½ per cent. On a $10,000, 25-year mortgage, this reduces the monthly charges by $12.37 per month.

Taxes are a problem, not only because they are a substantial cost to the home owner—and indirectly to the renter—but also because of great inequities in their assessment. Property taxes are charged as some percentage of "assessed valuation," which though it may be only a fraction of true market value, is supposed to be the same fraction as other properties, at least in your neighborhood. But even this is not true except in the larger and better administered cities. It is always difficult to re-assess properties, so assessments are seldom changed. This leads to a strong tendency during periods of inflation for assessing new houses (relative to their market value) higher than old houses but seldom reducing assessments on older houses as they depreciate.

Furthermore, property taxes are levied by cities, townships, school districts, and counties. The taxes may vary a good deal depending on the political jurisdiction where you live. This raises problems which we shall discuss later. In general, however, property taxes account for the vast bulk of the revenue of local governments and serve to make housing expensive in the process.   If more reliance were placed on income or sales taxes, housing would be cheaper, though it might be some time before rents came down.

Land is expensive primarily because of the improvements necessary to make it suitable for residential use: streets, sewers, water, gas, electricity, schools, fire protection, and so forth. Aside from increased efficiencies that would result from filling up one area completely before starting others, there seems to be little chance for reducing these costs.   Large-scale builders achieve economies here, of course, by putting all the improvements into an area at once, and filling it so that there are no empty lots and no excess capacity in the utilities.   Unfortunately, there is a strong tendency to try to reduce land costs by crowding houses together, even in isolated rural developments. At the same time, there is a tendency for scattered developments to spring up all around the outskirts of a city, and demand service from the city's utilities.   This is a rather inefficient way to expand a city, particularly because these developments may move out along a highway with few houses but long distances for the utilities to be carried.   The extreme case is what the British refer to as "ribbon development" where a road between two towns is completely built up, but only for one or two lots deep from the road.   Traffic is slowed, utilities are expensive, and the esthetic impact is often dismal.   Equally dismal are the motley mixtures of industrial, commercial, residential, and indescribable uses mixed up in the unzoned areas near many factories which have been put up out in the country.

The possibilities for reduction in any of these housing costs seem rather small, and we are left with the question whether anything can be done about the cost of the house itself.   Volumes have been written on this subject, and we can only provide an overview here.   Aside from some small programs of research by the government and by colleges, notably the University of Illinois, and the activities of some large-scale builders such as Mr. Levitt, little has been accomplished in reducing the cost of the house itself.   The consumer has insisted on a house with special features and different design from his neighbors, and he has insisted on an increasingly complex house with more and more plumbing and wiring, and more elaborate and automatic equipment. Attempts to produce and market prefabricated houses have not been successful, partly because the economies were not great, and partly because marketing proved extremely difficult.[36] People tend to feel that prefabrication means lower quality. Local builders and real estate salesmen foster this belief and make it difficult to find lots on which these houses can be put. The local building trades also fear them and prefer to work on traditional custom-built houses. As a result, it is usually only a rather stubborn and enterprising consumer who can save money this way. Recently, producers of partially prefabricated houses seem to be having more success. They make extensive use of local craftsmen at the building site, but achieve economies by concentrating on a few floor plans and by using a system for precutting lumber.

As the "housing industry" is now organized, it is difficult to see how the costs of houses could be reduced without coordination and monopolization of the whole industry. The reasons are simple: A house is made up of many parts and requires many services including financing and utilities. No one of these is any substantial part of the cost of the final product. In almost all of them, there are fewer sellers than buyers. An increase in the amount charged by any one supplier or any one labor union would increase the price of the whole house by only a small percentage, and could not be resisted by the many individual house buyers or builders even if they wanted to. Housing is usually built in periods of prosperity, and new houses are such a small addition to the total supply, that the demand is likely to be rather insensitive to price changes even when the price of the whole house is affected substantially. This seems to be particularly true when people believe that the increases in price are permanent.

There are, of course, restrictive devices used by the unions, and there is less price competition among suppliers of materials than many would like to see. The building codes aid and abet these restrictions while adding some unnecessary ones of their own. But the basic economics of the situation are such as to foster all these things. Periodic booms, demands for each service or material which are quite insensitive to price, general resistance to new methods, plus the complex array of different suppliers of materials and services make it difficult to build low cost houses.

Even if the prices of houses were raised by increased charges for various component elements to the point where people were really excluded from the market, there is nothing any of the unions or materials suppliers can do. The only things that keep this whole situation from resulting in completely unreasonable prices for houses are the desire of contractors to get enough volume to make money, and the fact that there are substitutes for some processes and some materials, and competition among the suppliers of some materials. One of the most comprehensive studies of the housing industry concluded that a many-pronged program is needed, including: [37]

Control of the price of land to avoid speculative subdividing
Larger producing organizations
Reducing marketing costs—more rentals
Reducing financing costs
Some public housing
Reducing operating costs by quality construction and better financing methods.

On the other hand, one recent study in the San Francisco Bay area led its author to conclude that the inefficiencies of house-building had been exaggerated, and that for a representative house, removing the restrictions of unions, building codes, and so forth might allow a 7 per cent decrease in cost or $650 at the outside.[38] Assessing all possibilities for increased efficiency, the author concluded that we might have a "realistic hope" of achieving a gain of 20 per cent in efficiency.[39] It is not clear whether even this gain would require the building of standardized houses which do not take account of what individuals want in their house. Building standardized houses almost certainly results in substantial saving in costs. One of the difficulties with house construction is that houses are all different, and are built in three dimensions from very inadequate two-dimensional blueprints. The proportion of an ordinary house which is built two or three times before it is right is rather large. Even honest builders who have no thought of trying to cheat on the specifications tend to give higher bids where there is an architect, because the architect will insist on following every detail of the blueprints whether it is important or not, and this increases the amount of "double-building" and the delays.

Given a stock of existing houses which is, by some standards, inadequate, construction of new houses cannot have any very large or rapid effect, because they only amount to an addition of 1 or 2 per cent each year. New houses are generally purchased by high income people, and there is some doubt as to the efficacy of the "filtering down" process whereby the dwellings vacated by those who buy new houses are occupied by lower income people, and the dwellings vacated by these people occupied by still poorer people, and so forth. The old houses of the wealthy are often not designed for the poor, and when cut up into many small apartments, they become rather poor places to live. Housing which does not have all the desired plumbing, and so forth, can, of course, be brought up to date, and a great deal of this has been done. Additions and repairs to existing houses paid for directly by consumers have been running around seven billion dollars a year, according to the Surveys of Consumer Finances. In 1953, 40 per cent of non-farm families, and 58 per cent of non-farm homeowning families made such expenditures.

Community Problems

But housing is more than a house. What people want is not just a roof, heat, running water, and a kitchen, but also a place in the community. It has already been pointed out how the value of a house itself depends on what happens to the community. Some communities provide more and better services than others and charge more taxes. The services are almost always worth more than the taxes cost; hence land is worth more in these communities. The author's brother was once in a co-operative which purchased and divided some land for home building. Of the 40 votes in the corporation, 21 belonged to people who wanted to hold the land for speculation and not to invest any more money in it, and 19 belonged to people who wanted to build homes. A deadlock persisted for nearly two years until one stormy night when only 18 of the 21 came out. The 19 who wanted to build voted through provisions for streets, sewers, water, and so forth. Before this time, the value of the lots had remained almost constant. Within a year after, the values had doubled and tripled, out of all proportion to any possible charges for these improvements.

The community problems which have attracted most attention, however, have not been inadequate services of some communities, but the high taxes, concentrations of bad housing, traffic congestion, parking problems, inadequate control of new developments, and inappropriate tax jurisdictions. Older cities, with growing problems of old inadequate housing, crowding, and so forth find it generally impossible to incorporate the growing suburbs into their jurisdiction. The people outside the city earn their living in the city, contribute to its traffic problems, but pay their taxes elsewhere. As more and more people drive to work, traffic and parking become serious problems, and the public transportation system has difficulty both in competing for use of the streets, and in getting enough business to remain solvent. The city then spends great sums of money to widen streets and to build parking structures, which increases the automobile traffic, decreases the revenues of the public transportation system, and leads to still more traffic and demands for more expressways and parking lots. The taxes are raised in the city, and more and more people, together with some industrial firms, move out of town.

As the suburbs get larger, and the people start to demand the same sort of services—schools, parks, fire and police protection, and so forth—as in the large cities, the taxes increase rapidly. Some people seek to achieve pleasant living without high taxes by moving outside the jurisdiction of any town. Here they generally have to put in their own water wells, septic tanks, and so forth. As these areas become more thickly settled, frequently, these independent systems do not work well. Neighbors are pumping out of the same limited water supply, and counting on the same drainage system to take their sewage. Usually, there is no governmental authority over these developments until the county health officer decides something is threatening to go wrong.

Sometimes areas become completely enclosed by a city, but maintain their own government, schools, police, fire department, and so forth and manage to keep their taxes down. This involves a type of exploitation of the rest of the city, of course, because these people use its business and shopping districts, contribute to its traffic and downtown parking problems.

Speculative subdivisions have in the past led to other troubles. Much more land was subdivided around cities than could ever be used. The city was induced to put in streets, sewers, and water mains. When it became evident, as it did after 1929, that these subdivisions were premature, the speculators, who had put very little money into their real estate, let the lands be taken over by the city for unpaid taxes. But the city had no use for the land, and it was frequently a difficult legal problem even to take clear possession. The special assessments for the costly improvements were a claim only on the land, not on its owner; hence, they could not be collected.[40] Some such areas were partly built up, but by the time conditions were ripe for another housing boom, the area was frequently "blighted" and the existing houses were too old to blend well with new houses. Of course, this is a very expensive and inefficient way for a city to develop.

The older areas within cities generally become inadequate, either through wear and tear, or through changing standards of what is adequate space, plumbing, or architecture. Many of these areas are conveniently located, but they frequently continue to decline over the years.[41] To some extent this is because it does not pay an individual owner to fix up his property if others do not. Partly, it is because redevelopment would necessitate assembly of lands now owned by many people in order to re-plan the area. A common charge is that properties in such areas are owned by banks and rich people and churches who will make huge profits either by renting substandard quarters or by selling at a big profit to the redevelopment agency. An extensive study by the National Housing Agency of the slum lands bought by the Federal Government for housing and slum clearance indicated, however, that of the total payments for these slum properties including payments to mortgage holders less than 3 per cent went to non-profit organizations (including churches) and less than 10 per cent to financial institutions.[42] In terms of amounts, less than 2 per cent of the recipients received $10,000 or more and two-thirds received less than $3,000. Of course, older cities in the northeast had more institutional or non-profit organization owners, but the major finding prevailed everywhere, that is, that slums are owned by a large number of private individuals. Indeed, that is one of the reasons they have become slums. The problem is that too many different people own the land, and acquiring enough for redeveloping an area is a difficult task. Even aside from legal powers and financing there is the task of securing clear title to each piece of land. One authority on land acquisition reports the following story:

The average layman has no idea of the vast horde of detail involved in the clearing of titles to real estate. One lawyer in New Orleans who had been advised that his abstract did not go back far enough, wrote of his title search as follows: "My abstract shows the title from the United States to the Present Time; the United States got it from France as part of the Louisiana Purchase; France got it from Spain by right of conquest; Spain got it by right of discovery, having financed the venture of Mr. Columbus; the King of Spain got his authority by being a descendant in the succession of St. Peter;

St. Peter got his authority from God, and God created the earth."
This is probably a slight exaggeration of some of the involved work
of our title experts.[43]

Many problems arise because of the conflicts between the
powers of governments and the legal rights of private land owners. Governments have the right to exercise police powers in
regulating what individuals can do with their property when
it will endanger the public safety or welfare. They can take
land under the powers of eminent domain for public purposes.

Redevelopment acts have been passed in many states in recent
years to allow land to be taken in condemnation proceedings
under eminent domain, even if the redevelopment is later done
by private firms to whom the land is sold. The Urban Land
Institute in a release dated July 1, 1951 estimated that thirty-
four states, the District of Columbia, and Hawaii have some
form of "Urban Redevelopment legislation." [44] Most of these
are enabling laws which allow the cities to set up redevelopment
corporations which can assemble lands, and sell or lease the land
to private developers. The constitutionality of these laws is in
doubt in some states as yet.

In any event, condemnation proceedings are costly and time
consuming. It may take a year or more to secure title. There
may be many different small properties, each requiring legal
action. Property owners, once they discover that some large
organization, government or private, is after their land, usually
make excessive demands, and the courts have an unfortunate
habit of splitting the difference between these demands and the
realistic estimates of the appraisers. The problems are so great
that even where the law allows condemnation, an attempt is
usually made to buy up the land secretly through a series of
agents, reserving condemnation for a few hold-outs. The New
York Port Authority has done this, much to the annoyance of
property owners who later feel that they could have gouged the
buyer for much more money had they only known who was
buying. Most of the large housing developments by insurance
companies have also used this method of acquisition.

In many states the redevelopment laws do not provide adequate legal powers or adequate financing arrangements. Local governments can also levy special assessments, usually on a front-foot basis, to pay for such locally beneficial improvements as streets, sidewalks, sewers. Some places, such as Kansas City, have used a concentric series of zones with different levels of assessment, to pay for a new park at the center of the zones.

But the private property owner is still master of his own property. He can resist pleas to sell. He can cause delays up to two years in the courts if the land is condemned and still end up getting far more than the land is worth. He can resist having his land included in the city, at the same time that he is requesting city water, or school privileges, or sewer service. He can hold land empty for years in the (often vain) hope of getting all his money out of it, including taxes, interest, and so forth. He can resist changes in zoning, or request and often get variations in the zoning to allow him to do what he wants to. Indeed, it is hard to resist the feeling, particularly after reading the history of land speculations, or of the difficulties in slum clearance, that the ownership of land brings out avarice, suspicion, and intolerance in people.

Owners resist changes which they feel will reduce the value of their property, or increase their taxes, often without really examining the facts. Since almost any change in a city is likely to affect property values slightly all over the city, there is almost sure to be some group of owners who feel they will take a loss in the process.

Government Efforts toward Better Housing and Communities

The larger and older cities have been seen as the focus of many housing and community problems, partly because these problems are more serious there, and partly because they are more noticeable. Some observers have suggested that there are too many people, and that the solution is to have them spread out in smaller cities through decentralization.[45] More commonly, however, people have realized that big cities are here to stay and have sought methods of improving them. We have already mentioned local zoning powers and redevelopment corporations. Very little has been accomplished by either. In some places, such as Baltimore, and more recently Trenton, drives have been conducted to enforce the "tenement house laws," using the police powers of governments to insist on minimum standards. But for the most part, any substantial improvement requires sums of money beyond the capacity of local governments or individual property owners.

Title 1 of the Housing Act of 1949 provides for loans and grants to facilitate redevelopment. Redevelopment generally involves purchase of an area, clearing off the old buildings, and then selling the land at a loss to someone who will develop it, because local governments usually do not want to go into the business of real estate development. The act provides for loans, because tremendous amounts of capital are involved, and the Federal Government will also pay two-thirds of the loss involved. Since the local government is credited with the value of parks, streets, improvements, and manpower used in clearing, most of the financial cost is actually borne by the federal governments. Some striking redevelopments such as that on the "point" in Pittsburgh have thus been facilitated.[46]

There are some who feel that the Pittsburgh development illustrates a trend not all to the good—a good idea perverted. They argue that when slum clearance involves housing improvement, it really helps the consumer, but that when run-down residential-business areas are redeveloped and used for business and commercial purposes, the justification for subsidy becomes more dubious. They argue that it was a mistake to have talked about slum clearance, when what was needed was better housing.[47]

An interesting question in any case is why it should require a subsidy to facilitate redevelopment. If land is being used for an inferior purpose, it should actually be profitable to redevelop it and use it more efficiently, provided that it can be purchased at a reasonable price. Of course, our condemnation proceedings frequently make it difficult to assemble land at a reasonable price. Also, land and property taxes are so arranged in many places that it is frequently profitable to use valuable land for unimportant purposes. A piece of urban land with a "taxpayer" on it (one-story inexpensive building) may have such low taxes that it is as profitable as the same land with a big building, more investment, higher assessments, and higher taxes. In some areas, perhaps housing is not the most efficient or profitable use for the land, and some authorities have argued that housing projects should be placed in inexpensive fringe lands, letting land values drop in the slums until they could be bought up and redeveloped without such great losses to the profit of the existing owners. Nathan Straus, the former Federal Housing Administrator, is a leading proponent of this view.

From 1941 to 1950 there was a kind of subsidy for commercial rental housing developments in the notorious Section 608 of the National Housing Act. The law limited the loan to 90 per cent of the estimated value of the property, including "other miscellaneous charges incidental to construction." These "miscellaneous charges" were interpreted to include 10 per cent for profit, 5 per cent for architectural fees, and 5 per cent for overhead. The net result of this plus liberal appraisals was that a man might get a loan of $900,000 on a project that cost $300,000 to build. He might build it and pocket the difference, or he might sell out the right to the loan for a quick profit. Furthermore, he only had to pay income tax on his profit as a capital gain rather than income, that is with a maximum tax rate of 26 per cent. Individuals have been known to have made windfalls of as much as $500,000 with an investment of as little as $1,000. Of a total of 7,032 projects, 1,149 made windfalls which totaled nearly $80,000,000.[48] Nathan Straus pointed this out in a book published in 1952:

The FHA has become a government agency unique in American history. Established to assist developers to erect low rent, limited-dividend housing, the agency has been converted into a mechanism for providing high-rent housing and fantastic profits for speculative builders.[49]

He adds that since the government loans the money and since only the land is liable for such debts, not the developers, the government is taking all the risk, too. Until recently the trade associations of builders and real estate men generally opposed all federal slum clearance and housing activity, but recently the National Association of Home Builders issued a statement highly in favor of slum clearance.

Any public improvement raises problems of equity, because it often involves increasing property values nearby, for example Central Park in New York, or the new United Nations development. Historically, there have been some attempts to recapture some of these gains by "excess condemnation," that is buying up a whole area, putting in the new improvements, and selling the extra land at a profit. Most of these attempts have been financial failures because of the high costs of condemnation and bad historical timing (just before a depression). The whole procedure is probably illegal in most areas of this country.

The 1937 and 1949 Housing Acts provided loans and direct subsidies from the federal government to localities for low cost housing. The local governments usually add to the subsidy through exemption or partial exemption from local taxes. This plus an annual federal payment limited to $3\frac{1}{2}$ per cent each year of the total cost, for 40 years, allows lower rents than any self-supporting project could provide. Even in some large-scale private housing developments, local governments have made special tax arrangements which amounted to a subsidy. The effects of all this on consumers are mixed. In the case of low rent housing, there is an improvement in housing immediately for those who get into the projects, and a type of income redistribution in their favor. Others as equally bad off are left out. In the case of some of the commercial projects, the housing is not low rent, and the subsidy becomes a subsidy for some middle and upper-middle income people, with some possible filtering of benefits down to those who occupy the apartments they vacate.

All in all, then, it seems difficult to force people to pay for their own adequate housing and most of the systems of subsidizing or bribing them have their drawbacks and erratic effects. The most efficient, direct methods of providing low rent housing involve putting the government into the construction and real estate management business, but still leave many problems.

On the other hand, it must be remembered that enthusiasts for better housing have overdone its importance. It is doubtful that bad housing is more than an intensifier of other more basic problems. Indeed, a famous study in Great Britain showed that when people were taken from slums and moved to more adequate housing, their health became *worse*.[50] The authors concluded that this happened because the people were forced to spend more of their meager incomes on rent and had less left for adequate food.

In general, there has been a tremendous volume of writing, many city plans printed and planning agencies set up, and not very much accomplished.

The hopes of city planners have been great; the general body of citizens has given rather lukewarm support. In actual practice very serious limitations have been encountered. First of all, there are very few chances to plan new cities from the start. For the most part we are restricted to the expensive task of remodeling existing cities. . . . Sometimes those who deal in real estate wish to have a plan which will aid them in their business but not do much else. Sometimes ambitious public officials promote the development of expensive ornamental features when there are many more urgent works at hand. Because of the plurality of governmental units . . . there is usually no single authority with power to make and enforce plans for an entire metropolitan district.[51]

Another authority concludes a study of the lower east side of New York with a

. . . question as to the kinds of urban land use that might replace slums on the thousands of acres now covered by low-quality housing in American cities—the kinds of land use which, in any system of private or public accounting, would be compatible with the typically high land prices caused by false expectations and fortified by tax assessments.[52]

It is difficult to resist the feeling that subsidized housing for the relatively few lucky or poor enough to get into it is not an answer to the problem of inducing a supply of adequate housing and being sure that people will and can afford to use it. Higher incomes and social security will help a great deal, and any method of increasing the supply of adequate housing or decreasing the supply of substandard housing will contribute.

Housing and Town and Country Planning in Great Britain

Many of the problems in this field are more serious in an older country like Great Britain. The British have been building subsidized public housing for thirty years, and it is estimated that one dwelling out of every seven in the United Kingdom today is publicly built and owned.[53] Under the 1946 New Towns Act, whole new towns were developed by development corporations with their own industry, schools, and so forth.

However, when it came to any development or redevelopment, there existed in Great Britain a law of compensation which said that, if any operation of the government could be shown to have reduced the value of a man's property, the relevant government authority could be made to compensate him. This led to difficulties because of the financial costs of such claims. It was particularly difficult if you wanted to zone the outskirts of a city to preserve some open area and concentrate the urban spread in a few well-planned and efficient developments. Property owners all around the city would insist that development was coming their way, and the total claims for compensation would be far greater than any possible actual gains in land values. While the law also said that *increases* in property values resulting from government action could be taken by the government in "betterment charges," somewhat akin to our special assessments, in actual practice these gains were so difficult to prove and took so long to be realized in cash, that few were ever collected.[54]

An attempt was made to get out of this impasse by the passage

of the 1947 Town and Country Planning Act. This act provided that no one could make any substantial change in the
use to which he put his land without permission and the payment of a development charge, representing the increase in
land value from the change in use. Since land was already selling at prices that took account of development possibilities, 300
million pounds were appropriated as "compensation" for this
expropriation of the right to develop land at will. The theory
was that land would be bought and sold at its "existing use
value" and could be taken at this value if needed for new developments. Also, rezoning was to be made painless because
no compensation need be paid, and no betterment was collected
except upon development of the land. In the words of the
Minister of Local Government and Planning, this "power to
plan without continual fear of compensation which crippled
pre-war efforts, has made it possible for the first time to allocate
land to the best advantage." [55]

In Great Britain the arguments had to do largely with the
adequacy of the compensation payment fund of 300 million
pounds—arguments both that it was too small and that it was
too large. In this country reactions varied from *Time,* which
called it socialization of the land, to the *Harvard Law Review,*
which pointed out that drastic land-use planning was possible
before the act, and is just as possible in this country.[56] The
first reaction is wrong because private property in land remained, as well as profits from proper care and use. The second reaction is irrelevant because powers to do things which
cause financial injury to a few without compensation are unlikely to be exercised. The history of attempts to improve zoning in American cities and the difficulty of achieving any redevelopment without tremendous subsidies make this clear.

In actual practice landowners in Britain refused to sell at
"existing use value," being stubborn as landowners usually are.
There was a shortage of materials and of housing, so that any
developer who got permission to develop and build houses was
perfectly willing to pay both the development charge and a

price for the land greater than its existing use value. In this situation, the Central Land Board could either assess development charges that were less than the difference between existing use value and land value with right to develop, or could stop development. As a legal commentator put it:

> On the question of values, we are at present in an unhappy state where there is a chasm between theory and practice. In theory, the act should have caused a market depreciation in the value of land which has any potentialities of development. The liability for development charges, and the risk of compulsory acquisition at the new levels of compensation, should have had the effect of reducing the value of a plot of building land from say £500 per acre to £50. However, that has not happened in practice.[57]

If instead of trying to arbitrate between the landowner and the developer, the Central Land Board had simply taken land at its existing use value and auctioned it off to developers, the system might have worked, but such stern measures were never taken. The final consequence of this inability to enforce the law was the abandonment of development charges, and probably will ultimately lead to cancellation of payment of the 300 million pounds compensation and a return to the old methods with all their difficulties.[58]

Summary

Problems of housing and the community are many and complex, and it seems clear that there are no simple answers. Indeed, it is not even always clear what is really wanted—whether it is simply physically clean and "adequate" housing, or much more than this. The consumer needs to be aware of these problems. Even if you can do little to change the course of events or to repair the damages of past mistakes, you can understand and predict in order to avoid mistakes in solving your own housing problem.

Even without such laws to help, any sort of long-range planning and zoning would prevent for the future the sort of costly legacy of the past that is existing today. But it would also put great power in the hands of a group of planners, who could only be effective if they could act in secrecy so that the speculators would not take advantage of the situation. Whether there ever could be developed such bodies of honest and trusted officials who could avoid major problems of future land use without dictating irrelevant details, and who would never make private profit for themselves or their friends, seems doubtful in view of the history of the F.H.A. Something might be done short of this to zone the open areas outside cities.

Where development of open lands is involved, and where problems of assembly of large tracts in one ownership can be solved, another hopeful development has been the entry of large-scale developers including insurance companies. When very large areas are developed, the developer has a real incentive to secure proper layout, traffic arteries, shopping districts, space for schools and parks, and so forth.

Perhaps the most important fact the consumer needs remember is that while the law may say he owns "private property," his property is not really private. His property's value depends on what others do with their property, and on the degree to which the owners co-operate to provide services they all need. He can only avoid the necessity for such co-operation, and for suffering perhaps the avarice and stubbornness of other landowners, if he is willing to move into the country and forego many advantages as well. If he manages to find adequate housing that he can afford in a pleasant community, he will be doing well.

SUGGESTED PROJECTS

1. Visit the office of the city or county planning commission, and see what you can find out about:
   Present zoning laws
   Zoning board, proportion of requests for rezoning refused
   Tax structure and the various tax jurisdictions
   The legal powers of the planning commission
   Major problems the planning commission sees in your community.

2. Visit the office of the property tax assessor. Ask some of the following questions:

How are assessed values arrived at? Does the assessor get inside the houses? Does he rely heavily on square feet of floor space or on exterior materials used?

Does the assessor get current information on the prices at which houses are actually being sold? How does he use this information?

Are the records kept in such a way that one can look up an address and find the assessed value?

Would it be possible, and would the assessor like to have you do the detailed work for him, to check the sale prices of the last 100 pieces of property sold (either through the realtors or through the federal transfer tax stamps on the deeds) against the assessments?

What is the average ratio of assessed value to current market prices? Is the ratio different for business or industrial property from what it is for residential property?

3. Make a study of real estate valuation, in one of two ways:

(A) Either take a sample of the blocks in your city, and a sample of three houses in each block, and check (a) assessed value, (b) the last recorded deed for tax stamps to estimate price—adjusted afterward for changing price levels, (c) if possible, the owner's own estimate of what the house would sell for, (d) an estimate of the number of square feet of floor space, excluding basement, and of the age of the house. Relate the ratio of assessed to market value to such things as the section of town, age of the house, number of years since the last time it was sold, and actual size of the house.

(B) Or, alternatively, take a sample of the last few deeds recorded noting the number of federal tax stamps affixed, and check the assessed value, and realtor's information files, if any. Visit the property and ask the owner what he thinks the house would sell for, how old the house is, and how many square feet of floor space it has.

4. Write a book review of any of the books referred to at the end of the chapter. Particularly good books for this purpose are those by:

Mabel Walker, ed.
Nathan Straus,

and   "The Uthwatt Report"
                       "The Barlow Report."

5. Select a new house which is being started. Visit it at least
once a week, talking with the workmen, contractor, owner, and so
forth. Why does the house end up costing so much? Do the various people involved in the construction agree on this?

6. Go through recent issues of magazines and newspapers for
sample house plans. Select ten and make a critical appraisal of
each. Check such things as:

Is the living room a major passageway from some rooms to
others?

Are the bedrooms isolated from the living room?

Is there more than one place where meals can be served?

Where will the washer and clothes dryer go? Can they be
reached easily, but also shut off from the rest of the house?

What about storage space for bicycles, card table, trunks,
garden equipment, and out-of-season clothes?

How many square feet of floor space are there?

How many corners are there on outside walls (minimum is usually four).

How many bedrooms are there large enough for two twin beds?

7. If the records of building permits are adequate, plot on a map
all those issued in your town in the past year. Then plot on a piece
of transparent plastic or cellophane superimposed on the map the
location of building permits issued during a whole year, five years
ago. Using a new piece of plastic each time, go back ten, fifteen,
or twenty years if possible. If records do not permit this, try plot-
ting each of the past ten years. By superimposing all the trans-
parencies, then removing them one by one, you can see the whole
pattern of development and the trends. If the building permits
allow separation of single family houses, and indicate a construction
cost estimate, use only the single family houses, and indicate inexpensive and expensive houses by using different marks on the map.

FOOTNOTES TO CHAPTER 8

1 For summaries of, or references to, most of the literature, see: Coleman Woodbury, ed., *Urban Redevelopment: Problems and Practices*, Chicago: The University of Chicago Press, 1953; Coleman Woodbury, ed., *The Future of Cities and Urban Redevelopment*, Chicago: The University of Chicago Press, 1953; James Dahir, *Communities for Better Living*, New York: Harper & Brothers, 1950; Lewis Mumford, *The Culture of Cities*, New York: Harcourt, Brace & Co., 1938; Mabel L. Walker, and others, *Urban Blight and Slums, Economic and Legal Factors in Their Origin, Reclamation, and Prevention*, Cambridge, Mass.: Harvard University, Harvard City Planning Studies XII, Harvard University Press, 1938; Twentieth Century Fund, *American Housing*, "The Factual Findings," by Miles L. Colean, and "The Program," by The Housing Committee, New York: The Twentieth Century Fund, 1944.

2 John P. Dean, "The Myths of Housing Reform," *American Sociological Review*, 14:281–288 (April, 1949); Robert K. Merton, "Selected Problems of Field Work in the Planned Community," *Amer. Sociol. Rev.*, 12:304–312 (1947); F. Stuart Chapin, "New Methods of Sociological Research on Housing Problems," *Amer. Sociol. Rev.*, 12:143–149 (April, 1947); Howard G. Brunsman, "Current Sources of Sociological Data in Housing," *Amer. Sociol. Rev.*, 12:150–155 (April, 1947); Svend Riemer, "Sociological Perspective in Home Planning," *Amer. Sociol. Rev.*, 12:155–159 (April, 1947).

3 U.S. Department of Commerce, Bureau of the Census, *1950 Census of Housing, Preliminary Reports HC-5*, Vol. IV (preliminary sample data).

4 See also, U.S. Dept. of Commerce, Bureau of the Census, *1950 Census of Housing*, Vol. IV, *Residential Financing*, Part 1, U.S. Gov't Printing Office, Washington, D. C., 1952. Table 30 of this survey of homes with mortgages (p. 60ff) gives the following data for owner-occupied houses with mortgages:

Region	Median percentage of property tax to house value
Northeast	1.64
North central	1.04
South	0.79
West	1.03
All of U.S.	1.13

5 Nathan Straus, *Two Thirds of a Nation*, New York: Alfred A. Knopf, Inc., 1952, pp. 100 and *passim*. See also U.S. National Housing Agency, *Housing Costs*, National Housing Bulletin No. 2, Washington, D. C., 1944.

6 W. F. Cottrell, "Death by Dieselization: A Case Study in the Reaction to Technological Change," *American Sociological Review*, 16:358–365 (June, 1951).

7 John P. Dean, *Home Ownership, Is It Sound?* New York: Harper & Brothers, 1945; Straus, *Two Thirds of a Nation*, pp. 71ff; Irving Rosow, "Home Ownership Motives," *American Sociological Review*, 13:751–756 (Dec., 1948), reporting on a study where 40 per cent of the people said they had to buy to get the neighborhood they wanted; Survey Research Center, *Relevant Considerations in Recent House Purchases*, report to the Housing and Home Finance Agency, Ann Arbor, Michigan: University of Michigan, 1951 (reporting a national sample survey where 19 per cent said they had to buy to find a place to live). The Sur-

vey Research Center material, together with some other data, will be found in
Edward T. Paxton, *What People Want When They Buy a House,* Washington,
D. C.: U.S. Gov't Printing Office, 1955; major portions of the same Survey Re-
search Center material will be found in "Relevant Considerations in Recent
House Purchases," *Journal of the American Institute of Appraisers,* in a forth-
coming 1955 issue.

[8] U.S. Housing and Home Finance Agency, Public Housing Administration,
Open Occupancy in Public Housing, Washington, D. C., 1953.

[9] Luigi M. Laurenti, "Effects of Nonwhite Purchases on Market Prices of
Residences," *Appraisal Journal,* XX:314–329 (July, 1952); E. F. Schietinger,
"Racial Succession and Value of Small Residential Properties," *American Socio-
logical Review,* 16:832–835 (Dec., 1951); Morton Deutsch and Mary Evans Collins,
Interracial Housing: A Psychological Evaluation of a Social Experiment, Minne-
apolis: Univ. of Minnesota Press, 1951.

[10] Merle Henrickson and Donald Monson, *What About Housing Cooperatives?*
Detroit: Co-op Builders, 1945; Alfred Hassler, "Commuters' Community," *Fel-
lowship,* 19:5–11, 17–18 (April, 1953).

[11] T. H. Robsohn-Gibbings, *Homes of the Brave,* New York: Alfred A. Knopf,
Inc., 1953.

[12] U.S. Bureau of Labor Statistics, *New Housing in Metropolitan Areas, 1949–
1951,* Bulletin No. 1115, Washington, D. C.: U.S. Gov't Printing Office, 1952,
Table 5, p. 26 and Table 1, p. 13.

[13] Mass-Observation, *People's Homes* (a study for the Advertising Service
Guild), London: John Murray (The Curwen Press Ltd.), 1943.

[14] See, for instance, Peter Rossi and associates, *Urban Residential Mobility*
(hectographed), New York: Bureau of Applied Social Research, Institute for
Urban Land Use and Housing Studies, Columbia University, 1952.

[15] Svend Riemer, "Maladjustment to the Family Home," *American Sociological
Review,* 10:642–648 (Oct., 1945).

[16] Women's City Club of New York, *Better Housing for the Family* (Prepared
and edited by Beatrice S. Friedman for the Housing Committee), New York:
Women's City Club of New York, Inc. (Hotel New Weston), 1948, p. 50.

[17] Federal Public Housing Authority, *The Livability Problems of 1,000 Families,* National Housing Agency Bulletin No. 28 (mimeo), Oct. 1945.

[18] Mass-Observation, *People's Homes* (a study for the Advertising Service
Guild), London: John Murray (The Curwen Press Ltd.), 1943, p. 53.

[19] U.S. Housing and Home Finance Agency, *Basements vs. No Basements for
Houses,* Parts I, II, and III (Reprinted from H.H.F.A. Technical Bulletins, Nos.
3, 4, and 5, March, May, and July, 1948), Washington, D. C.: U.S. Gov't Printing
Office, 1950.

[20] B. Kenneth Johnstone and others, *Building or Buying a House* (A guide to
wise investment), New York: Wittlesey House, McGraw-Hill Book Co., 1945;
Svend Riemer, "Designing the Family Home," in H. Becker and R. Hill, eds.,
Family, Marriage, and Parenthood, Boston: D. C. Heath & Company, 1948;
American Public Health Association, Committee on the Hygiene of Housing,
Planning the Home for Occupancy, Vol. III, Chicago: Public Administration
Service, 1950; Dorothy J. Field, *The Human House,* Cambridge, Massachusetts:
Riverside Press, Houghton Mifflin Co., 1939; C. G. Ramsey and H. R. Sleeper,
Architectural Graphic Standards, 2nd. ed., New York: John Wiley & Sons, Inc.,
1936; B. J. Harrison, H. D. Whitney, and C. Woodward, "From Rent to Space,"
Architectural Forum, July 1936; Univ. of Illinois, Small Homes Council, *Cir-
cular Series* (various issues).

21 Harrison, Whitney, and Woodward, *op. cit.*

22 Richard U. Ratcliffe, "Housing Standards and Housing Research," *Land Economics*, XXVIII:328–332 (Nov., 1952); Svend Riemer and N. J. Demerath, "The Role of Social Research in Housing Design," *Land Economics*, XXVIII:230–243 (August, 1952).

23 N. S. Perkins, *How to Judge a House* (Report of a Subcommittee of the National Committee on Wood Utilization on How to Judge a House), U.S. Department of Commerce, Washington, 1931.

24 K. Lee Hyder, "Depreciation, Obsolescence, and Lack of Utility in Residential Property," *Appraisal Journal*, XX:544–548 (Oct., 1952). (Reprinted from the October, 1933 *Appraisal Journal*) published by the American Institute of Real Estate Appraisers, p. 545.

25 *Ibid.*, p. 548.

26 Paul C. Glick, "The Family Life Cycle," *American Sociological Review* 12: 164–174 (April, 1947); Frederick Gutheim, *Houses for Family Living*, New York: The Woman's Foundation, Inc., 1948.

27 Robert V. Scott, "Residential Value," *Appraisal Journal*, XX:343–356 (July, 1952).

28 Coleman Woodbury, ed., *The Future of Cities and Urban Redevelopment*, Chicago, The University of Chicago Press, 1953, pp. 641–642 (In Part V written by Woodbury).

29 Walter Firey, *Land Use in Central Boston*, Harvard Sociological Studies, Vol. IV, Cambridge: Harvard University Press, 1947.

30 See, for instance, Homer Hoyt, *The Structure and Growth of Residential Neighborhoods in American Cities*, U.S. Federal Housing Agency, Washington, D. C., 1939; see also, Homer Hoyt and Arthur M. Wiemer, *Principles of Urban Real Estate*, rev. ed., New York: The Ronald Press Company, 1948.

31 See Women's City Club study cited in note 16. See also Woodbury, ed., *The Future of Cities and Urban Redevelopment*, Chicago: The University of Chicago Press, p. 386ff.

32 Mass-Observation, *People's Homes* (a study for the Advertising Service Guild), London: John Murray (The Curwen Press Ltd.), 1943, p. 208.

33 U.S. Department of Commerce, Bureau of the Census, *1950 Census of Housing, U.S. Summary, General Characteristics* (Vol. 1, Chap. 1).

34 See Peter Rossi and associates, *Urban Residential Mobility* (hectographed), New York: Bureau of Applied Social Research, Institute for Urban Land Use and Housing Studies, Columbia University, 1952.

35 For a fascinating first-person account, see: Abraham Goldfeld, *The Diary of a Housing Manager*, Chicago: National Association of Housing Officials, Published under sponsorship of Public Administration Services, 1938.

36 Burnham Kelly, *The Prefabrication of Houses*, New York: John Wiley & Sons, Inc. (published jointly with Technology Press, Massachusetts Institute of Technology), 1951.

37 Twentieth Century Fund, *American Housing*, "The Factual Findings," by Miles L. Colean, and "The Program," by The Housing Committee, New York: The Twentieth Century Fund, 1944. See also: Lee Loevinger, "Handicraft and Handcuffs—The Anatomy of an Industry," XII *Law and Contemporary Problems* 47–75 (Winter, 1947); Robert Lasch, *Breaking the Building Blocade*, Chicago: The University of Chicago Press, 1946; Leo Grebler, *Production of New Housing* (Monograph on Efficiency), New York: Social Science Research Council, 1950.

[38] Sherman Maisel, *Housebuilding in Transition: Based on Studies in the San Francisco Bay Area,* Berkeley and Los Angeles: University of California Press, 1953 (Publication of the Bureau of Business and Economic Research), p. 255.

[39] *Ibid.,* p. 299.

[40] Philip H. Cornick, A Report to the State Planning Council of New York *On the Problems Created by the Premature Subdivision of Urban Lands in Selected Metropolitan Districts in the State of New York,* Albany, New York: Division of State Planning, 1938; A. M. Sakolski, *The Great American Land Bubble* (The Amazing Story of Land-Grabbing, Speculations, and Booms from Colonial Days to the Present Time), New York: Harper & Brothers, 1932; Ernest M. Fisher and Raymond F. Smith, *Land Subdividing and the Rate of Utilization,* Ann Arbor: Bureau of Business Research, University of Michigan, 1932 (A study of the Grand Rapids area); Herbert D. Simpson and John E. Burton, *The Valuation of Land in Suburban Areas,* Chicago: Institute for Economic Research, Northwestern University, 1931.

[41] Leo Grebler, *Housing Market Behavior in a Declining Area* (Long Term Changes in Inventory and Utilization of Housing on New York's Lower East Side), New York: Columbia University Press, 1952.

[42] U.S. National Housing Agency, *Who Owns the Slums?* National Housing Bulletin No. 8, Washington, D. C.: Office of the Administrator, March 1946. (An analysis of 10,571 transactions buying property for slum clearance and housing in "100% slum sites.").

[43] Ira S. Robbins, "Problems in Land Assembly," Chapter XV in *Urban Blight and Slums,* Mabel Walker, ed. (see note 1), *op. cit.,* p. 176.

[44] See also: U.S. Housing and Home Finance Agency, *Comparative Digest of the Principal Provisions of State Planning Laws Relating to Housing, Slum Clearance and Urban Redevelopment, as of Jan. 1, 1951,* Washington, D. C.: H.H.F.A., 1952; Arthur C. Holden, "Urban Redevelopment Corporations," *Journal of Land and Public Utility Economics,* XVIII:412–422 (Nov., 1942).

[45] Svend Riemer, "Escape into Decentralization," *Land Economics,* XXIV:40–48 (Feb., 1948); Lewis Mumford, *The Culture of Cities,* New York: Harcourt, Brace & Co., 1938.

[46] "Pittsburgh's Answer to the High Cost of Squalor," *Business Week,* April 11, 1953, pp. 70–80.

[47] Catherine Bauer, "Redevelopment: A Misfit in the Fifties," in *The Future of Cities and Urban Redevelopment,* ed., Coleman Woodbury, Chicago: The University of Chicago Press, 1953.

[48] Clayton Knowles, "How FHA Loans Became Profits," *The N.Y. Times,* May 2, 1954, Sec. 4, p. 6. See also: U.S. Senate, Committee on Banking and Currency, *FHA Investigation,* Senate Committee Print, 83rd Cong., 2d Sess., Washington, D. C.: U.S. Gov't Printing Office, 1954.

[49] Nathan Straus, *Two Thirds of a Nation,* New York: Alfred A. Knopf, Inc., 1952, pp. 122–123.

[50] G. C. M. M'Gonigle and J. Kirby, *Poverty and Public Health,* London: V. Gollancz Ltd., 1936; see also: U.S. Public Health Service (M. Allen Pond), "How Does Housing Affect Health?" from *Public Health Reports* May 10, 1946, pp. 665–672; Jay Rumney and Sara Shuman, *The Cost of Slums,* Part III, Newark, New Jersey: Newark Housing Authority, 1946; Jay Rumney, "The Social Costs of Slums," in *Social Policy and Social Research in Housing,* eds. R. K. Merton, P. S. West, and M. Jahoda; and H. C. Selvin, *Journal of Social Issues* VII:69–85 (1951); John P. Dean, "The Myths of Housing Reform," *American Socioligal Review,* 14:281–288 (April, 1949).

[51] Stuart Queen and David Carpenter, *The American City*, New York: McGraw-Hill Book Co., 1954, p. 370; for general materials on redevelopment, see note 1 to this chapter.   •

[52] Leo Grebler, *Housing Market Behavior in a Declining Area* (Long Term Changes in Inventory and Utilization of Housing on New York's Lower East Side), New York: Columbia University Press, 1952, p. 152.

[53] Eric Bird, "British Housing Policies," Chapter X in *Two Thirds of a Nation*, by Nathan Straus, New York: Alfred A. Knopf, Inc., 1952.

[54] Great Britain, Ministry of Works and Planning, *Final Report of the Expert Committee on Compensation and Betterment*, Cmd. 6386 ("The Uthwatt Report"), London: Her Majesty's Stationery Office, 1947.

[55] Great Britain, Ministry of Local Government and Planning, Progress Report on the Work of the Ministry of Town and Country Planning, *Town and Country Planning, 1943–1951*, Cmd. 8204, London: Her Majesty's Stationery Office, 1951, p. 13.

[56] 60 *Harvard Law Review* 800–811 (May, 1947); *Time*, Jan. 20, 1947, p. 30.

[57] Robert M. Megarry, *Lectures on the Town and Country Planning Act*, London: Stevens and Sons, Ltd., 1949, p. 97; see also: Charles M. Haar, *Land Planning Law in a Free Society* (A Study of the British Town and Country Planning Act), Cambridge, Massachusetts: Harvard University Press, 1951.

[58] Ralph Turvey, "Development Charges and the Compensation-Betterment Problem," *Economic Journal*, LXIII:299–317 (June, 1953). H. R. Parker, "The Financial Aspects of Town and Country Planning Legislation," *Economic Journal* LXIV:72–86 (March, 1954); D. L. Munby, "Development Charges and the Compensation-Betterment Problem," *Economic Journal* LXIV:87–97 (March, 1954); R. Turvey, "Development Charges and the Compensation-Betterment Problem (Reply), *Economic Journal* LXIV:358–360 (June, 1954).

chapter 9

Other
Major
Consumer
Expenditures

‖‖‖

The importance of an expenditure item in your budget is not indicated by the proportion of your income that you spend on it, but by the degree to which that spending requires discretion, understanding, use of current information, and perhaps self-control. The social importance of a type of consumer expenditure depends on the extent to which the fluctuations in spending or the unwise allocation of such spending creates problems for masses of people or for the whole economy. The types of expenditures we will discuss in this chapter, while not so important as those to which we have devoted whole chapters, are still worthy of consideration.

Food

In great sections of the world today, people can barely provide themselves with a minimum of food, shelter, and clothing. And food is the most important of these. Shelter can be improvised, clothing patched a little more, but food must be taken daily. The basic source of body warmth is the "fuel" we eat. In the United States, the consumer's concern with food is not whether there will be enough available, but how he can secure adequate nutrition and a palatable diet without wasting money.

It has already been pointed out briefly in Chapter 7 that adequate nutrition is a complicated problem. A number of vitamins and minerals, copper and iodine and even traces of some rare elements like cobalt, magnesium, manganese, molybdenum and zinc have been proven to be essential to good nutrition. But new essentials, and new interrelationships are being discovered all the time. The most important fact is that all the nutritive elements interact in the most complicated ways.

One of the strongest trends in current nutrition research is the emphasis, based on clear-cut evidence, that both the essential and nonessential nutrients are in constant interplay, within the body, and hence the quantitative requirements are interdependent. One must view the quality of the diet as a whole and avoid the extremes and imbalances that are so often encountered by getting excited about only one or a few vitamins or minerals.[1]

Even a listing of the *major* elements known to be necessary gives some idea of the complexity. We need minerals: mainly calcium, phosphorus, iron and iodine. We need vitamins: A, B, (thiamine), B2 or G (riboflavin), C (ascorbic acid), D, E, K, niacin, and others in the B group. Others are being discovered all the time. We need proteins, new types of which are still being discovered. Finally we need calories from carbohydrates or fats for energy. Calories are used most often as the measure of nutrition, since one must have the energy they provide in order to live and work and stay warm, and also since getting enough calories by eating the kinds of foods most people eat usually means getting most of the other nutrients too.

A study in 1948–49 that checked people's reported food consumption against dietary standards indicated that there had been great gains since 1942, particularly in the adequacy of the diets of the lowest third of the income range.[2] Indeed, diets reported were generally good in everything except calcium where only about two-thirds of the families were getting the necessary minimum amounts. It also appeared that people with more education were getting better nutrition with less expenditure.

One gets the feeling from reading the literature on nutrition that the wisest thing a consumer can do is to attempt to have some variety in types and colors of foods over a period of time. The usual emphasis on such "protective foods" as milk, eggs, and green and yellow vegetables is important, but can be tempered by the added fact that the body does not need every nutritional element at every meal, or even every day. People adapt to widely different diets, and to long periods in the year when certain elements are missing. Any attempt to secure every nutritional essential at each meal would make meals complicated and expensive. On the other hand, there is no assurance that an expensive diet is an adequate one, and experts insist that there are large numbers of people with quite adequate incomes whose diets are deficient. Of course, it is a matter of judgment just what an adequate diet is. Many people live for years at levels far below most "adequate diet" levels. And there is the now famous story of the discovery in Mexico that the tequila, which seemed to be a harmful alcoholic beverage, contained some basic nutritional elements that were not present in anything else in the Mexicans' diet.

But we want more than just nutrition out of our food. We want food that tastes good. We also want food that is easy to prepare. And yet we want to keep expenditure on food as low as we can. A good many of the most concentrated sources of important nutrients are foods that are inexpensive but do not taste very good to some people: beet greens, cabbage, kale, soy beans, liver, cheaper cuts of meat. When good taste and good nutritional content are combined, the food is generally rather expensive: choice cuts of meat, eggs, milk. And finally, some foods that seem expensive are much easier to prepare. If the housewife's time is worth anything they may really be more economical.

Popular articles frequently urge you to try foods like beet greens which are cheap sources of vitamins, or to buy the cheaper cuts of meat in order to get more protein per dollar. These articles frequently play down or overlook the extra preparation time, the increased waste; they do not mention the necessity for getting used to the taste of new things or of convincing the children to eat them at all. They also omit the most important fact of all—that we want to enjoy eating too. Indeed, the picture of a family living on cabbage and beans and then splurging on expensive steak to make up for the sacrifice is only too common. It is matched by the opposite picture of the family that never tries anything new, and fails to discover such products as the new dried skim milk powders, margarine, or canned imported beef. In some cities people prefer white eggs, and in others brown, though there is no difference nutritionally or indeed in any other way once the shell is removed.[3]

There are other ways to increase the efficiency of your spending on food besides the selection of the foods you will eat. Two of the more obvious ways are to find the places where food prices are lower, and buy at the times when prices are lower. Years ago it used to be that one could save money by going to the farmers' market for produce, meat, and eggs. It is still true that for fresh produce in season, bargains sometimes exist at farmers' markets, or at farms that sell directly by advertising in the paper. In some cases, however, the farmers are now setting their prices according to the prices the supermarkets are charging, on the assumption that the superior freshness of their produce makes it a better bargain. When you count the cost in time and transportation of going to several places to shop, however, there may be no saving at all.

It is certainly true that the large supermarkets sell foods at lower prices than smaller stores. An examination of the prices charged by competing supermarkets, however, generally shows that one will be cheaper on some things, and another cheaper on others. Whether it is worth the time and energy to go to several supermarkets depends on how persistent these differences are, or how well you can train yourself to predict, while shopping in the first store, whether the second store will do better. It would almost never pay to return to the first store for things when you guessed wrongly that they would be cheaper in the second store. For some people, this game of strategy has a fascination and amusement all its own. There is a real satisfaction sometimes in guessing, correctly, that one supermarket that advertises a special price on something is actually charging more than the other store.

In recent years when there have been substantial fluctuations from month to month in the prices of foods, it has been tempting to try to take advantage of these changes. There is one perfectly safe and foolproof method of doing this, and that is to vary your weekly diet enough so that you can concentrate on the foods that are being sold at bargain prices. This method's usefulness is restricted by the limited variety of foods most families like, and the tradition of having certain foods, like meat, regularly. Any other method of taking advantage of price fluctuations involves speculating on the future course of prices. You buy a lot when something is cheap, and store it. Or you buy a home freezer, so you can store perishables that can be frozen. A little logic will reveal how dangerous it is to assume that you can really do very well at this sort of speculation. There are a large number of warehouses in the country, including frozen food warehouses. The people, who make a living by storing food when it is cheaper and selling it when it will bring more, are numerous. If these experts, who have detailed market information and efficient storage methods, predicted correctly, then the prices of foods would never increase more from one month to the next than the cost of storing them for that period. In order to save money at this game, you must be able to predict the future prices better than the experts, or be able to store the foods more cheaply. This seems unlikely. It seems particularly unlikely in the case of frozen foods, since a home freezer is a rather expensive way to store things. There are some canned foods that have a seasonal pattern of prices where it may pay to stock up, since it really costs you nothing to store them except the imputed interest on the money you have invested in them. If you hold $50 worth of foods for six months, the imputed interest at 3 per cent is only 75¢. Finally, there are now so many food items subject to one form or another of government price supports—and these supports can be changed by legislative or administrative decisions—that fluctutations in prices of foods are considerably smaller and less easily predictable than they once were.

The development of methods for precooking, preparing, or premixing food before it is sold gives the housewife the chance to hire an invisible part-time cook, by buying prepared foods. Indeed, she has a choice as to how much preparation time she will expend in order to avoid using more expensive and usually less palatable prepared foods. Of course whether the extra preparation time is worth it will depend partly on the size of the family, since it does not take much longer to prepare a large cake than a small one. One recent study based on a two-day menu for a family of four estimated the costs in time and money of concentrating on home cooked, partly prepared, and ready-to-serve foods.[4] The food and fuel costs were $4.90, $5.80 and $6.70, and of course the time cost for preparation, serving and cleaning up went the other way, from 5.5 to 3.1 to 1.6 hours. Put more meaningfully, changing from ready-to-eat to partially prepared foods cost 1.5 hours more time but saved 90¢ in food and fuel costs, or 60¢ per hour. Changing from partially prepared to home prepared food cost an additional 2.4 hours time and saved another 90¢, or 37¢ per hour.

With larger families, the housewife would "make more" per hour as a cook, but might find other duties were also more pressing. A panel of people rated the meals for palatability without knowing which were which, and the home prepared meal rated best (index of 4.9), the partially prepared next (4.3), and the ready-to-serve least palatable (3.8). It may also be that the housewife would get more enjoyment out of the creative aspects of cooking than out of other household tasks, and might prefer hiring a part-time cleaning woman with the money she saved by preparing food herself.

For women with large families, or those who work outside the home, time is so short that almost any time-saving is worth while. Indeed, packaged mixes are now so simple that very young children can enjoy themselves by "cooking."

It is also generally true that more expensive sources of nutrition are easier and quicker to prepare. Less waste is entailed and more of the rarer forms of protein are provided, so that it is not always clear that they are actually more expensive in relation to the amount of nutrition received. Recent studies tend to show that higher income people buy higher priced foods, and an examination of the basic data seems to indicate that this is not because they pay more for the same items, but because they buy larger proportions of the more expensive ones.[5] Supermarkets do a large part of the total food distributing, and sell at the same prices to everyone, so that the only way higher income people could pay more for the identical items is to buy them at smaller stores with greater mark-ups. Of course, incomes are higher in the large cities, and food prices are sometimes also higher there.

Another way the housewife can save food costs by using more of her own labor and skills is by preserving food at home. Such home canning and freezing, pickling and preserving are common in rural areas, and frequent even in cities. A recent study found the per cent of families doing some home food preserving varied by city size from 61 per cent in towns under 10,000 population to 20 per cent in the large metropolitan centers of a million inhabitants or more.[6] There was also a tendency for lower income families to do it more frequently, but even among city families with incomes of $7,500 and over, 40 per cent reported doing some home food preserving. There were even differences between different cities, with percentages ranging from 30 per cent in San Francisco and 40 per cent in Birmingham to 57 per cent in Buffalo and 74 per cent in Minneapolis-St. Paul.

It's also true that the consumer can benefit from knowing something about quality of foods. Aside from the obvious differences in looks or taste, which are often good indicators of vitamin content, and reliance on the hope that a brand that was good, will continue to be so, the consumer has little to go on.[7]

Sometimes you can buy in larger quantities and save money this way—although again this generally involves speculation on the course of prices in the future. And like any process that involves buying more than you need for the present, it runs counter to our final method of saving money on food, that is, planning meals.

Marketing experts are fond of saying about food that the problem of the store is to get the food into people's homes. "If you once get it there, the people will eat it," they say. The implication is that people will eat larger amounts, and will consume more expensively priced foods, if they have them around. The reverse implication is that planning meals and buying foods according to such a plan is likely to reduce food costs, if only by reducing the amount of food consumed—particularly the amount of expensive food. This would lead to the suggestion that you keep well stocked on nutritionally efficient and economical foods, and not well stocked in luxury foods. You could keep large supplies of peanut butter, skim milk powder, flour and sugar, but low supplies of canned fruits and choice meats.

This brings us to the basic problem of how much to spend on food. All of us spend more than is necessary for bare subsistence, because we want to enjoy eating too. But at the same time we don't want to use money on food that would bring us more satisfaction spent some other way. As in all consumer budgeting problems, satisfactions differ and individual preferences must be remembered. The only empirical material of any relevance besides our own experience is what other people are spending, and what the age and sex differences in food intake generally are.

Scant data on the effect of family size indicate that the proportion of income spent on food increases with the size of the family, and decreases with the level of income. Budget studies show people spending 25–40 per cent of their income on food, depending on the number of people in the family.[8] Of course, for incomes over, say, $6,000 a year, the proportion spent on food tends to become lower than any of these figures. Foods cost more in New York City than in farming communities, though the differences are much less than might be expected.

The need for good nutrition and pleasant taste will affect your selection of foods, but it might be assumed for simplicity's sake that it is largely the proportion of luxury foods and the total calories consumed that will determine food expenditures. The luxury level may well depend on your income, but it is generally safe to assume that you will continue on the same level. The calorie intake at any time may also depend on your habits, but basic calorie requirements depend on age, sex, weight, and activity level. As you and your family grow, the pattern of ages changes, and it is possible, knowing your family's present age and sex composition, to predict the future trends in calorie consumption. Table 25 below gives the recommended dietary allowances for both calories and proteins.[9] If your family's calorie requirements are going to increase 20 per cent over the next ten years, then it would seem sensible to expect your food expenditures to increase by about 20 per cent unless you cut down on the luxuries.

Of course, you can get added calories by consuming fats and carbohydrates found in inexpensive foods like margarine and potatoes, but the requirements for protein also increase, markedly, as children grow up. Some casual investigations of mine seem to indicate that if the recommended calorie intake per day is added up the monthly dollar cost is likely to be $10 to $15 for each 1,000 calories per day. In other words a young man and wife, with a recommended 5,700 calories per day, might spend $57–85 per month for food. Later when they have two children, a boy 17 and a girl 14, the table shows (assuming they are now 45 years old) 11,300 calories, or $113–169 per month for food.

TABLE 25

RECOMMENDED DAILY DIETARY ALLOWANCES FOR CALORIES AND PROTEINS [1]

	Age	Weight [4] (pounds)	Calories	Protein (grams)
Men	25	143	3,200	65
	45	143	2,900	65
	65	143	2,600	65
Women [2]	25	121	2,300	55
	45	121	2,100	55
	65	121	1,800	50
Infants [3]	1/12–3/12	13	720	21
	4/12–9/12	20	990	24
	10/12–1	22	1,000	26
Children	1–3	27	1,200	40
	4–6	40	1,600	50
	7–9	59	2,000	60
Girls	10–12	79	2,300	70
	13–15	108	2,500	80
	16–20	120	2,400	75
Boys	10–12	78	2,500	70
	13–15	108	3,200	85
	16–20	139	3,800	100

Source: adapted from, Food and Nutrition Board, National Research Council, Recommended Dietary Allowances (Revised, 1953), Publication 302. Washington, D. C.: National Academy of Sciences, 1953, p. 22 and passim.

[1] Designed for the maintenance of good nutrition of healthy, normally vigorous persons living in temperate climate.

[2] Add 400 calories and 25 grams of protein for the last 3 months of pregnancy and 1,000 calories and 45 grams of protein while nursing.

[3] More precisely 50 X their weight in pounds for calories and 1.6 X their weight in pounds for grams of protein.

[4] Add 10 per cent for each extra 15 pounds if a woman and for each extra 20 pounds if a man. Subtract if you weigh less than the standards. Add 5 per cent for every 10 degree decrease in outside average temperature from the reference base of 10 degrees centigrade. This temperature adjustment can be made seasonally as well as regionally. The table is based on a mean annual external temperature of 50°.

This takes no account of income, and clearly it is safer to use the table to see how much your family food expenditures will increase or decrease than to estimate dollar expenditures from it. A complex statistical study based on 1937–1938 expenditure data for Great Britain estimated simultaneously the equivalent adult coefficients of wives and children with respect to food expenditure and the effect of income on food expenditures.[10] This study derived two sets of such coefficients using different methods. (See Table 26.) The effect of income as estimated at the same time was that as income per person increased, expenditures on food would increase 46–53 per cent as much. We have added, in a third column of Table 26, coefficients estimated on the basis of recommended calorie intakes of Table 25.

Of course the level of luxury in eating is widely variable. You can pay anywhere from 30¢ to $1.50 a pound for meat, and even taking account of the amount of bone and fat in the cheaper meats, the net costs vary a good deal. You can get your protein from meat alone, or from a little meat mixed with any grain product, and your fats from 60¢ butter or 25¢ margarine. One of the first things many people try to cut when they become conscious of the need for economy in spending, is their food expenditure. Unfortunately, food habits do not change easily and what most of us have to do is to change a few at a time, and change them in such a way that we achieve satisfactions from initial successes to spur us on.

For example, dried skim milk powder costs about one-third to one-half as much as fresh skim milk, and contains all the same nutrients. But it doesn't taste exactly like fresh milk unless you mix a little fresh milk with it. In baking it proves to be quite easy to mix the powder with the dry ingredients and then add water instead of milk, provided that you learn that for some custards calling for whole milk, no skim milk will work because the fat is missing. In other words, substitution of cheaper foods always requires a little experimentation and skill.

Looking at the larger social scene, people are frequently

amazed and annoyed to discover that a large proportion of the money they spend for food goes to the distributors and processors. A one-pound loaf of bread that costs 17¢ will contain less than 3¢ worth of wheat.[11] About 44¢ of the dollar you spend for food goes to the farmer, most of which he pays out for seed, fertilizer, equipment, and so on, leaving about 14¢ of the dollar for his labor. Retail food prices seem to be "stickier" too, not moving up or down so fast as farm prices. Hence whenever farm prices are falling, people point to the fact that retail prices have not fallen nearly so much.

TABLE 26

RELATIVE FOOD EXPENDITURES ADDED BY VARIOUS FAMILY MEMBERS, ALLOWING FOR THEIR EFFECT ON FAMILY INCOME PER PERSON

	Method 1	Method 2	Estimated from National Research Council Calorie Requirements
Adult Male	1.00	1.00	1.00
Adult Female	.88	.86	.72
Male 14–17	.81	.82	1.20
Female 14–17	.65	.65	.84
10–13	.71	.69	.83
5–9	.57	.55	.62
1–4	.52	.51	.43
Less than 1	.35	.32	.34
10% increase in income per person increases food expenditures by ..	4.6%	5.3%	

Source: Prais, and National Research Council. See notes 1 and 10 to this chapter.

On the other hand, the food distributors point to the obvious efficiency of much of their operation, to the fact that there are no huge profits even in meat packing, and to the increasing amount of processing necessary before final delivery of the food. Instead of flour, you may buy mixes where part of the work of combining ingredients has already been completed.   Instead of fresh vegetables you may buy frozen or canned vegetables. Your chicken or turkey is cleaned and nicely wrapped in plastic. What you are buying, then, is not the produce of the farm, but a manufactured product that has that farm produce as an ingredient.   The spread between farm and retail prices is chiefly the costs of processing rather than middlemen's profits.   The food chains make only 1–2¢ profit per dollar of sale, a lower rate than other retail trade corporations.[12]

On the other hand, there have been periods in history, including the years 1951–1954, when substantial declines in the prices received by farmers did not result in a corresponding decline in retail food prices, a discrepancy so large that it has been difficult to explain it solely by increases in processing costs.   It seems likely, however, that such discrepancies will be temporary, since the processing and distribution of food is still a highly competitive industry for the most part.

One particular part of the food distribution system about which consumers know little is the wholesale markets for fresh produce in the larger cities.   In many cases these are extremely inefficient, and sometimes plagued by graft or monopolistic attempts to exclude new competitors.[13]   If I were going to devote some time and energy to improving the efficiency of the food distribution system, I should certainly start with the wholesale produce markets.

The retail distribution of food and a number of the functions of the wholesaler have been taken over by the large food chains, most of them operating "super markets."   By stressing volume they have cut gross retail margins on food.   Some people still prefer the small friendly store that gives credit or delivers or both, but they pay for these extras.   Some of the activities of the chains, however, have been less acceptable.   A national chain can force special favors from its suppliers.   This amounts to a lowering of prices below those paid by competitors.   These prices are not always justified by a larger volume purchased.[14]   The chain store can also lower prices in one area until it gets established, making up the loss in others where the competition is already less keen. In the long run, if consumers watch prices, the chains will only be able to keep their business by selling at lower prices. And provided these prices are the result of genuine efficiencies in distribution, and not in the use of size and power to keep out competitors, or to force unwarranted concessions from suppliers, the supermarket chain is a real boon to the consumer. Only in the case of locally produced fresh produce do chains seem to have failed to bring lower prices.

One final social problem arises because of the numerous food fads. Millions of dollars are spent every year on special foods, spent by people who have been deluded into hoping that these foods could cure their ills. Most of these fads are harmless, except to the pocketbook. Some, however, may lead to an unbalanced diet that actually does harm. Against the more extravagant and obviously fraudulent claims, the government tries to protect the consumer, as we shall see in a later chapter. But democratic freedom of consumer choice must still involve freedom to choose unwisely.

Clothing

If there are fads and foibles in food, there are still more in clothing. Both the traditionalism in men's clothing and the rapidly changing styles in women's clothing have been the object of discussion, ridicule, scorn, and historical analysis.[15] As a consumer, it may be interesting for you to know that the buttons on the sleeves of men's coats once served a purpose, or that the length of women's skirts has gone through a series of cycles similar to and seemingly correlated with the level of business activity, but it will not help you much. It will help, however, to realize that men's clothing is likely to remain largely traditional, with such minor modifications as clip-on bow ties, sport shirts, and "putter-pants," the last for around the house. It seems equally clear that women will continue to be more adventurous—or should we say gullible?

Faced with this situation, you can, if you wish, go out like a

modern Don Quixote to do battle with these customs, by refusing to accept the new styles if you are a woman, or by trying
to get along without a tie if you are a man.   You may, of course,
be laughed at, or refused entrance to your favorite restaurant.
More important, you may discover that in a world where a person's abilities are hard to assess, he is sometimes judged by what
he wears.   Refusal to conform may be interpreted as stupid
stubbornness or lack of good taste, or as an indication of radical-
ism in other and more important areas of life, or even as inability to afford new clothes.   Like many another social situation,
however, there is a reverse twist.   The well established and
socially secure can afford to set their own styles.   The sociologists are fascinated by the process whereby blue jeans for girls
started with wealthy coeds, and afterwards became acceptable
among others for whom the saving in money was much more
important.

If you decide to make your peace with custom, reserving the
right only to refuse the less palatable new styles offered in the
hopes that they will not endure anyway, then it seems obvious
that as a consumer you will look for quality and wearing ability
in men's clothing, and the proper styles in women's clothing.
A dress that lasts for years after it is no longer in style merely
clutters up the closet.   The woman who wants to use her clothing money wisely is in for a game of strategy.   She must predict
which elements of the new styles will persist.   To the casual
male observer, the fashion magazines seem to operate by showing new extremes in fashion, some modified and minor elements
of which end up as the acceptable style for the next few years.
The apparel of the entertainers on television may serve as the
same "trial balloon" purpose.   Good taste then consists in
predicting which of the new elements will appeal to most
women, and in rejecting those that are obviously so unflattering
or nonfunctional as to be unlikely to last long.   It is not enough
to go by what appears to be currently accepted, since new styles
seem frequently to be pushed by advertising and perhaps syn-

chronized style decisions of the manufacturers into prominence only to collapse when women refuse to wear them.

The selection of clothes for men, and to some lesser extent for women, involves looking for wearing qualities: durability, washability, comfort. This was difficult enough even before the advent of the "miracle fibers." When fabrics were simple, women used to be proud of their ability to tell by feeling and looking whether the fabric would wear and clean well.

There will probably never be a time when you can simply go by a grade label on clothing, whether put there by government, manufacturer, or retailer. The reason is that there is no obvious or simple answer to what qualities one wants in fabrics and clothing. Some qualities are almost antithetical to others. Light weight and softness are difficult to combine with durability and abrasion resistance. Some of us may be concerned mostly with fit, or feel, or warmth, or looks, or careful tailoring, or good linings, or strong pockets, or washability, or resistance to creasing. The blue serge that one may prefer for durability, another may detest because of the early shine that appears—"a reflection on him." To add to the problems, it seems psychologically impossible for manufacturers or sellers to point out the disadvantages of a new fabric, or to indicate what should not be done with it.

Alarmed by complaints of customers about the newer fabrics, the National Retail Dry Goods Association some years ago sponsored a program in the American Standards Association that led to the publication of a document called "L-22," the standard for rayon and acetate fabrics. It was based on 36 test methods and performance standards for 51 differently used products.[16] Unfortunately, the standard is not used or publicized widely, though some stores use it in their own buying. Work is now progressing on a standard "L-25" for all fabrics. This offers some hope for the future, if only the hope that buyers for retail stores will use such specifications. Nowadays, you cannot always find out whether or not a garment you buy is even washable. After a few experiences with nylon shirts that "didn't need ironing," "washable" fabrics where nothing shrunk but the seams, or miracle fabrics that not only wore like iron but felt like it, many of us are unsure of our ability to judge anything except the old, less miraculous fabrics. For these there are published buying aids.[17] Magazines, like *Consumer Reports*, both in reporting on specific clothing items, and, occasionally, in more general reports, provide information about fabrics and about what to look for in ready-made clothing. As time passes, articles will certainly appear that tell us more, and manufacturers will perhaps start indicating just what things are made of. In the meantime, you'll have to rely on well-known brands and on experience (sometimes sad) to indicate what is good and what is bad.

Clothing for children must obviously be durable, but it must also, and this is not so obvious, be of the same style all the other children are wearing. Trying to insist on snow-pants when others are wearing lined jeans leads only to trouble. Ready-made children's clothing seems to me to be remarkably inexpensive, and crafty mothers have made the situation easier by extensive use of mutual lending and giving. Rummage sales also put outgrown clothing back into use.

A combination of things—seasonal changes in clothing, style changes, and mere habit or custom—has led to a tradition among clothing stores of having regular sales several times a year. While these sales may sometimes serve merely to unload the styles that did not sell or the items that contained flaws, they are frequently a source of genuine bargains. This puts a premium on planning your clothing purchases to take advantage of the sales. Needless to say, such planning requires a sufficient inventory of clothing so that you can afford to wait until the next sale. It also requires knowing enough about what you are buying to be able to distinguish between the genuine bargains and the "special purchases."

What about budgeting for clothing? Surveys tend to show

families spending 10–15 per cent of their income on clothes. Strangely enough, they do *not* seem to spend a larger proportion when there are more people in the family. Apparently the increased need for clothes is restrained by the lower income available for clothing after still more pressing needs for food and rent are met. Income does not affect the proportion much either. Only when incomes become substantial does the proportion spent on clothing drop significantly. There are, of course, occupational differences. The engineer who wears a suit even when going through a factory has a different problem than the worker who applies more abrasion to cheaper fabrics. As in all questions of "how much," your own experience is a useful guide, provided you have not been running short of money and skimping on the clothing budget as a consequence.

This leads to an important problem some consumers have with clothing. They can usually get along for a while with what they have. But buying clothing usually involves thought, shopping, and expenditures of appreciable sums of money. What often happens is that other enticements to spend may take over. Even if there is a budget, it is the clothing item that is most often "robbed." This results in the consumer being forced to buy clothing when his supply gets desperately low, usually at "standard" prices rather than at the sales. More important, it may result in his spending less on clothing than he planned, or than is necessary for proper appearance. Since he may be judged at least in part by how he looks, this might even affect his future income adversely and make the budget still harder to balance!

It is possible of course to spend a good deal more than is "necessary" on clothing, and some people get satisfaction out of wearing fine fabrics or selecting a wide variety of clothing. Others like to be up with the latest styles or the most expensive of the traditional pieces (Harris Tweeds or Daks for men, for instance). There is little to say about this except to remark that this is another illustration of the basic principle of choice that asks whether additional dollars spent on clothes brings as much satisfaction as if they were spent on something else, or saved.

When viewing the larger social scene, it is found that the clothing industry in America is a highly competitive scramble. Manufacturers have managed to produce clothing at remarkably low prices while paying substantially higher wages over the years, all this while faced with the problems of rapidly changing styles. Distribution costs are substantial, however, and it is difficult to see how they can be reduced so long as styles change as rapidly as they do. Even in the case of men's clothing, the attempt to reduce service, credit, and range of styles, and to sell good quality suits at lower mark-ups in volume, does not seem to have been particularly successful. It is possible that the manufacturers may, with the aid of consumer research organizations, secure volume sales of quality merchandise and introduce a new type of retailing efficiency.

Recreation

The estimates given on consumer expenditures for other major items were only rough estimates, but for recreation expenses the economist cannot even do that well. The reason is that recreation is not something that can be defined or some simple group of expenditures the amount of which can be asked of consumers. Some people do a lot of entertaining. Is this a business expense, recreation, a necessary social obligation, or what? Perhaps it depends on whether they enjoy it! Other people take pictures of their children and send them to all their relatives. Is this recreation, gifts to the relatives, or part of the cost of having children? Others like to raise vegetables or flowers. Is this part of their housing or food expenses, or are the costs assigned to recreation, or is it a method of avoiding medical care costs?

Quibbles aside, the American people spend vast sums every year for commercial recreation of one sort or another. Some stay home but visit the ball games, the races, the movies, the bowling alleys, and so on. Others travel, sleeping in tents, trailers, or air-conditioned motels that feature television. The intensity with which people try to get somewhere on their vacations makes it look as though most of them would like to have a longer vacation, though some would insist that they just don't know how to slow down. The vacation "industry" is so important in certain parts of the country, for instance New England, that attempts are made to predict people's expenditures. The weather becomes a matter of genuine concern. National and state parks, and the recreation areas of federal irrigation and flood control projects are becoming increasingly popular.

There are philosophers who poke fun at the hurried vacation from which you come "back to work for a rest." Others point the finger of scorn at reliance on commercial forms of recreation. "It is better," they say, "to play some instrument only fairly well, than to listen to someone else do it. The more your recreation involves having someone else do it for you, the more it costs and the less real sense of satisfaction you will get from it." Not heeding these philosophers, many Americans today relax and watch their television sets or listen to their radios, or watch the movies or the ball games or the concerts. Yet many others are developing an interest in forms of recreation which are relaxing and enjoyable, yet also creative and inexpensive and helpful in keeping the family together.

On the national level, vacation and recreation expenditures are important because they are potentially so volatile. People can become worried about the future and take their vacations at home, painting the house instead of patronizing the resorts. Or they can relax and decide to have a "real vacation," and so create a prosperous year in the recreation industry. We need to know more about how people make such decisions.

As individual consumers concerned with making the money go around, and getting satisfaction out of it, you need to realize the 5–7 per cent of consumers' income reported as spent on recreation, reading, and education in most budget studies, covers a variety of patterns of behavior as well as many difficulties in definition.   We need to ask ourselves why it is that some people enjoy only expensive recreation while others have somehow developed a capacity to enjoy simple things.   Perhaps dissatisfaction with one's job and home have something to do with the pressure for elaborate vacations and expensive recreation in between.   But so many personality variables and such a long process of developing habits and aspirations is involved as to suggest that any attempt to change your own patterns would be a slow process.

Consumer Investment in Cars, Appliances, and Additions and Repairs to Homes

One of the most important categories of consumer expenditure is that involving purchase of a car or household appliances, or making additions or repairs to one's home.   Most budget studies and many budgets divide these items and bury them in other categories, in spite of the fact that they involve problems for the consumer quite different from the other expenditures in these categories.   They involve large expenditures concentrated in time and are particularly heavy for young families that have other financial pressures and an income that may not yet have risen much.   They allow a wide range of discretion regarding amounts to be spent, styles, and so on.   They demand a great deal of information and shopping if one is to get good values.   Finally, the objects involved depreciate, yet such depreciation does not call for money outlays, so that budgeting for them is difficult.

In 1953, the average consumer spent 5.5 per cent of his income on a car, 3.75 per cent on major household appliances, and somewhat over 3 per cent on additions and repairs to his home.   Altogether, about 12.5 per cent of his income was thus spent not counting such durables as cameras, boats, power lawn mowers, home work-shop equipment, and so on.   National income aggregates would indicate that these amounted to another 1.5 per cent of personal income.   (See Table 27 on page 321.)

In any one year 40 per cent of spending units buy a household appliance, 21–24 per cent buy a new or used car, and some 36 per cent spend something on additions and repairs. (Nearly 60 per cent of non-farm home owners spend something on additions or repairs every year.) The largest expenditures come less frequently, of course. The amount people spend on these "investment" items depends on their income, and on the degree to which they have already accumulated the vast inventory of such items as the modern household owns. People seem to have spent in recent years about the same *proportion* of their income on cars, durables, and additions and repairs at all income levels up to $7,500 a year. At higher incomes, of course, the proportion tends to drop somewhat, but not much. The bulk of the expenditures on durables are, however, concentrated at the stage in the family life cycle when a home is being bought, children are being born, and family income is still expected to rise.

On the other hand, you will notice from Table 27 that for those, in particular, who own their own homes, substantial proportions of their incomes continue to be spent on "consumer investments" even when they are old and *retired or unemployed*. To some extent people substitute these expenditures for rent, and this is particularly true of repairs to houses. They remain nonetheless substantial items of expenditure. They involve large amounts of money and require discretion concerning how much is to be spent and when.

The fact that these expenditures are essentially investments —since the items purchased, and in most cases also the home repairs, will last a long time—does not eliminate the difficulty that they call for large expenditures, often at a time when free liquid assets are not likely to be available. It is for this reason among others that consumer installment credit has been so popular. For those who want to avoid the costs of such credit, the problem of accumulating the necessary cash is a serious one.

A second difficulty arises from the extensive "hidden costs" in owning durables and cars. The most important hidden cost is depreciation; the others are largely hidden because they are small, intermittent, unpredictable, or in the case of opportunity cost, unrecognized. As an example, we reproduce a statement passed out, for obvious reasons, by the Chicago Transit Authority.

WHAT'S IT COSTING YOU TO DRIVE?

Figure It Out For Yourself:

>   . . . here's how to do it!

Costs   (Your Car annual mileage: —————)

	Cost per year	*Cost per mile*
1. Depreciation		
2. Extra depreciation allowance		
3. Insurance		
4. License fee and taxes		
5. Interest on investment		
6. Gasoline		
7. Oil		
8. Tires		
9. Maintenance		
10. Miscellaneous expenses		
11. Total Car Costs		

Suggestions to help you with your figures:

1. DEPRECIATION: Check classified ads for today's value of your car. Subtract the present market value from the price you paid for your car. Divide the difference by the number of years you've owned your car.

2. EXTRA DEPRECIATION: If you drive more than 18,000 miles annually, show $9.40 for every thousand miles over 18,000.

3. INSURANCE COSTS: Show total annual premiums you pay for all automobile insurance.

4. LICENSE FEES AND TAXES: Show state and city license fees, plus personal property tax.

5. INTEREST ON INVESTMENT: The money spent for your car would earn about 3% if invested in government bonds.

TABLE 27

PROPORTION OF INCOME AFTER TAXES SPENT ON CONSUMER INVESTMENTS,[1]
ACCORDING TO AGE, MARITAL STATUS, AND HOME OWNERSHIP [2]

(AVERAGES 1947–1953)

	18–34	35–44	45–54	55–	55 and Over and Unemployed or Retired
Renters:					
Single		9		4	
Married, no children	17	12	9	7	3
Married, children	16	11	8	8	
Owners:					
Single		17		18	
Married, no children	23	18	18	16	15
Married, children	18	17	16	16	

Source: 1948–1954 Surveys of Consumer Finances, Special Tabulation.

1 Investments in cars, home appliances, or additions and repairs to homes.

2 In order to emphasize the *typical,* this table excludes farmers, secondary spending units, people who neither own nor rent, people with extremely large incomes or expenditures or ratios of expenditures to income (200% or more), and some for whom some information was missing.

6. GASOLINE: Divide the cost per gallon of gas by the number of miles your car gets to the gallon to determine cost per mile. Then multiply by miles driven annually to get your total gas cost for the year.

7. OIL: Multiply the number of quarts used by the actual cost per quart. Divide by total miles operated annually to determine cost per mile.

8. TIRES: For a light car, figure 4/10 of a cent per mile; for a heavy car, 5/10 of a cent. Multiply by total miles operated annually to determine cost per year.

9. MAINTENANCE: Includes greasing, repairs, washing, etc. If you don't have actual figures, use 7/10 of a cent per mile for a small car, and 8/10 of a cent per mile for a heavy one. Multiply by miles operated annually to determine total cost for year.

10. MISCELLANEOUS: These costs include parking fees, polishing, anti-freeze, tolls, etc. Use estimated figures to the best of your knowledge.

NOW:

ADD up all the figures in column one and DIVIDE the total cost per year by the number of miles you drive annually to determine what it's costing you to drive per mile.

FIGURE FACTUALLY—show all costs, don't cut corners!

We think you'll agree that CTA IS THE CHEAPER WAY . . . by far!

RIDE LOCAL TRANSIT—YOU'LL AVOID TRAFFIC WORRIES AND SAVE MONEY

If preciseness is wanted, it should be added that unless you are carrying complete (not deductible) collision insurance, there is one final hidden cost: the possible cost of an accident not covered by your insurance. We have already pointed out that for many reasons the cost of collision insurance is not a good measure of the risk, but some fraction of this amount should be put in reserve to allow for the chance that sometime one of those large bills may come your way.

Similar, but not so complex, problems arise with durable goods, and with additions to homes: that depreciation and the cost of the money invested must be included in estimates of cost.

A third problem for the consumer arises because of the necessity for shopping carefully when purchasing and maintaining all of these items. Whether it is a car, household appliance, an addition or repair to the home, or repair service, the selection and timing may have a great deal to do with what you get for your money. Again, take the purchase of a car as an example. Although there are list prices for cars, the real price even of new cars varies according to trade-in allowances, "extras," or even straight discounts. Furthermore, the real net price tends to be low just before new models come in, and at other periods when the car market is a little "slow." Relatively speaking, there are even greater "swings" in the prices of used cars. All this adds up to the fact that a little observation and patience can pay off in helping you decide *when* to buy. It is also true that shopping around can pay off, since at any point in time there may be wide differences among dealers as to how eager they are for business. Finally, the selection of the brand also necessitates some investigation and decision making; for this purpose published information is available in sources like *Consumer Reports.*

Similar purchasing problems arise with household appliances: Which is the best brand? Where is the best deal? Will there be sales a little later? Most of these items are supposedly "fair traded," that is, sold at the same price everywhere, but there are frequently "sales," discount houses, "demonstrators," or retailers that offer big trade-in allowances.

It is for these large items that consumer information services are the most valuable. In addition to the usual sources discussed in an earlier chapter, technical material is available if you use the library properly.[18] A great many people are willing to pay somewhat more for the well-known nationally-advertised brands. This is only partly because they feel that the quality will be higher or parts easier to get. What is more important to some people is that they take less risk this way. They feel that they are less likely to make a very bad choice, that is, of a model that just does not work right, and that if they get a "lemon," one of the occasional models that has a flaw, the manufacturer or dealer will repair or replace it without difficulty. For many people, avoiding grossly bad choices, difficulties in service or in fulfillment of guarantees is more important than saving a few dollars on the original price.

In buying a car or appliance, there is also the question whether to buy a new one or not. Buying new is expensive. It costs about a third of the price of an appliance or a fourth of the price of a car just to take it out of the showroom. This is not just depreciation but is largely the cost of selling. The dealer who sells you a new durable must make his expenses and profit, and the dealer who would take it if you sold it must again make something when he resells. In addition to these costs of buying and selling there is the time cost of the shopping and information seeking that go with these decisions.

But it is not just transaction costs that make a new item expensive; it is the way in which their market value falls. A $2,000 car may last for ten years, but its market price falls a good deal more than $200 the first year. It may fall by $500. The next year it may cost you $400 in depreciation, the next year $300, the next year $200, and the next year another $150. At this time you have a five-year old car that is worth $450. This is clearly more expensive than buying a five-year old car for $450 and keeping it for five years. Of course maintenance and repairs will be somewhat greater on an older car, so that choices about new versus used cars, or newer versus older used ones depend at least in part on whether you can find an honest and reasonable mechanic or have some mechanical aptitude yourself. But it is difficult to see how extra repairs on an older car could amount to several hundred dollars a year.[19] With household appliances, the difference between the new and used prices is even greater, and the physical depreciation and increase in repair costs even smaller for most of them.

In any case, the consumer is paying for newness, the latest "improvements," and a somewhat smaller chance of breakdown. It is fortunate both for the producers of these items, and the people who need the services of inexpensive durables, that many people want and are willing to pay for newness. This provides an almost constant supply of inexpensive used durables.

Repairs to cars, durables, and houses, and even new construction around a house face the consumer with shopping problems of the sort we have been discussing: selection of brand and source, and timing the market, plus an additional problem— assessing the quality of the service. How can you tell whether the painter will work fast or slowly, leave paint on the windows or not? How can you tell whether the repair man's diagnosis that your washing machine needs a new motor represents the best strategy? In a great deal of repair work the decision must be made whether to replace a part that is suspected of not functioning perfectly, try to repair it, or continue to expend time and energy finding out just what is actually wrong. It is not necessarily either dishonest nor bad strategy to replace a part which may be all right, or to replace it with a new one when the old one could be repaired. Sometimes it takes longer and is more expensive to find out exactly what is wrong than to keep replacing one part after another, in some order of their possible chance of being the cause of the trouble, until the appliance works again.

On the other hand, it is easier work to replace parts, and easier to charge for it, consequently there is a temptation to put in a new part rather than repair the old part. There is sometimes, unfortunately, a temptation to rely on experience rather heavily as a guide to what might be wrong rather than apply any scientific methods of isolating the source of the difficulty.

Major repairs to a car or house usually require a considerable amount of shopping if you are to avoid excessive charges and bad work. It pays to insist on bids, and to check on the quality of work previously done by the bidders. If you can find someone who is not overburdened with work, and if you are not in too much of a hurry, you can frequently save considerable sums of money. Already mentioned was the possibility of pooling information by co-operatives which would provide ready access to the experience of others with various service organizations and contractors.

We have attempted to summarize a large and complex group of expenditures, and to show that they involve similar problems. The durables involve problems of arranging for large cash outlays, of remembering depreciation in figuring what something costs (and in budgeting and planning), of taking account of the cost of tying up money in that durable, of shopping for the right brand, the best deal and the weakest market period.

SUMMARY

The consumer makes decisions about how to spend his money in a number of major areas of spending. The more technical information about the products and market information about brands and prices he has, the more efficiently he can spend his money. Again, however, it may not be worth the effort expended, since there is a real cost in trying to know everything, and in the time and energy spent in shopping. In the case of durable goods we noticed some general principles which are useful: depreciation is a cost, and new cars and durables depreciate much more rapidly than older ones. You may prefer the new one, but it is good to realize the economic implications of the choice. Opportunity cost may also be important for large items, since money can always beget more of itself in the form of interest or dividends if it is not tied up in a car or new garage or some appliance.

A basic problem exists: how to get information on when to buy, and where, and on the quality of such services as auto repair, appliance repair, or work around the house. It is quite likely that consumers could do themselves more good by combining their information about these things than in almost any other way. The product testing organizations can provide information on the differences between different brands, but when it comes to the prices charged by different dealers, or the market fluctuations in prices from month to month, local information is necessary. And when it comes to the service trades, only local information is of much use.

Suggested Projects

1. If you can find a car needing some major repair, take it to a number of garages and get estimates of what it would cost. Are there differences in the details of the job that would account for some of the price differences; for instance, are some thinking of new parts and others of fixing the old?

2. Keep a record of the prices of a number of major fresh vegetables each week for several months. If possible, visit one store each week and make notes on the visible evidences of quality.

3. Make a study of the retail prices of various food items using published materials. Plot the prices and see whether you can observe regular seasonal patterns for some products, and irregular but somewhat cyclical fluctuations in the prices of others.

4. Read a recent textbook on nutrition and try to summarize it in terms of what the consumer should know about nutrition.

5. If there is a farmers' market near you, see what you can find out about how they decide on their prices, or what you can infer from the relation of their prices to those charged in the super-markets. Are they consistently a few cents on one side or the other of supermarket prices? Does this mean that the supermarket is actually setting the prices?

6. If you live in or near a large city visit the wholesale produce market. Try to find out how it operates and assess its efficiency. How much mark-up is there between the buying and selling price?

7. Ask an auto dealer for one of his old copies of the National Auto Dealers' Association, *Official Used Car Guide*. Look up the prices of some popular make of car for various year models. Take the differences and plot them as an estimate of the annual depreciation over the life of a car. Particularly well-liked year-models may distort your curve somewhat, but if you plot curves for several makes of cars, the general pattern should appear.

8. Estimate your own future family pattern including number and sexes of children. Then estimate the calories and protein requirements over the next 30 years. Plot the totals.

FOOTNOTES TO CHAPTER 9

1 Charles G. King, "Trends in the Science of Food and Its Relation to Life," *Nutrition Reviews*, 10:1–4 (Jan., 1952), p. 4; see also: Henry C. Sherman, *The Nutritional Improvement of Life*, New York: Columbia University Press, 1950; see also, however, *Recommended Dietary Allowances* (Revised, 1953), Publication No. 302, Washington, D. C.: National Research Council, National Academy of Sciences, 1953. A Report of the Food and Nutrition Board, National Research Council.

2 U.S. Department of Agriculture, Agricultural Research Administration, Bureau of Human Nutrition and Home Economics, *Nutritive Content of City Diets*, Special Report No. 2 (lithoprint), Washington, D. C.: U.S.D.A., October, 1950. A Summary report including some previously unpublished data, based on Food Consumption Surveys of 1948–49.

3 U.S. Department of Agriculture, Production and Marketing Administration, *Some Highlights from Consumer, Egg Studies*, Agricultural Information Bulletin No. 110, Washington, D. C.: U.S. Gov't Printing Office, 1953.

4 Gertrude S. Weiss, "Time and Money Costs of Meals Using Home- and Pre-kitchen-prepared Foods," *Journal of Home Economics*, 46:98–100 (Feb., 1954).

5 Guy Black, "Variations in Prices Paid for Food as Affected by Income Level," *Journal of Farm Economics*, 34:52–66 (Feb., 1952); for the basic data, see: U.S. Department of Agriculture, Agricultural Research Administration, Bureau of Human Nutrition and Home Economics, *Food Consumption of Urban Families in the United States, Spring, 1948*, 1948 Food Consumption Surveys, Preliminary Report No. 5 (lithoprint), Washington, D. C.: U.S. Dept. of Agriculture, 1949.

6 U.S. Department of Agriculture, Agric. Research Adm., Bureau of Human Nutrition and Home Economics, *Home Food Preservation by City Families, 1947,* 1948 Food Consumption Surveys, Preliminary Report No. 15 (lithoprint), Washington, D. C.: U.S. Dept. of Agriculture, 1950.

7 See, however: U.S. Department of Agriculture, *Egg Buying Guides for Consumers,* Home and Garden Bulletin No. 26, Washington, D. C.: U.S. Dept. of Agriculture, 1954.

8 U.S. Department of Agriculture, *Guiding Family Spending,* Misc. Pub. No. 661, Washington, D.C.: U.S. Gov't Printing Office, 1949, esp. Table 7, p. 24; but see also: U.S. Bureau of Labor Statistics, *Family, Spending and Saving in Wartime,* Bulletin No. 822, Washington, D. C.: U.S. Gov't Printing Office, 1945; U.S. Bureau of Labor Statistics, *Family Income, Expenditures and Savings in 1950,* Bulletin No. 1097 (Revised), Washington, D. C.: U.S. Gov't Printing Office, 1953; U.S. Department of Agriculture, Agricultural Research Administration, Bureau of Human Nutrition and Home Economics, *Food Consumption of Urban Families in the United States, Spring, 1948,* 1948 Food Consumption Surveys, Preliminary Report No. 5 (lithoprint), Washington, D. C.: U.S. Dept. of Agriculture, 1949; for estimates based on a mixture of facts about what people do and judgments about what they should do, see: Heller Committee for Research in Social Economics, *Quantity and Cost Budgets for Two Income Levels, Prices for the San Francisco Bay Area, Sept., 1953,* Berkeley: University of California, 1953.

9 See also: Henry C. Sherman, *Principles of Nutrition and Nutritive Value of Food,* U.S. Department of Agriculture, Misc. Pub. No. 546, Washington, D. C.: U.S. Gov't Printing Office, 1944.

10 S. J. Prais, "The Estimation of Equivalent Scales from Family Budgets," *Economic Journal,* LXIII:791–810 (December, 1953).

11 U.S. Congress, House Agriculture Committee, *Farm Prices and the Cost of Food, A Review of the Extent to Which Recent Farm Price Declines Have and Have Not Been Passed On to Urban Consumers,* Committee Print, 83rd Congress, 2nd Session (July 23, 1954).

12 *Monthly Letter,* National City Bank of New York, November, 1954, p. 130.

13 Published evidence is scarce on this topic. Descriptions of needed improvements in specific markets have been published by the U.S. Department of Agriculture, Production and Marketing Administration. See, for example: U.S. Department of Agriculture, Production and Marketing Administration, Marketing and Facilities Research Branch, *The Wholesale Produce Market at Indianapolis Indiana* (mimeo), Washington, D. C.: U.S. Department of Agriculture, 1950. For a general treatment of distribution, see: Paul W. Stewart and Frederick J. Dewhurst, *Does Distribution Cost Too Much?,* New York: Twentieth Century Fund, 1939.

14 M. A. Adelman, "The Large Firm and Its Suppliers," *Review of Economics and Statistics,* XXXI:113–118 (May, 1949); Joel B. Dirlam and A. E. Kahn, "Integration and Dissolution of the A & P Company," 29 *Indiana Law Journal* 1–27 (Fall, 1953).

15 Edwin Wolff, *Why We Do It,* New York: Macaulay Co., 1929; Bernard Rudofsky, *Are Clothes Modern?,* Chicago: P. Theobald Co., 1947; Paul H. Nystrom, *The Economics of Fashion,* New York: The Ronald Press Company, 1928; James Laver, *Taste and Fashion,* rev. ed., London: George G. Harrap Co., 1948; Thorstein Veblen, *The Theory of the Leisure Class,* New York: The Viking Press, Inc., 1912; Elizabeth Hawes, *Fashion Is Spinach,* New York: Random House, 1938; Morris DeCamp Crawford, *The Ways of Fashion,* New York: Fairchild Publications, Inc., 1948.

16 Jules Labarthe, "Your Money's Worth in Clothing and Textiles," *Journal of Home Economics*, 46:640–644 (November, 1954).

17 U.S. Department of Agriculture, Bureau of Home Economics, Textiles and Clothing Division, *Judging Fabric Quality*, revised, Washington, D. C.: U.S. Gov't Printing Office, 1942; see also any recent text in Home Economics or Textiles, for example: Mildred G. Ryan and Velma Phillips, *Clothes for You*, 2nd ed., New York: Appleton-Century-Crofts, Inc., 1954.

18 See, for instance: Enid S. Ross, Katherine Taube and Dorothy S. Greene, *Home Washing Machines—Operating Characteristics and Factors Affecting Performance*, U.S. Department of Agriculture Technical Bulletin No. 1088, Washington, D. C.: U.S. Gov't Printing Office, July, 1954. The brand names are not given in this study, but the specifications of the machines allow most of them to be identified.

19 A detailed statistical study indicates that it pays to keep a car for many years. See, Armen A. Alchian, *Economic Replacement Policy*, Santa Monica, California: The Rand Corporation, 1952.

chapter 10

Protection
for the Consumer

Introduction

We have already seen that the government is heavily involved in protecting the consumer against some risks in the areas of medical care, unemployment and old age, and housing. In addition, we have seen that voluntary insurance schemes add to this protection. In this chapter we shall be concerned about protection for the consumer against fraud, extortion, and profiteering. We shall see first what the government does for consumers in this area, and then what he does or can do for himself.

GOVERNMENT PROTECTION FOR THE CONSUMER

Federal, state, and local governments have a wide variety of agencies and laws designed to protect consumers against extortion and exploitation. We shall put them into three types: protection against fraud and dangerous products, prevention of monopoly and its variants, and the regulation of public utility charges.

Government Prevention of Fraud

Although there are many government agencies which have something to do in protecting the consumer against fraud and deception, they have, for the most part, limited themselves, or have been limited by insufficient funds, to elimination of the worst and most obvious abuses. The consumer who relies on them completely will find that there are still many opportunities for being bilked.

On the local level there are inspectors of weights and measures, who though they cannot keep the butcher's thumb off the scales, can check that the scales will weigh correctly what is on them. At the state level there is the state insurance commission that tries to make sure that insurance companies pay legitimate claims and do not write "joker" clauses in their contracts, and that they invest the policyholders' money in safe investments. Recently, moreover, the U.S. Supreme Court in *U.S. v. South Eastern Underwriters Association,* June 5, 1944 (322 U.S. 533), declared that the entire business of insurance was interstate commerce and therefore was subject also to federal regulation under the anti-trust laws. Since there has been a rather surprising similarity of types of policies offered by the various companies, and since many of them operate on a national basis, this was probably a sensible decision. Congress passed a law in 1945 suspending application of the anti-trust laws to the insurance business until January 1, 1948, but they presumably apply now. The South Eastern Underwriters Association not only had fixed premium rates, but also had used boycotts and other types of coercion to force other insurance companies into the conspiracies, for instance, by refusing to provide reinsurance for them.

In 1948 the McCarran Act gave the Federal Trade Commission supervisory powers over insurance to the extent that it is not already subject to state law, but the regular anti-trust laws also apply.

States also regulate trust funds, particularly the open-ended kind where one can buy shares and the trust simply invests the money, charging a small commission for its services. Clearly the possibilities for excessive charges, fraud in reporting the value of the holdings of securities, etc. are such that regulation is required.

Also on the state and local level health departments check on sanitation not only in water supplies and in sewage and garbage disposal, but also in food handling establishments, barber shops, and so forth. It should be added that in several states acts purporting to insure sanitation in barber shops have actually been designed to prevent price competition and to fix minimum prices.

On the federal government level, there are a number of agencies which try to protect the consumer against fraud and dangerous products. Their functions are so defined that sometimes several of them might be involved in the same case. If a man sent out advertising for a new drug that purported to be a cure for cancer, but was not, he would find himself embroiled with the Food and Drug Administration, because it is illegal to introduce a new drug without their permission, with the Post Office for using the mails to defraud, and with the Federal Trade Commission acting under the Wheeler-Lea Act of 1938 for issuing deceptive advertising injurious to the public welfare whether it injures competition or not. An agreement was worked out in 1954 to eliminate duplication and to provide closer working relations between the F.T.C. and the F.D.A.

The Food and Drug Adiministration is perhaps the most important single agency protecting the consumer against dangerous or misrepresented foods and drugs, because the activities of the Post Office are limited to mailed solicitation and their investigations have to be done without opening mail, and such activities of the Federal Trade Commission are peripheral to their major task of preserving competition. The Annual Reports of the Food and Drug Administration are fascinating reading.[1] Every year there are new and dramatic reports of seizure of misbranded or adulterated or dangerous foods, drugs, or cosmetics.

Danger to health was charged in seizures of dressed birds that had undissolved diethylstilbestrol pellets in edible portions of the necks. The pellets were implanted in young male birds to cause artificial caponization. Directions called for insertion at the base of the head, so that undissolved portions would be discarded at the time of slaughter. Some poultrymen were careless, however, in handling this potentially dangerous substance. After more than 61,000 pounds of poultry were seized in 14 actions early in the year, some raisers abandoned the use of pellets, and others corrected their practices.[2]

In June 1952 carloads of "pink wheat" began to arrive at milling centers, colored by a poisonous mercurial compound used for seed treatment. Weather conditions had prevented farmers from planting expected quantities of the treated seed and they were confronted with surpluses. Many mixed it with good wheat and delivered it to elevators for food use.[3]

A single regulatory action may bring spectacular results in consumer protection. Following a series of seizures of filth-contaminated candies, a Federal court enjoined the manufacturer from making further violative shipments. The factory closed down for three weeks while 300 people engaged in a thorough clean-up of the premises. Resulting sanitary improvement extended beyond the output of that plant, however, with other candy manufacturers reviewing their sanitary programs.[4]

Sometimes the products are not dangerous to anything but the pocketbook.

Most of the poultry removed from the market to protect the food purchaser's pocketbook had been deceptively weighted with feed or water. Thanksgiving market surveys resulted in seizures of turkeys with a pound and a quarter of oats in their crops. Addition of water took two forms. Some birds were injected in the thighs and breast with an average of a quart of water which froze in the flesh—destroying flavor as well as adding to the net cost. In other cases wet eviscerated poultry was packed in plastic bags before freezing, resulting in a 7 to 10 per cent ice glaze.[5]

More recently watered oysters have been discovered.

The reports of dangerous drugs, adulterated drugs, "treatment centers," sales of therapeutic devices, sales of drugs without prescription, and counterfeit drugs are equally fascinating.

One druggist sold ascorbic acid tablets for cortisone.[6]

Physical danger faced by FDA investigators may be expected to increase as it becomes necessary for inspectors to trace distribution of harmful drugs through underworld channels. Investigations during the past year of criminal drug rings resulted in one inspector being held at gun point for 2 hours and another having his skull fractured by a blackjack. Unfortunately, it is not a federal offense to attack an FDA inspector, although this protection is afforded to Narcotics agents.[6]

In another case, a pharmacist was making surreptitious sales of barbiturates to an addict on street corners at designated times, without knowledge of the owner of the store.[7]

In the same city women seeking to reduce were purchasing amphetamines by "speakeasy" methods. They presented a white box with an "X" marked in pencil on the top and gave the password "tops." The drug in question should be used only under careful medical supervision.[7]

One drug store fined for illegal sales could not account by prescription records for 172,552 barbiturate capsules received from wholesalers or manufacturers.[7]

An injunction in November restrained further shipments of a cancer diagnosis kit, consisting of a test tube and two bottles of well-known chemicals labeled "Reagens I and II." Directions were given to add Reagens I (hydrochloric and nitric acid) to a sample of the patient's urine, heat and cool it, add Reagens II (ether), and if a color change occurred in an hour the patient was doomed as a cancer victim. The kit was employed by many alleged practitioners of the healing arts who had little medical training and no specialized training in the diagnosis or treatment of cancer.

The danger to public health of such a scheme is emphasized by the fact that controlled tests with this kit showed negative results in 59 of 76 cases known to be malignant, and positive results in many healthy medical students. Retesting on the same group produced varying results. FDA based its injunction request on the fact that the only reliable cancer test is the microscopic examination of suspected tissue by a qualified pathologist.[8]

Devices were seized because of false and misleading claims to remove cataracts and treat other eye conditions; shoes to ward off disease by dispersing the electricity the body generates; violet ray instruments to prevent or cure baldness; and various types of massagers and vibrators to remove excess fat, tone the system, and protect against or cure numerous diseases.

The electrical vibrator purporting to do the most for the ills of mankind was claimed to be an effective treatment for polio, goiter, diabetes, angina pectoris, appendix pain, locomoter ataxia, cardiac asthma, drowning, sun stroke, hay fever, cold in the head, and excess fat.[9]

One major difficulty in preventing this sort of thing is that the jurisdiction of the federal government is only over items shipped in interstate commerce, or offered for interstate transportation. This means that so long as the drug or device is sold only within a single state, and no new drugs are involved, only state health officers have any powers.

The Narcotics division of the Treasury Department is responsible for proper and safe use of narcotics. Their problems are simpler because of the limited number of different drugs involved and the strict rules about records that must be kept by distributors.

The Post Office Department concerns itself with the use of the mails to defraud, and the annual reports of the Postmaster General contain stories of the activity of the Office of the Chief Post Office Inspector.

Some of the various fraudulent schemes investigated in the past year in which convictions were had or indictments are outstanding include: In a typical case, buyers lost $225,000 which they paid in substantial down payments on new homes, and received nothing. In the name of the Sister Kenny Foundation an operator promoted donations amounting to $187,000 and converted a large proportion to his own use. . . . Two officials of the Cancer Welfare Fund collected $123,000 in 10 months and spent most of it on high living. A financier obtained $1,600,000 in loans on forged notes backed with counterfeit whisky-warehouse receipts. Promoters of worthless Canadian stock have received a severe set-back in the ratification of an extradition treaty with Canada making it possible to remove them to this country for prosecution.[10]

Medical fraud by mail, mostly promising home cures, and mail lotteries are also kept in check by postal authorities. Continuous efforts are required because the frauds are highly profitable.[11]

The resources available to these agencies, particularly the

Food and Drug Administration, are insufficient if they are to do what they feel is an adequate job of protecting the consumer.

The Federal Trade Commission, together with the agencies we have mentioned, tries to reduce the amount of false advertising, and together with the Anti-Trust Division of the Justice Department tries to reduce monopoly and price-fixing. (See below.) It likewise suffers from inadequate funds. As of June 30, 1952, the Commission employed fewer people than in 1918 or 1939.

Thus the Commission resembles a city which, while doubling in population and tripling its volume of trade, has slightly reduced the size of its police force and fire department. Maintenance of effective operations has become steadily more difficult.

The problem is aggravated by the fact that the Commission's statutory duties are substantially greater than when it was created. Highlights of this expansion of functions have been as follows:

1. In 1936 the Robinson-Patman Act materially enlarged the scope of the law against price discrimination.

2. In 1938 the Wheeler-Lea Act materially expanded the Commission's functions in the prevention of false advertising.

3. In 1940 the Wool Products Act assigned to the Commission the duty of maintaining surveillance over the labeling of wool textiles. . . .

4. In 1946 the Trade Mark Act assigned to the Commission new duties with regard to the unlawful use of registered trade marks.

5. In 1948 the McCarran Insurance Act gave the Commission jurisdiction over insurance which is highly complex because its scope varies from State to State in accord with variations in State law.

6. In 1950 the Anti-Merger Act gave the Commission jurisdiction over acquisitions of assets by corporations where there is an adverse effect upon competition. The Commission's previous jurisdiction in such matters had been limited to acquisitions of stock. . . .

7. The Fur Products Labeling Act, effective August 9, 1952, gives the Commission authority over the labeling of fur products similar to that already assigned in the case of wool textiles. . . .

At a conservative estimate, the Commission is now spending upon functions assigned to it by these additional statutes at least $1,250,-000 or about 29.9 per cent of its total appropriation; and a full enforcement of these additional statutes probably would cost double this sum. The diversion of personnel to these new duties has necessitated a corresponding shrinkage in the other activities assigned to the Commission by the original Clayton Act and the Federal Trade Commission Act.[11]

The descriptions in the Annual Reports of the Federal Trade Commission of its activity in "antideceptive practices work" are always interesting. Cases range from the obliteration of marks indicating foreign manufacture of sewing machines to false representation of foreign manufacture of smoking pipes actually made in this country.[12] The Commission attempts to prevent (1) false and misleading advertising, (2) unfair and deceptive acts and practices, (3) misbranding, and (4) other forms of misrepresentation.

The Commission operates through Trade Practice Conferences, where the members of a trade get together to agree on certain standards, or through "stipulations" to which offenders agree, or finally through "cease and desist" orders enforceable through the courts. However, the Federal Trade Commission can eliminate most practices only after they have been engaged in for some time, and then only the most clearly fraudulent cases and after lengthy legal processes. If the manufacturer only *insinuates* that his product will do something, without actually saying so, it is difficult to do anything about it. If he puts on a whirlwind campaign with false claims, the readers may well remember the claims and never see the report of the F.T.C. action.

In banking, as a result of bank failures which wiped out people's savings, we now have rather extensive regulation on both state and federal levels as well as through the Federal Reserve System. We also have the Federal Deposit Insurance Corporation and the Federal Savings and Loan Insurance Corporation that insure savings accounts in participating banks up to $10,-

000 for each account. The consumer need no longer fear that his bank will fail through fraud or mismanagement and leave him without funds, provided his account is insured by the F.D.I.C. or the F.S.L.I.C.

In the field of securities, again after some experience with fraudulent issues of stock, the Securities Exchange Commission was established, requiring complete disclosure of the financial facts by companies wishing to sell new issues of stock or bonds and to advertise them. There are some who argue that the resulting "protection" is deceptive, because a bad investment might still look attractive to an unsophisticated buyer who had all the facts but did not know how to interpret them. On occasion, as in the famous Tucker controversy, the S.E.C. has issued releases which made the nature of the situation quite plain.

The Commission is particularly sensitive to "deals" whereby promoters are given rights to buy stock at prices far less than the price at which identical shares are offered to the ordinary investors. There are also state "blue sky" laws against fraudulent promotions, but the laws in Canada are much less strict; hence, there has been an active solicitation by mail urging people to buy stock in Canadian "oil companies"—companies which on investigation turn out to hold nothing beyond some options on some potential oil lands, and to have arrangements for stock purchases at special prices by the promoters. By and large, however, stock issues in this country, particularly by established companies, are honestly and openly made.[13]

Finally, there are numerous government agencies that provide useful information for the consumer that can enable him to avoid being "taken in." Perhaps the most important of these are the Bureau of Human Nutrition and Home Economics of the Department of Agriculture and the Bureau of Standards. However, information comes from such a variety of agencies that the only safe procedure is to consult the annual indexes to the *Monthly Catalogue of Government Publications.*

Government Anti-monopoly Activities

Under a series of laws beginning with the Sherman Anti-Trust Act of 1890 two general types of activity have been prohibited by law: The *restraint of trade* (price agreements, allocation of market areas, collusive bidding, preventing competitors from entering the field), and *unfair competition* (price discrimination between different customers not justified by differences in costs of serving them, attempts to drive competitors out of business in hopes of recouping losses later). Two government agencies, the Federal Trade Commission and the Anti-Trust Division of the Justice Department, attempt to enforce the laws, with some resulting problems of overlapping authority.

Most of the actual cases have dealt with large producers of relatively homogeneous products: steel, aluminum, cement, cigarettes, oak flooring, and so forth. Given limited funds and the necessity for proving that interstate commerce was involved —and hence federal intervention was legal—it is easy to see why this would be so. In addition, there may well have been an implicit distrust of the concentration of economic power as such, regardless of the degree of monopoly, because of the potentiality for misuse.

A number of exemptions from the anti-trust laws have been made: labor unions, by a declaration in the Clayton Act of 1914 that labor is not a commodity or article of commerce, and by the Norris-LaGuardia Act of 1932; agricultural cooperatives, by the Capper-Volstead Act of 1922 and the Agricultural Marketing Agreements Act of 1937; shipping, by the Shipping Act of 1916; railroads, by the Reed-Bulwinkle Act of 1948; airlines, by the Civil Aeronautics Act of 1938; banking, by the Federal Reserve Act of 1913; and exporting agreements among producers, by the Webb-Pomerene Act of 1918. At present the state of the anti-trust laws is as controversial as ever and somewhat more in flux.

There is no space in this book for the details of anti-monopoly policy, the enforcement of the laws, and the changes in Supreme Court interpretations. There are excellent textbooks on the subject.[14] A few general statements need to be made: First, insofar as economies of large-scale production, research, product development, or merchandising make it economically impossible for any large number of producers to exist in a given field of production, no law can produce price competition. Competition will exist if there is someone like Harvey Firestone in tires or Henry Ford in automobiles who believes in low margins, high volume, and competition. Secondly, however, competition may exist in dimensions other than price. If it is competition in changing the product—and most changes are improvements—then the consumer is still well served. If it is competition in advertising, then economists would generally regard it as wasteful—justified only if consumers can be induced to spend their money and to keep business going only by such advertising. Thirdly, there are many local "monopolies" and "conspiracies" which are not subject to federal control and may well do more damage to the consumer than any possible amount of monopoly in the steel industry. Exclusive dealers with franchises to sell and/or service products, or sole providers of specialized services, may charge almost what they please. Local associations of professionals, building trades workers, barbers, and so forth can and do get together to raise prices and restrict entry.

Finally, and perhaps most important, there are high prices and inefficiencies that arise from what the economist calls "monopolistic competition." [15] There are situations where there is not just a single product but many differentiated products all serving the same general purpose. They will be differently made, packaged, advertised, or distributed, so that each "producer" has a market somewhat sheltered from competition. This can have several results: If the producers or distributors are very successful in differentiating their products from one another, there will be very little competition in the areas of price and quality but great concentration on advertising and changes in the product. If there remains a good deal of competition, the final result may be "too much competition," that is, many firms, no one of which can get enough business to operate efficiently, all charging enough to cover their high costs, but no one making any substantial profits. Many areas of retailing, as well as the manufacture of style goods, seem to be examples of this sort of situation.

But is it not possible that the consumer himself is to blame for all this? If he did not demand variety, and would go a little farther to a store with better quality or lower price, or did not shift so rapidly from one brand to another in response to new features (ammoniated, chlorophyll, and so forth) perhaps the more efficient producers and distributors would drive the others out of business. In Great Britain factory space was released for war production during the second world war by restriction of furniture and clothing to a few "utility" lines. The moderate success in this country of attempts to sell quality and low price without the usual frills of fancy store, credit, delivery, and so forth would indicate that except in times of inflation, consumers are themselves responsible for some of the high prices they pay. They are paying for service, variety, and up-to-dateness in their products.

In the main, however, it is fair to say that the anti-trust laws have probably done a great deal of good not so much for what they have punished as for what they have prevented. Many observers of British industry have concluded that the ease with which cartels and other monopoly devices could be formed there led to technological stagnation in many British industries.[16]

Companies also have economic power in buying, particularly in the purchasing of labor services in non-unionized trades. Possible exploitation has been minimized by the Fair Labor Standards Act and other laws which have established maximum hours and minimum wages, and by the growth of unions.

Over the years there has been a great deal of material published on the monopoly problem in general, perhaps the most massive of which is the hearings and monographs of the Temporary National Economic Committee of the 1930's.

Recently the Senate Select Committee on the Problems of Small Business published reports on monopoly particularly on relation to its impact on small business.[17]

There are a number of basic questions which have never been adequately answered. For instance, to what extent is the large corporation, operating many plants making many different products or located in different areas, more efficient than smaller individual enterprises? If there are few or no such economies, many people argue that the preservation of competition, incentive, opportunity, and even political democracy can be aided by splitting large aggregations into smaller independent units. It is no exaggeration to say that available data on the relation of corporate size to efficiency are inconclusive. Even the definition of efficiency is unclear. If one concentrates on pure technical and manufacturing efficiency, almost by definition one corporation need not own more than one plant. If you admit the possibility of economies in advertising, marketing, product development, research, securing of finances, unified cost control, unified purchasing, then the possible economies of scale are much broader. On the other hand, we must ask to what extent these are genuine economies—more efficient use of resources—and to what extent they are themselves the result of concentrated power, for example in forcing suppliers to sell at lower prices simply because of the ability to bargain and threaten. Or to what extent are marketing advantages the result of the capacity for large expenditures on advertising to create a protected market?

There are technological changes in our economy which require taking risks with very large amounts of capital, for example, color television, and the large corporations have proven an effective instrument for taking these risks.

The law is very complex, and businessmen argue that they never know what is legal. Others argue that the businessmen hire expensive lawyers to obfuscate the issues so they can say this. The Attorney General's National Committee to Study the Anti-trust Laws, headed by Professor S. Chesterfield Oppenheim of the University of Michigan Law School is currently examining the present state of anti-trust laws and can be expected to come out with some recommendations, perhaps with several sets of minority recommendations as well. There are many complex problems here. If a manufacturer thinks that one of his customers is misusing his product, perhaps by using it with some other cheaper parts, and thus ruining his reputation, does he not have the right to refuse to deal? How can we distinguish this from unlawful discrimination between customers which makes it impossible for them to compete with one another?

Finally, there is the general sociological problem arising from the power of corporation management. In practice the largest and most secure corporations have seemed to be developing leadership that took a rather broad social viewpoint regarding itself as an arbiter between the interests of the investors, workers, and customers. And, of course, in periods of inflation, the large corporations held the line on prices longer and were easier to control by authority than industries with a lot of small competitors. One could easily reverse this argument and argue that large aggregations of power can and may make it all too easy for the government to take over control.

Government Regulation of Public Utility Rates

Whenever it is economically not feasible to have many small competing producers, we face a choice whether to try to enforce competition and to prevent collusion, or to regulate the prices and profits of the producers, or to take over and operate them as a government enterprise. We have discussed, very briefly, the attempts by government to enforce competition. In most public utilities—electric light, railroads, telephone and telegraph service, airlines, busses, and trucks—the predominant solution has been to set up commissions to regulate the rates charged and to prevent extortion.[18] However, some electric power is produced by the TVA and by local publicly owned plants. Regulation of privately owned utilities is bound to be expensive and somewhat inefficient, involving two sets of accountants, long hearings, and occasional legal battles. We see a fascinating paradox where the utility spends hundred of thousands of dollars to convince the regulating commission and the public that it cannot lower the rates and still earn a fair return on the investment. Of course, the expense is deducted in computing recent past profits.

On the other hand, the ownership and operation of a utility by a government body may lead to inefficiency and "bureaucracy" unless accounting systems can be designed and comparisons made with other utilities as a test of efficiency. It is likely that the coexistence of both publicly owned and privately owned utilities keeps both of them more efficient than the domination by either type. More will be said in the next chapter about utilities in connection with multi-purpose federal projects. Here we are concerned with the protection of the consumer against unreasonable charges by private utilities.

The regulating commissions—Interstate Commerce Commission, Civil Aeronautics Board, Federal Communications Commission, and the various state commissions—face a serious and basic paradox in attempting to regulate the charges of the various utilities under their jurisdiction. The people who manage the utilities must be motivated to run them efficiently and to make advances in techniques. If the commission adjusts rates so that only some reasonable level of profits is allowed, no matter what happens, then no effort by management can result in higher profits or more funds for future experimentation. Management can be as inefficient as it likes, or fail to serve the customer adequately, and then appeal for higher rates when the profits fall. On the other hand, if the commission is lax in insisting on lower rates when profits rise, then management will have more profit and more incentive, but the consumer will pay higher prices to provide potentially excessive profits.

The regulating commission must then achieve some acceptable compromise between immediate gains to consumers in lower charges, and potential future gains through preserving the incentives of management. Many observers feel that the commissions have been too free in allowing increases in rates, and too slow to force them down, and that in some cases they have even allowed rate increases which provided temporary relief at the expense of making basic readjustments more difficult. Some states have been experimenting with systems which try to maintain incentive by allowing the utility to keep some of the gains if they reduce costs.[19]

In view of the fact that regulating commissions are closely in contact with the utilities they regulate but not with the consumers they protect, it would seem that some pressure from informed consumers would have a good influence on them. However, it is difficult for consumers to understand the issues even if they can get at the accounting facts. Regulation of public utility rates is customarily done by establishing some fair rate of profit on the investment. The difficulty arises both in deciding what is a fair rate of profit, and in deciding what the investment—customarily called the rate base—is. A utility may have built a plant which cost $1,000,000 at the time of construction, but would cost $2,000,000 to reproduce now. And technical progress may be such that it would never be reproduced as is, but replaced by a quite different type of plant which costs, say $3,000,000, but has double the output and lower current operating costs.

Should the company be allowed enough income to pay a reasonable profit and to accumulate funds to write-off the original investment—forcing the company to seek additional new investment funds when it comes time to replace the plant? Should they be allowed enough income to have funds to replace the same plant at today's higher prices, but be forced to seek additional funds for the expansion in capacity and increase in efficiency? Or should they be allowed to accumulate enough to expand completely out of earnings?   The purists, economists or accountants, would choose the first or perhaps the second solution, the utility managers the second or third.

Decisions about allowable depreciation charges—which is the way the "writing-off" of old plant and equipment is done —affect the rates charged by the company in two ways: First, the more depreciation expense allowed in any one year, the higher the rates must be to cover this plus the operating expenses plus a fair profit to the investors.   Secondly, the depreciation charges reduce the net book value of the plant and equipment which is part of the investment base on which "fair" profits will be figured in the future.   On the other hand, revaluation of the plant to take account of increased prices or equipment costs will increase this investment base.

Thus, what started out to be a simple task of determining how much the investors had invested, what the profits were, and whether they were high or low relative to a "fair" rate, turns out to be complex enough to allow considerable bargaining and argument.   What is a fair rate of return?   The Association of American Railroads has argued that 6 per cent is fair.   There has been at least one court opinion that a fair rate is what industries with a comparable degree of risk have been earning, whatever this means.

However, after deciding what the investment is, the regulating commission has a relatively simple task to determine what depreciation charges are allowable, and what is a fair rate of return.   If the rates provided profits of $50,000 and a "fair" rate times the amount of investment would have given $60,000 "normal" profits, then the commission figures out how much the rates would have to be increased to bring in an additional $10,000 in profit.   Since rate increases generally have very little effect on the sales of the company's services, this would be a simple calculation.

One further complexity arises because rates, particularly for electricity, vary between different kinds of customers and between the initial and marginal amounts used by the same purchaser. This means that the conscientious commission has to make some decisions about the structure of rates, though often they are left to the company to decide. It is customary to allow lower rates to industrial or large-scale users because of economies in transmission, billing, and so forth, and because some of them use power during periods of the day when there is excess capacity, and also because some of these users might produce their own power if rates were too high.

As for the lower rates to each user for the last few units used, there are excellent reasons for allowing such practices: Most utilities operate with large fixed costs, which means that the cost of producing an additional kilowatt is very low compared with the average cost per kilowatt. The larger the output, the lower the cost per unit and the greater the efficiency. If it costs 2¢ to produce an additional unit, charging 8¢ will keep consumers from using something which cost 2¢ and is worth 7¢ to them. On the other hand, it is necessary to pay the fixed costs of the company too. By charging a consumer a high fixed charge, either as a flat sum or as a high unit charge for the first few units each month, the company can cover its costs, and still charge a low rate for additional units, inducing the consumer to use more of it and allowing the plant to expand and to operate efficiently.

There are two economic principles at work here, (a) that the cost of production of a good or service should generally be covered by those who buy it, and (b) that output should be expanded so long as the additional output is worth more than the additional costs involved. The first is a matter of equity and income distribution. Both involve problems in resource allocation.[20] Perhaps an extreme example will make this clearer.

A bridge costs so much to build, and something to keep up, but the costs do not depend on the number of cars that cross it, to any significant extent. The decision whether to build the bridge depends on whether it is worth the large total cost, or, to put it another way, whether by any possible diabolical system of discriminatory charges one could pay for the bridge. This may involve taxes as well as charges for crossing the bridge, because it is possible to have a bridge that would not pay for itself in tolls, but which people desire enough to be willing to pay taxes for. But a second decision has to do with how the bridge is actually paid for. Any system that charges people for using the bridge will keep some people from using it, people to whom it is worth something but not as much as the toll. Since it costs nothing to carry an extra car on the bridge—provided it is not operating at capacity which is unlikely—economists feel that resources are being misused. On the other hand, someone has to pay for the bridge, and if it is paid for out of taxes, some people will pay who never use the bridge, and others will benefit from the bridge without paying because the taxes do not get them. This is particularly true for bridges like the George Washington Bridge, across the Hudson River in New York, which serves a wide area and many tourists. In this particular case the bridge is financed out of tolls, but the distorting effects on its use are reduced somewhat by providing lower rates for commuters who cross ten times a week.

You will notice that there are two different types of price discrimination, one which charges lower prices to the same person for additional units, and another which charges different prices to different people. The second type involves more difficulties, because more problems of equity as between the different people are involved.

To return to regulation of public utilities, the commissions control their rate levels and structures so as to provide normal profits, equity as between different types of consumers, and reasonable prices. They also have some controls over the service offered. In the case of airlines, the Civil Aeronautics Board has the additional possibility of deciding how many competing airlines there shall be by their control over chartering, over the particular routes each airline is allowed to fly, and over proposed mergers of airlines. The problem is to allow enough airlines to provide competition in service and some comparisons of cost, and so forth, and few enough so that they each have enough business to operate efficiently.[21]

The schedules are also subject to control in the case of railroads. A railroad which wishes to abandon an unprofitable branch line will find it difficult to secure permission if the regulating commission finds that there are people or firms who have come to depend on that service.[22] Whether the Interstate Commerce Commission is a regulator or defender of the railroads is still subject to debate.[23]

Non-Government Protection for the Consumer

Organizations

There are numerous organizations which, for one reason or another, provide the consumer with protection or with information he can use for his own protection. Professional associations are frequently concerned not only with maintaining high standards but also with preventing or eliminating excessive charges, deception, or fraud. Better Business Bureaus or local Chambers of Commerce serve to warn the public of the worst sorts of frauds, particularly if perpetrated by people from outside the city. Various magazines (*Good Housekeeping, Parents Magazine*) and trade associations have "seals of approval." And, of course, magazines that specialize in serving the consumer, such as *Consumer Reports* or *Consumers Research,* contain articles about various types of frauds. The ingenuity of those who prey upon people's gullibility or avarice is such, however, that the consumer himself must use his own discretion, too.

Self-Protection and Cooperatives

We can say very little about this subject that is useful. There are, however, certain standard techniques for fooling people: First, there is the establishment of a "normal" price. Sometimes this is done by advertising the object in some small

newspaper for a very high price, then having copies made of
the advertisement. Second, there is the lure of promises that
you can get rich quick. It is difficult to see why people can be
made to believe that anyone is really going to give them anything for nothing, but they do. Third, there is often a specious
element of urgency: the promised opportunity will vanish if
you do not act immediately. Fourth, particularly with illegal
schemes, there is secrecy, designed of course to keep the victim
from talking to someone and finding out the truth. Perhaps
the most useful rule to follow is to take your time and not rush
into anything.

Cooperatives, particularly in Sweden, have done a great deal
to protect consumers, even against monopolies. They went
into the production of rubber overshoes and electric light bulbs,
and forced substantial price reductions for consumers.[24] In
Great Britain they got started when retail distribution was quite
inefficient, and to some extent got enough volume to do in
Britain what the large chains have done in this country—reduce
margins and improve efficiency in retailing. In this country
they have worked out well for the farmers by providing such
services as grain elevators or the supplying of farm equipment
without the possibility of monopoly charges. They have also
been a boon to the farmers in marketing their produce effectively, as in the case of the California Fruit Growers Exchange,
but these are not consumer cooperatives.

The consumer cooperatives have not done so well. As we
have pointed out, they have generally gone in for retailing,
usually of groceries, adding one more retail outlet when there
have usually already been too many in existence. However,
they have done something in protecting their members against
bad products, and the reason for mentioning them here is to
suggest that there is a type of cooperative that would provide
great service to the consumer: A local group of consumers could
form a consumer information bureau, not to deal with nation-
ally advertised products, where organizations like Consumers
Union are already doing a good job, but to provide information

about the local service trades, and make attempts to break up the more serious of local monopolies or collusions. Basically, the cooperative would attempt to reintroduce more competition into local markets. This would benefit the whole community not just the members.

Several types of things could be done:

(A) A dossier could be kept on prices charged by local plumbers, repair men, doctors, lawyers, dentists, shoe repair men, watch repair men, and so forth, and evidence collected as to the quality of their work. Such evidence would not be conclusive in most individual cases, because of the difficulty in evaluating, but an accumulation of negative or positive comments by many different people over a period of time would lead to presumptive evidence as to the quality of the commodities or services. Evidence of shady practices such as fake sales, failure to fulfill promises, charging much more than estimates made before the work was done, refusal to discuss costs beforehand, and so forth, would also be collected.

(B) In cases where everyone charged the same price, the group could make positive attempts to break up the situation by agreeing to concentrate the patronage of all its members on anyone who would break away, provided that he lowered his charges to everyone, not just members of the cooperative. I add this proviso partly for ethical reasons—a cooperative which served only its own members would be only one more monopoly (or monopsony) and could never elicit real enthusiasm—and partly because an effective demonstration that local competition could be made workable is more likely if people other than the members of the cooperative are induced to shift to the seller who believes in competition. Indeed, one function the cooperative could easily perform is that of publicizing the fact that one seller had lowered his rates and believed in competition.

Even casual observation of many of the repair services indicates that it is probably consumer ignorance of prices and qualities that leads to some of the unsatisfactory situations which exist. For instance, the repairman who charges the highest prices and puts his profits into larger and fancier premises seems to get more business, more profits, and still fancier premises. The consumer, not having any evidence of quality or not realizing that price differences exist, goes to the fancy place in order to be sure of high quality service. Often he does not get it. To some extent the larger places have more expensive equipment: "watchmasters," "motor analyzers," and so forth, but a vast majority of their services require only competent mechanics and standard equipment which they all have.

Such a consumer cooperative could also aid in eliminating such price-fixing devices as resale price maintenance, by keeping members informed about discount houses and bargains. It might even be able to make people aware of the wide differences in charges made and interest paid by different banks, particularly if people are willing to consider banking by mail with banks in other towns.

Summary

I should not like to infer that the practice of fraud, price-fixing, and so forth is widespread nor that all of it is even illegal. However, in spite of all existing protection, the consumer in America is free to be "taken in" if he wants to, and can rather easily find someone to do the job. Somewhere between the extremes of gullibility and hyper-suspicion we must all find our own manner of living. For those who do not like to be perpetually shopping or checking, there is the comforting thought that they face a reasonably competitive group of sellers because of the efforts of others who do shop and check. For those who enjoy being informed and careful, there is the cheering thought that they are helping others as well as themselves, by helping maintain competition so that prices will fairly represent quality.

Suggested Projects

1. Check at the library for recent issues of:
   (a) Press Releases of the Anti-Trust Division of the Department of Justice,

(b) *News Summary,* of the Federal Trade Commission, and

(c) Notices of Judgment under the Federal Food, Drug, and Cosmetics Act published by the U.S. Department of Health, Education, and Welfare, Food and Drug Administration.

Make a list of the types of frauds and dangerous or adulterated products mentioned. If there are any serious offenses, check the newspapers to see whether they were reported there.

2. Write to your state Public Utilities Commission and to the major utilities in your state for information about the most recent rate hearings, and if possible, the briefs presented at those hearings.

3. Read one of the books referred to in notes 14, 18, 20, or 22.

4. Watch for advertisements of what appear to be extremely good bargains, particularly in "reconditioned" appliances. Visit the store and try to buy one. Is it really reconditioned? Do they try to sell you something else?

FOOTNOTES TO CHAPTER 10

1 See *Annual Report of the Food and Drug Administration,* separately, or incorporated as a chapter in the *Annual Report of the Federal Security Agency.* See, for instance: *Annual Report of the Federal Security Agency, 1952,* Washington, D. C.: U.S. Gov't Printing Office, 1953, pp. 225–250. For 1953 and following, the Annual Report is included as a chapter in the *Annual Report of the Department of Health, Education, and Welfare.*

2 *Ibid.,* p. 231.

3 *Ibid.,* p. 229.

4 *Ibid.,* p. 230.

5 *Ibid.,* pp. 231–2.

6 *Ibid.,* p. 236.

7 *Annual Report of the U.S. Department of Health, Education, and Welfare, 1953,* Washington, D. C.: U.S. Gov't Printing Office, 1953, p. 212.

8 *Ibid.,* pp. 214–215.

9 *Ibid.,* pp. 215–216.

10 *Annual Report of the Postmaster General, Fiscal Year Ended June 30, 1952,* Washington, D. C.: U.S. Gov't Printing Office, 1952, p. 99.

11 *Annual Report of the Federal Trade Commission, 1952* (for the Fiscal Year ended June 30, 1952), Washington, D. C.: U.S. Gov't Printing Office (no date), pp. 10–11.

For an old but interesting account, see: T. Swann Harding, *The Popular Practice of Fraud,* New York: Longmans, Green & Co., Inc., 1935.

12 *Annual Report of the Federal Trade Commission, 1952* (for the Fiscal Year ended June 30, 1952), Washington, D. C.: U.S. Gov't Printing Office (no date), p. 45.

13 See: Louis Loss, *Securities Regulation,* Boston: Little, Brown & Co., 1951.

14 See: H. L. Purdy, M. L. Lindahl, and W. A. Carter, *Corporate Concentration and Public Policy,* 2nd ed., New York: Prentice-Hall, 1950; see also: Alfred R. Oxenfeldt, *Industrial Pricing and Market Practices,* New York: Prentice-Hall, 1951; Fritz Machlup, *The Political Economy of Monopoly,* Baltimore: Johns Hop-

kins University Press, 1952; Corwin D. Edwards, *Maintaining Competition: Requisites of a Government Policy*, New York: McGraw-Hill Book Co., 1949; Vernon A. Mund, *Open Markets: An Essential of Free Enterprise*, New York: Harper & Brothers, 1948; Henry C. Simons, *A Positive Program for Laissez-Faire: Some Proposals for a Liberal Economic Policy*, Chicago: The University of Chicago Press, 1934, reprinted in H. C. Simons, *Economic Policy for a Free Society*, Chicago: The University of Chicago Press, 1948; Joseph A. Schumpeter, *Capitalism, Socialism and Democracy*, New York: Harper & Brothers, 1943; J. K. Galbraith, *American Capitalism*, Boston: Houghton Mifflin Co., 1952; A. R. Burns, *The Decline of Competition*, New York: McGraw-Hill Book Co., 1936.

[15] Edward Chamberlin, *The Theory of Monopolistic Competition*, 6th ed., Cambridge, Massachusetts: Harvard University Press, 1950.

[16] *Technological Stagnation in Great Britain*, Chicago: Machinery and Allied Products Institute, 1948.

[17] U.S. Senate, Select Committee on Small Business, *Monopoly and Cartels*, Hearings before Subcommittee, 82nd Congress, 2nd session, on Impact of Monopoly and Cartel Practices on Small Business, Part 1, Washington, D. C.: U.S. Gov't Printing Office, 1952; U.S. Senate, *Monopolistic Practices and Small Business*, Report to Federal Trade Commission for the Subcommittee on Monopoly of Select Committee on Small Business, March 31, 1952. Washington, D. C.: U.S. Gov't Printing Office, 1952.

[18] Emery Troxel, *The Economics of Public Utilities*, New York: Rinehart & Company, Inc., 1947.

[19] *Ibid.*, pp. 406–417.

[20] See Abba P. Lerner, *The Economics of Control*, New York: The Macmillan Company, 1944.

[21] Lucille Keyes, *Federal Control over Entry into Air Transportation*, Cambridge, Massachusetts: Harvard University Press, 1951.

[22] Charles R. Cherington, *The Regulation of Railroad Abandonments* (Harvard Political Studies), Cambridge, Massachusetts: Harvard University Press, 1948.

[23] Samuel P. Huntington, C. Dickerman Williams, and Charles S. Morgan, "The I.C.C. Reexamined: A Colloquy," 63 *Yale Law Journal* 44–63 (Nov., 1953).

[24] Marquis Childs, *Sweden: The Middle Way*, New Haven: Yale University Press, 1936.

chapter 11

The Consumer
as a Voter
and Citizen

Throughout this book some important national economic problems have been discussed, but only those which have effects on society because of the way many consumers make their choices. There are several other important economic problems where you as a consumer need to have intelligent opinions even though the only choices you have are whether to write your congressmen, and, occasionally, how to vote. These issues cannot be discussed in detail, and since they are both complicated and controversial, you should read other sources too. In this chapter the problems will be outlined, and some general analytical principles and interpretations brought out which are more general than the particular issues and more relevant than the current state of the laws, or other facts, which change rapidly.

Resale Price Maintenance

Resale price maintenance or "fair trading" is a process whereby the manufacturer or wholesaler set minimum retail prices for trade-marked products. Except in Vermont, which has no explicit "non-signer provision," if a single retailer signs a contract agreeing to abide by the manufacturer's prices, then all other retailers in the state are also bound to sell at those prices, and no lower. State laws permitting resale price maintenance were passed during the depression of the 1930's, beginning in 1933 in California. During this time competition both from retailers desperately trying to stay in business, and from chains selling "loss leaders"—items sold at less than wholesale just to bring customers into the store—was generally regarded as excessive, and as damaging to the good name of manufacturers whose products were sold too cheaply. In 1937 the Miller-Tydings Amendment to Section 1 of the Sherman Anti-Trust Act was passed to allow price maintenance of items in interstate commerce without jeopardy under the anti-trust laws for restraint of trade.

As present Vermont lacks a non-signer provision, and Missouri, Texas, and the District of Columbia have no resale-price-maintenance laws, but all other states have such laws. In 1952 Congress passed the McGuire Amendment, not to the Sherman Act but to the Federal Trade Commission Act, to make non-signer control over prices legal in interstate commerce. The Miller-Tydings Amendment had failed to provide explicitly for non-signer provisions, as Schwegmann Brothers proved before the Supreme Court in 1951.[1] The legality of non-signer provisions in state laws is in doubt. As we shall see below, state courts have been deciding both ways.

From the beginning there have been legal and verbal battles over resale price maintenance. Professional economists and such business publications as *Business Week, Wall Street Journal,* and *Fortune* have generally taken a dim view of it as an unnecessary restraint on competition purportedly to achieve elimination of practices (loss-leaders), which could be eliminated directly by law. Retail druggists, represented by the Bureau of Education on Fair Trade, and some manufacturers, represented by the American Fair Trade Council, have been actively lobbying for it with some encouragement from such advertisers' publications as *Tide* and *Printers Ink*. Perhaps the strongest statement against resale price maintenance is in a memorandum written by an economic consultant to the Anti-Trust Division of the Department of Justice:

The passage of resale price legislation has become a classic example of the use of misrepresentation by a pressure group. Since this group has boasted of its achievements, there is no longer any doubt about what happened. The so-called "fair trade" laws which legalized resale price legislation in the states were drafted and urged by lobbyists for organized retail druggists and were enacted with practically no support from any other source. Druggists were organized under captains, district by district, to bring pressure to bear upon legislators. Care was taken, however, to describe their bill as one generally supported by the entire retail trade of the state. The bill was given the ambiguous and appealing name of "fair trade" law. A systematic effort was made to prevent public hearings and to secure the enactment of the bill without public debate. This effort was successful. There was a public hearing on the bill in only three states out of the first thirty-two in which it was passed, and in one of these the hearing followed the passage. Indeed, there was so little consideration of any kind that, although the original draft of the bill contained a stenographic error which made utter nonsense out of one of the most important provisions, this error appeared without change in the statutes of eleven states before it was caught and corrected. Another stenographic error, not quite so serious, was included in the laws of seventeen states. Some members of state legislatures subsequently told consumers' organizations that they did not know what they were voting on.

Meanwhile, every effort was made to throttle public discussion and to intimidate business opposition. In California an aspirin manufacturer was forced by boycott to issue resale price contracts against his will. . . . In the same state the manufacturers of Pepsodent toothpaste, who had experimented with resale price contracts under the California law, decided to withdraw these contracts, apparently under advice of counsel who believed that the contracts violated the antitrust laws. Thereupon the druggists organized a campaign to put Pepsodent under the counter and to switch customers to other brands. This campaign was so effective that the offending company made public apology at a subsequent convention of the National Association of Retail Druggists and, as a token of its contrition, subscribed $25,000 to a fund to lobby for resale price maintenance in other states. . . .

The campaign of misrepresentation became the basis of the lobbying to amend the Sherman Act. The draft amendment was urged upon Congress with the argument that it did not involve any acceptance of resale price maintenance as a Federal principle but merely committed the Congress to the view that if states desired to authorize resale price maintenance, the Federal control over interstate commerce should not stand in the way. The state laws were described as though they consisted merely in grants of authority for manufacturer and retailer to agree upon the resale price of branded goods. Actually, there is not one of the state statutes which is limited to such a grant. A statute of that kind was tried in California and proved to be a miserable failure because many retailers would not sign such contracts. All of the state laws now provide that when a manufacturer and a retailer sign a resale price contract all other retailers who have notice of the contract price must refrain from selling below that price. In other words, these state laws give to a manufacturer and a retailer the right to coerce the retailer's competitors by fixing the resale price of these competitors against their will. There is no provision for public hearing, for standards in the establishment of the price, for any process of appeal by the nonsigner, or for any other safeguard such as is always included in a plan for price fixing by public authority.* . . .

The Senate reports and the very text of the amendment demonstrate that those who amended the Sherman Act had been misinformed about the status of non-signers under the state laws. The amendment explicitly prohibits agreements between retailers to fix minimum resale prices. Yet in practical effect such agreements would not be as severe a restraint upon competition as a grant of power to a single retailer to make an agreement with a manufacturer which then becomes binding upon all other retailers. When persons are bound by law they do not need to be bound by contract. . . .

It is noteworthy that the advocates of the Miller-Tydings Amendment were unable to pass it as a separate bill and eventually secured its enactment by attaching it as a rider to the appropriation bill for the District of Columbia. . . .

When the state laws were tested in the Federal courts, they were represented as statutes which allowed a manufacturer to protect the

---

* The state of Wisconsin is an exception to this rule. Its law provides that the state may set aside contracts which establish unreasonable prices.

good will attaching to a brand by making contracts concerning the resale price of articles carrying the brand. Thus described, the bill is intended to defend the manufacturers' property rights. Actually this interpretation of the bill was mere pretense. . . . The bill originated with retailers, was backed by a retailers' lobby, was passed by retailers' pressure, and has been used by retailers to force the issuance of contracts whether the manufacturer wants them or not. Retail organizations in the drug trade and elsewhere have used white lists of manufacturers issuing contracts, and black lists of manufacturers who do not, in an endeavor to coerce those manufacturers who are reluctant. . . .

A different purpose for the statutes was urged upon Congress and state legislators. They were told that resale price maintenance contracts were necessary to enable the small independent retailer to survive against the competition of the large chain. The legislation was presented as a part of the effort to defend little business and to avert monopoly in retailing. Actually this announcement of purpose involved a mixture of misrepresentation and self-deception. In the first place, though the independent retailer may be threatened in some industries, he was not actually threatened in the drug trade. The number of independent retail druggists was increasing during the period. . . . The average life of an independent drug store is greater than that of almost any other kind of retail store. The markup realized upon drug products is higher than that upon other fast-moving retail lines, so much so that organized retail druggists are now trying to prevent the handling of packaged drugs by grocery stores which are attracted by the relatively high margin upon this merchandise. . . . The chains themselves supported these laws . . . the secretary of the National Association of Chain Drug Stores testified before the committees of the House and Senate in favor of the Miller-Tydings Amendment.

Resale price maintenance has served the chains in two ways: first, it has relieved them from the competition of the pineboard independent and thus protected them from the newest and most effective channel through which fast-moving packaged drugs can reach the consumer at low prices. Second, it has enabled the chains to organize a low-price raid against any independent drug store without fear of retaliation. . . . With national brands of drug products price controlled, the chain can collect substantial margins upon such products while reducing the price of its own private brands whenever it desires to use them as leaders or to make a raid upon the national brand business enjoyed by other stores. Since these other stores are bound not to cut prices upon the national brands and do not control private brands which have acquired prestige through extensive advertising, retaliation by the victims is not possible.

Druggists determine the amount of selling effort they will spend on a product in the light of the size of the operating margin which the manufacturer is able to establish between his wholesale price and his fixed resale price; and under this pressure, manufacturers have begun to bid for business by raising the retailer's margin. The amendment has encouraged flagrant violations of the Sherman Act which it does not actually sanction. . . . In practice it is nearly always impossible for one manufacturer to establish a system of vertical price fixing unless he can be sure that his competitors will do likewise; and a single price fixed commodity is exposed to the inroads of competing commodities when these articles can be sold for less than the fixed price. Consequently, horizontal collusion in violation of the law has been an indispensable part of the movement for resale price maintenance.[2]

Clearly there are some strong arguments against resale price maintenance: It tends to eliminate price competition between retailers, even if some remains between the manufacturers of the products they retail. Furthermore, it is probably difficult for new competitors to enter manufacturing—certainly more difficult than for competitive retailers to start business. Efficient retailing relying on a large volume, minimal extra services, and low mark-ups is not possible. Chains may drive retailers out of business in some lines, while in others, small inefficient retailers can stay in business because they can give discounts without being caught. Finally, large discounts may be available to people with connections, who are frequently those who need discounts the least.

There remain, however, problems which could still arise from "too much price competition" if resale price maintenance were eliminated. There would still have to be some method of preventing stores from selling items at less than a reasonable price—wholesale price plus some contribution to the costs of the retailer—and thereby giving people the idea that the man-

ufacturer's price is unreasonably high. Excessive competition
on a price basis might lead to deterioration of quality.[3] We
shall see in other sections of this chapter that this is only an
example of a basic problem of providing "workable competition" in a free enterprise economy.

The legal situation is still in flux, and it is not even clear just
what it is anyway. Some lawyers have complained that the
McGuire Amendment has made the Miller-Tydings Amendment—to a different act—a useless appendage without repealing
it. The laws all allow resale price maintenance only where
the commodity is in "free and open competition" with other
commodities, the meaning of which has never been legally
settled. So long as there are some states without resale price
maintenance laws, there will always be legal problems about
sellers in one state and buyers in another. The same Schwegmann carried a second case to the Supreme Court suggesting
that the whole system was unconstitutional, and raising such
issues as due process, equal protection under the law, invalid
delegation of power to the states, and interstate commerce rights
of the Federal government. The Supreme Court refused to
review a decision adverse to Schwegmann, but the matter is unlikely to stay settled for long. A number of recent court decisions have been unfavorable or critical. The Florida Supreme
Court twice declared the state act unconstitutional, the second
time after a law had been passed to patch things up by letting
the State Attorney General enjoin enforcement when competition might be injured.[4] The court decided that the non-
signer clause had no standard of free competition as a yardstick
for protecting the consumer; hence, it was an invalid use of
police powers for a private purpose. In Louisiana, Judge
Wright argued that the Supreme Court must change its decision
made in *Old Dearborn* v. *Seagram Corp.* (299 U.S. 183 (1936)),
because

. . . after twenty years of experience under fair trade acts . . .
we may conclude that the real purpose of these acts is not to protect

the goodwill of the manufacturer, and that price fixing under these acts is not an appropriate means to that perfectly legitimate end, but is in fact an end itself.[5]

Other critical decisions have appeared in Michigan, Nebraska, and Georgia.[6]   It seems clear that resale price maintenance will remain a major legal and political issue for some time.

Agricultural Price Supports

The Farmer [7]

His work is never done
Not even with the sun
Because it's not begun
He hasn't got to
We pay him not to.

The doggerel above represents the reaction of many a consumer who sees the government buying up surpluses, imposing import quotas, restricting production, and letting food rot or be sold at give-away prices to distillers, at a time when food is expensive or even scarce in other parts of the world, and none too cheap at home.   This is far too simple-minded a view, and what you must try to do is to understand something of the problems that have led to the introduction and preservation of such systems.   It may then be possible to think of solutions to these problems which do not have quite such absurd and undesirable secondary effects.

Here again, we can only skim the surface, and shall try to recommend other reading necessary for more complete understanding.[8]   Agricultural price supports really "came of age" during the depression of the 1930's.   Neither the demand for agricultural products, nor their supply, adjusts itself very well in response to price changes.   When a depression comes, some people will have to spend less on food, but a decline in its price will not induce them or anyone else to spend more for it.   On the production side, the farmer has most of his capital tied up in a farm, often in rather specialized form, and he has to provide a living for himself and his family.   Hence, when prices for his products are low, he may even try to produce more in order to have enough money to buy the things his family needs. Falling income and spending of farmers in turn reduce the incomes of other producers. During the 1930's there were many farmers who were unable to make payments on their loans. Desperate attempts by banks, who had loaned them money, to get some liquid funds and to avoid bankruptcy themselves, led to foreclosures. A number of public auctions resulting from these foreclosures were attended by neighbors with shotguns. The auction would either be called off, or the farm resold to its previous owner for a small sum. This was obviously not a permanent or even satisfactory temporary solution to the problem.

The solution took the form of government attempts under the Agricultural Adjustment Act of 1933 and the Agricultural Marketing Agreement Act of 1937 to bolster up the prices of agricultural products to "parity" levels. The idea was that the prices farmers received for their products, relative to the prices they paid for things they purchased, should remain at about the 1909–1914 "normal" level, or 1919–29, or 1934–39, or 1936–41, or, later, at some other more recent "normal" level. The Agricultural Acts of 1948 and 1949 provided for the "new parity" based on average prices received and paid over the most recent ten years, and including wages of agricultural labor in prices paid. These acts recognized that this would reduce the parity price too drastically in some cases. Hence, a transitional period was arranged during which "transition parity" prices would be used. For some commodities it will be 1960 before the new parity is actually in effect. Once the parity price was determined, the government would make crop "loans" to the farmers at this price. This amounted to a promise to buy the crop at this minimum support price, for if the market price fell below parity, the farmer could merely let the government take over the crop and keep his "loan," without even paying interest on it. If prices rose above parity, the farmer could sell his crop and pay off the loan plus 4 per cent interest.

Such price supports led to greater surpluses of unsold crops, of course, because the government agencies did not like to buy a crop and immediately sell it at a loss, particularly in view of the uncertainty about next year's crop. In order to keep the surpluses from getting too large, marketing quotas, and acreage allotments were imposed. Actually, the situation is far more complex than this.

The United States Department of Agriculture carries on a number of operations aimed at protecting prices received by farmers for agricultural commodities. These operations, commonly referred to as "price programs," include the price-support, International Wheat Agreement, section 32, national school lunch, marketing agreement and order, and sugar programs.

The price problem is approached a little differently through operations under each of these programs. Under the price-support program, price minimums or "floors" are established for a number of commodities. Support is achieved through loans, purchases, or agreements to purchase—or, for some commodities, through a combination of these methods. The International Wheat Agreement seeks to assure markets for wheat to exporting countries and supplies of wheat to importing countries at equitable prices. Under the Agreement, the United States is obligated to sell specified quantities of wheat to importing countries if the importing countries offer the maximum Agreement price; and the importing countries are obligated to buy specified quantities of wheat from the United States if the United States offers the wheat for sale at the minimum Agreement price.

Removal of surpluses, with consequent strengthening of prices, is the objective of programs carried on under section 32 (of Public Law No. 320, 74th Cong.). This legislation makes an amount equal to 30 per cent of the receipts collected under the customs laws available for encouraging the exportation of agricultural commodities and products; encouraging the domestic consumption of commodities and products by diverting them from the normal channels of trade or by increasing their use among persons in low-income groups; and reestablishing farmers' purchasing power by making payments in connection with the normal production of any agricultural commodity for domestic consumption.

The national school lunch program encourages increased domestic consumption of agricultural commodities. By doing so it affords some protection of prices received by producers and, at the same time, improves the nutritional status of the Nation's children.

Marketing agreement and order programs enable farmers to establish and maintain orderly marketing conditions for certain commodities and their products. Milk-order programs establish equitable minimum prices that handlers or distributors are required to pay producers for milk going into various uses. For commodities other than milk—principally tree fruits, tree nuts, and vegetables—minimum prices are not established; but prices are strengthened, nevertheless, under the order programs through control of quantity, quality, and rate of shipment from producing areas. The sugar program stabilizes prices through the regulation of imports of sugar from foreign areas and marketings of sugar produced in domestic areas.[9]

In the main the support prices, loans, and purchase agreements can be looked at as methods of preventing excessive price fluctuations (particularly downward) and the output restrictions combined with higher support prices as a method of subsidizing farm incomes. Output restrictions take three major forms: (a) acreage allotments under the Agricultural Acts, (b) marketing quotas, available under the Agricultural Acts only for corn, cotton, wheat, rice, peanuts, and tobacco, and (c) marketing orders under the 1937 Agricultural Marketing Agreement Act for milk, fruit, vegetables, tree nuts, and hops. Acreage allowments are not mandatory unless combined with market quotas, and a farmer who does not abide by his allotment gets a "free ride" enjoying the effects of output restriction on the price and losing only his right to commodity loans. If two-thirds of the farmers in an area vote for marketing quotas, and they must in order to keep the price supports at 90 per cent of parity when there are large carryovers, then all must abide, or pay fines amounting to 40–50 per cent of the loan rate (support price). Marketing orders also require a two-thirds vote and impose even more severe penalties on those who do not abide by the controls over quality, quantity, and rate of shipment to market. The farmer can be restrained by injunction, fined damages equal to three times the value of his excess shipments, and fined $50 to $500 per violation. Each day can be considered a separate violation. In 1953 there were 49 milk marketing orders, and order programs for such other products as citrus fruits, grapes, peaches, pears, potatoes, almonds, filbert, pecans, walnuts, and hops, each in specified areas.

The Agricultural Act of 1949 also set up for the basic commodities—corn, cotton, wheat, rice, peanuts, and tobacco—a sliding scale whereby the prices would be supported at 75–90 per cent of parity depending on the relation between the supply and "normal supply," unless the producers disapproved marketing quotas in which case cooperators were to receive support at 50 per cent of parity. However, Public Law No. 585, 82d Congress, fixed the support at 90 per cent of parity for the 1953 and 1954 crops. In 1954, Congress, in spite of an accumulated investment by the Commodity Credit Corporation in surplus crops amounting to more than six billion dollars, compromised between the demands of farm senators for 90 per cent support and the necessity for more flexible supports to discourage production, and set the range of the sliding scale at 82.5 per cent to 90 per cent. The details of which parity definition is being used and what support level are of course subject to frequent changes.

Needless to say, the system of price supports has run into a number of difficulties, and serious objections have been raised to it.

1. The acreage restrictions were difficult to administer fairly and did not reduce production nearly so much as expected. A farmer can leave some land in clover for an extra year, use more cultivation and fertilizer on the remaining acreage, and increase his output per acre a good deal. The following year, the land which was held in clover also proves to be more productive, *etc.* Where there were tenant farmers or sharecroppers, the combination of a system which seemed to be paying the landowner for producing less, but still allowed him to throw some of his workers off the land, seemed rather nasty.

2. In spite of restrictions, surpluses accumulated to a dangerous level in the late 1930's. This proved to be a boon when World War II came, but might not the next time.

3. Large producers who are generally more efficient benefited most, receiving substantial checks from the government, while the price supports also enabled inefficient marginal farmers to scrape along when they should have left farming. On the other hand the acreage and output restrictions reduced the use of good lands as well as poor lands.

4. Only staple crops that could be stored could be supported effectively, and yet the country was in the process of a long-term shift away from these crops toward fruits, vegetables, meats, and the "protective foods." Marketing orders were not so effective as the combination of quotas and price supports. This tended to retard the natural development and keep people producing the old staples.

5. Not only did the supports, which were initially justified to eliminate misery and extreme insecurity for the farmer, continue to aid him in a period of prosperity, but they also failed to take account of gains in productivity and particularly of differential gains in productivity in different crops. As a result, acreage allotments in such crops as burley tobacco in Kentucky, Tennessee, Missouri, Kansas, Indiana, and Ohio are actually reported as selling for as much as $1,000 an acre in some areas— a clear indication that the supports had gone beyond providing a decent return and were producing the monopoly profits of restriction.[10]

Potatoes provided another extreme example, intensified by the impossibility of storing them for long or shipping them long distances. After 1950 potatoes were no longer given price supports. Nearly half of the $1,110,000,000 net loss of the Commodity Credit Corporation during the period October 1933 through June 1953, was lost on potatoes.[11] The reason why potatoes ran into such difficulties is that the output per acre had more than doubled between 1928 and 1953. With such increases in efficiency (and reductions in cost of production) parity was a meaningless concept.

To add insult to injury, the Anti-Trust Division of the Department of Justice announced on May 10, 1954 a consent judgment against the Shade Tobacco Growers Agricultural Association and some others enjoining them from continuing to agree to reduce production and distribution of Connecticut Valley shade grown tobacco (used as cigar wrappers). The government is restricting output of burley tobacco and at the same time enjoining individual producers from restricting output of "shade grown."

6. While consumers pay high prices for food, surpluses accumulate, spoil, or are sold at give-away prices to cattle feeders, distillers, or dumped abroad. When commodities are kept from uses where they are worth much and put to uses where they are worth less, social welfare is clearly reduced.

7. The system not only cost money—over a billion dollars between 1933 and 1953—but involved a government bureaucracy, quarrels over what "parity" was and at what per cent of parity prices should be supported, and so on.

In 1950, at a time when, once more, accumulating surpluses combined with very high food prices were making people conscious of the paradoxes in the price support system, the then Secretary of Agriculture Brannan came out with a plan which was supposed to stabilize farmer's incomes without the disadvantages of the existing plan. It involved a complex formula for determining parity prices, one which would have given supports comparable with the ones in use, if not a little higher. The essential part of the plan was that these prices were used not to determine the level at which market prices should be supported, but to determine what payments should be made to farmers when their incomes suffered from low farm prices, relative to the prices of things they bought. In other words, market prices were to be allowed to fall, and direct payments would be made to farmers if prices fell too low. Since no storage was involved, this plan could have been extended to perishables, which needed expanded production. Quotas and acreage allotments were to be continued, with only those who abided by them and followed approved soil conservation practices receiving the payments. Finally, the payments only applied to

$26,666 worth of crop for any one farmer unless the crop was under acreage allotment. This would have cut the amount the very large farmers could get.

The Brannan plan clearly could have improved the balance of production and aided the long run shift toward the protective foods. It also would have been of great benefit to consumers, providing them with low food prices. However, the plan never had a chance. It brought the subsidy to farmers out in the open. It took away some bonanzas from large wealthy farmers. And, worst of all, it would have looked as though it cost a lot more, for instead of consumers being forced to support farmers by paying more for food, they would do it by paying taxes. Estimates of the amount of direct payments ran as high as three billion dollars a year.

Other problems, such as adjustments for changes in productivity, equity in acreage allotments, and the fostering of better soil conservation, would have been unaffected and unsolved. Almost everyone seemed to be opposed to the Brannan plan, yet President Eisenhower's farm program of early 1954 called for the introduction of exactly the same principle in the case of wool. In this case competition from foreign wools made the absurdity of high domestic prices even clearer.

As matters stand, the surpluses are accumulating, farmers are once again voting for acreage restrictions, and the consumer continues to pay high food prices relative to the cost of producing food. But we must not forget that there remains a basic problem of how to preserve some stability in farm incomes. Of course, if we can maintain a high level of income and employment in the rest of the economy, a serious agricultural depression is unlikely; but even if this were assured, we would need some emergency system to take care of temporary surpluses and world price fluctuations. Finally, so long as times are good, and if some adjustments are made, the present system can go on without doing a great deal of damage. It costs the consumer something, both in taxes and in higher food prices, and some reductions in the level of supports and other improvements in the system are needed, but some protection to farm income is probably justifiable too.

We should add that both coal and crude oil are subject to similar government-sponsored devices for restricting output to hold up prices. Partly under the guise of conserving natural resources through orderly exploitation, output is "prorated" over the various oil wells, the total amount allowed being only what the market can absorb at current prices. In the case of oil, the more important of the two, the Connally ("Hot Oil") Act of 1935 prohibits interstate shipment of "contrabrand oil," defined as oil produced, transported, or withdrawn from storage in excess of the amounts permitted by state laws. Most states which produce crude oil have laws restricting output, the major exception being California. In California, a voluntary scheme to do the same thing has been under attack by the Department of Justice as a violation of anti-trust laws, while it is illegal in other states for producers *not* to restrict output at times. In practice, the U.S. Bureau of Mines estimates the "market demand" for crude oil by states. States make other estimates, and oil purchasers in a state will submit "nominations" for the amount they will buy. The state commission—in Texas it is the Railroad Commission—will then announce how much can be produced, usually in terms of the number of days per month the wells may produce.[12]

There are also upper limits on production when "maximum efficiency rates" of production have been reached. Here the justification of physical efficiency is obvious. When "market demand" sets the upper limit, however, the restrictions on output may reduce waste. But these restrictions are not so much the most efficient ways to produce the maximum amount of oil as they are methods of holding up the market price of crude oil. The ultimate consumer has no voice in determining whether "market demand" should be met at a higher or lower price. The result has sometimes looked more like a racket to move prices up than a governor to stabilize them. At times the output of crude oil has been progressively restricted when the refineries were operating at much less than capacity.

But again, forgetting the arguments about conservation and efficiency, it is clear that pure competition in the oil industry could be a rather unhappy state, with wide price fluctuations, periodic shortages and gluts, business failures, and perhaps less new exploration and well drilling and ultimately higher prices. It would seem, however, that some representation of the final consumer, not just the refiners who can pass price increases along to their customers, would be in order.

Milk Price Control

A special, interesting, and important case of agricultural price supports is that of milk. The problems of the producer are accentuated in the case of milk, because he has highly specialized equipment, and the production process requires that the producer concentrate on it rather than spend most of his time growing food or some other crop when the price of milk is low. He cannot sell his cows for a reasonable price when the price of milk is low. He is likely to be dependent upon milk for his cash income, and is more in need of a cash income than some other kinds of farmers.

In addition, milk is an unusual commodity with an unusual market. Fluid milk is heavy and perishable; hence cannot be shipped far. This means that the producers around a large city have a "protected" market with an "inelastic demand," that is, the amount they can sell does not vary much if the price changes. However, milk can be turned into cheese, butter, ice cream, casein paint, and a number of other products which are not so heavy or so perishable, and are sold in a national market or even abroad in competition with products from other areas. Hence, they can be sold in widely fluctuating amounts without much effect on the price.

The limited area in which fluid milk can be produced for a large metropolitan market is generally called a "milkshed," an analogy to the term "watershed," referring to an area that drains into a particular stream.   Limitations are also further enforced by law, partly to keep out sporadic surpluses, and partly to make it easy to inspect the producers' sanitation methods.   In any one milkshed, the producers have two markets for their milk, crudely speaking.   There is a local market for fluid milk, with an inelastic demand, and a national market for most of the other milk products where the demand for the milk from any one area is quite elastic—price will not be affected much by changes in output; hence, surpluses can be sold without depressing the price much.

In this situation, it was rather easy to figure out a method to ease the plight of the farmers during the depression of the 1930's when the low price of milk was threatening to bankrupt them.   A legal authority was set up by the A.A.A., which could set a minimum price to be paid farmers for "fluid milk," that is, milk to be sold as fresh milk.[13]   Later, states set up milk price control laws, and the 1937 Agricultural Marketing Agreement Act allows communities to empower a Federal market administrator to do the same.   In 1953 there were 49 such communities.   When the farmer sells his milk to a dairy, he has no way of knowing how much of it will be used for fluid milk and how much for all the other uses—generally called Class 1 and Class 2 milk respectively.   The dairy figures out how much of his milk they sold as fluid milk, and pays the farmer the legal minimum for that milk, and the Class 2 market price for the rest.   In other words, the price the farmer gets is an average depending on the two prices and the proportions of milk sold at each price.   During the spring peak production of milk, a larger proportion will be at the lower price; and if there is a surplus at any other time, the average price paid the farmer falls.   This average is called the "blend price."

The economic effect of raising the Class 1 milk price is the same as when a discriminating monopolist raises the price in the wealthier of two markets; there is a small reduction in the amount of fluid milk consumed, but considerably more money is paid for what is consumed. The extra is dumped on the Class 2 market, but depresses that price very little. Hence, the total revenue of the farmers increases. Consumers pay much more for fluid milk, very little less for cheese, casein paint, butter, and so forth. Both economists and nutrition experts object to this. The economists object because the effect is to take money from the consumers of fluid milk to subsidize farmers and consumers of other dairy products. The consumers of fluid milk may well be people with large families and lower incomes. The nutrition expert is bothered because he regards milk as one of the best health foods and feels people should be encouraged to drink it, rather than discouraged. Workers in social agencies report that when milk gets expensive, poor parents often succumb to their children's demands and feed them carbonated beverages which contain almost no food value but are cheaper.

In addition to the political problems over the setting of the wholesale price for Class 1 milk, there are other problems. When the price of milk used to fluctuate from a low in the spring to a high in the late fall, producers tried to adjust their production somewhat, to produce less in the spring and more during the rest of the year. This kept the seasonal movements small. When each farmer is paid an average price that depends on the seasonal movement of all the producers together, he has no incentive to keep his own production steady. It is cheaper for him to let his cows have their calves in the spring, which is the natural time for them, and which allows cheap spring pasture at a time of their maximum demands for food. This leads to a flood of milk in the spring, a large proportion of which goes into the surplus uses, unless the Administrator or Price Control Board adjusts the price of milk several times a year to discourage it.

But the main problem arises because the higher returns to the milk producers lead others to go into the business. This means that gradually a larger and larger proportion of the total milk goes into the lower priced surplus uses, driving the "blend price" down until, after a time, the farmers are again not making very much money.

This situation clearly has all the aspects of the "worst of all possible worlds": interference and price fixing, discrimination between products that tends to inhibit the use of an excellent health food and perhaps to tax the poor, and all this without any lasting benefit to the farmers. Nor is there any easy way out of the dilemma: There is a real problem how to maintain some stability in wholesale milk prices both to keep an adequate production, and to prevent bankruptcy and distress among the farmers. Any removal of the minimum prices would cause trouble for the present producers, who find it physically as well as psychologically difficult to change to some other business.

One recently suggested solution was based on the idea of establishing an automatic mechanism for determining the price, based on a combination of indexes of prices farmers pay, United States wholesale prices, and New England department store sales.[14] It also had built-in seasonal price adjustments and an automatic adjustment for market conditions which would reduce the Class 1 price if too large a proportion of the milk were going into Class 2 uses, and vice versa. The plan proposed a formula which would have worked well when applied to the previous 25 years, and which was based on the following objectives:

1. The delivery of sufficient milk from producers to provide a reserve above Class 1 sales of between 15 and 20 per cent of receipts in the months of lowest production, assuming a reasonable seasonal pattern of receipts.

2. A less highly seasonal pattern of production than that of recent years.

3. Market stability, accomplished through orderly and timely adjustments in prices for changing supply and demand conditions.

4. Maintenance of producer prices and incomes at a satisfactory level relative to general economic conditions.[15]

Later on, the same document explicitly recognizes the consumer interest:

Protecting the public interest in establishing milk prices requires that there be a minimum of the exploitation which is possible through the combined effects of the physical and sanitary limitations on supply, the rigid control of price competition, and the inelasticity of milk consumption.[16]

The Boston formula still maintains two prices for the same commodity, but it eliminates the quarrels over the minimum price, deals with the problems of seasonal fluctuations and of changes in the general price level, and even provides a method for automatic lowering of milk prices when prices of other things fall, or surpluses develop. The Boston formula was actually adopted by being incorporated into the five New England Federal milk orders effective April 1, 1948. It was revised in 1952 with the substitution of an index of New England per capita disposable income in place of the index of New England department store sales, as a measure of consumer buying power. Other minor changes were made in the price indexes used, and the supply-demand adjustment was made more flexible. Depending on how much the proportion of Class 2 milk gets above or below the normals for the previous two months, prices can now be moved down or up by 2–12 per cent. The formula is complex, but not so complex that it cannot be followed and understood by farmers and consumers. One of the benefits of the plan has been that it reduced the suspicion and misunderstandings that went with administrative and apparently arbitrary price fixing.

The distribution of milk raises other problems which we have not discussed: There are few dairies relative to farmers, which gives the dairies a bargaining advantage except where the farmers band together in producing associations, and perhaps even there. On the other hand, from the point of view of pasteurization and delivery there are probably too many dairies. One excellent study indicates substantial savings in distribution costs if milk were collected by only one dairy in an area, pasteurized in a few large plants, and distributed by only one dairy in any one area.[17] Of course, this would be at the expense of competition and would require that the dairy industry become either a public utility under regulation and control, or a socialist enterprise, neither of which most people would like.

For the dairies, there is a situation like that we have seen before: high overhead costs and a great incentive to try to expand sales, particularly in the delivery area now covered. At times this has led to price wars, secret price cuts, and even inserting foul substances in competitors' milk. It is still true in most areas that a group of consumers in an area can band together and get their milk cheaper by simply bargaining with the dairy, but for the most part the dairies try to increase their profits by selling several different grades of milk. The butterfat differential, between "Grade A" and "Regular," if it exists, is generally much less in value than the price difference. And, of course, homogenized milk frequently sells for a cent more a quart, yet it costs almost nothing to homogenize milk. A homogenizing machine will pay for itself in a week at 1¢ a quart!

Recently, attempts have been made to capitalize on the low price of Class 2 milk by making milk concentrates which would keep better and could be shipped farther economically, and by making better quality powdered skim milk. Because skim milk contains the protein and most of the vitamins of whole milk, and because newer drying processes have been developed which do not leave the burnt taste, it can be used effectively by those seeking economy, at a cost of about 10¢ a quart or less.

By early 1954 the surplus of the storable dairy products like butter was substantial, and the support level on dairy prices was reduced from 90 to 75 per cent of parity. Whether producers will reduce output or succeed in demanding higher supports is difficult to say, but at least some of them felt at the time that some readjustment in prices and output was essential in view of the surpluses and "overproduction." By fall of 1954, production of dairy products was already lower (relative to consumption) than in the previous year, so perhaps people felt that the flexible supports would induce readjustments.

Tariffs and Quotas

Three programs under which the government actually encourages and gives legal sanction to devices which restrict competition have been already dealt with very briefly: resale price maintenances, agricultural price supports, and milk price control. Of the others, which include restrictions on the output of natural gas and crude oil, legal export cartels, and so forth, we want to mention briefly two more: import restrictions by the use of tariffs and quotas, and the basing point system or "delivered prices."

The textbooks of economics have for years been strong in pointing out that free trade is advantageous to all concerned by promoting specialization, division of labor, and the concentration of countries on producing things at which they were comparatively better. After a peak of protection under the Smoot-Hawley Tariff Act of 1930, substantial reductions have been made under the Reciprocal Trade Agreements Act, and the importance of fixed dollar duties has been reduced by inflation. A dollar tax is less important if the article costs $25 instead of $10. It is difficult to say just what the impact of the present tariffs is, however, because tariffs still cause some goods to be excluded almost entirely, and some of the reductions have been on inconsequential items. But substantial reductions have been made, and perhaps more important, manufacturers who export part of their output have come in increasing numbers to recognize that we must buy if we want to sell, or, to put it more crudely, that we must import something if they are to sell their products abroad.

On the other hand, agricultural price supports have had to rely on tariffs or quotas to keep foreign supplies from driving prices down. In the case of sugar we have even used quotas to keep the domestic price up. Tariffs on consumer items that benefit a few producers of those items are likely to involve great cost to consumers relative to the net benefit to producers. This is particularly true in the case of things like wool and sugar.

One detailed study of the possible impact of removing the quotas on sugar imports indicates that the gain to consumers would be far greater than any possible loss to the farmers—who could shift to other if somewhat less profitable crop rotation schemes.[18]

You must not forget, however, that tariffs and quotas are not the only devices for excluding foreign goods. The most effective device of all is to change the value of the currency, that is devalue it by raising the price of gold. If we double the price of gold, and another country whose currency is "backed" by gold does not, then they can buy twice as many dollars with their currency as before—if only by buying gold and selling it to us. This makes it easy for them to buy from us, cutting not only the tariff but also the price in half. It makes it difficult for us to buy from them, for it doubles the price of their goods in dollars. Changes in exports and imports will affect the prices too, of course, but the over-all effect is a powerful one; and the International Monetary Fund has yet to secure agreements from all countries not to change the valuation of currencies, and to give up fancy multiple-currency systems with different values.

In the 1930's the Nazi regime in Germany made use of a substantial number of devices for exploiting other countries by manipulations of currency values and convertibility. Recently the economists have shown that even tariffs, so long as they are not met by matching retaliatory tariffs, are a method by which a country can exploit the rest of the world.[19] The fact that a competitive raising of tariffs can leave every country worse off than before does not undo the fact that we have an unstable situation where everyone can see at least short-run gains from such manipulations.

Finally, given the American situation, where some industries have been protected by tariffs for many years, it seems clear that we are rapidly approaching the point where any further reductions in tariffs would injure some of these industries and their workers. While the benefit to the rest of the country would be greater than these losses, it seems clear that unless some method of easing the burden on these few can be devised, they will resist removal of the tariffs and get support for their resistance. The problem is further complicated by pleas for protection of industries necessary in case of war, particularly because almost any industry can look necessary in case of war. Our tariff policy is in a state of flux, but it seems likely that unless the world becomes more peaceful, and unless means are devised to facilitate the transfer of workers and capital out of formerly protected industries, further tariff reductions will be small. Indeed, by the summer of 1954 pressures for tariff increases were growing and had succeeded in the case of watches. A study of the Smoot-Hawley Tariff and its passage in 1930 indicates why it is difficult to resist such increases.[20]

More is at stake in tariffs and quotas than economic efficiency, because many other countries want and need American products and want to be able to sell us something in order to earn the dollars necessary to buy our products.   In addition, our foreign aid programs lend money abroad, while tariffs make it difficult to pay it back in the only way it can finally be paid: in dollars earned by exporting goods to the United States.

It is frequently argued that it is unfair to ask American workers to compete with workers in other countries who are not more efficient but are simply paid much less.[21]   This is either another method of pointing to transition difficulties, or is irrelevent.   Any trade we have with other countries involves our not producing what we can import much more cheaply, whether because other countries are more efficient or have lower living standards.[22]   This only causes difficulties (a) in transition if we have to move workers and resources out of certain formerly protected industries or (b) if we have import surpluses which threaten our over-all level of employment.   Both these problems can be solved, and if they are, the opening up of trade will improve our living standards as well as those of the people with whom we trade.   Only under unusual circumstances will removal of tariffs change the "terms of trade" so that we do not benefit, and in this case the other country is made so much better off that they might very well be willing to make other concessions.

Looked at in very general terms, it seems obvious that specialization and division of labor will increase the total output of goods and services, and that some distribution of the increase is possible which will make everyone better off. The great difficulty in this country arises from our unwillingness to admit that if a change for the general benefit injures a few, these few should be compensated somehow.

"Delivered Pricing" and the Basing Point System

On May 26, 1936, the Bureau of Supplies of the U.S. Navy opened thirty-one sealed bids on a particular lot of steel they wanted. All thirty-one quoted the same price: $20,727.26, although some bidders would have had to ship the steel much farther than others, and the price was a delivered price.[23] This was in the middle of the depression when most businesses were trying desperately to find customers. Nor was this an unusual incident, or something which happened only to the government purchasing agencies. No matter where the customer, or how many bids were submitted, and whether the article was a type of steel, cement, cast iron pipe, rigid steel conduit, or oak or maple flooring, the same suspicious identity of bids existed.

How was this possible, particularly in view of the complex nature of transportation costs and varied means of transportation, without actual collusion, which was illegal under the antitrust acts? It was possible through the "basing point system," whereby a price was set, called a "base price," at one or more "basing points," usually the locations of the major producers. These base prices were published, together with a standard book of transportation charges, which everyone in the industry used. What all of them did was to charge the base price plus the rate book figure for transportation cost *from the nearest basing point,* regardless of where they were located, or how they actually shipped the material (the rate book was based on rail freight charges).

This meant that any consumer found all producers quoting the same price to him, regardless of where they were, basing the price on the base price plus rail freight charges from the nearest basing point, although their plants might be closer or farther away.   If their plants were closer, they would be charging "phantom freight"; if farther, they would be absorbing freight charges, that is, getting less for the steel than the base price.   At one time or another, such pricing has been used in iron and steel, rigid steel conduit, cast-iron soil pipe, lead, copper, zinc, gasoline, cement, sugar, corn products, including corn syrup, and a number of lumber products, to name only the more important ones.

The distinction between reductions in prices to meet competition, for example, by "absorbing freight," and uniform prices that result from an implicit agreement not to compete on a price basis is frequently difficult to make, and for a time even the Supreme Court decided that because competition leads to uniform prices, uniform prices must mean that competition exists—a type of logical fallacy which is only too common. After years of ambiguity, however, the Supreme Court in 1948 declared the use of the basing-point system for cement was unfair competition and unlawful discrimination.[24]   In the same year, a Circuit Court of Appeals confirmed a Federal Trade Commission order against manufacturers of rigid steel conduit, and the U.S. Steel Corporation accepted a consent decree confirming a Federal Trade Commission order of 1924.[25]

Economists have argued that more serious problems are caused than the mere elimination of price competition.

We may conclude that the power of the large concern to meet competition by the seemingly innocent device of so-called "freight equalization" can be used to strangle small competitors, to force them into merger, to halt or retard their growth, to compel them to obey, and to discourage potential competitors from venturing into the industry.

Strangely enough, this power can be exercised with such ease and elegance, and so fully without violence and commotion, that neither of the parties need be conscious of what is going on.[26]

The major reasons why this is so are (a) it is easier for larger firms to excell in service, variety of products, and other types of non-price competition, and (b) because the large firms are almost always at basing points and many competitors are not, they can invade the competitors' territory without absorbing freight, but those who invade their area do have to absorb freight, and thus make less money.

In addition, because it is advantageous to locate at basing points, industry tends arbitrarily to locate there, although it might be more economical to produce elsewhere, and industries using the product, for example, steel, also tend to locate there, leading to an uneconomic pattern of industry location. And, of course, because customers had no incentive to buy from the closest mill, there was a lot of uneconomic "cross-hauling," that is, shipping the same product in both directions at the same time.   Finally, because rail freight was paid for, there was no incentive to make use of less expensive means of shipment, particularly if they were a little slower or slightly less convenient.   The best case against the whole system is the book by Machlup cited in note 26.

Why, we might ask, have the manufacturers in these industries been so insistent on maintaining the system and on fighting the issue through the courts for so long?   No manufacturer likes competition, but they do not customarily insist on eliminating it.   The basic reason is that these industries have very large fixed costs, low variable costs, an inelastic but fluctuating total demand for the product, and homogeneous products not protected from competition by qualitative differences and brand names.   In this situation, there are great temptations for each individual firm to cut prices, because a small price difference will enable that firm to take over substantial numbers of his competitor's customers.   In addition, because the products are heavy and expensive to ship, these price cuts can be restricted to markets close to, and ordinarily served by, competitors, without cutting prices to nearby customers.   Of course, such price cutting leads to retaliation, and the firms can end up selling no more than before, as a whole, and in addition "absorbing" many freight charges and receiving net prices perhaps below their average costs (including overhead). This is what businessmen call cutthroat competition.

Since there are bound to be periods of excess capacity for basic products like steel and cement and building materials, periods of ruinous competition are only too likely. There are some economists who say, "Why not let them drive prices below costs? It'll help revive business in general, and they can pay for their overhead costs of plant during boom times." Others insist that this would lead to high prices and less expansion in prosperity, and that falling prices do not provide a very effective stimulus to bring the industry out of a slump.

The producers, of course, prefer stability. A remarkably frank and often-quoted letter from a trustee of the Cement Institute to its Chairman read:

Do you think any of the arguments for the basing-point system, which we have thus-far advanced, will arouse anything but derision in and out of the government? I have read them all recently. Some of them are very clever and ingenious. They amount to this however: that we price this way in order to discourage monopolistic practices and to preserve free competition, etc. This is sheer bunk and hypocrisy. The truth is of course—and there can be no serious, respectable discussion of our case unless this is acknowledged—that ours is an industry above all others that cannot stand free competition, that must systematically restrain competition or be ruined.[27]

Well, if the basing point system leaves too little competition, and competitive price cutting in competitor's areas by freight absorption leaves too much, what other solutions are possible? One is a simple rule that all plants publish F.O.B. prices on their products. Some argue that this would mean each plant would have a local monopoly in the area near the plant, within which freight costs would be less from that plant than from others. However, any plant could cut its price and compete in the border areas half-way between it and the next plants in all directions, and perhaps this is about as much competition as one could allow or expect the industry to tolerate.

One final problem: any change in pricing methods is likely to lead to shifts in industry location, and some losses to those who located in uneconomic positions because of peculiar features of the former pricing system. It is easy to show that uniform F.O.B. pricing leads to optimum plant location in the long run, but it might lead to some difficulties in the transition stage.

The consumer's interest in this problem arises because the materials involved are basic in many things he buys directly or pays for indirectly through his taxes. In the coming years there will probably be changes made or suggested to be made in the laws, and the consumer-citizen needs to understand the problems so that he will know how to vote and how to instruct his representatives in congress.

Private Versus Social Costs and Benefits

Three basic conditions must exist if an economy is to function properly, that is, use resources efficiently to produce what the people want and need:

1. The distribution of income must be such as to encourage effort and to attract resources where they are most needed, but must also be "fair" so that money demands for products can be assumed to represent their "real" value to society.

2. Prices must be representative of the real costs of commodities so that those who use them, either in consumption or in further production, will be guided to use them only where they are most needed.

3. All the relevant costs of production, and values of output, should be considered by producers in deciding whether to expand, continue, or discontinue any productive process, whether or not these costs and benefits are actually paid for or charged for.

The first of these conditions would not exist in a free economy without some government interference. If payments are made only to those who are productive workers or owners of resources, we should have a rather unequal distribution of income, and one which would become cumulatively more unequal as wealth accumulated in the hands of a few—because wealth itself produces more wealth. Differentials to attract resources

to newer industries need not be great, and in many jobs, incentive payment systems are possible, which encourage effort
without actually paying more income, but any payment to
workers according to what they are worth as productive agents
leads to very large payments to a few, and very small payments
to those at the other end of the scale of ability and health.

On the other hand, the highly ethical ideal "from each according to his ability, to each according to his need" depends
on the development of other motivations for work—a development which has not yet been achieved on any important scale.
Even in Russia it became necessary very early after the revolution to provide economic incentives in the form of higher incomes for more production and for work at jobs where necessary skills were scarce.   In our own country, we prohibit the
hiring of people at wages below what would be necessary to
keep the worker alive and healthy, not only to avoid exploitation, but on the ground that an industry that hired them so
cheaply would be really subsidized by the rest of society.   Society would somehow have to make up the difference and to
provide for the rest of the person's support.

At the other end of the income scale, income taxes and inheritance taxes reduce the larger incomes more than the smaller
ones, without destroying the ranking.   In addition, free government services and a number of open or hidden subsidies also
affect the distribution of real goods and services among people.
We shall come back to this in the next section of this chapter.

The second condition, that prices should be representative of
costs so that they can guide people, is violated wherever there
are monopolistic methods of eliminating price competition,
whether by private industry, labor, or the government.   When
the Bureau of Mines estimates how much crude oil the market
can take—at current prices—and the states restrict production
to that amount, they preserve a stable price which may or may
not have any relation to the real cost.

The third condition is the one we want to discuss in this section, that is, that all relevant costs and benefits should be con-

sidered in evaluating any activity, not just those which law or accounting practice recognize. Back in 1904 George Bernard Shaw wrote a book entitled *The Common Sense of Municipal Trading* wherein he commented that the wages paid stevedores on the docks did not represent the cost of their work.[28] They could not live decent healthy lives on their wages, and at an early age, became wards of the state dependent on charity. Labor legislation has largely eliminated this difficulty.

Another striking instance, now largely eliminated by legislation, was the competitive drilling of oil wells. Oil occurs in pools underground, generally with natural gas, the pressure of which facilitates removal of the oil. If several pieces of property are over a single "pool," as they generally are, each property owner must rush to take as much oil as he can before his neighbors get it. However, if too many wells are drilled and the oil is taken too fast, gas pressure is lost, and some of the oil may never be recovered. Unfortunately, the "proration" system devised to deal with this difficulty also serves as a device for restricting total output and keeping up the price of oil. It might be more interesting to look briefly at some other areas where the laws have not yet completely caught up with the situation.

A. *Smoke nuisance.* Those who produce the smoke are not charged with all the cleaning bills and hospital bills and pay nothing for the inconvenience and discomfort they cause. When the situation becomes bad enough to cause immediate suffering and death, as in Donora, Pennsylvania, it is most noticeable, but it exists in many areas of the country. Rather than try to assess costs and to levy charges on those who produce smoke, cities like Pittsburgh have sometimes passed laws insisting on the use of better grades of coal, or more effective furnaces and firing devices. Interestingly enough, shut-downs of the steel mills in and near Pittsburgh had demonstrated that the mills were not responsible for as much of the smoke as people had thought. Private homes using soft coal with a high sulfur content had been responsible for much of it. At times, it was necessary to put the street lights on at noon in downtown Pittsburgh, but the situation has been vastly improved.

B. *Stream pollution.* The towns whose sewage and the factories whose wastes pollute the streams are not charged with the loss of fishing, swimming, and recreation, nor with the extra costs of securing pure water farther downstream, nor with the costs of illness, and so forth. Some regulations have been enforced, particularly when water systems are affected, or all the fish are killed off, but progress has been slow here. Narragansett Bay, from Providence, Rhode Island to the Atlantic, is bordered by summer homes, but is polluted and unsafe for swimming. Even the state institutions dump raw sewage into the bay. One of the difficulties here is the difficulty in determining who is responsible upstream, another is that sewage and wastes are generally a local responsibility so that areas affected downstream have no jurisdiction over the area upstream causing the trouble.

It is difficult, once a factory is built and producing wastes, to force the company to go to the expense of treating its wastes. Sometimes ingenuity finds useful by-products that can be gotten from the wastes thus reducing the costs, but frequently it is very expensive to do anything. Since frequently each factory is contributing only part of the wastes, none of them feel responsible, and there is a tendency to think that if only some of the others would treat their wastes, all would be well.

Recent research has led to a new method for discovering just which foreign chemicals are in a stream, and should make it easier to identify the industries that were responsible.[29] Basic problems must still be solved, however, because a stream is a natural resource which can be exploited in various ways, one of which is the absorption of industrial or municipal wastes. How to balance the various calls on the river's services for recreation, fishing, water supplies, irrigation, transportation, and absorption of wastes is a complex problem that need not and probably will not be solved by insisting that no wastes be dumped into the river at all. Perhaps a tax on those who use the river for waste disposal would be an aid, especially if the proceeds went into research for better methods of treating waste or reducing its impact.

Large dams for flood control and electric power have raised further problems of an interesting and unexpected sort. Ordinarily streams purify themselves if they have enough miles to absorb air and sunlight, but in the deep waters behind the dams, the air and sunlight cannot penetrate. When the dam gates are opened, cold and still polluted water goes rushing downstream, and even rushes underneath the warmer water upstream, up tributaries, polluting city water systems that are not even on the main river.

At times Clinch River water has been found in the Emory River as far as 14 miles upstream from its mouth.[30]

On the other hand, disease organisms apparently die off in a shorter distance below the sewer outlets in streams with dams than in those without them. One interesting facet of the problem is that, like many social problems, it arises when too many people do something. If only a few factories and towns dump wastes into a river, natural purification is sufficient, but when too many do so, other methods must be used.

From as far away as Virginia wastes from alkali manufacturing plants influence the quality of the water in the stream at Knoxville. Joining these wastes are those carried downstream from pulp and paper mills, rayon plants, and kaolin mining and processing. While the streams receiving these wastes have been undergoing natural purification between sources of pollution, they never completely recover before additional wastes are dumped into them.[31]

Similar problems arise when too many homeowners in an area try to use septic fields, particularly if natural drainage is not good.

C. *Floods and silting of reservoirs.* It is frequently true that the most profitable crops, at least in the short run, also cause a great deal of erosion. Strangely enough, one crop, the planting of which was greatly encouraged by the government—soy beans

—is highly erosive in its effects.   One observer noted a specific case where much of the 58,000 acres of rich farm land in the Upper Sangamon Valley of east central Illinois was planted in soy beans, and the farms were losing thousands of tons of fertile topsoil, along with a great deal of water, every year.[32] This same soil put an annual deposit of some half a million tons of soil in Lake Decatur, the reservoir formed by the two million dollar Decatur dam.   The capacity of the dam had been reduced by 14 per cent in the 14 years from 1922 to 1936. Dredging the reservoir could have cost more than a million dollars at prewar prices.   In this case, the city of Decatur provided twelve thousand dollars a year to organize soil conservation activity and education.

Another example is the over-grazing of the range lands in the west.

Mechanical means can be very effectively used, however, in conjunction with restoration of plant cover, and a good illustration of this is found in the short, steep mountain canyons of the Wasatch front in Utah, which have their outlet on a rich-soiled, heavily populated valley floor.   These canyons, many of them only a few miles in length, have belched forth highly destructive flows of mud whenever torrential rainfall gathered quickly on spots bared by serious overuse at the heads of the drainages.   An economic survey of one of these districts showed that small areas of land practically denuded of vegetation and topsoil, aggregating as few as 846 acres but strategically located at the headwaters of the canyon streams, were endangering values totaling 5¾ million dollars in the valley below, or nearly $7,000 worth of property for each acre of denuded slope. With such values at stake, it has been deemed expedient to construct on these high denuded areas enough trench terraces and other works to catch all of the rainfall from the ordinary torrential summer rainstorms before it has a chance to accumulate a large volume of runoff and gain great momentum.   The results have thus far quite equaled expectations.   In general these trench terraces serve the same purpose as the plant cover and a normal soil profile, namely, to aid in getting the maximum quantity of precipitation into the ground where it falls.   They are however, considered only as a stop-gap or safeguard pending establishment of a good plant cover, and as temporary means of hastening establishment of the cover.[33]

The point to remember here is that those who created this problem are not charged with its solution. The damages, plus the cost of repairing the eroded lands to prevent future floods, came to $1,040 per acre of eroded land, or about 200 times what the land was worth for grazing.[34] Tenant farming leads to a whole array of such problems: Insofar as a tenant farmer receives no credit for improving the soil or preventing erosion, even activities which are of long-range benefit to the farm may not be undertaken.[35]

All these examples have been of cases where costs to society or to some individuals were not charged against the people, communities, or companies responsible for them. Where the benefits from some action are greater than the revenue that could be collected for it, government action seems to have been easier. It would be difficult to send out a boat to collect a fee from every ship that made use of a lighthouse, and no one would like to restrict the use of parks by charging for them. In the case of some things like schools, one might even argue that the benefits are greater than possible tuition collections, because some people might not send their children to school if there were tuition to pay. In cases like these we rely on tax-financed government activity.

Perhaps the most discussed example is the case of increments in land values that result from the general growth of cities or public improvements. Except in the case of very specific improvements such as sidewalks, it has proven to be very difficult to isolate these gains and to charge for them. As a result, most public improvements on a large scale have been financed out of tax revenues of a rather general type, such as property taxes.

There is another class of cases where possible revenue to individuals is greater than the actual benefits, provided the benefits are looked at from the point of view of society: The sale of narcotics is usually quite profitable, but it is generally assumed that the narcotic addict has a distorted view of the value of the narcotic.

Finally, an extremely complex application of the problem of

social costs and benefits arises with multi-purpose Federal projects such as the Tennessee Valley Authority or the Central Valley Authority in California.[36] These projects not only provide water for electric power and irrigation, but also improve navigation and flood control. The latter two clearly benefit the area, but are difficult to charge for in any market. Hence, reclamation law provides that the Federal government pay for that share of the capital costs attributable to flood control and navigation. That part attributable to irrigation is supposed to be paid for by charges for the water, spread over many years, but without interest charges; and finally, the part attributed to the production of electricity, plus 3 per cent interest on the investment, is to be paid for by the users of electricity. These allocations are difficult, and there are many political, legal, and bargaining problems. There is some evidence, for instance, that the failure of the authorities to make contracts with the users of irrigation water before the Central Valley project was well along put them in a bad bargaining position so that the charges made for water are "a colossal bargain" to the irrigationists and perhaps represent "a great mistake in administration." [37] Further problems arise as to whether the Federal government or the state or private power companies should distribute the power, and whether irrigation water—likely to involve an implicit subsidy paid from Federal funds—should be provided to large commercial farms. Present reclamation law limits an individual holding to the amount of water necessary to irrigate 160 acres, with some variation to meet varying conditions of climate and land. This has led and still leads to terrific battles with the larger landowners, particularly in the Central Valley in California.[38]

There is not only the problem of the distribution of a subsidy but the more basic problem of whether the family farm can be preserved in irrigated areas and whether it should be. On the last point, convincing evidence was presented by comparing two communities in California. Where the land was owned by individual farmers, the community was healthier and good citizenship flourished.[39]   In the community where the land was owned by large commercial interests and the farmers were paid a wage, all the indexes of social participation and civic interest were low.

When one looks at the problem of how much to charge for water from publicly financed irrigation projects, two paradoxical facts appear: first, substantial increases in land prices and value occur when irrigation is introduced, the result of providing water at considerably less than it is worth (and also of the more intensive use of land with other factors of production), and second, there seem to be great difficulties on the part of the farmers in paying such charges as are levied to help pay for the dam and irrigation facilities.   If farmers really could afford to pay no more for the water, presumably they are buying an added factor of production at about what it adds to the value of their output, and it is difficult to see why the market prices of the land should skyrocket.   The facts are a mixture of things, as is usually the case in the real world: To a very large extent the water *is* subsidized and is worth far more than is charged for it.   On the other hand, the farmer may have real difficulties in paying, partly because he may have bought the land at speculative values, which already fully or more than fully took account of this, and partly because of a short-run cash shortage resulting from the necessity for large investments in equipment and construction on his farm.[40]

Some commentators have urged that if the charges for water are figured out, stated, and put into contracts before the irrigation work is built, it would be possible to make it pay for itself, and the value of the water would go to pay for the dam rather than increase land values.   Others urge that some system of collecting from others who benefit locally, for example the storekeepers, and so forth, would also help.   There would still be a necessity for government operation because of the tremendous amounts of capital involved, and the diversity of economic interests affected, but there might be less taxing of the whole country for the primary benefit of a few.   Similar problems arise with grazing on public range lands, where the fees are far below the value of the grazing rights, and with the state and federal forests.[41]

From the point of view of the consumer, whose taxes go to build these projects, or care for the national forest and range, there would seem to be a concern that the money should not provide excessive subsidies either to many small or to a few large farmers. However, the chances for competition driving the prices of the produce down may be better with more and smaller farmers. The picture of price-supported cotton being grown on California lands with subsidized water is a difficult one for the consumer to accept as justified. On the other hand, these projects are quite clearly of great total benefit, far greater than their cost, even if they can never be paid for out of revenues.

Taxes, Free Government Services, and the Distribution of Income and Wealth

The standard of living in a country and the welfare of its citizens are frequently equated to the level and distribution of income. International comparisons of income levels are diffi-

TABLE 28

Approximate Per Capita Incomes of Continental Divisions of the World, 1949

(In Equivalent American Dollars)

Africa	$75
North America	1,100
South America	170
Asia	50
Europe	380
U.S.S.R.	310
Oceania	560
World Total (Average)	230

Source: U.N. Econ. and Soc. Council, *Volume and Distribution of National Income in Under-Developed Countries.* Report by the Secretary General of the U.N. Doc. E/2041, June 1951, Table 3, p. 15.

cult and treacherous because of the widely different methods of living, different proportions of income received in money and goods, and the varying degrees of inadequacy of the statistics. It is quite obvious, however, that average per capita incomes are greatly higher in the United States than in most of the rest of the world, particularly Asia.

These data are based on estimates of national income divided by estimates—equally tenuous for Asia in particular—of population. More revealing in many ways and probably at least as accurate are infant mortality and life expectancy data, where many countries of Europe show up rather well.

For the ordinary citizen, however, it is not just income but its distribution that counts. A mere statistical division of the income of wealthy landlords over the peasant population does not provide them with food and clothing. If "a third of the nation is ill-fed, ill-clothed and ill-housed," this must mean that their income is inadequate. Rather than provide any tables on the distribution of income, what I should like to do here is to point out how difficult it is to derive any conclusions from such tables.

The first problem has to do with what income is. If we include only money received by wage earners, then we omit the value of food produced and consumed at home. We neglect the services of the housewife, so that if she hires someone to take care of the house and children and gets a job, the income of the family looks very large. Some available data include estimates of the non-money income in the form of the services of one's own house, others do not. When they do not, then renters who have their savings invested in assets that earn a money return look better off than home owners who take the return on their savings in the form of the use of a house without rent. Then there are gifts in money or food and clothing, annuity payments only part of which are taxable income, and capital gains from the increased value of real assets or investments during a period of inflation. All these things are differently distributed. Farmers are most likely to provide some of their own food.   Higher income people are more likely to own their own homes and to receive capital gains.   Finally, there are substantial taxes, income taxes, and others, which affect the amount of money left to use.   (See the last two columns of Table 29 on page 397.)

Even if we can settle on a definition of income, we discover that a large proportion of the lower income spending units are single people, some of them living with their parents or their children.   This raises a number of questions, one of which is the definition of the unit.   Are we talking of income of individuals, spending units, or families—or families excluding those consisting of single individuals?   Table 29 shows distributions on several of these bases.   What about those with no income, or with negative income (business or farm losses)?   How about the actual number of people to be supported on that income even if there are more than one?   Would not it be better to talk about per capita or per "equivalent adult"—counting children as various fractions?   Finally, what about the amount of effort involved?   Certainly a family with a large income, because everyone is working, is not necessarily that much better off!   A farmer or small businessman may work long hours and have most of his family helping.   If we are really concerned with welfare, it is the real income relative to the amount of work effort and relative to the "needs" as indicated by the number of people, which should concern us.   Then, too, in any one year there will be some people temporarily without adequate income because of business losses, crop failure, illness, or unemployment.

Finally, the definition of inequality of a distribution has been a matter of argument among the experts for years, and there is no satisfactory solution to it.   During the depression of the 1930's there were fewer very large incomes, but a large number of people with extremely low incomes (the unemployed); hence, the distribution of income became more unequal at the bottom and more equal at the top.   Is it more unequal for one man to have all the income and all the rest none, or for half the people to have some equal amount and the other half none at all?   In view of all the difficulties most people have settled on some simple arbitrary measure.   One of these is the share of the total income that goes to the top fifth of the income receivers, that is, if we rank people (or families) according to their income, take the 20 per cent with the largest incomes, and ask what proportion of the total income they receive, we have one measure.   This measure will fail to register the effects of important developments raising or lowering incomes at the bottom, such as minimum wage laws, unions, or elimination of unemployment.   If we use spending units (treating as separate spending units related people other than the wife who have separate finances and separate incomes even if they live together), then the top fifth in both 1952 and 1953 received more than eight-tenths of the income after federal income taxes, according to the Surveys of Consumer Finances.   Comparisons with similar data from England reveal a surprising similarity in distribution.[42]

Table 29 presents data on income from two basic sources: the annual Current Population Survey conducted by the U.S. Census and based on a sample of 15–18,000, and the annual Survey of Consumer Finances conducted for the Federal Reserve Board by the Survey Research Center, University of Michigan, based on a somewhat more complex sample of 3,000.   The 1950 Census, asked every fifth person (20 per cent sample) about individual income, and a sample of one-sixth of these (making a $3\frac{1}{3}$ per cent sample) were tabulated.   The reductions in sampling errors in going from 3,000 to 15,000 or from 15,000 to more than 4 million are quite small, as we found in Chapter 3. The differences in results stem primarily from differences in definition, and, secondarily, from differences in methods of collecting the data.

Detailed studies have shown that concentrating the time and attention of the interviewer on financial information, and checking specifically for extra sources and types of income, and for extra earners in the family will increase the amounts of income reported.   Of course, the Bureau of Internal Revenue receives reports of income carefully worked out by people, but they are on a taxpayer or joint husband-wife basis.   They only include income subject to tax, and provide no data on people who do not even need to file a return because their income is so low relative to their exemptions.   Specialists have pieced these data together with estimates of aggregate income to make estimates of the shares of income going to the top 1 per cent or 5 per cent of the recipients.[43]

TABLE 29

DISTRIBUTIONS OF INCOME IN 1952 BY VARIOUS DEFINITIONS AND METHODS

	(1)	(2)	(3)	(4)	(5)	(6)
	CURRENT POPULATION REPORTS			1953 SURVEY OF CONSUMER FINANCES		
Income Level	Individual	Families and Unrelated Individuals	"Families" (excluding individuals)	Spending Units	Families	Families (income after taxes)
Under $1,000 ...	27.5%	14.7%	8.5%	11.0%	9.9%	10.1%
1,000–1,999	16.8	12.8	10.8	13.8	11.8	12.6
2,000–2,999	17.2	14.5	14.1	16.4	13.6	17.8
3,000–3,999	18.2	17.4	18.5	17.9	16.5	18.1
4,000–4,999	9.3	13.4	15.4	14.7	15.0	16.1
5,000–9,999	9.7	23.8	28.5	21.8	27.1	21.6
10,000 and over..	1.3	3.4	4.1	4.4	6.1	3.7
	100.0	100.0	100.0	100.0	100.0	100.0

Sources: (1) U.S. Dept. of Commerce, Bureau of the Census, Current Population Reports, Consumer Income, Series P-60, No. 14, "Income of Persons in the United States: 1952," Washington D.C.: Dec. 31, 1953, Table 1, p. 13.
(2) and (3) U.S. Dept. of Commerce, Bureau of the Census, Current Population Reports, Consumer Income, Series P-61, No. 15, "Family Income in the United States: 1952," Washington D.C., April 27, 1954, Table 1, p. 9.
(4), (5), and (6) 1954 Survey of Consumer Finances, Federal Reserve Bulletin, July, 1954, and unpublished tables.

A final complication has to do with the creation of legal entities, largely for tax purposes, which make it difficult to say just who actually received the income.   Privately held corporations, trusts, and other devices are legal entities that can receive income and under certain conditions pay their own taxes, while the rights to the accumulated funds ultimately revert to someone. And, of course, there are always undistributed corporate profits, which belong to someone, but are not income to him at the time.

All in all, it is a difficult task to define income, and we can attempt to measure only some of the less meaningful definitions. We are ultimately concerned with the level and distribution of psychic satisfaction, and this is determined not only by the level of physical comfort, but also by short working hours at a satisfying and creative job, pleasant recreation possibilities, pleasant communities, adequate provisions for old age, a general feeling that the distribution of income and wealth is fair, and so forth.

However, it has been clear for a long time that the free play of competition would lead to a distribution of income and wealth that was not acceptable. Some people because of limited abilities or illness or disability or poor bargaining position would get less than enough to live on. Others more richly endowed, or luckier, could command large incomes and accumulate wealth, which would itself earn more income. It might be true, and usually is, that the well-endowed man is worth to society the high income he can command, and that the services of the rentier's wealth are worth what it earns, but society has long since decided that they need not be allowed to keep all of it. We have a progressive income tax that reduces the inequality in income, and inheritance taxes that reduce the amount of accumulated wealth passed along to children who did not earn it. It is easy to overestimate the impact of these taxes, and people who object to them frequently do so. If we use the standard tax tables and survey data on actual income and the number of exemptions for each family, it appears that the proportion of income taken in federal income taxes looks like that reported in Table 30 from the 1954 Survey of Consumer Finances.

Critics point out that in order to be thus progressive, the tax must have higher and higher rates on additional increases in income, and that this will reduce people's incentives to work, or to take risks in investing their money. The latter is true to the extent that possible losses cannot be entirely subtracted from other income to reduce taxes. If they could, the tax would mean that the government was taking part of the risk, gain or loss, and this might induce people to take more risks. We shall present some other evidence on this later. The former is true to the extent that people are concerned with absolute income and not relative income, relative to its previous level and to other people. Any increase in income means an increase in net income, after taxes, no matter how high your income is. The argument is also true anyway for another reason: Your "take-home" pay is reduced; hence, the cost of leisure in terms of foregone income is lower. To complicate matters, capital gains are taxed at a lower rate, and it is frequently possible, particularly for high income people, to turn income into capital gains.

TABLE 30

ESTIMATED TAX LIABILITY IN RELATION TO BEFORE-TAX INCOME

Income Group	Mean Income Before Tax	Estimated Tax as Per Cent of Income
Under $1,000	$503	0.2%
1,000–1,999	1,478	3.0
2,000–2,999	2,486	6.7
3,000–3,999	3,447	7.5
4,000–4,999	4,438	9.8
5,000–7,499	5,953	12.1
7,500–9,999	8,423	15.1
10,000 and over [1]	19,204	27.9

Source: 1954 Survey of Consumer Finances.

[1] Averages for the open-ended income group in a survey are not accurate because of fluctuating numbers of very rich from one sample to the next.

The impact of inheritance taxes is also not so great as even the stated rates would make it seem because of various legal loopholes, particularly those involved in setting up personal trust funds. By setting up a trust fund for the grandchildren to be administered by the children, one can always avoid inheritance taxes completely every other generation.

There are a number of other ways in which the government is involved in affecting the distribution of income. There are state and federal minimum wage laws that prevent the exploitation of those in weak bargaining position. Some people argue that it is better to allow a man with low productivity to earn something rather than nothing at all, but it is difficult to determine whether it is his productivity that is low, or his bargaining power. Hence the laws generally provide few exceptions. The theory is that if an industry cannot afford to pay its workers enough to keep them in good health, then it is placing charges on society (for the later care of its workers), which involve a hidden subsidy without prior justification.

In many other ways, people's real income, rather than their money income, is supplemented by the government, usually in ways which tend to make the distribution of real income more nearly equal, if only by providing the same free service to everyone—a service which may be relatively more important to the poor man. All the way from schools and police and fire department, on the local level, to the medical research, national defense, and so forth, at the national level, free or partially subsidized services are being provided for the consumer.

At the same time there is an elaborate structure of federal, state, and local taxes, the over-all impact of which seems to be to take a larger proportion of the higher incomes, largely because of the federal income tax, and of the very bottom incomes, because of taxes like sales taxes which are more important when people spend more of their income on taxed items. The over-all final impact of the tax structure is difficult to assess, but most people are sure that it reduces inequality somewhat.[44] Furthermore, since governments are providing so many services, and taking so much money in taxes, they have a substantial impact on the distribution of income, and many government policies that lead to controversy do so because of their impact on the distribution of income. We have already pointed out that housing programs involve not only getting more housing built, but redistributing income in favor of those who get into the subsidized housing units.   Unfortunately, in most cases, small but well organized groups can frequently affect policy in such a way as to get more income for themselves, and only an enlightened electorate which can see through the verbiage to the issues can preserve some sort of balance between all the conflicting claims.

Labor unions claim to have increased the income of their members, though it is difficult to prove or disprove this, and economists do not agree.

The distribution of income also affects the over-all level of spending and saving; hence, the level of income, output and employment—though there are other things which also affect them.   When recession threatens, arguments are frequently heard for lowering the taxes or raising the wages of the lower income groups so that there will be more spending.   The opposite argument is not heard during inflation, that is, that we cut down the overspending by increasing the taxes of the poor who are doing most of it.   Indeed, there is serious doubt as to just how much effect income redistribution really has on saving. It is not the average saving of the rich and poor that counts here, but the effect of changes in their net income on their saving.   A rich man might save half his income, but reduce his consumption rather than his saving when he was taxed more heavily. A poor man might save nothing until his income rose, but then save most of the increase.

Furious arguments are made about the effect of taxes on people's willingness to invest in risky ventures or common stock. The best study of this problem came to the following conclusion:

The tax structure, as of 1949, cut substantially into the investment capacity of the upper income and wealth classes—the strategic source of venture capital for investment in business—and, on balance, it also decreased the willingness of these investors in the aggregate to make equity-type investments.   In other words, for equity-type investments considered as a whole the investors who were induced by taxes to shift to less risky investment positions appear to have overbalanced the opposite reaction of appreciation-minded investors.   The latter group, however, may have been so

stimulated by the tax structure to seek out investments offering unusually large capital gains potentialities, such as promising new
ventures, as actually to increase the flow of capital to such situations.
However this may be, it is clear that the combined impact of these
effects fell far short of drying up the supply of equity capital which
private investors were willing and able to make available to business.   The evidence indicates that the accumulation of investable
funds by the upper income classes has been consistently large during
the postwar years, despite the existing tax structure, and that individuals with large incomes and substantial wealth continue as a
group to hold and invest a large proportion of their funds in equity-
type investments.[45]

In other words, while taxes may have reduced the capacity of
upper income people to invest, they have apparently not reduced willingness to do so.   The same study, using evidence
from various sources, concluded that the very top income and
wealth groups owned most of the common stock, in spite of the
frequently quoted figures about the large number of stockholders various large companies have.

In terms of size classes of stockholdings, a minimum of 55 per
cent to 60 per cent of all marketable stock owned by private individuals in 1949 was concentrated in the hands of spending units
owning $100,000 or more of marketable stock.   Only a small frac-
tion of 1 per cent of all spending units, perhaps one-fifth of 1 per
cent, own this much stock.   A more probable estimate of the holdings of these spending units is 65 per cent to 70 per cent of the total
marketable stock owned by private individuals.

In terms of wealth groups, a minimum of 55 per cent to 60 per
cent of all marketable stock owned by private individuals in 1949
was held by spending units with a total wealth in excess of a quarter
of a million dollars.   A more probable estimate of the holdings of
this wealth group is 65 per cent to 70 per cent of the total marketable stock owned by private individuals.[46]

And by income levels:

Based mainly on SRC [Survey Research Center] data and on the
active investor sample, we estimate that, as of 1949, the upper 3
per cent of spending units with incomes of $10,000 and over owned
a minimum of 70 per cent of the aggregate marketable stock held

by individual investors.   A more probable estimate would be that the $10,000 and over group owned approximately 75 per cent of this total, with the figure being several percentage points higher if stock held in trusts managed by corporate trustees for individual beneficiaries is included in the total.

Based on dividend receipts reported on income tax returns, we estimate that in 1949 the degree of concentration in the ownership of marketable stock within the top 3 per cent of spending units ranked by size of income was roughly as follows:

(a) Spending units with incomes of $50,000 and over—approximately one-tenth of 1 per cent of the population—held about 35 per cent of all privately-owned marketable stock.

(b) Spending units with incomes of $25,000 and over—approximately one-half of 1 per cent of the population—held slightly over half the marketable stock owned by private investors.

(c) Spending units with incomes of $15,000 and over—approximately the top 1 per cent of the population—held about 65 per cent of all privately-owned marketable stock.

These figures would all be several percentage points higher if stock managed by corporate trustees for individual beneficiaries were included in the total.

There is no evidence of any marked change in the concentration of marketable stockholdings by income groups between 1949 and 1952.[47]

In view of this, arguments about double taxation of corporate dividends, and the need for tax relief for the poor investor would seem to be not very compelling.   Yet, beginning in 1954, dividends have been taxed less heavily than any other form of taxable income.

In discussing the distribution of income we noticed that one problem in interpretation arose because of the fact that sometimes several people in a family were working and earning income.   Most frequently this means either the wife or grown children in addition to the head of the household.   We might argue that this betokens financial pressures, that the wife would ordinarily be busy raising a family and keeping house, at least while there are children at home, and that children should either be in school, or able to set up separate households.   But, of course, things are not this simple.   Some women work because they prefer it to staying home, some work because the family could not live on what the husband makes, and others work because there are a number of things they are so eager to buy that it seems worth while having someone else in the family go to work.

There have been a number of studies of women workers, though unfortunately the ones with the most interesting content have been based on groups not representative of all women who work.[48]   One does, however, get an impression of a substantial number of women working, many of them because they feel they have to do so in order to make ends meet.   On the other hand, where the husbands were making between $4,000 and $4,999 during 1951, more than one-fourth of their wives were working too; and where the husband was making $5,000 to $5,999, more than one-fifth of their wives were working.[49]

In April 1953, the proportion of married women (living with their husbands) who were in the labor force varied from 20 per cent in the age group 14–19 to a peak of 33 per cent of women between the ages of 35 and 44, then dropped rapidly to very small proportions among older women.[50]   This amounted to more than ten million married women in the labor force, more than nine million of whom had a husband living at home and employed.   For those with children, working raised problems of day care, which have been studied in the Wichita study cited in footnote 48.

In addition, there were in April 1953 nearly 22 million women living alone, many of whom were supporting themselves.[51]   Only 10.8 million were single women, 7.4 million were widowed, 1.3 million were divorced, and the rest were separated from their husbands for one reason or another.

How can we summarize the distribution of income in the United States?   People are paid for their productive effort or the productive increase of wealth they already own.   Theory says a man will only be hired if he adds to the output in value more than his wage; and that if there is a free market and competition, he will be paid no less than this.   In the real world, people are not mobile, nor aware of all their opportunities.[52] Furthermore, if by law or union their pay is increased, it sometimes turns out that it was possible by better organization or greater use of machinery for them to produce that much.

There remain substantial barriers against some minority groups in many types of employment, and a tendency to pay them lower wages for the same type of work when they are employed.   Negroes, American Indians, and Mexican and Puerto Rican immigrants are treated the worst on this score, but even women workers sometimes find they are discriminated against. In terms of the persistence of discrimination and the size and importance of the group involved, however, it is in the acceptance of the Negro worker where progress is most important.[53]

Ultimately, the distribution of income is an ethical problem. We want to maximize social welfare and happiness and to preserve democracy.   This means reducing inequalities that lead to political power or envious unhappiness.   It may mean eliminating incomes so low as to be incapable of supporting a family.   At the same time, differential rewards may be desired to induce people both to work hard, and to work at the right job—where they are most needed.   Finally, the distribution of income can affect the total demand for goods and services by consumers, and the flow of savings ready to be invested.   In so-called backward countries the problem is securing resources for investment, whereas in our own country, so long as consumers will keep buying, we seem to have developed rather effective devices for providing investment funds out of undistributed profits, depreciation allowances, savings institutions, and so forth.

Perhaps the most important thing that you need to remember is that a great many arguments in both economics and politics have as their base disagreements as to what is the best distribution of income or wealth.   If you can interpret these arguments in such terms, they become much easier to understand.

Summary

We have skimmed over a whole array of problems in this chapter, not intending to discuss them adequately, but hoping to illustrate some basic principles that you will find useful in dealing with any such problems as they arise.   These principles can be thought of as of two sorts: those dealing with the fair distribution of the goods and services which society produces, and those dealing with the efficiency with which the economy allocates resources in the proper proportions in producing the proper things.   These two are not really separable, and neither can be adequately solved without solving the other at the same time.   If we have competition; and if there are some laws to deal with cases where prices do not represent all the real costs or where real benefits exist which cannot be charged for; and if there are the necessary differentials in rewards to insure that resources go where they are needed most, then all is well, *provided the money demands for goods and services represent their real worth*.[54]   We can only be sure that this last is true if we feel that the distribution of income and wealth is reasonably fair and that consumers use their money intelligently.   In a feudal society, we might feel that the price of caviar and dancing girls is likely to be higher relative to their "contribution to society" than is the price of milk.   The market place can only determine what *should* be produced if the purchasing power of each consumer is an acceptable measure of his importance.

If the distribution of income is acceptable, and if there is competition so that the prices of goods represent their costs without any excessive profits thrown in, and if there is some equality of bargaining so that the prices of labor and other factors of production represent their worth in alternative uses, neither more nor less, and, finally, if all the relevant social costs and benefits are either included in the calculations of people, or some legal corrective is provided, then the consumer can feel that these larger economic problems are well solved, and he can concentrate on his own personal decisions.   When questions which involve these basic economic functions arise, however, the consumer's interests are involved, and he needs to understand the issues involved.

In many cases the issues arise because groups in the economy are attempting to improve their own position at the expense of others. A group must be organized to do this, and producers find it easier to organize than consumers. If it is illegal to organize, or difficult, then sometimes the power of government authority is used to help. We have seen in this chapter a number of ways in which this has happened. Even on the level of fact-gathering, communication of news to people and of people's views to Congress, we see labor served by the Labor Department, farmers helped by the Department of Agriculture, businessmen by the Department of Commerce, but the consumer has no representation at all except in specialized areas such as public health, education, or social security. The usual channels of information—newspapers, radio, and magazines—can hardly be said to have the consumers' interest foremost.[55] Even the homemaking magazines seem to be primarily directed to showing us how to spend our money on the newest fanciest things. In such a situation the best way we the consumers can keep up is to read the trade journals of the various interest groups. Frequently, you will find revealing articles objecting to the activities of another interest group, or revealing the latest moves in legislation or salesmanship.

Suggested Projects

1. Look in *U.S. Law Week* and *Commerce Clearing House* for references to the latest court decisions and articles in law journals on

> anti-trust laws
> resale price maintenance
> basing point pricing
> joint tenancy.

2. Write a review of one of the books referred to in the notes to this chapter, by

> 8. Benedict or Black
> 12. Rostow (preferably jointly with Cassady)

17. Bressler
20. Schattschneider
26. Machlup
36. de Roos
    Frank and Netboy
    Williams
39. Goldschmidt
40. Hoffman
41. Gulick
45. Butters, Thompson, and Bollinger
48. Komarovsky
52. Jefferys
53. Sterner
54. Lerner
55. The Nieman Fellows.

3. Read several issues of one of the following journals. Make a list of items of information of interest to you as a consumer which you found and which you might not have found in ordinary newspapers.

Advertising Agency
Bankers Monthly
Best's Insurance News
Broadcasting-Televising
Coal Age
Credit and Financial Manage-
, ment
Department Store Economist
Electrical World
Food Engineering
Gas Age
Hardware Age
Hardware Retailer
Home Furnishings
Iron Age
Jewelers' Circular-Keystone

Men's Wear
N.A.R.D. Bulletin (National As-
soc. of Retail Druggists)
National Furniture Review
National Petroleum News
National Real Estate and Build-
ing Journal
National Underwriter
Printers Ink
Public Utilities Fortnightly
Railway Age
Restaurant Management
The Spectator
Stores
Tide

4. Find out whether the wholesale price of milk is fixed in your area, and by whom. Are there public hearings? Are there consumer representatives on the price-fixing board?

5. Write to the following, and ask about the present status of the basing point system, and whether delivered pricing is still a practice.

U.S. Federal Trade Commission, Washington D. C.

American Iron and Steel Institute, 350 Fifth Ave., New York, N. Y.

American Cement Institute, 33 West Grand Ave., Chicago 10, Illinois.

Ask, also whether uniform F.O.B. prices are charged, or are prices varied to meet competition. Finally, ask whether customers are allowed to transport the steel or cement in their own trucks.

FOOTNOTES TO CHAPTER 11

1 *Schwegmann Brothers* v. *Calvert Distillers Corporation*, 341 U.S. 384 (1951); see also: James A. Rahl, "Resale Price Maintenance, State Action, and the Antitrust Laws, Effect of Schwegmann Bros. v. Calvert Distillers Corp.," 46 *Northwestern University Law Review* 349–384 (1952) (sometimes called *Ill. Law Rev.*).

2 Corwin Edwards, Memorandum for Assistant Attorney General, Antitrust Division, Re: *Grounds for the Repeal of the Miller-Tydings Amendment Which Authorizes Resale Price Contracts* (mimeographed), Washington, D. C.: Department of Justice, Feb. 10, 1941, *passim;* see also: *Report of the Federal Trade Commission on Resale Price Maintenance,* Submitted to Congress, December 13, 1945, Washington, D. C.: U.S. Gov't Printing Office, 1945, particularly p. liv; C. H. Fulda, "Resale Price Maintenance," 21 *Univ. of Chicago Law Review* 175–211 (Winter, 1954); G. E. Weston, "Resale Price Maintenance and Market Integration: Fair Trade or Foul Play?", 33 *Geo. Wash. Law Rev.* 434–50 (March, 1954).

3 C. R. Alsberg, "Economic Aspects of Adulteration and Imitation," *Quarterly Journal of of Economics,* XLVI: 1–33 (November, 1931).

4 Florida Supreme Court, *Liquor Stores Inc.* v. *Continental Distillers Corp.* 40 So. 2d 371, and *Miles Laboratories Inc.* v. *Eckerd,* March 15, 1954 (17 U.S. Law Week 2487 and 22 U.S. Law Week 2458).

5 *In Eli Lilly & Co.* v. *Schwegmann Bros.,* 205 F.2d 788, June 30, 1953.

6 Michigan Supreme Court, *Shakespeare Co.* v. *Lippman's Tool Shop Sporting Goods Co.,* 334 Mich. 109, June 27, 1952 (see *U.S. Law Week* 21: 2020); *Grayson-Robinson Stores* v. *Oneida Ltd.,* 209 Georgia 613 (see 21 *U.S. Law Week* 2434), upheld by Georgia Supreme Court, 75 S.E.2d 161 (see 22 *U.S. Law Week* 3035, 3090); Nebraska District Court, *General Electric Co.* v. *J. L. Brandeis and Sons,* Feb. 24, 1954 (see 22 *U.S. Law Week* 2396).

7 Stephen Leacock, *Hellements of Hickonomics* (in *Hiccoughs of Verse Done in Our Social Planning Mill*), New York: Dodd, Mead & Co., 1936.

8 See for instance: John D. Black, *Parity, Parity, Parity,* Cambridge, Mass.: Harvard Committee for Research in Social Science, 1942; see also: *Consumers Look at Farm Price Policies,* Consumer Problems Series No. 1, Miami University, Oxford, Ohio: Council on Consumer Information, 1954; Murray R. Benedict, *Farm Policies of the United States, 1790–1950, A Study of their Origins and Development,* New York: Twentieth Century Fund, 1953.

9 U.S. Department of Agriculture, *Price Programs of the U.S. Department of Agriculture,* Agricultural Information Bull. No. 13 (Rev. Dec., 1953), Washington, D. C.: U.S. Gov't Printing Office, 1953, pp. 1–2.

10 Glenn L. Johnson and Cecil B. Haver, *Decision-Making Principles in Farm Management,* Lexington, Kentucky: Kentucky Ag. Expt. Station Bulletin 593, January 1953, pp. 30–31.

11 U.S. Department of Agriculture, *Price Programs of the U.S. Department of Agriculture*, Agricultural Information Bull. No. 13 (Rev. Dec., 1953), Washington, D. C.: U.S. Gov't Printing Office, 1953, pp. 1–2.

12 For a highly critical analysis of this, see: Eugene V. Rostow, *A National Policy for the Oil Industry*, New·Haven: Yale University Press, 1948. For a more sympathetic treatment which curiously does not mention Professor Rostow's book, see: Ralph Cassady, Jr., *Price Making and Price Behavior in the Petroleum Industry* (Petroleum Monograph Series, Volume 1), New Haven: Yale University Press, 1954.

13 John D. Black, *The Dairy Industry and the A.A.A.*, Washington, D. C.: The Brookings Institution, 1935; see also: U.S. Department of Agriculture Production and Marketing Administration, *Compilation of Agricultural Marketing Agreement Act of 1937*, Washington, D. C., 1952.

14 Boston Milkshed Price Committee, *A Recommended Basis of Pricing Class 1 Milk in the Boston Market*, Boston, Massachusetts: Sept. 1947 (available from the Federal Market Administrator).

15 *Ibid.*, p. 2.

16 *Ibid.*, p. 17. See also: *The New England Basic Class 1 Milk Price*, Amherst, Massachusetts: Special Circular 201, Extension Service, University of Massachusetts, September 1952.

17 Raymond G. Bressler, *City Milk Distribution*, Cambridge: Harvard University Press, 1952.

18 John D. Black and Catherine Corson, *Sugar—Produce or Import?*, New York: Carnegie Foundation for International Peace, 1947. Published by University of California Press, Berkeley and Los Angeles.

19 R. F. Kahn, "Tariffs and the Terms of Trade," *Review of Economic Studies*, XV:14–19 (1947–8); T. Scitovszky, "A Reconsideration of the Theory of Tariffs," *Review of Economic Studies*, IX:89–110 (Summer, 1942); F. C. Child, "The Gains from Limited Trade," *Review of Economic Studies*, XVIII: 87–98 (1950–51); for a graphic description of the inevitable logrolling process which led to reforms taking tariff policy out of congress, see: E. E. Schattschneider, *Politics, Pressures and the Tariff*; New York: Prentice-Hall, Inc., 1935; Harry G. Johnson, "Optimum Tariffs and Retaliation," (*Review of Econ. Studies*, XXI:142–153 (1953–54).

20 E. E. Schattschneider, *Politics, Pressures, and the Tariff*, New York: Prentice-Hall, Inc., 1935.

21 Leland I. Doan, "A Protectionist Comments," *Michigan Business Review*, VI:1–5 (March, 1954).

22 Gottfried Von Haberler, *Currency Convertibility*, New York: American Enterprise Association, 1954, pp. 28–29 for a short simple explanation, or see any text book on international trade for the details.

23 *Exhibit 2241*, Hearings before the Temporary National Economic Committee, 76th Congress, 3rd Session, Pursuant to Public Resolution No. 113, Part 27, Washington, D. C.: 1940, p. 14,548.

24 *Federal Trade Commission* v. *The Cement Institute*, 33 U.S. 683, 68 S. Ct. 793.

25 *Triangle Conduit and Cable Company* v. *Federal Trade Commission*, 168 F.2d 175 (1948).

26 Fritz Machlup, *The Basing-Point System*, Philadelphia: The Blakiston Company, Inc., 1949, p. 16. G. W. Stocking, "Law on Basing Point Pricing: Confusion or Competition," 2 *J. Public Law* 1–28 (Spring, 1953); U.S. Senate, *Price Discrimination and the Basing Point System*, Hearings before a Subcommittee of the Senate Select Committee on Small Business, Washington, D. C.: U.S. Gov't Printing Office, 1951.

[27] Letter from Mr. John Treanor to Mr. Rader, dated May 17, 1934, quoted from *Aetna Portland Cement Co. et al v. Federal Trade Commission,* in the U.S. Circuit Court of Appeals, Brief for Respondent (Federal Trade Commission, Feb., 1946), p. 127.

[28] George Bernard Shaw, *The Common Sense of Municipal Trading,* Westminster: Archibald Constable, 1904; see also: A. C. Pigou, *Economics of Welfare,* 4th ed., London: MacMillan, 1938.

[29] U.S. Department of Health, Education, and Welfare, *Annual Report, 1953,* Washington, D. C.: U.S. Gov't Printing Office, 1953, p. 135.

[30] Tennessee Valley Authority, *Stream Sanitation in the Tennessee Valley,* Chattanooga, Tennessee: T.V.A. Division of Health and Safety, December 1952, p. 8.

[31] *Ibid.,* p. 5. See also: C. J. Velz, "Recovery of Polluted Streams," *Water and Sewage Works,* 100:495–500 (December, 1953); A. R. Meetham, *Atmospheric Pollution, Its Origin and Prevention,* London: Pergamon Press Ltd., 1952; S. I. A. Laidlaw, "Effects of Smoke Pollution on Health," *Institute of Fuel,* 27:96–9 (Feb., 1954).

[32] R. H. Musser, "A Farm City Plan for Erosion Control," *Journal of Land and Public Utility Economics,* XVIII:323–327 (August, 1942); A. N. Garin and G. W. Forster, "*Effect of Soil Erosion on the Costs of Public Water Supply,* Washington, D. C.: U.S. Department of Agriculture, Soil Conservation Service, 1940; A. N. Garin and L. P. Gabbard, *Land Use in Relation to Sedimentation in Reservoirs, Trinity River Basin, Texas,* Texas Agricultural Experiment Station Bulletin 597, 1941.

[33] C. L. Forsling, "Vegetative Aspects of Erosion Control in the West," Symposium on Some Aspects of Vegetative Methods of Erosion Control, Annual Meeting of the American Society of Agronomy, December 1937, pp. 2–3.

[34] U.S. Dept. of Agriculture, Forest Service, *Watershed Management for Summer Flood Control in Utah* (by R. W. Bailey, G. W. Craddock, and A. R. Croft), Misc. Pub. No. 639, Washington, D. C.: U.S. Gov't Printing Office, December 1947, p. 22.

[35] Arthur C. Bunce, *The Economics of Soil Conservation,* Ames, Iowa: The Iowa State College Press, 1942.

[36] R. W. de Roos, *The Thirsty Land, The Story of the Central Valley Project,* Stanford, California: Stanford University Press, 1948; Bernard Frank and Anthony Netboy, *Water, Land and People,* New York: Alfred A. Knopf, Inc., 1950; Albert N. Williams, *The Water and the Power,* New York: Duell, Sloan & Pearce, Inc., 1951; U.S. Department of the Interior, Bureau of Reclamation, *The Columbia River,* A comprehensive Departmental Report on the Development of the Natural Resources of the Columbia River Basis . . . Washington, D. C.: U.S. Gov't Printing Office, Feb. 1947; U.S. Department of the Interior, Bureau of Reclamation, *The Colorado River,* A Comprehensive Departmental Report etc. . . . Washington, D. C., U.S. Gov't Printing Office, March 1946; The President's Water Resources Policy Commission, *A Water Policy for The American People,* Washington, D. C.: U.S. Gov't Printing Office, 1950. (Three volumes: Vol. 1, General Report; Vol. 2, Ten Rivers in America's Future; Vol. 3, Water Resources Law.) Arthur D. Angel, "Who Will Pay for the Central Valley Project in California?", *Journal of Land and Public Utility Economics,* XXII:266–272 (August, 1946).

[37] R. W. de Roos, *The Thirsty Land, The Story of the Central Valley Project,* Stanford, California: Stanford University Press, 1948, pp. 149 and 158.

[38] Paul S. Taylor, "The 160-Acre Water Limitation and the Water Resources Commission," *Western Political Quarterly,* III:435–450 (September, 1950).

39 Walter R. Goldschmidt, *As You Sow,* New York: Harcourt, Brace & Co., 1947. The original report, a Senate Committee Print (No. 13) for the Senate Special Committee to Study the Problems of American Small Business (79th Cong., 2nd Senate Committee Print No. 13, Dec. 23, 1946) is difficult to find even in libraries.

40 Roy E. Hoffman, *Irrigation Development and Public Water Policy,* New York: The Ronald Press Company, 1953, p. 68.

41 John D. Black, *Introduction°to Economics for Agriculture,* New York: The Macmillan Company, 1953, p. 584; Luther H. Gulick, *American Forest Policy,* New York: Duell, Sloan & Pearce, Inc., 1951. (A Study of Gov't Administration and Economic Control published for the Institute of Public Administration.)

42 Theodore Morgan, "Distribution of Income in Ceylon, Puerto Rico, the United States and the United Kingdom," *Economic Journal,* LXIII:812–834 (December, 1953).

43 Simon Kuznets, *Shares of Upper Income Groups in Income and Savings,* New York: National Bureau of Economic Research, 1953; see also: Selma Goldsmith, George Jaszi, Hyman Kaitz, and Maurice Liebenberg, "Size Distribution of Income Since the Mid-Thirties," *Review of Economics and Statistics* XXXVI:1–32 (February, 1954); U.S. Department of Commerce, Office of Business Economics, *Income Distribution In the United States by Size, 1944–1950,* Washington, D. C.: U.S. Gov't Printing Office, 1953; Herman P. Miller, "An Appraisal of the 1950 Census Income Data," *Journal of American Statistical Association,* 48:28–43 (March, 1953); Selma Goldsmith, "Appraisal of Basic Data for Size Distributions of Income," in *Studies in Income and Wealth,* Vol. 13, New York: National Bureau of Economic Research, 1951.

On a more general level, see: R. J. Lampman, "Recent Changes in Income Inequality Reconsidered," *American Economic Review,* XLIV:251–268 (June, 1954); and also J. N. Morgan, "Review of Kuznets, Shares of Upper Income Groups in Income and Savings," *Review of Economics and Statistics* XXXVI:237–239 (May, 1954).

44 R. A. Musgrave, J. J. Carrol, L. D. Cook, and L. Frane, "Distribution of Tax Payments by Income Groups, a Case Study for 1948," *National Tax Journal,* 4:1–49 (March, 1951), and succeeding controversy, which pertains only to details. See also: Senator Hubert H. Humphrey, *Tax Loop Holes,* Washington, D. C.: The Public Affairs Institute, 1952.

45 J. Keith Butters, Lawrence E. Thompson, and Lynn L. Bollinger, *Effects of Taxation, Investments by Individuals,* Boston, Mass.: Graduate School of Business Administration, Harvard University, 1953, pp. 50–51.

46 *Ibid.,* pp. 399–400.

47 *Ibid.,* p. 440.

48 See the following publications of the U.S. Department of Labor, Women's Bureau, Washington, D. C.: U.S. Gov't Printing Office: *Women as Workers, a Statistical Guide,* 1953; *Women Workers and Their Dependents,* Bulletin No. 239, 1951; *Negro Women and Their Jobs,* Leaflet No. 19, Jan. 1954; *Working Women's Budgets in Twelve States,* Bulletin No. 226, 1948; *Part Time Jobs for Women, a Study in Ten Cities,* Bulletin No. 238, 1951; *Employed Mothers and Child Care,* Bulletin No. 246, 1953.

And see Mirra Komarovsky, *Women in the Modern World, Their Education and their Dilemmas,* Boston: Little, Brown & Co., 1953; Margaret Mead, "Towards Mutual Responsibility," in *Professional Women in Modern Society,* Vol. VI of the *Journal of Social Issues* (No. 3), 1950 (also articles in the same issue by Viola Klein, Marguerite Wykoff Zapoleon, Josephine J. Williams, and Hazel Davis and

Agnes Samuelson; Amy Gessner Gerling, *Day Care for the Children of Wichita, a Study of Needs,* Wichita, Kansas: Community Planning Council, 406 Orpheum Building, Publication No. 11, April 1953; "Graduate Wives," *Planning,* Vol. XX, No. 361 (April, 1954). (Published by Political and Econ. Planning, 16 Queen Anne's Gate SW1, London: a study of married women graduates of English universities.)

49 U.S. Department of Commerce, Bureau of the Census, *Current Population Reports,* "Family Income in the U. S., 1951," Washington, D. C.: U.S. Gov't Printing Office, June 1953, Table D, p. 4.

50 U.S. Department of Commerce, Bureau of the Census, *Current Population Reports,* "Labor Force: Marital Status of Workers, April, 1953," (P50 No. 50), Washington, D. C.: U.S. Gov't Printing Office, Nov. 30, 1953, Table 2, p. 7.

51 U.S. Department of Commerce, Bureau of the Census, *Current Population Reports,* "Population Characteristics: Marital Status, Year of Marriage, and Household Relationship, April, 1953," Washington, D. C.: U.S. Gov't Printing Office, Dec. 6, 1953, Table 1.

52 Margot Jefferys, *Mobility in the Labour Market,* London: Routledge and Kegan Paul, 1954.

53 Richard M. E. Sterner, *The Negro's Share,* New York: Harper & Brothers, 1943.

54 Abba P. Lerner, *The Economics of Control,* New York: The Macmillan Company, 1944.

55 The Nieman Fellows (Leon Svirsky, ed.), *Your Newspaper,* New York: The Macmillan Company, 1947.

chapter 12

Maximizing
Consumer Satisfaction

|||||||||||||||||||||||||||||||||||||||||||||||||||||||||||||||||||||||||||||||||||||||||||||||||||||||||||||||||||||||||||||||||||||||||||||||||||||||||||||||||||||||

Introduction

We have been dealing with consumer choices in the use of money income throughout most of this book. In this chapter we shall discuss very briefly two questions. First, what possibilities are open to the consumer for increasing the level and stability of his money income? Second, are there other ways of becoming better off in addition to increasing earnings? In dealing with the second question, we'll discuss both "home production"—methods of increasing available goods and services directly without the necessity for earning money first—and also the more general problem of keeping one's level of aspiration within hailing distance of one's potential achievements.

Increasing Money Income and Income Security

Income depends upon what occupation you choose as well as how far you go up the scale in that occupation. Very little is known about occupational choice as it is actually made, except that the choice is really a series of choices.

The outstanding conclusion from our findings is that occupational choice is a developmental process: it is not a single decision, but a series of decisions made over a period of years. Each step in the process has a meaningful relation to those which precede and follow it.[1]

Young people may therefore sometimes make decisions which will restrict their possible future choice of occupation more than they realize. There is also considerable evidence that, except where conditions are very bad, many people tend to choose occupations similar to those of their parents.

The difficulties in choosing an occupation are obvious. First there is more to it than maximizing income or security or some mixture. We all have abilities in certain directions more than others, and we all have some things we like to do more than others. There are of course psychological tests for both of these. Many of them are developed by finding out the likes and dislikes of those who have been successful in certain occupations, and assuming that people with those same patterns will also be successful and happy in those occupations. They should clearly not be taken too seriously. I have taken some of them and they indicate that I should be a farmer. When it comes to finding out about the income prospects of different occupations, not much can be said either. The Department of Labor puts out a series of Occupational Outlook handbooks which attempt this. A few years ago the engineering profession was considered dangerously overcrowded; now engineers are scarce and command very high incomes. During the 1920's and early 1930's farmers earned very little; now the better equipped farmers do extremely well and the government promises to insure that they continue to do so. There is a great shortage of doctors and dentists now which seems likely to continue, but it is not outside the range of possibility that fluorinated water and simpler antibiotics would greatly reduce the need for dentists and increase the possible number of patients one doctor could handle. Neither is it beyond the range of possibility that health insurance plans, partially subsidized by the government, would vastly increase the ability of people to pay for adequate medical care and make the doctors better paid, however overworked they might become.

On the other hand, aside from a few dying occupations like cigar-making, or those likely to remain low paid because they require little or no skill or intelligence, a person who likes his job and does it well need not worry about these long-range problems.   A more immediate problem is to choose between occupations requiring a long period of investing time and money in training with the promise of great rewards later, in medicine, law, teaching and many of the other professions.   If an opinion were to be ventured, it seems at present that a person must either invest a great deal in a profession, that is, enough to become a specialist in medicine or get an advanced degree in engineering or social sciences, or face the question whether he could not find a job where the skill develops on the job and the over-all earnings are about as great.   On the other hand, in our society a college education seems to be a sort of prerequisite for many jobs which do not require the education. Further there seems to be such a social status associated with a college education that many people feel dissatisfied all their lives because they did not finish college.   Whatever the reason, it is quite obvious from the data in Table 31 that it is not very many years after he graduates before the college graduate is earning more than those who went to work sooner.   Right now many of the skilled trades seem to offer real advantages, particularly those that are necessary for repair and maintenance as well as construction.   A tendency to look down at some of these occupations, plus a rapid development of greater needs for them, has left them undermanned.   The tremendous increase in the number and complexity of appliances and equipment that are used has not been accompanied by a sufficient increase in people who know how to service and repair them, and who have capital for the complex tools required.

If this discussion seems unsatisfactory to you, it is because the choice of occupation is a personal matter dependent largely upon one's tastes and abilities, and because it is very difficult to say much about what incomes one can expect from an occupation relative to other occupations in twenty or thirty years.

TABLE 31

MEDIAN INCOME IN 1949 OF MALE PERSONS (INDIVIDUALS) WITH INCOME,
BY YEARS OF SCHOOL COMPLETED AND AGE

Age (in years)	8 Years of Grade School	4 Years of High School	College Graduate
14–17	$ 305	$ 411	.....
18–19	881	767	.....
20–21	1,364	1,617	$ 854
22–24	1,840	2,309	1,526
25–29	2,255	2,892	2,928
30–34	2,557	3,308	4,227
35–44	2,803	3,523	5,142
45–54	2,912	3,687	5,549
55–64	2,601	3,436	5,142
65–74	1,505	2,262	3,597
75 and over	800	1,217	1,892

Source: U.S. Bureau of the Census, *U.S. Census of Population: 1950.* Vol. IV. *Special Reports.* Part 5, Chapter B, Education. Table 13, p. 128 of Special Report PE No. 5B, Washington, D. C.: U.S. Government Printing Office, 1953.

Finally, we can speak only in the most general terms about the stability or security of incomes of various types. It used to be that the farmer's income was most insecure, and it fluctuates even today, in spite of price supports; but the farmer has other types of security. It is common knowledge that it is the unskilled production worker who has the least job security, though even here unemployment compensation has made a difference and may make still more. Security is a difficult thing to talk about, and people may not admit to themselves that they are insecure, but it is interesting to see the answers to a question asked by Survey Research Center in November, 1949.

Some people feel quite secure in their job or business, others have many worries about how they will get along financially. How is it in your case?

The answers varied according to the occupation of the head of the household as shown in Table 32.

Security not only involves both possible loss of job and possible fluctuations in income earned, but it is in addition a psychological attitude which may vary almost independently of the facts of the situation. It is not even a simple attitude, since people who have weathered a period of economic adversity can either become more fearful that another may come, or more confident of their ability to handle it if it does. Some of the most secure people I know and the least worried about a possible depression, are people who had a very difficult time in the 1930's.

TABLE 32

EXPRESSED FEELING OF SECURITY, BY OCCUPATION OF HEAD OF SPENDING UNIT

| | | | OCCUPATIONS | | | | |
	ALL SPENDING UNITS [1]	Profes- sional	Self Em- ployed	Other White Collar	Skilled & Semi- skilled	Un- skilled	Farm Oper- ator
Very secure	33	47	41	43	31	21	33
Rather secure	39	38	41	44	41	40	49
Rather insecure ..	13	6	11	8	17	17	9
Very insecure	12	6	4	5	10	20	7
Not ascertained ..	3	3	3	*	1	2	2
	100	100	100	100	100	100	100

Source: Survey Research Center, based on 1,242 interviews.
  [1] Includes other "occupations" such as housewife, student, etc.
  * Less than 0.5%.

It is dangerous to look only at the money returns from an occupation, of course. What you are after is satisfaction, and this depends not only on the money you get, but how much effort you have to put out to get it, and whether you enjoy the work to some extent, and how much investment went into training for the job. It is possible to make very good salary—with a low life expectancy—in some dangerous jobs. It is possible to make very low incomes in a pleasant job like that of a teller in a bank, or even in such unpleasant jobs as are found in laundries. So an occupation involves some choice between more leisure and more money.

Once you have chosen an occupation, how much you earn will depend on how hard you work at it, how much ability you have, and your willingness to be mobile and flexible. One of the amazing things to an observer is the extent to which people will stay at a low-paying job when there are similar or even more pleasant jobs that pay more, often in the same town. Study after study shows wage differentials between employers that are possible because of the different amounts of machinery and of managerial efficiency, but also persist because people do not move easily from one job to another, and still less easily from one town to another. During the great depression, workers frequently hung around closed plants for years, even when there were other jobs not far off. Of course, seniority and pension rights frequently make it difficult to change jobs without loss.

The lesson is clear. Mobility is likely to pay off, provided you do not overdo it. Every job has its special characteristics which must be learned, and it does not pay to move so fast that you never learn any of them well. In addition both employers and psychiatrists look on excessive changing of jobs as evidence of emotional instability.

"Home Production"

Even if interests are restricted to increasing personal ability to secure goods and services, earning more money is not the only way to do it. After all, the original method of getting a house was not to earn money and pay someone else to build it, but to build it yourself, with some help from neighbors. It is difficult to examine the possibilities of doing things for yourself purely as a matter of increasing income in the form of goods and services, since inevitably more is involved than that. Is home production looked upon as an infringement of leisure, or using of time that might better be put into advancing one's own occupational interests, or is it recreation and hence less than costless? Even one's security and mental health may be involved, some argue. Among the reformers in our country is a group who decry the degree of specialization, and the dependence on an impersonal system of mass production and exchange with the monotony and lack of brotherhood it engenders. One of the leading spokesmen of this "school" is Ralph Borsodi, who has made much of what he insists are demonstrations that one can even save enough to feel that he has earned a good salary in such tasks as baking one's own bread. Of course, there are additional arguments about better quality and personal satisfaction with other direct visible achievements, too.[2] In addition to their concern with home production, many of these people are also in favor of leaving the unsatisfactory big cities for small "intentional communities" with much more limited specialization and more community life.

We are concerned here, however, with a single aspect of their program: the attempt to produce things at home or provide one's own services as a method of increasing "real" income. Some of the more frequently suggested methods are:

a. Grow your own food
b. Do your own baking, canning, preserving, freezing
c. Sew your own clothes
d. Build your own home (with variations)
e. Make additions to your home
f. Repair your own car
g. Repair your own clothing
h. Repair your own appliances
i. Do repair and upkeep work on your house (painting, etc.)
j. Do your own washing and ironing
k. Capitalize on artistic skills (music, art)

Looked at as a general problem, it is only common sense that people who specialize in these things and have special equipment can do the actual task more efficiently than you can do it. However, this is not the end of the matter since there are frequently very large costs of distribution, problems of communicating to others just what you want, and restrictions on variety because of the necessity for mass markets. A commercial laundry, for instance, must pick up and deliver, keep records, mark the laundry, and even at that cannot do your laundry just when you want it and how you want it.   In repair work, the cost of just getting a man and his equipment to your house is substantial.   Even if the repair man merely inserts two crossed sticks and twists a garbage disposer loose, or tightens a drive belt, he must still charge this "overhead cost" to you.   What is worse, if he must do the job of observing symptoms to locate some intermittent failure, a great deal of his time may be involved whereas the owner with a little interest and very little mechanical ability can learn to watch for symptoms for a little while before he calls the repair man.   The same sort of comments apply to many different repairs.   A small investment in asking questions and looking up "how to" books can enable you to do things in your spare time that would require an expert's working time, plus travel time.   Makers of appliances are gradually becoming aware of this and providing their customers with detailed instruction books, parts lists, and diagrams indicating how the item is assembled or disassembled.   The latest to come to my attention is a gadget at the TV repair shops inviting you to bring in your own tubes and test them yourself.

In many cases all the repair man does is remove a whole part and substitute another one rebuilt at the factory, and anyone who can determine which part is not working can do this. With automobile repairs, special tools may be necessary, or more complicated knowledge, and the same may be true of some home repairs.   I offer the following set of suggestions, all but the first of which apply even if you have no mechanical ability or dexterity at all:

1. Make a few attempts at repair yourself, but don't get careless, particularly with electricity or with things requiring delicate adjustments.

2. Always open up and inspect anything which is causing trouble before calling the repair man.   You may find what is wrong and even be able to repair it.   If not, you save the repair man the time and trouble of getting at the mechanism, and indicate that you are not indifferent to what is going on.

3. Insist on keeping any old parts which are replaced. This will allow you to take them apart and see what happened, and will reduce the temptation of the repair man to replace a large component when only one part of that component was broken, or to replace something which *might* be causing the trouble without making sure of it.

4. Always watch the repair man if possible, or have someone in the family do it. You might learn something.

There are, of course, many types of repairs, and many services, which an ordinary consumer cannot do himself because of the skill and equipment necessary. Most of us do not try to repair radios, television sets, watches, and so on. Furthermore, it is my experience that most books and articles on "do it yourself" subjects are like traps. They tell you just enough to get you into trouble, and not enough to enable you to get out. For example, I have checked several books on how to lay cement blocks. They were full of instructions about how to string lines to get the wall straight, but failed to mention the critical fact that if you try to lay more than two or three courses a day, the weight is too much for the unset concrete, and the wall will develop cracks. It is frequently best to talk to someone who has done such a job recently, or does it for a living, rather than rely on books.

When we come to home gardening, canning, baking, and so forth, the amount of specialized knowledge required is smaller, and the written directions are much more adequate. The possible amounts of time and energy involved are larger however, and the necessity for asking whether one is really saving money is greater.

In any "home production" it is a safe rule to start with simple easy tasks where you feel confident that you can finish the job and do it right. One of the main arguments for doing things yourself is that it gives you a feeling of satisfaction from the creative activity—even repairing things is a type of creativity. The enjoyment of doing things oneself, like that from eating ripe olives, comes from getting used to it gradually. There seems to be a sort of generalized ability that carries over from one of these "do-it-yourself" activities to another. You learn how to look critically and carefully at some mechanism, or how to ask the right questions of those who know how to do something. You get a feeling for when you should give up and call in an expert. And most important of all you learn that many things simply require that you start and give them a try, and turn out to be surprisingly easy.

The arguments against all these "home production" activities are that they take up leisure that you might better enjoy playing golf or fishing, or skiing, or that you might better be spending in the furthering of your own career. The first argument applies only in a limited sort of way since it assumes that you can get enjoyment only out of activities that cost you money, and not out of those that save money. The second is more cogent, at least for people who can actually do something outside working hours working at their main occupation, at which they are presumably more skilled. Even those of us in professional lines who could presumably be keeping up with our reading and writing find, however, that there are times when a change of activity, particularly one which involves different muscles and perhaps less concentration, is both enjoyable and restful. It is of course possible to overdo anything, and a man who could make $1.50 an hour after taxes working overtime or on extra jobs at his own specialty would not be wise to do jobs around the house that he could have someone else do for $1.25 an hour, unless he thought of them as recreation for which he was willing to pay 25¢ an hour.

We have already inferred a number of arguments in favor of doing things for yourself: it saves money, often provides healthy exercise, can become an enjoyable recreation from which you can get a feeling of creativity that is lacking in many jobs. Frequently these projects can become family enterprises, which help develop the spirit of co-operation in the family, and keep the members from drifting off into their own private recreations. Often the end results are better—you may well get a more careful paint job on the house. Home grown fruits and vegetables, as the nursery catalogues aver, taste better and have more nutritional value than those picked not-quite-ripe for shipping to stores. Finally, it might be added that in order to pay someone else $100 to do something for you, you have to earn $120 or more, because the government will take some of it in income taxes. And the man you pay will only be able to keep $80 or so after he pays his income taxes. All this adds up to a very large tax saving.

It might be added here, that the use of one's time in home enterprises, and the growing satisfaction with one's achievements in these projects, provides a double-barreled advantage in another way. You do not have time to develop a taste for more expensive and less productive types of recreation. If the family enjoys having a garden or engaging in other activities around the house, they are less likely to develop a taste for expensive vacation trips. This leads us to consider more generally what is probably the most important of all the things that determine whether we are happy or miserable.

Aspirations and Satisfactions: The Control of Wants

It should be obvious, as is most of what we are saying in this chapter, that one's security and happiness depend not only on one's income, wealth, job security, and status in society, but on the relation of those to one's aspirations. Let me hasten to add that I am not against aspirations, which under the name of ambition lead to enterprise, effort, creativity, and progress. Even if it is possible for someone who is slothful and indigent to be happy, neither his relatives nor his dependents, nor the society in which he lives, will be happy about him.

But is it not possible to have high aspirations for producing and earning money, without having equally strong "needs" that rapidly develop to demand every extra dollar you earn? Put another way, it should be possible to get our satisfactions from what we do as well as from what we spend. People who can keep their wants under control are not only happier, but more adaptable when the going is rough. The fact that security and happiness and ability to adjust depends on the relation of "needs" to one's ability to satisfy them was dramatically illustrated by the number of ex-millionaires who jumped from windows in 1930. This is not to say that adjusting to a lower standard of living is easy.

In our society, and perhaps in most, people find themselves gradually enmeshed in situations, contractual and social, which make it difficult for them to allocate their income realistically. It is this insidious process whereby our needs and obligations settle themselves upon us, which is difficult to control. Throughout this book we have tried to point out how certain crucial decisions commit you to a great many other decisions. The choice of the community where you live involves more than bus routes and nearness to schools. It involves a pattern of life, neighborhood standards, and pressures—particularly on children—to conform to these patterns and standards. The purchase of a house involves pressures to buy things to put in it. The choice of friends also involves a choice how to spend your time. A realistic system for allocating your money, and saving some of it not only provides saving, but keeps you from developing expensive habits.

There are fascinating studies in the *Ladies Home Journal* giving many details each month of a different family: where their money goes, how pressed they are financially, and so on. Sometimes it will be a family with a high income hard pressed to get along, sometimes the reverse. One man wrote in *Harpers* that he was "Going Broke on $10,000 a Year," and his article is a dramatic presentation of the social and cultural pressures that left him, he felt, with no other recourse.[3] This man did not even own an automobile or a house!

Studies of saving behavior reveal tremendous differences in the amounts people save even at the same income level. Sometimes there are even drastic changes in people's behavior in whole communities, as in the Italian town of Terruggia. This town, with less than 1,000 inhabitants had an average number of babies each year of thirty-two until the first years after World

War II when there was an economic boom.   There were thirteen children born in 1944, twenty-six in 1947, seventeen in 1948, twenty in 1950, eight in 1951, eleven in 1952, and none in 1953.[4]   One of the villagers is quoted as saying "We reaped the benefits of long years of hard work, a great deal of sweat, and small returns.   Now we are organizing our lives so that we may have small families and pleasant homes, instead of large broods and pigsties."   Whether this is the only explanation for the phenomenon is not known, but such a transition is certainly remarkable.

Little is known about why some people develop sources of satisfactions that are inexpensive, and aspirations they can achieve, while others do the opposite.   There is evidence in social psychological studies, however, that aspirations in any one direction are cumulative, that the joy of reaching a goal at a particular activity leads to greater confidence, and willingness to continue, but also leads to new and higher goals in that direction.   It is also true, however, that you can substitute successes in a different endeavor, and substitute one type of aspiration for another.

The conclusion from this for the ordinary consumer would seem to be that it is worth some conscious effort to find means of achievement, self-expression, and even recreation which are adapted to his abilities, and which can stand the enlargement of aspirations as time passes.   It is not easy to see how this is to be done, but it certainly can be.   If we cannot do it for ourselves, then perhaps we can help our children do it.   Child psychologists generally suggest that if a child can excel at one or two things, he will not feel the need to conform to the crowd so much, and he will be better able to stand the realization that he is worse than most other children at some other things.

Another conclusion that seems to follow is that confidence in new lines of achievement needs to be developed carefully and gradually, so as to avoid discouragement.   Many people try home gardening, or budgeting their money, or painting their own house, but take on too much at once and end up discouraged. Many people try budgeting with an elaborate system that takes a lot of time and energy, creates frustration because the amounts do not come out right, and does not save any money. Others suddenly start an economy wave and try all the cheap cuts of meat, and end up splurging on steak to "make up" for the sacrifice.

Only the slow development of satisfactions which are not expensive, and the discovery of a pattern of life that fits individual needs and abilities, will lead to real happiness. The problem of the consumer is ultimately not an economic one but a religious one. True, he needs analytical ability of the type I have tried to impart in this book. He needs information and the habit of insisting on having adequate information. He needs a clear awareness of his own potential and the power to set his sights on realizable goals. But most of all he needs to know what things are really important in his life, and to have the maturity to face the fact that choices involve giving up some things for others. Whether you choose to call this religious maturity, mental health, or rational behavior, it involves many choices not customarily regarded as in the realm of economics.[5]

This does not mean that you must conform to anyone's idea of what is best. One consideration though must certainly be, other things being equal, that there are some reasons for conformity if only to make your neighbors more comfortable. Neither does it mean that anything you happen to decide you want will make you happy. There is a moral order in the universe, and there are other people around. Some types of activity tend to lead to harmony with others, and to increase the "general welfare," and others do not.

Indeed, one of the problems of society in general is to induce its members to have the proper balance between ambition and contentment, and, in addition, to choose ways of living that lead to harmony with fellow men. Anything you as an individual can do to make wise choices of this sort will probably have more effect on your own and your neighbors' happiness than whether you buy the best pair of shoes on the market, or the best television set for the money. On balance, it is probably true that our society is more likely to cause us unhappiness by breeding too many wants than by stimulating too little ambition. The words of John Ruskin, written in 1862, though quaint, are still apt.

We need examples of people who, leaving Heaven to decide whether they are to rise in the world, decide for themselves that they will be happy in it, and have resolved to seek-not greater wealth but simpler pleasure; not higher fortune but deeper felicity; making the first of possessions self-possession; and honoring themselves in the harmless pride and calm pursuits of peace.[6]

FOOTNOTES TO CHAPTER 12

[1] Eli Ginzberg, Sol W. Ginsburg, Sidney Axelrad, and John L. Herma, *Occupational Choice*, New York: Columbia University Press, 1951, p. 185; see also the most recent *Occupational Outlook Handbook* of the U.S. Bureau of Labor Statistics.

[2] Ralph Borsodi, *Prosperity and Security, A Study in Realistic Economics*, New York: Harper & Brothers, 1938.

[3] Jay Taylor, "Going Broke on $10,000 a Year," *Harpers*, July 1952, pp. 60–65; see also: "The Metropolitanities," in *Fortune*, Vol. XX (July, 1939) where the "compulsion to be stylish" could use up almost all of an $18,000 income at 1939 prices on "necessary" items of living. See also: G. M. White, "How Young America Lives: Broke But Happy on $11,200 a Year," *Ladies' Home Journal* LXXII:117–120, 131–135 (Feb., 1955) where an analysis of the budget presented shows that this family was actually saving nearly a third of their income.

[4] *The New York Times*, November 22, 1953, Sec. I, p. 42.

[5] See: Robert H. Thouless, *How to Think Straight, the Technique of Applying Logic Instead of Emotion*, New York: Simon and Schuster, Inc., 1939.

[6] John Ruskin, *Unto This Last*, London: J. M. Dent and Sons, Ltd., 1907, p. 191.

Index